The Structuring of Labour Markets

THE LIBRARY OF POLITICAL ECONOMY

POLITICAL ECONOMY is the old name for economics. In the hands of the great classical economists, particularly Smith, Ricardo and Marx, economics was the study of the working and development of the economic system in which men and women lived. Its practitioners were driven by a desire to describe, to explain and to evaluate what they saw around them. No sharp distinction was drawn between economic analysis and economic policy nor between economic behaviour and its interaction with the technical, social and political framework.

The Library of Political Economy has been established to provide widely based explanations of economic behaviour in contemporary society.

In examining the way in which new patterns of social organization and behaviour influence the economic system and policies for combating problems associated with growth, inflation, poverty and the distribution of wealth, contributors stress the link between politics and economics and the importance of institutions in policy formulation.

This'open-ended' approach to economics implies that there are few laws that can be held to with certainty and, by the same token, there is no generally established body of theory to be applied in all circumstances. Instead economics as presented in this library provides a way of ordering events which has constantly to be updated and modified as new situations develop. This, we believe, is its interest and its challenge.

Volumes in the Library

Dangerous Currents: The State of Economics–Lester Thurow
The Political Economy of Nationalism–Dudley Seers
Women's Claims: A Study in Political Economy–Lisa Peattie and Martin Rein
Urban Inequalities under State Socialism–Ivan Szelenyi
Social Innovation and the Division of Labour–Johnathan Gershuny
The Structuring of Labour Markets: A Comparative Analysis of the Steel and Construction Industries in Italy–Paola Villa
Monetarism and the Labour Market–Derek Robinson

The Structuring of Labour Markets

A Comparative Analysis of the Steel and Construction Industries in Italy

Paola Villa

CLARENDON PRESS · OXFORD
1986

Oxford University Press, Walton Street, Oxford OX2 6DP
Oxford New York Toronto
Delhi Bombay Calcutta Madras Karachi
Petaling Jaya Singapore Hong Kong Tokyo
Nairobi Dar es Salaam Cape Town
Melbourne Auckland
and associated companies in
Beirut Berlin Ibadan Nicosia

Oxford is a trade mark of Oxford University Press

Published in the United States
by Oxford University Press, New York

British Library Cataloguing in Publication Data
Villa, Paola.
The structuring of labour markets: a comparative analysis of the steel and construction industry in Italy.—(The Library of political economy)
1. Construction industry—Italy 2. Steel industry and trade—Italy
I. Title II. Series 338.4'7624'0945 HD9715.I8Z
ISBN 0–19–828508–6
ISBN 0–19–828552–3 Pbk

Library of Congress Cataloging in Publication Data
Villa, Paola
The structuring of labour markets (The Library of political economy)
Bibliography: p. Includes index.
1. Construction workers—Italy 2. Iron and steel workers—Italy.
3. Labor supply—Italy. I. Title II. Series.
HD5718.B892I88 1986 331.12'924'0945 86–871
ISBN 0–19–828508–6
ISBN 0–19–828552–3 Pbk

Set by Spire Print Services, Salisbury
Printed in Great Britain
at the University Printing House, Oxford
by David Stanford
Printer to the University

Acknowledgements

This study could not have been written in isolation. If the ideas expressed in it have some cogency and make some contribution, then part of the credit must go to the people whose questions, criticism, and encouragement have helped to develop my ideas about society.

My interest in the nature of labour markets owes much to my friend and teacher, Ezio Tarantelli. It was while I was following his lectures that I turned my attention towards labour economics. The challenging discussions I had as a student and, later, the friendly co-operation with him when I was an assistant lecturer turned out to be a transformative intellectual experience. It is to his memory that this book is dedicated. I remember him as a great teacher, a brilliant scholar, combative in proposing his ideas and always ready to discuss them, and, above all, as a kind and generous friend.

My most significant intellectual debt is to Frank Wilkinson, who encouraged me to begin this research and surpervised my work as a Ph.D. student. The sustained interest he showed in this study from its inception was a major source of encouragement. The discussions I had with him, so often and over so long a period of time, have been a continual source of intellectual stimulation.

I am also indebted to a number of students and colleagues, upon whose research I have drawn and who have been helpful in the development of these ideas. For their extensive critical comments upon parts of the manuscript and their advice at various stages of the work, I would like to thank Carlo Beretta, Francesca Bettio, Angiola Contini, Elisabeth Garnsey, Jane Kenrick, Edward Lorenz, Antonella Picchio, and Paul Ryan. As examiners of my Ph.D. thesis, Sebastiano Brusco and Roger Tarling went far beyond the call of duty in offering suggestions for the improvement of this work, giving me the benefits of their knowledge and insight. I am also indebted to the paticipants in the various conferences of the International Working Party on Labour Market Segmentation for access to their research, and for many enjoyable discussions which have helped to develop and clarify the ideas expressed in this book. Particularly important were Tony Lawson, Wayne Lewchuk, Nigel Mason, Roger Moore, and Nichos Theokharakis, as friends who shared my interests and with whom I participated in a study group on the labour process. My thanks go also to the Università Cattolica of Milan for allowing me to spend part of my time in Cambridge, and to my colleagues at the Dipartimento di

Scienze Economiche for the sustained encouragement. I would like especially to thank Luciano Boggio for his intellectual and moral support.

A large number of people made this study possible. Many union officials and management representatives, and various people who work in the two sectors in an official or professional capacity, gave generously of their time and provided me with data and information. My arguments draws heavily upon interviews with them. Without their co-operation the study would not have been possible. Unfortunately, the list of people who contributed in this way is too long to be included here. To them I wish to express my sincere gratitude for their help and co-operation.

I would also like to thank the institutions from which I have received financial assistance at different stages of the study: the *Ente per gli Studi Monetari Bancari e Finanziari L. Einaudi*, Newnham College, and the *Consiglio Nazionale delle Ricerche*.

Last but not least, I offer my warm thanks to all the friends with whom I shared the ups and downs of being a research student, and who made my life in Cambridge so pleasant.

Contents

List of Tables

List of Figures

Abbreviations

AFL	*Acciaierie e Ferriere Lombarde*
ANCE	*Associazione Nazionale Costruttori Edili*
ASSIDER	*Associazione Industrie Siderurgiche Italiane*
ASSIMPREDIL	*Associazione Imprese Edili e Complementari della Provincia di Milano*
BOS	Basic Oxygen Systems
CCNL	*Contratto Collettivo Nazionale di Lavoro*
CGIL	*Confederazione Generale Italiana del Lavoro*
C.d.D.	*Consiglio dei Delegati*
C.d.F.	*Consiglio di Fabbrica*
CISIA	*Centro Siderurgico Sviluppo Impiego Acciaio*
CISL	*Confederazione Italiana Sindacati Lavoratori*
CRESME	*Centro Ricerche Economiche, Sociologiche e di Mercato sull'Edilizia*
DLM	Dual Labour Market
EGAM	*Ente Autonomo e di Gestione per le Aziende Minerarie e Metallurgiche*
EFMEC	*Ente Formazione Maestranze Edili e Complementari*
EIU	Economist Intelligence Unit
ENI	*Ente Nazionale Idrocarburi*
FAST	*Federazione delle Associazioni Scientifiche e Techniche*
FENEAL	*Federazione Nazionale Lavoratori Edili, Affini e del Legno*
FILCA	*Federazione Italiana Lavoratori Costruzioni e Affini*
FILLEA	*Federazione Italiana del Legno, dell'Edilizia, industrie Affini ed Estrattive*
FINSIDER	*Finanziaria Siderurgica*
FIOE	*Federazione Italiana Operai Edili*
FIOM	*Federazione Italiana Operai Metallurgici*
FLC	*Federazione Lavoratori delle Costruzioni*
FLM	*Federazione Lavoratori Metalmeccanici*
IRI	*Istituto per la Ricostruzione Industriale*
ISCO	*Istituto per lo Studio della Congiuntura*
ISFOL	*Istituto per lo Sviluppo dell'addestramento e della Formazione Professionale dei Lavoratori*
ISTAT	*Istituto Centrale di Statistica*
IU	*Inquadramento Unico*
ISSOCO	*Istituto per lo Studio della Società Contemporanea*

JA, JE	job analysis, job evaluation
LD	Linz–Donawitz furnaces
LF	labour force
LMS	labour market segmentation
MPM	multistand pipe mill
OBM	Oxygen Bottom Max Hütte
OECD	Organization for Economic Development and Cooperation
OH	open–hearth
OTML	*Osservatorio Territoriale sul Mercato del Lavoro*
PPE	*premio di professionalità edile*
PPM	press piercing mill
UIL	*Unione Italiana Lavoratori*
UHP	ultra-high-power

Introduction

The research presented in this book originated as a Ph.D. dissertation completed over the period 1978–83 at the University of Cambridge. My thinking and research on questions of labour market structures were initially stimulated by the emerging of two new streams of literature on labour issues which followed the publication of two important books: that by Doeringer and Piore in 1971 and that by Braverman in 1974. Despite the deep theoretical differences between the two approaches and the different focuses of their analyses, both the dual labour market literature and the labour process literature were based, by and large, on direct empirical investigations. Their attempts to describe and analyse the real world were characterized by many insights into the functioning of the labour market, in contrast to the inability of orthodox economic theory to explain how the labour market works in reality.

I was strongly attracted by the ideas expressed by the dual labour market theory as an interesting alternative view of divisions and inequalities among workers. At the same time, I was perplexed by the divergencies which started to emerge as the initial debate on the duality of the labour market was extended to explain the origin of segmentation. Different hypotheses were advanced: they were proposed as competing explanations, but they lacked generality, and so were suited to explain some empirical cases only. Therefore, they all revealed some inadequacies. As the empirical research expanded, a consensus gradually emerged that these explanatory hypotheses were not necessarily mutually exclusive, and that it was the interaction between different forces that had to be investigated. And it was with this idea in mind that I started my empirical analysis on the structuring of labour markets. Moreover, I was puzzled by the fact that, on the one hand, the debate which followed Braverman's book had shown the centrality of the labour process (and therefore the crucial role of the social relations of production) in order to understand the transformation of the workplace; and, on the other hand, the labour market segmentation debate had shown the centrality of the firm in order to explain the existence of different categories of labour market. Thus, both approaches put at the core of their analysis the firm, opening the 'black box' of orthodox labour economics. Nevertheless, the possibility of integrating the labour process theory with the theory of labour market segmentation was worked out by the radical economists only; and their hypothesis, based on the analysis of the historical evolution of the labour market in the USA, was too country-specific.

It was the question, therefore, of the complementarity of apparently competitive hypotheses about the origin of segmentation, and the question of the role of the labour process within the process of segmentation, which induced me to analyse the dynamics determining the structuring of labour markets. For this reason, I decided to investigate how and why labour market structures differ. The aim of my analysis, based on the comparative study of the steel and construction industries in Italy, was to develop the theory of labour market segmentation.

The two case-study industries have been chosen because both are characterized by wide cyclical fluctuations, and both have experienced a period of rapid expansion followed by a deep recession. Moreover, the labour force in both industries mainly consists of male semiskilled manual workers, employed in hard and tiring jobs, with low status but with the possibility of good earnings. Despite these similarities, the structure of the two labour markets is quite different. In the steel factories, workers are employed in well-structured jobs with opportunities for advancement and a well-defined career. Jobs are secure and labour turnover is very low. In the building industry, only the more skilled workers have secure and stable jobs. The other workers have uncertain employment prospects, no defined career and very high mobility. As my empirical investigation proceeded, I found not only that labour market structures differed as I moved from one sector to another, but that labour market structures changed with time. Thus it was in order to explain why labour markets differ in their structures that I started investigating how they changed with time.

The idea underlying my empirical work is that the structure of jobs, employment conditions, and the rules determining recruitment, training, career, and mobility can be understood only in terms of product market conditions, industrial structure and technology in use. But economic and technological factors alone are not sufficient to explain the structuring of labour markets: they define the economic and technological framework—i.e. what I define as the 'realm of possibilities'—within which employers, workers, and unions interact. This is to say that the economic and technological factors do not determine the content and structure of labour markets: rather they define the realm of possibilities within which the division of labour and the labour market structure can result from labour/management interaction. Differences in economic and technological conditions are crucial in defining the problems that employers face in organizing the labour process, and that unions face in organizing workers and representing their interests. But the motivations of management, labour, and union organization also affect the structuring of the labour market, so that an understanding of this process requires a consideration of the dynamics of labour/management relations. It is the ways in which employers, workers, and unions can through their social relations resolve (or try to resolve by strategy) the problems created within a changing economic and technological environment which makes segmentation a continuous process. Therefore, segmentation has to be regarded as an iterative process, where this iteration is not towards a balance of power, but towards a continuously disturbed system. The previous literature, which focused on the closure of labour segments and therefore on the presence, absence, or extent of mobility, missed the dynamic instability of segmentation. But if segmentation is defined as qualitatively non-uniform, that is, if the labour market is analysed as a segmented market whose segments are distinguished by the fact that they treat workers differently, independently of their own characteristics, segmentation becomes an iterative process.

The book is developed as follows. Chapter 1 opens with a review of the labour market segmentation debate and develops the basic analytical perspective. The following four chapters (2 to 5) are concerned with the *analysis* of the structure of the labour market in the steel and construction industries. Chapter 2 presents a discussion of the economic and technological conditions that characterize the two sectors. Chapter 3 focuses on the division of labour, and points out the general characteristics of jobs in the two industries as they are shaped by economic and technological factors. Chapters 4 and 5 examine how these jobs are internally organized—in steel and in construction respectively—into a system of job clusters: that is, how workers are recruited, allocated to jobs, and organized for work. The following three chapters (6 to 8) are concerned with the *dynamics* of labour market structures. Chapter 6, in the light of the empirical results presented in the previous chapters, reasserts the analytical framework, pointing out the role of the labour process in the structuring of labour markets; and it concludes that for an understanding of the process of labour market structuring it is necessary to consider the dynamics of labour/management relations and their interplay with economic and technological factors. Chapters 7 and 8 examine the evolution of the labour market structure in the steel and construction industries respectively, pointing out the interplay among economic, technological, and social factors. A concluding chapter (9) returns to the hypothesis of non-competing groups and argues that, once this hypothesis is accepted, it calls for a definition of the labour market different from the traditional one. And, in the light of the empirical findings on the steel and construction industries, Chapter 9 puts forward a comprehensive framework for the analysis of the labour market structure, incorporating the ideas expressed in the labour market segmentation debate and specifying the variables affecting the structuring of the labour market.

CHAPTER ONE

The Labour Market and the Labour Market Segmentation Debate

1.1 The labour market: a critique of the traditional view

Traditionally, the labour market has been considered as the totality of jobs for which, given the achievement of equilibrium—and, in Hicks's terms, 'allowances for other advantages' (1963, p. 7)—the single wage prevails and the market is cleared. This conventional view is based upon the assumed condition of competition among employers to secure labour and among workers to get a job. The wage-setting process and the physical movement of workers interact in a market process:

> Wages, say the textbooks, tend to that level where demand and supply are equal. If supply exceeds demand, some men will be unemployed, and in their effort to regain employment they will reduce the wage they ask to that level which makes it just worth while for employers to take them on. If demand exceeds supply, employers will be unable to obtain all the labour they require, and will therefore offer higher wages in order to attract labour from elsewhere. Now, this . . . is quite a good simplified model of the labour market. (Hicks, 1963, pp. 4–5)

Labour economics has developed on the basis of this model. The original picture of the labour market described by Hicks has been made more complex by incorporating different aspects in the attempt to make it more similar to the real world. The basically competitive labour market model has been modified by taking into account the existence of imperfections, rigidities and costs—both for employers and for employees—associated with labour mobility, trade union organizations and goals, the existence of uncertainty and imperfect information, and finally the process of acquisition of information. The labour market model that emerges through the incorporation of these elaborations is modified, but still 'retaining the central core as a descriptive theme'.[1] Thus, the labour market is still supposed to have as its main function the allocation of labour, the efficiency of which is ensured by the competitive nature of the market.

But it has been argued that the labour market is not a true market.[2] The term 'market' is usually understood[3] to imply: (*a*) an idea of market as *exchange*; (*b*) that buyers and sellers meet or are *in relation* to exchange commodities; and (*c*) that for each commodity there is *a price* at which the market will be cleared.

The assimilation of the labour market to a commodity market can be criticized, schematically, on three different levels. First, the idea of exchange is very misleading when we apply it to labour. This has to be related to the fact that labour is not a commodity in the sense of other commodities. In marxian terms, what wage labourers sell is not their labour but their labour power. As commodity owners, workers are free to sell or not sell their labour power, but this freedom is formal rather than real, since they must work or starve.[4] This proposition could be better specified by taking into account differences in the conditions of the labour supply.[5] But, at a general level, it still holds that for most households wage labour is the only available means of obtaining sufficient income to meet family needs. Therefore, since there is no real choice, on the workers's side, whether to work or not, supply curves cannot be drawn in the usual upward sloping way. And this implies that only very few households can afford to supply less labour as real wages decline; similarly, an excess supply of labour cannot be eliminated in this way.[6]

Moreover, the idea of a relation of free exchange is misleading with respect to the existing relationship between employers and workers, as has been stressed in the labour process debate.[7] And this has to be related to the fundamental reason for Marx's distinction between labour and labour power: that is, the characterization of capitalism as a mode of production. This gives a central position to the social relations of the labour process, and it recognizes the despotic role of the capitalist in the organization of the labour process (Rowthorn, 1980, pp. 42–3). Thus, according to Marx, the worker/employer relationship is not one of free exchange, but a power relationship where the position of labour is crucially determined by the fact that wage labourers have no alternative but to sell their labour power, at a given wage rate. And as soon as workers engage in labour they no longer own their labour: it is under the control of the capitalist.

Finally, the price of labour—the wage rate—is incapable of performing any market clearing function: variations in the wage rate cannot eliminate unemployment. In keynesian terms we could say that quantities (employment) and prices (wages) are determined by two different sets of factors. Neither the demand for nor the supply of labour depend on wages: the demand for labour is related to the level of output that firms plan to produce, and labour supply is by and large determined by demographic and social factors (though it is to some extent responsive to changes in employment opportunities).

Wage determination (money and real wages) and wage flexibility, though affected by conditions in the labour market, are determined by other forces, both economic and social.[8] It should follow, from what has been previously said, that the adjustment of inequalities between demand for and supply of labour do not take place through wage fluctuations. This has been supported by a large body of empirical evidence[9] pointing out that it is not through wages but through employment opportunities that demand and supply are adjusted. In the main, employers adjust their labour force, whether upward or downward, by varying the number of workers whom they are willing to take on or whom they dismiss, thereby directly changing job opportunities.[10] In addition, labour market segmentation (LMS) theories have shown that this process of adjustment does not take place uniformly across the sectors: while the labour force in the primary sector is protected from cyclical fluctuations of demand—being treated as a quasi-fixed factor—the workers in the secondary sector suffer from instability and uncertainty, since it is onto them that the burden of flux is shifted.

To conclude, the labour market is not a competitive market, since: (*a*) there is no free exchange, since there is no real choice for wage labour; (*b*) the employer/worker relationship is not a relation of free exchange, but a social relation exercised under constraint and specified within the labour process; (*c*) the price associated with the commodity—labour power—is incapable of performing any market clearing function. Indeed, in these circumstances, the appropriateness of the notion of a labour market comes into question: the main contribution of the LMS debate is to challenge the traditional notion of the labour market.

1.2 The labour market segmentation approach: a historical perspective

In the 1960s economists became increasingly concerned with the problems of poverty, inequality, underemployment, and social discrimination, and began to call attention to the functioning of the labour market in an attempt to understand the concentration of disadvantaged workers among specific groups.[11] The traditional neoclassical model appeared unsatisfactory: the real world seemed inconsistent with the predictions of competitive theory. The urban crisis and the racial tensions that exploded in the USA during the 1960s pushed for a rexamination of the problems of poverty, underemployment, and discrimination. As attention focused on these problems, changes emerged in their economic definition and in their perception. A new set of categories, such as the dual labour market, primary/secondary, internal/external, core/peripheral/irregular, and a new set of concepts, such as segmentation, stratification, and internalization, were introduced. This resulted in an extensive debate, in which different hypotheses were advanced in an attempt to explain the persistence of disadvantaged workers among specific groups. Despite their differences, all these hypotheses explained the persistence of low-paid groups as the result of the emergence of non–competitive, or structured, labour markets, where no competitive equalization of wages took place.[12] The basic idea underlying this new approach is that the labour market seems to be better described in terms of a set of segments in which the process of wage determination and labour mobility are no longer assumed to be closely connected.

1.2.1 The idea of non-competing groups

The ideas and concepts incorporated into the LMS debate are not new. The hypothesis of a market stratified into non-competing groups was first formulated by Cairnes (1874, pp. 65–9). Developing the idea of a 'hereditary distinction of caste' between the different grades of workers expressed by Mill,[13] he argued that the whole population did not compete indiscriminately for all occupations, but there existed a series of industrial groups, superimposed on one another:

> I am far from contending for the existence of any hard lines of demarcation between any categories of persons in this country. No doubt the various ranks and classes fade into each other by imperceptible gradations, and individuals from all classes are constantly passing up or dropping down; but while this is so, it is nevertheless true that the average workman, from whatever rank he be taken, finds his power of competition limited for practical purposes to a certain range of occupations, so that, however high the rates of remuneration in those which lie beyond may rise, he is excluded from sharing them. We are thus compelled to recognize the existence of non-competing industrial groups as a feature of our social economy; and this is the fact which I desire here to insist upon. (Cairnes, 1874, pp. 67–8.)

The labour market was therefore perceived as divided into horizontal strata, where workers could compete within each strata, but where the entry to other groups was precluded. The allocation of workers to the different strata depended on their social origin; differences in educational opportunities and disposable means limited the choice of employment and the competition within a tolerably well-defined range of occupations. The labour market was seen as divided into 'a series of industrial layers, superposed on one another', where the limitation of free competition of labour was imposed by 'social position and circumstances'. The labour force was therefore assumed to be segmented horizontally, and this segmentation determined by factors exogenous to the economic system.

Marshall himself considered social factors affecting access to jobs and trades, and the problem of vertical mobility from one grade to another.[14] He pointed out that access to a certain occupation depended on, and was limited by, the resources of parents in the various grades of society, by their power of forecasting the future, and by their willingness to sacrifice themselves for the sake of their children; and that these limits were comparatively greater in the lower ranks of society.[15] But Marshall, at the same time, neglected the extent to which different occupations could be regarded as distributed in 'great planes': he preferred to look at them 'as resembling a long flight of steps of unequal breadth', therefore implying mobility as an adjustment mechanism. Horizontal mobility—i.e. from one trade to another within the same grade of labour—was supposed to be very great: although there were some trades which were difficult to enter, there were also adjustments of supply and demand which were affected by movements of workers between trades. Vertical mobility—from one grade to another—was seldom rapid or on a large scale,[16] but he assumed it would be sufficient to adjust differences between demand and supply within a short period of time.

Thus, in Marshall there was still the idea of a labour force divided horizontally into grades, similar to the view expressed by Mill and Cairnes. This was still explained, as by the previous authors, on the basis of social and institutional factors, exogenous to the working of the labour market. Nevertheless, Marshall assumed that the labour market, both within each grade and between grades, was governed by the inflow/outflow of labour, so that there was a general tendency to 'equality of efficiency earnings'.[17] And inequalities in wages were therefore mostly explained by differences in the characteristics ('industrial abilities') of the labour force.[18] Thus, in the Marshallian system there was a sort of dichotomy between the social analysis and the economic analysis: on the one hand, the distinction and separation of labour in different grades was discussed and analysed in terms of the influence of social factors, on the other hand these qualifications were left out of account in the economic analysis of the labour market. And the study of labour was finally placed within competitive market reasoning.

With Marshall, the social analysis of labour problems was abandoned by orthodox economics: Hicks's *Theory of Wages* (1963) was in fact conceived in the neoclassical deductive tradition, where 'the theory of determination of wages in a free market is simply a special case of the general theory of value' (p. 1.) The idea of non–competing groups explained on the basis of social factors was lost. What was left was the persistence of wage inequalities. These were explained in terms of differences in the supply of labour[19] and imperfections in the functioning of the labour market.[20]

It is along these lines that orthodox economics has recently been developing a better specification of the supply of labour and the acknowledgement of imperfections in the market process.

1.2.2 From empirical evidence to the definition of a new approach

The study of social complexities and realities was not completely abandoned by economists. The institutionalists, in the 1920s and 1930s and later in the postwar period,[21] continued to analyse the functioning of the labour market on the basis of social and institutional factors.

This approach developed more as an empirical challenge to orthodox economics than as a new body of theory. The descriptive analysis undertaken pointed out the limits and the inconsistencies of the traditional theory in terms of features of the real world. It was found that the processes of wage determination and labour mobility were not so closely related as the theory seemed to suggest.[22] On the contrary, high earning levels tended to be associated with low turnover rates. Labour market behaviour was then explained by historical and institutional factors in wage setting;[23] the existence of ports of entry limiting access to the internal markets;[24] the relevance of seniority and other institutional rules in governing job allocation;[25] the increasing importance of hiring practices and on-the-job training activities within the firm;[26] finally, by the weight of factors such as career, attachment to the firm and uncertainty in workers' behaviour.[27] Thus a large body of empirical work emerged where institutional elements were introduced to explain both workers' mobility[28] and wage structure.[29] The existence of non-competitive markets was explained by the *balkanization* (institutionalization—Kerr, 1954) of free-choice markets, as the result of formal and informal rules.

This approach can be looked at as a development of Cairnes's non-competing groups idea, since a fragmentation of the labour market into non-communicating segments is here implied. At the same time, the new approach has to be distinguished from Cairnes's idea, since a vertical segmentation, and not a horizontal stratification, is emphasized. The focus of the analysis is the institutionalized enterprise: the market is here reduced to an 'irreducible minimum' by established rules. These rules set sharper boundaries between internal and external markets, define the ports of entry and mobility criteria, and at the same time set forth interrelationships between the internal and external wage structures. Rules are the result of group behaviour; the locus of decision-making is no longer with single individuals but with collective subjects like groups of workers, trade unions, and managers.

Part of this early literature attempted to describe the structure of the labour market by working out a typology of these non-competitive segments. Kerr (1950, pp. 280–3) introduced the concept of the institutional labour market; Fisher (1951) wrote about the structureless market for harvest labour, thereby making an implicit distinction between structured and structureless markets; Kerr (1954) introduced two new categories into the structured market: guild markets for craftworkers and manorial markets for industrial workers; Dunlop (1966, p. 32) introduced the concept of the internal labour market; Doeringer (1967) developed this category and the determinants of its structure.

1.2.3 The non-competitive labour market

This section will try to follow this path through a brief discussion of the typologies introduced to describe these non-competitive markets.

In an article published in 1950, Kerr discussed the characteristics of labour markets. His starting point was the observation that the term 'labour market' was often used with different meanings. And this was explained by the fact that two processes are taking place all the time—wage rates are changing and workers are moving between jobs—but the two processes are not always and necessarily connected. One should refer to the labour market as a *wage market*, when the process of setting wage rates is considered, and as a *job market*, when the process of distributing jobs is considered. On the basis of this distinction, Kerr pointed out five different models of labour markets (perfect market, neoclassical market, natural market, institutional market, managed market), characterized and identified by the different degree of connection between the process of determination of wage rates and the process of distribtion of jobs. At one extreme of the typology is the perfect market, in which the dichotomy wage market/job market does not exist: the two processes are interconnected and simultaneous, the single wage prevails, and the market is cleared. This is the labour market described by orthodox theory, when no imperfection is assumed to exist. At the other extreme of the typology is the institutional market, distinguished by the substition of institutional rules for market processes. Here, formal rules and informal practices—the result of the policies of unions, employers and government—define the wage structure of, entry into, movement within, and exit from these markets. The wage market and the job market are separated.

Fisher (1951), a year later, discussing empirical findings on the harvest labour market in California, defined this as a *structureless market*, characterized by five distinct features: (*a*) there were no unions imposing seniority or other rules; (*b*) the relation between the employer and the employees was transitory and impersonal; (*c*) the labour force had no skills; (*d*) the wage rates were defined by unit of output; and (*e*) the technology in use was simple: little machinery was employed. In this type of structureless market, wage rates vary greatly over time and, at the same time, they tend to be quite uniform over space; and this is possible as there are no structural barriers to the mobility of workers. Thus, the two processes (variation of rates and workers' mobility) are connected.

A few years later Kerr (1954) developed his idea of the *institutional market* on the basis of the structureless market described by Fisher. This was considered an important point of reference and contrast for other possible situations. It was argued that the competitive model, as described by orthodox economics, was not a norm, but an anomaly that could be found only in some very special situation, as in the harvest labour market in California. In opposition to this market where there are no barriers to the mobility of workers and to wage variations, Kerr described a structured (or institutional) market. This is the outcome of the institutionalization of the 'natural' or 'free choice' market, through the establishment of formal or informal rules. The rules delimit the market, prescribing different treatment for 'ins' and 'outs', and thus create non-competing groups. They also replace individual decision-making processes (in wage-setting and worker allocation) and establish criteria other than pecuniary ones (such as equity, security, seniority, and certainty). On the basis of this analysis, Kerr identified two types of institutional markets: the guild market and the manorial market. The first is a closed labour market under the control of craft unions, where the unions carefully define their occupational and geographical area, and set the rules for apprenticeship and entry into the trade. Thus, workers enter the market through the unions, and employers must hire union members. Here, workers' mobility is primarily horizontal, between employers. The second type of market is found in industrial enterprises. New workers are hired by the enterprise and allocated to entry jobs; as jobs open up, workers are promoted in order of hiring, and, as jobs disappear, they are moved down, again in order. A set of well-established rules creates sharper boundaries between internal and external markets, ports of entry, and criteria for internal mobility. Here, the emphasis is on attachment to the place of work and movement is vertical, within the firm. In both types of institutional market, guild and manorial, wage rates play a secondary role in the process of worker allocation to jobs; and, at the same time, workers' mobility plays a secondary role in the process of wage determination.

The concept of the internal labour market, later introduced by Dunlop (1966, p. 32) and better specified by Doeringer (1967), has therefore to be considered as the logical continuation of a stream of analysis which dates back to the first insitutionalists. For this reason, it is interesting to refer directly to the definition of internal labour market given by Doeringer:

> The theoretical construct of the internal labour market, as introduced by Kerr, may be more precisely defined as an administrative unit within which the market functions of pricing, allocating, and often training labour are performed. It is governed by a set of institutional rules which delineate the boundaries of the internal market and determine its internal structure. These institutional or administrative hiring and work rules define the 'ports of entry' into the internal markets, the relationship between jobs for purposes of internal mobility, and the privileges which accrue to workers within the internal market.' (Doeringer, 1967, p. 208.)

This specification of a typology of non-competing markets developed side by side with the empirical description of these markets. Despite the richness of insights into the functioning of the labour market embodied in this early literature, it was dispersed amongst a large number of separate empirical studies. The debate on urban poverty and discrimination which emerged in the 1960s pushed for a reconsideration of the factors influencing the structuring of labour markets. A more comprehensive approach, usually referred to as the dual labour market theory (DLM), was proposed by Doeringer and Piore (1971) incorporating the variables identified in the previous contributions.

1.2.4 The dual labour market theory

The basic hypothesis of this theory is that the market is separated into two sectors, in which workers and employers operate according to fundamentally different behavioural rules, and which display distinct and identifiable features. The labour market is no longer perceived as a unified phenomenon, but as a plurality of markets, each distinct in its structure and characteristics. The DLM is a theoretical construct which distinguishes between a primary sector, characterized by high wages, good working conditions, employment stability, and possibility of advancement and equity, and a secondary sector, characterized by low wages, uncertainty, poor working conditions, and high turnover. The persistence of poverty is therefore analysed in terms of a dichotomy in the economic and social structure.

The theory is developed around the idea of the internal labour market, defined as an administrative unit—i.e. an enterprise or a craft market—within which the market functions of pricing and allocation are performed by a set of institutional and administrative rules, which substitute for market processes. Here the workers are protected from the external market, where the allocation and the payment of labour are regulated by economic variables, by rigidities upon entry, and by possibilities of internal mobility. The fundamental element in these markets is the rigidity of the rules which, based largely on past experience, tend to govern every aspect of the work relationship. The allocative structure found in internal labour markets defines quite precisely the movement of workers within the firm: mobility chains delimit the different career processes for labour, where the movement from one step to another represents a progression toward jobs characterized by higher wages and better status. These chains tend to be fully specified, and mobility between different grades depends on ability, seniority, and frequency of work. The resulting structure is the outcome of management's interest in internal allocation, as in the promotion of efficiency by reducing training and turnover costs, and of the interests of the employees in internal markets, as a means of enhancing job security and advancement. In the external market, the different jobs are not linked together in such a chain, and employees move from one job to another in a more casual way. Pricing, allocation and training decisions are controlled more directly by economic variables.

This theory has been extended to explain the problem of disadvantaged workers. The labour market has been analysed as a whole, and its segmentation into primary and secondary sectors has been pointed out. The primary sector consists of a series of internal markets, and of those subsectors of the external markets in which a career pattern is well defined. A stable labour force characterizes this sector. The secondary market consists of all those employment situations characterized by lack of structure. Instability, both of jobs and of workers, seems to be the salient feature of secondary markets. And disadvantaged workers are here confined.

1.3 The LMS debate: the need for a more comprehensive approach

The notion of a dual labour market, as first expressed, was widely acclaimed by economists as providing a useful conceptual construct for the analysis of the labour market. But, at the same time, the original hypothesis was criticized because it tended to be more descriptive than explanatory.[30] The analysis of the internal markets and their separation from the external market, even if described as the result of the institutionalization of rules over time, was presented in static and non-historical terms;[31] finally, it was a particular analysis, mainly related to the USA experience, and therefore it raised doubts concerning the general applicability of this model to other national contexts.[32]

Being more descriptive than explanatory, the DLM theory, as first outlined, has rasied questions rather than answered them. These questions can be grouped under four main headings:

(i) Why do labour market structures differ? How does segmentation originate, i.e. what are the variables at work in the structuring of the labour market?
(ii) Which worker gets which job?
(iii) Is there any mobility between primary and secondary sectors? And if this is the case, is the DLM hypothesis still useful?
(iv) Are the categories proposed useful for the analysis of the labour market structure? Are they a comprehensive description of the complexity of the real world?

In the debate that followed the earlier work, different and opposed hypotheses have been put forward, trying to give insights and answers to the questions raised and, in more general terms, to identify the factors determining the structuring of the labour market. But as research on segmentation has expanded and developed, this has brought a new range of problems and issues under discussion, and this has revealed the emergence of a general consensus. The structuring of the labour market is in fact increasingly perceived as a complex phenomenon, where different factors are seen to interact. Thus, rather than involving competing hypotheses about segmentation, recent work has shown converging explanations.

The following section will present a brief discussion of the different hypotheses,[33] as they were initially put forward. In the subsequent sections (1.3.2 to 1.3.5), I will discuss the answers suggested by the current debate to the questions originally raised, with the intention of singling out a more comprehensive approach which, incorporating common ideas, will lead to a better understanding of the functioning of the labour market.

1.3.1 The different hypotheses about labour market segmentation

On the origins of segmentation, three different hypotheses can be singled out. The first, which is directly related with the DLM theory proposed by Doeringer and Piore (1971), emphasizes the role of technology. The second, which originated from the radical analysis of the evolution of the American capitalist economy, emphasizes the class conflict and the role played by employers in controlling labour. The third approach, which is based on several empirical studies—by and large carried out by researchers of the University of Cambridge—emphasizes the active role of unions in the process of labour market segmentation.

The DLM theory, as initially formulated, identified technology as one of the most important factors in the explanation of behavioural differences in the labour market.[34] Following Oi's (1962) analysis, it has been argued that when the technology in use is specific and complex, the labour force employed is skilled and the type of training required is firm-specific. This implies that management will be interested in having a stable labour force, and will try to ensure this by offering labour high wage rates and other privileges. However, the role of technology has been better explored when the DLM theory has been developed to analyse the dynamics of the labour market. Here, the economic structure and its evolution, and thus the development of the technology in use, is at the centre of the analysis. It is argued that with the development of oligopolistic markets, technology evolves towards firm-specific techniques of production, skills become more firm-specific, and workers' productivity more closely related to on-the-job training. Efficiency criteria push towards structured labour markets, as a stable labour force is regarded as more necessary. It follows that higher wages and prospects of advancement will be provided in order to internalize the market. Dualism, i.e. the existence, on the one hand, of primary labour markets—characterized by good employment conditions, security of employment and stability—and, on the other hand, of secondary labour markets—characterized by low wage rates, instability, lack of career prospects, and uncertainty—is here interpreted as the result of divergent development in the industrial structure, given heterogeneous technological evolution and its interaction with the structure in product market.

Radical economists identify as the principal cause of dualism the conflicting interests of employers and workers.[35] The starting point of the radical approach—which is related on the one hand to the analysis of monopoly capitalism and on the other hand to the labour process debate— is the hypothesis that the processes connected with the evolution of the factory system and the increased mechanization/automation of the production process led to a progressive homogenization of the labour force. The technological innovations introduced at the turn of the century had the effect of squeezing the skill level of workers, by eliminating some craft-trades and impoverishing the skill content of others. With management facing an increasingly homogenized, and therefore more easily organized and antagonistic, labour force, the answer has been to use the internal labour market as a mechanism through which divide and conquer the labour class, minimizing their capacity for cohesion and the possibility of class struggle. Thus, just as jobs were becoming deskilled and more homogeneous, complicated and artificial job hierarchies were introduced to stratify and divide the working class. According to this approach, the job ladders found in primary sectors, and the promotion paths associated to them, have more to do with workers' behavioural traits, such as obedience and rules orientation, than with skill content, as suggested by the DLM theory. Thus, the development of internal labour markets in the twentieth century, as well as the division of labour in the various segments, is interpreted as the capitalists' answer to the problem of discipline, inherent in their need to control the labour process. The historical origins of this process are thus associated with the upsurge of industrial conflict in the USA at the turn of the century, since segmentation served to reduce the possibility of the development of class consciousness among a workforce with an increasingly homogeneous and proletarian character. To conclude, according to the radical approach, the segmentation of the labour market is the outcome of the capitalists' efforts to 'divide and conquer' the working class. In other words, employers try to develop a segmented and stratified labour market in order to minimize the possibility that workers employed in the less desirable (secondary) jobs might identify themselves and form a coalition with the workers employed in the better (primary) jobs, thus reducing the possibility of the development of class consciousness and class struggle.

The third interpretative approach, which can be identified as the 'Cambridge approach', focuses on the active role of workers' organizations in the process of segmentation.[36] The underlying hypothesis is that trade unions organize themselves on the basis of the conditions of production within which they operate. The economic, technological, and market conditions of the firms and the industrial sectors where labour is employed strongly affect trade union organization, power, and strategy. Thus, the evolution of the economic structure, its impact upon the employment structure, and the union reaction to these changes have all to be considered. With the development of capitalism, as capital moves from old into new areas, labour is displaced, jobs are eliminated, and skills become redundant. These continuous changes in the economic structure modify the labour process, and have complex and far reaching effects for the employment structure. This process, inherent in the progress of captialism, creates problems for workers, as competition for jobs necessarily reduces their bargaining power. At the same time, these changes interrupt the prevailing social relations of production, thus giving rise to conflict, due to trade union opposition and resistance. In this situation, it is to be expected that workers will act defensively to protect themselves from competition from the external labour market in order to obtain job security and higher wages. The defence developed by workers, and by their organizations, against competition in the labour market tends to involve some means of control of the supply of labour. And this creates segmentation in the labour market.

In the following pages, the questions originally raised by the debate (see pp. 18–23) will be discussed. The different interpretative hypotheses will not be confronted; rather, the various answers suggested will be discussed in order to define an alternative, more comprehensive approach which incorporates ideas common to all three hypotheses and leads to a better understanding of the functioning of the labour market. And it is with this purpose in mind that the first question, 'why do labour market structures differ?', will be discussed last.

1.3.2 Which worker gets which job?

Research has underlined that both demand factors and supply factors have to be considered in order to understand the problem of workers' allocation to jobs.

On the demand side, it has been suggested that economic and technological factors shape the characteristics of jobs. Thus, it is argued that industry and firm characteristics,[37] the technology in use and firm specific techniques of production,[38] firm-specific skills, and the need for on-the-job training[39] will define job features. And these factors, together with employers' general labour policies,[40] will define the worker stereotypes which—in terms of skills, educational attainment, age, behavioural patterns—will best fit the jobs at hand. Information available and employers' prejudices[41] will determine (given the jobs available and their characteristics) their preference ranking of the labour force and, therefore, their hiring devices. In this respect, it is important to point out that all the approaches advanced (despite the prevailing differences) assume, implicitly or explicitly, *employment choice on the side of demand*, substantially based on the definition of a preference ranking of the labour force.

On the supply side, differences in the characteristics of workers have been widely discussed. These can be grouped under three main headings: workers' background characteristics, workers' behavioural patterns, and workers' social position. The importance of these factors is related not to the problem of workers' choice in the labour market but to the *determination of their position in the labour market* (and therefore in the ranking preference of firms).[42]

On the basis of what has been pointed out in the debate, we could argue that workers' basic characteristics (such as sex, race, age, marital status, and also, to some extent, educational attainment and previous training) define workers' position in the labour market *directly*, with respect to the technical/physical/attitudinal characteristics required to fill the vacancies, and *indirectly*, with respect to behavioural patterns (in terms of stability, reliability, obedience, diligence, and so on), as they are used by employers as screening devices to define their hiring policies.[43] With respect to the behavioural patterns, there are two opposed arguments. On the one hand, it is argued that differences in behavioural patterns are exogenous to the functioning of the labour market: what the labour market does is to exploit them. In other words, secondary workers tend to show unstable and unreliable behaviour, and are willing to accept secondary jobs because of their social origin (Piore, 1975a) and/or because of the culture background and the work ethic attached to it (Sabel, 1979). Therefore it is argued that the society *finds* groups within an already existing social structure who are willing to play these roles (Piore, 1978). On the other hand, it is argued that it is the social structure, and particularly the way in which the labour market works and treats workers, that *creates* these groups in order to have people who will play these economic roles (Edwards, 1979; Reich *et al.*, 1973; Watchel, 1975; Harrison and Vietorisz, 1973; Gordon, 1976). That is, the behavioural attributes of workers develop differently in the 'core' and 'peripheral' markets: behavioural characteristics of workers are endogenously induced.

Finally, as far as differences in the social position of workers are concerned, it has been pointed out that workers occupy different positions in the labour market, depending on their willingness and/or ability to accept certain working conditions. This has to be related to the differences in workers' position in the system of social reproduction, and thus is reflected in differences by sex, age, and marital status. In this context, the large debate on the economic and social position of women[44] has pointed-out the existing relations between the system of production, the system of social reproduction, and the labour market, and therefore the relations between the system of social reproduction and (i) the wage structure and the labour supply structure, (ii) the structure of production and consumption. It is an acknowledged fact that women are, within the labour market, a distinct group—often identified as a 'secondary labour force'—and that they occupy specific positions in the labour process, identified in terms of job segregation. Despite the existence of different interpretative hypotheses on the nature of the position of women in the labour market, and consequently on the position of the other groups of workers, the fact that women are segregated in secondary jobs is related to the role of women in the system of social reproduction and, in particular, within the family.[45] Similarly, it has been pointed out that workers' position within the social structure (and therefore their definition in terms of status) affects their culture, ethic of work, and work habits; and, therefore, it defines their acceptability—in terms of status—of jobs.[46]

To conclude, we could say that differences in the background characteristics and behavioural patterns of workers allow firms to differentiate their hiring policies, given the jobs available. At the same time, differences in the workers' social position, with respect both to the family structure and to the social structure, define the minimum level of acceptability, in terms of jobs, on the supply side.

1.3.3 Mobility

The LMS debate has stimulated a large amount of empircal work[47] testing the hypothesis of a labour market structured in different segments, where some groups of workers are prevented from moving up from secondary to primary jobs. The empirical work consists in: (*a*) a description of the labour market in terms of the distribution of job characteristics (wage, stability, skill requirements, education, working conditions, and so on) to groups of workers (where workers are classified by race, sex, and age); and (*b*) the estimation of occupational mobility for all groups of workers. The assessement of occupational advancement for different groups of workers has been employed to test the DLM hypothesis.

The empirical evidence seems to be, in this respect, quite contradictory. In fact, this approach has been used both to support and to disprove the original hypothesis. For example, Leigh (1976) tested various mobility hypotheses for workers classified by race, previous wage, previous industry and occupation, and other characteristics. He found no support for immobility across variously defined boundaries for low wages and black workers. His conclusion was that there was little empirical support for the DLM hypothesis. Rosenberg (1980) criticized Leigh's work and proposed a direct test, supporting the hypothesis. He argued that, because of the full characteristics of secondary and primary jobs had not yet been identified, tests of the DLM theory generally consisted of a comparison of the experiences of groups of workers, such as, for example, blacks and whites. Blacks were assumed to represent workers in the secondary sector and whites to represent those in the primary sector. But what was actually assessed in these investigations was not the DLM theory, but different groups' experiences. Rosenberg's conclusion was that there *was* segmentation, even if the barriers separating the primary and the secondary labour markets were not impermeable. For education, training, and experience were found to be relatively unimportant in determining whether a person living in a low-income area moves from a secondary to a primary sector.

This debate about the existence or nonexistence of immobilities has made clear the differences in the hypotheses advanced, in particular with reference to the concept of segmentation itself. Orthodox economics has incorporated some of the ideas developed by the LMS debate and has adopted its terminology. But the separation of the market into segments is analysed in terms of *rigidities*; the problem therefore is to explain the existence of these rigidities. The LMS approach, on the contrary, despite the different hypotheses advanced, seems to agree on a common general definition of segmentation, in which the labour market is analysed in terms of a set of markets, *differentiated in their working processes and in their outcomes*. This idea of segmentation is based on two main points: (*a*) the functioning of these segmented markets diverges from the competitive norm; (*b*) what distinguishes the different segments is not only the problem of rigidity/mobility of workers between them, but the fact that they are qualitatively different. That is to say, they are distinguished by specific labour market characteristics, economic processes, and behavioural rules: thus the labour market segments treat workers differently.[48] Therefore, the crucial problem is not to show if there is or is not mobility between the segments, but to show that labour markets are qualitatively non-uniform: that is, that workers are treated differently in terms of wages, working conditions, stability, and so on, because economic processes such as wage determination, training, and career are fundamentally dissimilar in the separate market segments.

1.3.4 Categories

The early debate about LMS was based on the major division of the labour market into primary and secondary sectors, implicitly or explicitly centring the analysis around the definition and description of the internal labour market.[49] The large, capital-intensive and oligopolistic firms were supposed to operate internal markets providing high wages and secure employment, thus limiting the mobility of workers both within the primary market and between the primary and the secondary segments. The analysis focused on the aggregate level, using a categorization that did not allow for differences in product market, technology, industrial relations conditions, or labour supply conditions for similar enterprises in separate industries.[50]

The attempt to employ the LMS categories, as previously formulated, has therefore raised problems at the empirical level. In fact, these categories are scarcely applicable if one tries to operate at a less aggregate or less abstract level. It is in the attempt to formulate a more extensive typology that a further specification of the labour market segments has been introduced, such as, for example, an upper tier for professional and managerial employment in the primary market and a lower tier for blue-collar and part of the white-collar jobs[51]; independent and subordinate spheres[52]; and primary internal, primary external, secondary internal, and secondary external.[53]

These new categories are, in some respect, a better specification of the labour market segments. Nevertheless, it should be noted that the usefulness of these categories depends substantially on the level of generalization, the level of abstraction, and the kind of problem that one wants to investigate. This helps to explain why all these typologies lose their strength when we try to apply them to concrete cases. At the same time, it suggests that, even if reality looks more complex and variable than is as described by these typologies, nevertheless they can be useful if employed as analytical constructs to allow some generalization about the structure of the labour market, and not as exhaustive definitions of labour market segments.

In fact, what seems to emerge[54] is that what is needed is not to broaden this typology, but to interpret segmentation in terms of *discontinuity*, as is clearly stated by Berger and Piore:

> When we began, we called this pattern of social and economic segmentation *dualism*. . . . As we proceeded, it became clear that the significance of dualism is not that a society is divided into *two* autonomous and discontinuous segments but that a *society is divided segmentally and not continuously*. Whether there are two or more such lumps is not central to our conception, though the numbers of segments cannot be multiplied indefinitely without restoring the continuum and returning to the paradigm we have rejected. (Berger and Piore, 1980, p. 2; their emphasis.)

That is to say, what is relevant about these discontinuities is that they distinguish labour market segments which are qualitatively different. This means that the processes of allocation, training, promotion, wage determination, and so on, as well as workers' and employers' behavioural patterns, are qualitatively different as we move across market segments. And it is exactly the hypothesis that the labour market segments work non-uniformly, i.e. that they are qualitatively different, that has stimulated a large amount of empirical work on the structure of the labour market.[55] And this leads us to the last point.

1.3.5 The structuring of labour markets

The empirical work that followed the original hypothesis pointed to different explanations in an attempt to account for segmentation, and different explanatory variables were put forward (see section 1.3.1 above).

The early institutionalists stressed the role of *formal and informal rules* established in industrial enterprises; the DLM theory suggested *technological variations* between sectors as the key factor in the distinction between 'internal' and 'external' markets; the radical Americans argued that *class conflict* and the consequent strategy of capital to 'divide and rule' the labour force together provide the main explanations for labour management segmentation; whilst a more general approach took into account the *direct role of workers*, as organized in trade unions.

The empirical findings of most recent years have shown that these explanatory variables are not necessarily mutually exclusive. On the contrary, they have been found to be complementary:

> . . . segmentation requires multi-causal explanations, and . . . the various explanatory hypotheses—based on the structure of technology, product markets, control over the labour process and labour supply conditions—are complementary rather than competitive. (Rubery and Wilkinson, 1981, pp. 116–16.)

A consensus is emerging that the search for one explanation is misplaced. It is the interaction between different forces (technological, economic, and institutional) that has to be investigated. Therefore, a more comprehensive approach which works out the functioning of these non-competing markets is needed in order to identify the determinants of the structuring of the labour market.

1.4 Preliminary conclusion

The LMS debate has pointed out the emergence of non-competitive markets. The labour market is not analysed as an aggregatable phenomenon, but as a set of distinct markets, characterized by different structures. Within each market, employers and workers face fundamentally different conditions and behave according to different rules, so that the mechanisms at work within them operate non-uniformly.

A large part of the early literature has attempted to reconsider the labour market by working out a typology of these non-competing segments; at the same time, different and apparently opposed explanations have been put forward in an attempt to account for segmentation. The most recent empirical work has pointed out that the crucial problem is neither a problem of categorization nor a question of competing explanations, but a problem of explaining labour markets in terms of their different structures. In this respect, the questions that this work sets out to investigate are the following: (*a*) how do labour market structures differ? (*b*) why do they differ? A comparison between the functioning of two industrial sectors, steel and construction, in Italy has therefore been carried out in order to shed light on the above questions.

Notes

1. Addison and Siebert, 1979, p. 3. They present the neoclassical labour theory, incorporating into the general framework the major developments in labour economics: the analysis of the supply of labour as the outcome of household decision-making; the theory of investment in human capital; and the new microeconomics of uncertainty and information processes.
2. Appelbaum, 1979, p. 39.
3. A market as defined by Marshall (1920) is 'a district, small or large, in which there are many buyers and many sellers all so keenly on the alert and so well acquainted with one another's affairs, that the price of a commodity is always the same for the whole of the district. . . . Thus the more nearly perfect a market is, the stronger is the tendency for the same price to be paid for the same thing at the same time in all parts of the market.' (Marshall, 1920, Vol. III, Ch. 4, § 7, p. 112 and Vol. V, Ch. 1, § 3, p. 325).
4. See Marx, 1976, Vol. I, Chs. 5, 8, 17.
5. This would allow for the housewife who works part-time in a temporary job just to finish the payments on the dishwashing machine; the homeworker who accepts a low-paid job simply because it is the only form of waged work available for her; and the construction worker who accepts work on 'the lump' for an unskilled job with no prospects, since it is the only available mean of obtaining, for the time being, sufficient income to meet family needs.
6. See Appelbaum 1979, p. 41.
7. This is the debate that followed the publication of Braverman's (1974) study. See *Politics and Society*, 1978; Zimbalist, 1979; Edwards, 1979; Nichols, 1980; Littler, 1982; Gordon *et al.*, 1982.
8. Keynes himself conceived of wages, in terms of the wage structure, as exogenously determined, and real wages, though to some extent affected by events in the labour market, as determined by 'the other forces of the economic system' (1936, p. 14). Since Keynes's *General Theory*, econom-

ists have been investigating these 'other forces' and non-market factors (social and normative factors) in the process of wage determination. While the demand for labour, relative to supply, plays a major role by strengthening or weakening labour's bargaining position, other factors have also been taken into account, with the resulting conclusion that neither money wages nor real wages can be said to be uniquely determined by demand and supply of labour.

9. See Reynolds, 1951; Reddaway, 1959; OECD, 1965, among many citations that could be listed.
10. In this context Reddaway (1959) stated: 'whether we like it or not, wages are not fixed . . . in response to the forces of supply and demand . . . Changes in the demand for labour in the various industries and occupations operate to secure a redistribution of the labour force mainly through direct changes in "job opportunities" made available by employers, and the vigour (or lack thereof) with which the employers seek to recruit workers.'
11. See for example Bluestone, 1968; Piore, 1970; Harrison, 1972; Watchel, 1970; Watchel and Betsey, 1972.
12. These different hypotheses have been given many different names: job queue model, dual labour market theory, radical approach, institutional approach, LMS theory. I will use the last definition to include them all.
13. John Stuart Mill was the first to see inequalities of wage as the outcome of social differences, instead of as the equitable principle of compensation represented by Smith as the general law of remuneration of labour. Mill pointed out that the worst jobs, instead of being better paid than the others, were '. . . almost invariably paid the worst of all because performed by those who have no choice'. He explained this as the result of the division into social ranks and the immobility between ranks. In Mill's words: 'so complete, indeed, has hitherto been the separation, so strongly marked the line of demarcation, between the different grades of labourers, as to be almost equivalent to an hereditary distinction of caste. . .' (Mill, 1909, Vol. I, Book 2, Ch. 14, pp. 369–77.)
14. See Marshall, 1920, Vol. IV, Ch. 6, § 8 and Vol. VI, Chs. 3–5.
15. 'Parents generally bring up their children to occupations in their own grade, and therefore the total supply of labour in any one grade in one generation is in a great measure determined by the numbers in that grade in the preceding generation, yet within the grade itself there is greater mobility.' (Marshall, 1920, p. 217.)
16. Marshall argued: 'The vertical movement from one grade to another is seldom very rapid or on a very large scale; but when the advantages of a grade have risen relatively to the difficulty of the work required of it, many small streams of labour, both youthful and adults, will begin to flow towards it; and though none of them may be very large, they will together have a sufficient volume to satisfy before long the increased demand for labour in that grade.' (Marshall, 1920, p. 217.)
17. See Marshall, 1920, Vol. VI, Ch. 3, § 2.
18. Ibid., Vol. VI, Ch. 3, § 8.

19. As it is so effectively expressed in this well-known quotation: 'Casual labour is often badly paid, not because it gets less than it is worth, but because it is worth so appallingly little.' (Hicks, 1963, p. 82.)
20. Hicks (1963, p. 77) acknowledged that 'movement is far from easy', so that mobility from one job to another was not sufficient to eliminate earning differences.
21. The term 'institutional economics' usually refers to the various efforts undertaken to infuse economic theory with a greater realism. This approach developed initially in the USA at the beginning of the century. It received a new push in the postwar period, when the focus of the analysis became precisely the study of labour. See McNulty, 1980, pp. 153–76 for a discussion of the early institutional economists; see Kerr, 1980 for a discussion of postwar developments.
22. Lester, 1946, 1947; Reynolds, 1951, Ch. 9; OECD, 1965.
23. Dunlop (1957) introduced the concepts of 'wage contours' and 'job clusters'; Livernash (1957) defined the internal wage structure as the 'job family'; Ross (1947, 1948) discussed the concept of the 'orbit of coercive comparison' in the wage-setting process; Eckstein and Wilson (1962) showed the existence of key groups of related industries to account for wage differences.
24. Kerr (1950), discussing the 'institutional market', advanced the idea of rules limiting the entry into them; the idea of ports of entry limiting the access to labour markets was expanded in a later article (1954). Lester (1951–2) discussed managers' and workers' practices in limiting access to the labour market.
25. See Kerr, 1950, 1954; Lester, 1951–2; Palmer, 1954; Myers, 1954; Parnes, 1962.
26. Palmer *et al.*, 1962; Oi, 1962.
27. Palmer, 1954; Palmer *et al.*, 1962; Parnes, 1962.
28. Kerr, 1950, 1954; Fisher, 1951, Myers, 1954.
29. Ross, 1948; Dunlop, 1957; Livernash, 1957; Lester, 1951–2.
30. Cain, 1976; Del Boca, 1980.
31. Gordon, 1972; Reich *et al.*, 1973.
32. Reich and Wilkinson, 1978; Bruno, 1979.
33. For a review of the literature, confronting the different hypotheses advanced, see Gordon, 1972; Cain, 1976; Rubery, 1978; Del Boca, 1980; Loveridge and Mok, 1979.
34. Doeringer, 1967; Doeringer and Piore, 1971; Piore, 1975*b*.
35. Reich *et al.*, 1973; Watchel, 1975; Stone, 1975; Edwards, 1979; Gordon *et al.*, 1982.
36. Kah, 1976; Friedman, 1977; Wilkinson, 1977; Rubery, 1978; Elbaum and Wilkinson, 1979; Craig *et al.*, 1982.
37. Averitt, 1968; Bluestone, 1970, 1971.
38. Piore, 1970, 1975*b*; Doeringer and Piore, 1971; Thurow, 1972.
39. See Doeringer, 1967; Piore, 1975*a*, 1980.
40. Reich *et al.*, 1973; Stone, 1975; Noble, 1977; Burawoy, 1979; Edwards, 1979; Gordon *et al.*, 1982.

41. The 'signalling and screening' hypothesis has analysed the effects of the existence of imperfect information in employment relations. In particular, the impossibility of the firms of knowing the desired features of labour results in the emergence of proxy variables (signals) in order to select and screen the labour force for the required characteristics. See Spence, 1973; Stiglitz, 1975; Taubam and Wales, 1973.
42. In more general terms, I would say that if there is a possibility of choice on the side of labour, this is by and large overcome by other factors: on the one hand, jobs available and employers' choice, on the other hand, workers' social position. So that the role that labour choice plays in the functioning of the labour market is minimal.
43. See Piore, 1978; Doeringer and Piore, 1971; Sabel, 1979; Edwards, 1979; Reich *et al.*, 1973; Bowles, 1971; Bowles and Gintis, 1975; Thurow, 1972, 1975.
44. See, among many works that could be cited, Amsden, 1980; Mitchell and Oakley, 1976; Kuhn and Wolpe, 1978; Blau and Jusenius, 1976; Eisenstein, 1979. Despite the relevance of the issues raised by this debate, the problem of social reproduction was left out of account by the LMS debate. It is only very recently that attention has been drawn to these issues and to their implication for the analysis of the structuring of the labour market. See on this Picchio del Mercato, 1981; Kenrick, 1981; Rubery and Wilkinson, 1981; Rubery and Tarling, 1981; Humphries and Rubery, 1984.
45. See Beechey, 1977; Humphries, 1977; Himmelweit and Mohun, 1977; Picchio del Mercato, 1981.
46. Piore, 1975*a*, 1978; Sabel, 1979.
47. Leigh, 1976, 1978; Lucas, 1974; Alexander, 1974; Oster, 1979; Rosenberg, 1977, 1980, 1981.
48. This point has been recently stressed by different authors. See Piore, 1979, pp. xii–xiii, and 1980, pp. 16–17; Edwards, 1979, pp. 166–70; Ryan, 1981, p. 4.
49. Doeringer and Piore's analysis (1971) was in fact based on this category. Later works, even if based on a quite distinct approach, were still using the concept of the internal labour market as the basic feature for characterizing the functioning of segmented markets. See for example Stone, 1975, p. 75 and Edwards, 1979, pp. 5–6.
50. For a discussion of this issue see Rubery and Wilkinson, 1979; Craig *et al.*, 1979, 1982.
51. Piore, 1975*a*, and 1980.
52. Reich *et al.*, 1973.
53. Loveridge and Mok, 1979.
54. See Piore, 1980, pp. 16–17; Berger and Piore, 1980, p. 2; Ryan, 1981, pp. 6–8.
55. See Rubery and Wilkinson, 1979; the collection of papers in Wilkinson, 1981; Craig *et al.*, 1982; Solinas, 1982; Brusco, 1982.

CHAPTER TWO

The Economic and Technological Framework for Analysis of the Labour Market Structure

The empirical work on the steel and construction industries in Italy aims to shed light on the functioning of the labour market, focusing attention on its structure. This chapter presents a discussion of the contrasting economic and technological characteristics of the two industries that are regarded as relevant in defining the framework within which the employer/worker interaction takes place.

2.1 The steel and construction industries in Italy

2.1.1 The nature of the product

Steel is an intermediate product whose main markets are the construction, motor vehicle, electrical and non-electrical machinery, shipbuilding, household equipment, mining, oil, gas extraction, railway and aircraft industries. These industries produce, for the most part, capital investment goods and consumer durables, and as a result their demand is subject to wide cyclical fluctuations. Steel products differ in quality (such as alloys, and special steels such as stainless, high-speed, and tool steels) and in shape (sheet, coils, and strips; bars and sections; tubes and fittings; plates; wire rods and wire; tinplate; rails and axles). But once these two characteristics are defined, there is little possibility for further differentiation, so that steel products are highly standardized and produced in large quantities. The high standardization and the low level of tariff protection encourage foreign trade. The market for steel is therefore highly competitive at the international level.[1]

The construction industry's output is a durable good, immobile, highly differentiated, and with no close substitutes. Even within each branch of the sector the product differs in location and technical features. This lack of standardization makes building a typical one-off product. Construction products, with the exception of speculative ventures, are supplied to customer specifications via a complex system of tendering arrangements. The works to be built on a site are owned by the building contractor only in a small number of cases. The client, i.e. the owner of the works to be built, can be an individual, a cooperative, a company or the government itself (local authorities or the central government). The client addresses itself to a consultant, who is in charge of the conception of the project and the design. An agreement (a contract) between the client or the consultant and a building contractor (the main contractor) defines the types of work to be done at certain rates, generally within stated times.

There are several branches of the construction industry: housing, commercial and industrial buildings, and civil engineering (such as roads, harbours, pipelines, and transmission lines). Each branch employs different techniques of production and operates in different product markets; and within each branch the industry deals with new construction, repair, maintenance, and demolition. Finally, within a single branch, building products differ widely so that, for example, housing includes small cottages as well as large blocks of flats and skyscrapers.

2.1.2 Technology in use

The steel industry is a process industry: the transformation of raw materials (iron ore, limestone, coke) into finished products (plates, coils, strips, sheets, bars, sections, tubes) occurs through a series of physical and chemical processes set out in a fixed and rigid sequence, so that the production process is continuous and integrated. Appendix A presents a discussion of technology. In this chapter, the main features of the production process flow are discussed, as set out in Figure 2.1. This shows the principal installations for the main productive departments in rectangles, while inputs and outputs are shown by arrows. Three separate but integrated stages are identifiable: reduction of iron ore into pig-iron, refining of pig-iron into steel, and rolling of steel ingots into semifinished and finished products. Pig-iron is obtained by direct reduction of the ore with the enrichment of carbon in the blast-furnace—a vertical cylinder lined with protective firebricks, continuously charged from above and tapped at the bottom at intervals.[2] Pig-iron is carried in the molten state in ladles into the steelworks, where it is refined into steel, a process consisting of the reduction of carbon content and the removal of impurities. This can take place in different types of steel-making plants. In Italy, Basic Oxygen Systems (BOS), such as LD and OBM converters, open-hearth furnaces (OH) and electric furnaces are employed. While the first two can be charged with liquid metal, the third has to be charged with solid metal (steel scrap) and is therefore not employed in integrated plants.[3] When the steel-making cycle is completed, the molten metal is casted either in the casting pits, in large ingot moulds where it

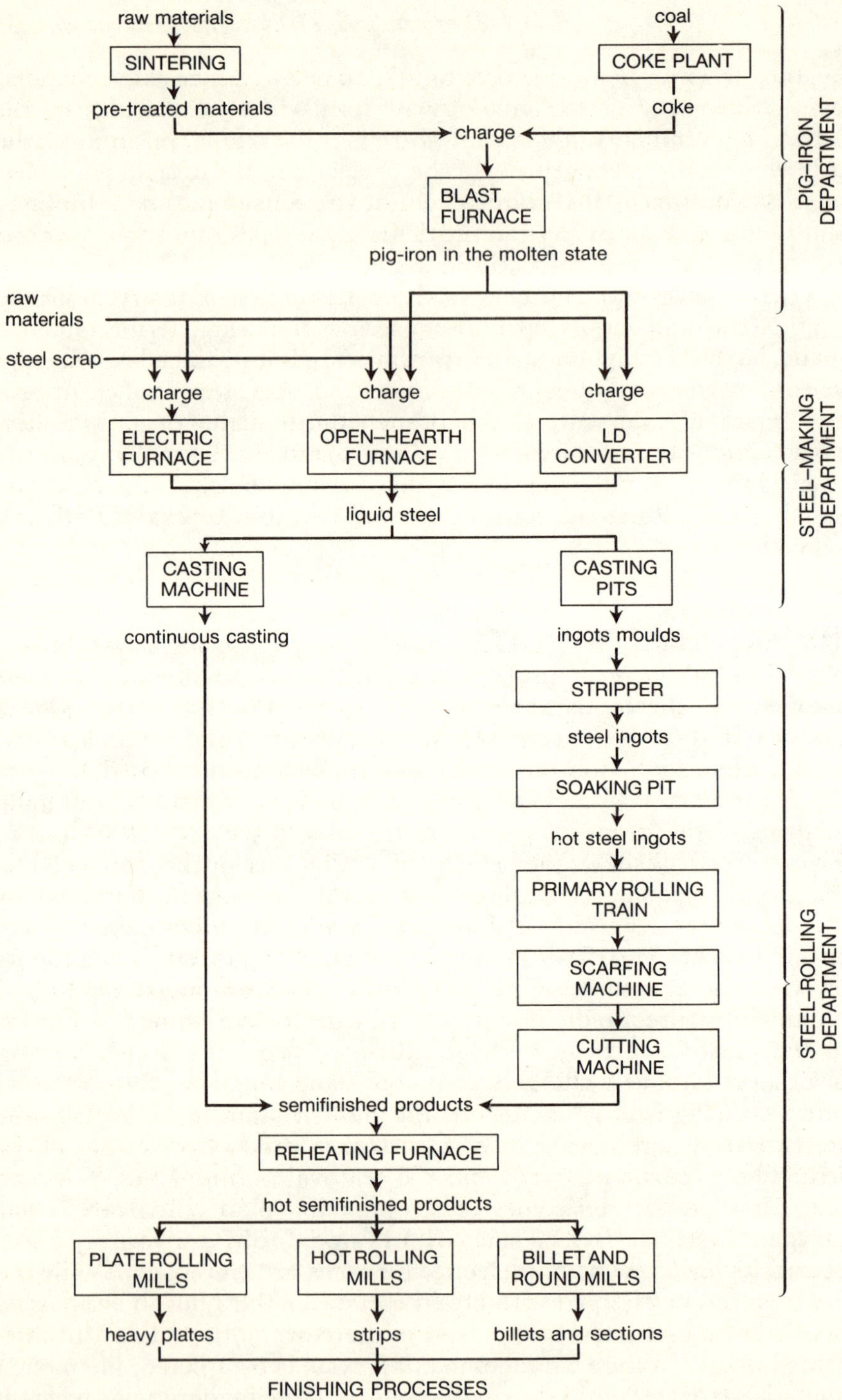

FIG. 2.1 Production process flow for an integrated steel plant

is left to solidify, or—increasingly—in a continuous casting machine, from which the molten metal emerges as a solid semifinished product, thereby doing away with the first rolling of the ingots. A large variety of rolling trains changes the shape of the ingots into semifinished slabs, blooms, or billets (slabbing train, blooming train) and then into finished products (finishing trains for hot and cold rolling) by passing the metal between two rotating rolls.

A steel plant can be looked at as a sequence of departments, clearly distinguished in terms of installations and processes, but highly integrated. Within each department, the transformation of inputs into outputs is organized around the activity of large and very complex equipment (blast-furnaces, converters, steel furnaces and rolling trains), highly mechanized and partly automated. Here the intervention of labour consists, mainly, in the control and regulation of installations, and processes. Each department is organized in elementary productive units, so that in the pig-iron department there will be as many productive units as the number of blast-furnaces; in the steel-making department as the number of converters and furnaces; and in the rolling mills as the number of rolling trains. Each productive unit consists of sections corresponding to the way in which that phase of the production process is organized. The pig-iron department has a separate section for the preparation and sintering of raw materials, one for the coke plant and one for the blast-furnace; the steel-making department has separate sections for the preparation of raw materials, the smelting of steel and the casting of the molten metal into ingots; the rolling department has a soaking pit section for the ingots to be reheated, a rolling section where the ingots are rolled by the different trains, and a final section where the output is stocked. Besides the productive departments, there are maintenance and service sections, corresponding to different specific functions and acting mainly in support of the process departments. Maintenance services, by far the largest, are organized to provide the process department with the type of maintenance intervention required (e.g. electrical maintenance, engineering maintenance, brickwork maintenance). The service sections include a large variety of services: auxiliary services acting directly in support of the process departments;[4] transport services in charge of all the handling of inputs and outputs;[5] technical and administrative services for accounting and technical assistance;[6] and personnel services, such as surveillance, safety, cleaning, and sickbay.

The three stages of the production process, as previously discussed, can be carried out jointly by the same plant or separately by different plants. Three main types of plants may therefore exist: integrated steel plants, steelworks integrated with rolling mills, and rerolling plants, distinguished not only in terms of the general dimensions of the works but also in terms of technology in use, quality of steel produced, degree of product standardization, and degree of mechanization and automation. *Integrated steel plants*, usually located near a supply of large quantities of raw materials (i.e. either near the ore deposits or near the sea), produce finished products from the raw materials (iron ore, coal, limestone). Blast-furnaces for the production of pig-iron are integrated with steelworks (LD or OBM converters, or OH furnaces). The characteristics of the integrated mills—very large, highly mechanized, and increasingly employing process computers—make them better suited for the production of highly standardized products in very large quantities. *Steelworks* integrated with rolling mills produce finished products mainly from scrap by a process of melting and refining in electric furnaces. Smaller works, less mechanized and with little automation, usually characterize these plants, making them better suited for the production of special steel and/or special finished products (steel sections). *Rolling mills* transform semifinished products into finished products through a rolling and finishing process. Given the large variety of finished products, a large variety of rolling mills exist. The coexistence of these three main types of plants reflects both the evolution of technology, and thus the historical period in which the works were built, and the existence of different market situations in terms of availability of raw materials and access to the market for them, as well as access to the product market.

To conclude, steel is a process production consisting in the chemical and physical transformation of inputs into outputs. Very large and complex capital equipment is employed, so that steel production is a typical capital intensive process. The plant is organized in separate processes (i.e. departments), and each process has separate stages that form the basis for labour organization. As will be discussed in Chapter 3, the activity of labour remains an activity of control, regulation, and maintenance concerned with works and processes, where workers tend to be characterized not by trade or skill but by the position they occupy with respect to the production process (process, maintenance, and ancillary workers).

In construction, each single output is the result of a unique process of production. The building product, and therefore the technology in use, is largely differentiated by branch (housing, commercial, and industrial building, civil engineering, repair and modernization), by lack of standardization, and by location. Indeed, building traditions, weather, and general land conditions, as well as the supply of local inputs—stones, wood, bricks—vary widely between areas, thus affecting the way the buildings are erected. Construction is a sequential and cyclical process: each stage builds upon earlier stages, and each stage has to organize and integrate a wide variety of materials, techniques of production, skills and trades. Table 2.1 shows a typical site cycle for residential building, distinguishing the main sequences for each stage.

The first stage (site preparation) requires the extensive use of capital equipment, while labour is employed only to drive and maintain this equipment. In the second stage, the loadbearing structure of the building is erected. With the most traditional technique (brickwork), this consists of load-bearing walls, floors, and roof. This is a typical labour-intensive process, where the erection of walls is done by putting together small units (such as bricks, small concrete blocks and stones) on a lay of lime-mortar. If reinforced concrete is employed, the superstructure consists in a reinforced concrete frame of columns and beams. The structure is erected by casting (or pumping) concrete into

TABLE 2.1
Typical building site activity grouped in construction sequences

site preparation	(1) site clearance	tree felling and grubbing up roots demolition of existing building general site levelling
	(2) foundations	excavations and earthworks piling and construction of direct bearing foundations
loadbearing structure	(3) superstructure	columns and beams main walls, floors and roof
	(4) external cladding	the structural frame is closed and cladded
	(5) interior walls	brickwork and partitions paving roofing
finishing	(6) fixing	windows and door frames floor coverings wall and ceiling finishes glazing and decorating sanitary plumbing heating electrical fixtures gas and water mains
	(7) services	electrical conduits heating work lift shaft structure

prepared shutters internally reinforced with steel. When the structural frame (columns, beams, floors, and roof) is completed, the building is externally closed and internal partitions are erected using brickwork, cladding, and plastering. The third and final stage consists of a long and variable series of operations (varying according to the industrial design of the building), including fixing (window frames, door frames, floor covering, wall and ceiling finishes, etc.) and finishing (installation of services).

For each specific sequence of the production process not only are alternative techniques available, but a combination of different techniques (in variable proportions) tends to be used.[7] This is because technological evolution is not linear: there is no temporal succession so that the new techniques will replace the old ones; rather, for the same set of operations, older techniques can be combined with other more recent ones. That is, the introduction of reinforced concrete has not eliminated brickwork; neither has the introduction of prefabricated components eliminated reinforced concrete works. But these innovations have increased the range of techniques available, so that a wider variety of combinations is now possible for the production of similar outputs. Appendix C presents a discussion of technical change in construction, outlining the main features of the techniques available. Table 2.2 presents a simplified sketch of the evolution of the techniques available for the realization of the main building structure. It distinguishes, for each main technique (brickwork, reinforced concrete work, industrialized systems), the subdivisions into groups of works and the available techniques.

To conclude, construction activity is a typical one-off production process consisting in the production of units to the customer's requirements by a large combination of techniques and inputs. Capital equipment is employed, but only to a small extent, so that building remains basically a labour-intensive process, consisting in the manufacture of an output by assembling different materials manually. The labour process remains dominated by handicraft labour, where specialization by trade is clearly related to the materials handled: bricklayers (bricks), carpenters (wood), steel fixers (steel). When industrialized methods of erection (industrial casting and prefabricated building) are used to a large extent and for a very large site, the production process is more correctly defined as a batch system. In this case, the construction process is quite drasitically modified, consisting of a sequence of operations repeated in rigid succession.

2.1.3 The industrial structure

Economies of scale are important in steel production (Cockerill, 1974): large plants and installations distinguish it, and the tendency is

TABLE 2.2

Technical evolution in building activity (load-bearing structure)

Technical evolution	Site cycle activity	Techniques available
brickwork	load-bearing and non-bearing walls	common bricks stones concrete blocks
	external cladding	plastering cladding
↓	carpentry	timber shutters (traditional) standardized timber shutters metal shutters
	steel fixing	steel bending and fixing prefabricated steel structures electro-weld wire-netting
reinforced work	cement production	manual semi-mechanized industrially produced
↓	concrete casting	on site (manual) on site (cement gun machine) precast (beams, columns) precast (concrete floors, panels)
	industrialized metal carpentry	'table banche' 'demi-tunnel' 'tunnel'
industrialized systems	production of prefabricated large units	site factory prefabrication manufacturing factories
	assembling of prefabricated large units	by casting mechanical assembly other methods

towards a further increase of their dimensions. Steel is a highly capital-intensive sector; investments need large amounts of finance and a long time for realization. This explains the oligopolistic feature of the industry: a few large enterprises produce for most of the market, both at the national and at the international level.[8] This oligopolistic structure implies both a financial concentration, so that the major corporations include a large number of steel plants, and a concentration of production, so that steel is produced in a small number of large steel plants. Given the large investment involved and the long time of realization,[9] entry into the sector is extremely difficult. This implies that the structure of the sector tends to change slowly and in relation either to (*a*) the investment plans of existing enterprises; and/or to (*b*) plans for restructuring and closing down plants, due to changes in economic conditions and the process of technological obsolescence.

The Italian steel industry consists of 130 iron and steel companies and over 146 rerolling companies (CISIA, 1980) employing, on the whole, about 146,000 people (ASSIDER, *Sintesi dell'attività svolta*, 1982), highly concentrated in few very large plants. The steel enterprises differ by type of management (public, private), technology in use (integrated works, scrap-based mills, mini-mills), product specialization (common steel, special steel; long products, flat products, sections), and geographical location (coastal plants, continental plants). As a result, it is possible to analyse the industry in terms of the different subsectors, as summarized in Table 2.3: integrated steel plants (public sector), continental mills (private sector), continental mills (public sector), and mini-mills (private sector).[10] Table 2.4 shows the breakdown of crude steel production by technology and enterprise, in the public and private sectors, giving their market shares.

There are four very large *integrated plants* (Cornigliano, Piombino, Bagnoli, and Taranto) located on the coast along the peninsula, where large quantities of raw materials are supplied by sea. They all belong to state-controlled companies (Italsider, Acciaierie di Piombino). Very large steel converters (LD, OBM) are used for the mass production of common steel. Continuous casting and highly automated rolling mills have been installed for the production of high capital-intensive products.[11] The policy of concentrating production in a few very large integrated plants has resulted in a tendency to specialize in common grades of steel and highly standardized products, such as *flat products*, so that FINSIDER[12] is the only producer of coils (hot rolled coils), partly sold to the market and partly rerolled. It is this type of production, highly standardized and in very large quantities, that allows for the use of highly automated capital equipment. Large plants and works dimensions, new works and up-to-date techniques, highly mechanized and partly automated processes using process computers, characterize such plants. Given the large investments involved, and their recent date, the problem is one of the full utilization of their productive capacity.

The *continental steel works*, so called because of their location in the northern industrial triangle, are medium sized scrap-based works for the production of high-value added products. They are located in an area poor in raw materials but rich in hydroelectric power. They are mainly privately owned (Tecksid, Falck, Redaelli), even if this subsector includes a few state controlled enterprises (Dalmine, Breda, Terni). This group uses mainly electric furnaces for the melting and refining of scrap. These are efficient at a smaller scale and allow for better quality control. They are therefore more suitable for the production of high-quality and special steel products (particularly for the production of *long products* such as bars and sections). These plants have quite an old tradition, most of them dating back to the beginning of this century; their problem has always been one of introducing innovations and of keeping a competitive position in the market. No radical changes have been introduced, but the existing works have been subject to smooth modification over time. In the 1970s, new electric arc furnaces (UHP electric furnaces) were installed to replace the outdated furnaces, and they are being increasingly installed in combination with casting machines.

Finally, there is the group of *mini-steel works*. These are concentrated in the Brescia district; they are all privately owned; and they produce rather *simple and standardized products*, such as reinforcing bars for the building industry and light sections. They developed in the postwar period, taking advantage of the low price of scrap. They rapidly increased their productive capacity by introducing innovative production methods at an early date, i.e. UHP electric furnaces connected with continuous casting machines. This allowed them to reach a highly competitive position in the international market in a short period.[13]

To conclude, the Italian steel industry is described as up-to-date and technically competitive, for its technical productive differentiation is quite sound.[14] In fact, the present structure is the result of a long and continuous process of expansion, innovation, and rationalization, which has allowed for differentiation in terms of location, technology, and product specialization. It has also anticipated some of the rationalization that the actual conditions of the world steel market has been imposing on the European industry. But large investment plans reached completion in the early 1970s, when a major recession hit the world steel market, and the Italian economy has entered a period of stagnation. Thus demand has slumped while new capacity continued to expand (see Figure 2.2), so that the country is now in the difficult position of having a relatively young steel productive structure but one that is far too large for its market.

The construction industry is a large and diversified sector of the economy: its share of the GDP has ranged between 10 and 6 per cent over the last two decades, employing between 2.15 and 1.7 million people.[15] There are a great many enterprises selling construction services, spread all over the country. The features of building products in

TABLE 2.3

The productive structure of the Italian steel industry: main characteristics (1980)

	Integrated plant	Continental medium steel works	Mini-mills
Public sector:			
main enterprises	Italsider (3 integrated plants); Acc. Piombino (1 integrated plant)	Breda Siderurgica; Dalmine; Nazionale Cogne; Terni	—
productive capacity	over 1,000,000 tons/year	between 150,000 and 1,000,000 tons/year	—
location of the main works	along the coast	northern industrial triangle and central Italy	—
technology in use	large blast-furnaces integrated with Basic Oxygen converters CLD and OBM)	electric furnaces (and a few open-hearth furnaces) using steel scrap	—
production	pig-iron, common steel	special steel (and common steel)	—
product specialization	coils, flat products	special steel products, tubes	—

Private sector:			
main enterprises	—	AFL Falck; Tecksid; Redaelli; Acciaierie Bolzano; Ferrotubi; SISMA	(a large number of small enterprises)
productive capacity	—	between 150,000 and 1,000,000 tons/year	less than 150,000 tons/year
location of the main works	—	northern industrial triangle	Brescia district, Valtrompia
technology in use	—	UHP electric furnace, using steel scrap	UHP electric furnace, integrated with continuous casting
production	—	special steel (and common)	common steel only
product specialization	—	special steel products, long products	reinforcing bars, specialist products

TABLE 2.4

Crude steel breakdown by process and by enterprise (1977) (tons)

	Open hearth process	Electric process	Oxygen* process	Total	(%)
Public sector:					
FINSIDER	1,303,149	1,213,213	8,816,939	11,333,301	(48.57)
Acc. Piombino	—	—	1,489,258	1,489,258	(6.38)
Ex Egam*	115,544	588,088	145,510	849,142	(3.64)
Private sector:					
Falck holding	—	1,162,516	—	1,162,516	(4.98)
Teksid	—	786,568	—	786,568	(3.37)
Radaelli	—	194,756	—	194,756	(0.84)
others	163,422	7,346,317	8,535	7,518,274	(32.22)
Total	1,582,115	11,291,458	10,460,242	23,333,815	
(%)	(6.78)	(48.39)	(44.83)		(100)

* Almost all LD and OBM converters; other processes account for only 9,000 tons.

† Breda Siderurgica and Cogne.

Source: Ministero dell'Industria, 1979.

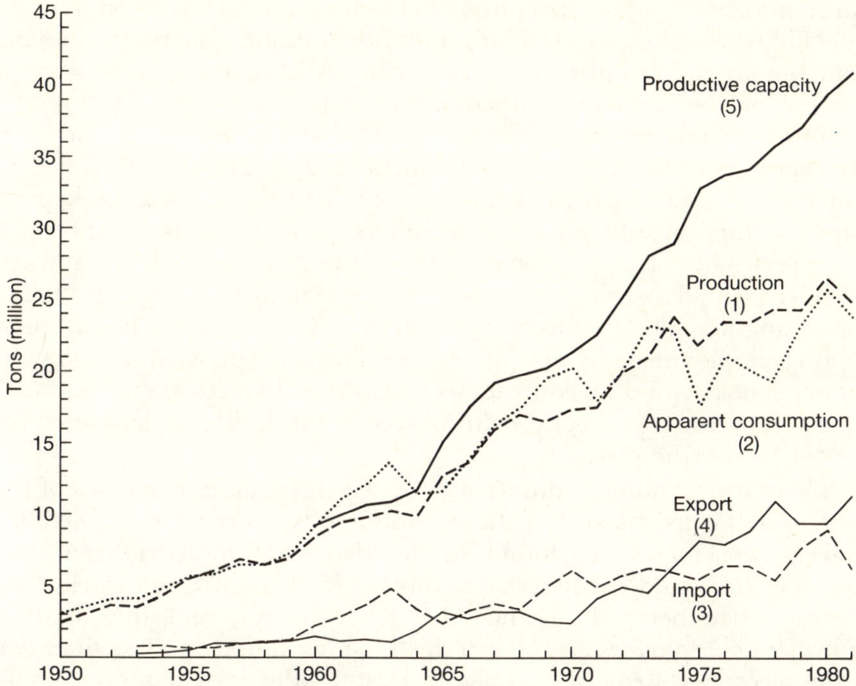

FIG. 2.2 Production, consumption, productive capacity, and foreign market for steel, 1950–81 (million tons)
Source: ASSIDER data.

terms of immobility and lack of standardization have created local markets relatively insulated from competition from elsewhere and completely closed to international competition.[16] Within each local market the industry operates competitively. Since relatively little capitalization is required,[17] there is widespread freedom of entry, and even specialized branches of the industry face competition from contractors who move from one branch to another. Thus, while enterprises tend to be relatively specialized by branch and type of output, there is a degree of shifting, so that residential building firms may expand into school and commercial construction, and specialist contractors in commercial construction may shift into industrial construction. It is the characteristics of building technology (and the separation of the process into separate stages, each requiring distinct techniques, equipment, and trades) that allows for a considerable variety of specialization so that, beside general contractors, there is a large number of small specialist contractors, limiting their activity to specific works such as excavation and demolition, plastering, paving and tile laying, painting and decorating. All this tends to produce a system of contracts and subcontracts. But competition is not only among similar types of contractors (in terms of branch, size, and local markets): general and specialist contractors, national and local contractors compete with each other over whether work will be kept in one contract or subcontracted to others. A very few large specialist enterprises operating nationally, or even in the international market, coexist with a large mass of small and very small building contractors operating locally, often as subcontractors. Table 2.5, on the distribution of employment by size of construction enterprise, shows that 93 per cent of all building contractors emply less than 20 people, and that these represent 46.4 per cent of the total building labour force (recorded by the census).

There are significant differences between the main branches of the sector, as far as the size of their workforce is concerned (Table 2.6). Larger workforces are found in the two most industrialized subsectors, roads and earthworks, and other civil engineering works (the average size being 17.3 and 44.9 respectively), and the smallest number of employees is found in the finishing subsector (less than two employees per firm on average). Despite the growing number of specialist contractors, the majority of the labour force is still employed by general building enterprises. But building enterprises differ not only technically, according to the branch in which they operate, but

TABLE 2.5
Enterprises and employment in construction by size, 1971

Size of firms (No. employed)	No.		%	
	Enterprises	Employment	Enterprises	Employment
1–2	54,769	66,938	50.06	7.97
3–5	22,324	86,271	20.40	10.27
6–9	14,685	106,297	13.42	12.66
10–19	10,038	130,077	9.17	15.49
20–49	5,463	161,932	4.99	19.28
50–99	1,385	93,258	1.27	11.11
100–499	689	125,805	0.63	14.98
500–999	42	28,002	0.04	3.33
1000– . . .	22	41,201	0.02	4.91
Total	109,417	839,781	100	100

TABLE 2.6
Average dimension of construction enterprises by branch, 1971

Branch	Enterprises	Employment	Average size
general construction	68,926	610,628	8.86
roads and earthworks	5,642	97,381	17.26
other civil engineering	1,289	57,803	44.87
finishes	31,244	62,221	1.99
services	2,316	11,748	5.07
Total construction	109,417	839,781	7.67

Note: Data refer to construction only, excluding installation.
Source: ISTAT, *Censimento generale dell'industria e del commercio*, 1971.

also in terms of their relation to the market and to the other enterprises. Five distinct groups can be singled out: general contractors, large construction contractors, speciality contractors, house-building contractors, and small craft building enterprises.[18]

General contractors, organized chiefly through a research and project structure, are responsible for the entire project, from conception and design to construction and commercial sale. They are in charge of all the financial aspects and economic risks of the operation, and are responsible for the bulk of the work on a site, but they tend not to be involved directly with the building activity itself. They often subcontract the entire execution of the building project to enterprises linked to them in a variety of ways (ranging from partners and sharing companies to labour-only subcontracting). It is frequently the case that real estate companies act as general contractors in the housing branch,[19] making decisions to invest in a project and bearing all the financial risks associated with it, while the production process is turned over to building contractors through a system of contracts and subcontracts. The possibility of good profits largely depends, particularly in the urban areas, on the commercial and speculative aspects of the project, and on the ability to bid for profitable contracts and to negotiate subsequent changes in the contract (adjustments in prices and times). All this has little to do with the productive structure, but it is related to the administrative and commercial structure, and to the possibility of stable contacts with local councils and political parties.

Large construction contractors, the size of which is related to business turnover and the scale of projects, are found both in civil engineering and in building construction (housing and general buildings). Building enterprises specializing in heavy construction are relatively large (both in turnover and in employment), and operate over wide areas or even internationally. They are almost exclusively organized for the construction process, and bid for large contracts. Highly skilled workers are employed by them permanently, while unskilled labourers are usually recruited locally.[20] Large contractors are more common in commercial and industrial construction, but they also operate in housing. In this case, they act as general contractors, as they take the initiative and are responsible for the project; but at the same time they are organized as real building enterprises for the execution of the project itself. They operate at a national level for large-scale projects, usually requiring some specialized techniques; and they are usually well equipped with up-to-date machinery and skilled labour. They execute the main sections of the project and subcontract the others.

Speciality contractors started developing as soon as capital-intensive equipment came to be used for some sequences of building activity (demolition, digging, site levelling, cement production). General building enterprises do not buy capital equipment unless they can provide for its full utilization, given that such equipment is needed only for some sequences of the building cycle and that the demand for future production is uncertain. The tendency is to subcontract to specialist contractors those tasks for which heavy equipment is required or to hire the machinery (such as fork-lift trucks and special cranes) from them, when it is needed.

Home building contractors account, by and large, for the largest part of the sector. These are small firms, locally orientated and chiefly operating in the housing branch. Some contractors are organized for the commercial aspects of the project as well as the construction activity. They build mostly individual houses and a few small apartment blocks, and/or work as subcontractors for larger enterprises and general contractors.

Finally, there is *a large and heterogeneous group*, difficult to define since it is composed of 'real' small craft building enterprises, 'fictitious' small enterprises, self-employed artisans, gang-groups working on the lump, and finally, labour-only subcontracting teams of workers. This heterogeneous group is found in all branches of the sector, but it is heavily concentrated in housing. They operate under different systems of subcontracting for all building contractors.

The development of general contractors in large urban areas during the 1960s, and their gradual acquisition of monopoly in the control and management of urban property, has served to emphasize the distinction and separation between *promoters*, i.e. agents taking decisions to invest in construction (general contractors) and *builders*, i.e. agents building the works on a site (building contractors). In fact, a very important peculiarity of the sector is not only the distinction between promoters and builders but also the crucial role of the first in decision-making with respect to building activity. In civil engineering and public buildings (schools, hospitals, etc.) the client and the promoter is the state (i.e. local or central government), and the works to be built are assigned to a main contractor through an open tendering procedure. In housing and general buildings, by contrast, the direct participation of the state is very low.[21] This has to be related to the heavily private character of the building sector in Italy, with respect both to construction activity and to housing property. Thus, decisions to invest in construction are by and large taken by the private sector. Within it, three main groups are identifiable.

Large and powerful agents (such as industrial corporations producing materials for construction, insurance companies, banks, and *immobiliari*[22] acting as general contractors) started to emerge as a group in the large urban areas at the beginning of the 1960s, usually acting as general contractors. This group has developed a monopoly position since then, eliminating via competition small agents in all activities related to investment decisions in construction. They determine the housing supply and direct town-planning policies, often through direct mediation with the political parties and the local authorities.[23] Their monopoly position is assured by: (*a*) their technical and financial ability to realize long-term building plans; (*b*) strong connections (usually through shareholdings) with building contractors and enterprises producing construction materials; (*c*) very strong self-financing ability, as the direct emanation of large and powerful industrial and financial corporations; finally, (*d*) the large scale of their projects.

A large group of small and medium sized agents, who do not compete with the first group acting in the urban areas: on the contrary, these agents concentrate their activity in the rest of the country, i.e. areas marginal to the urban areas, small towns, tourist areas, and the southern regions.

The group of home owners generates quite a substantial amount of building activity. In fact, they are still one of the principal initiators of decisions to invest in housing construction. They have their main impact in small towns and villages, and the southern regions.

To conclude, the production process is still organized in a traditional way, despite the increasing financial concentration among general contractors. Construction is still a labour-intensive sector, where industrialized methods have limited application, and building activity is organized by and large through a system of contracts and subcontracts, so that a large number of marginal and quite small building enterprises still exist. The existence of this large and fragmented structure of small marginal firms, and the consequent high level of competition among them, allows for the erection of buildings at low cost and to strict schedules. General contractors and main contractors find it convenient to organize the production process through subcontracting, because it both allows control over costs and timing and does away with problems related to flexibility, work supervision, labour force recruitment, and so on (as shown in Chapter 5).

2.1.4 Demand, product market pricing, and production activity

Steel consumption is related, as already said, to the production of consumer durables and capital investment. Demand for steel, in any one country, depends on the demand for capital investment and is related to the rate of growth of the economic system.[24] The Italian case shows this quite clearly: its steel industry, only a small producer at the beginning of the century, developed steadily and rapidly in parallel with the process of industrialization of the country, in order to meet the continuous increase in the demand for steel.[25] This long upward trend, both in consumption and in production, slowed down in the 1970s, and was then interrupted by the slump of the world steel market.

Steel consumption fluctuates pro-cyclically, following the fluctuations occuring in the economy as a whole. Steel consumer industries producing capital goods and consumer durables are subject to wide and deep swings, and as a result so is the demand for steel.[26] Due to the integrated structure of steel production, adjustments in quantity are difficult and expensive to obtain: when there is a decline in demand, the tendency is for each producer to export excess production. But this process of adjustment is costly, given the wide fluctuations in international steel prices and the generalization of dumping phenomena during recessions (Tarr, 1979). In booms, steel products bought in the international market become very dear for the national industries, while in periods of recession prices tend to be depressed below their cost, so that steel enterprises produce at a loss. The market for steel is therefore highly competitive with *considerable price variations*. Consequently, on the whole, fluctuations in production tend to be much smaller than fluctuations in steel consumption, leaving employment relatively stable. Figure 2.2 (p. 41) shows for Italy how swings in demand for steel have been faced. In periods of expansion (1959–63 and 1968–70), the excess demand has been met by increasing imports and decreasing exports; in periods of recession (1974–9), the tendency has been to allocate the excess supply to the foreign market, thus keeping steel production relatively stable. Employment has not been affected by these cyclical fluctuations (as shown in Figure 2.3), but it has increased according to the expansion of productive capacity.

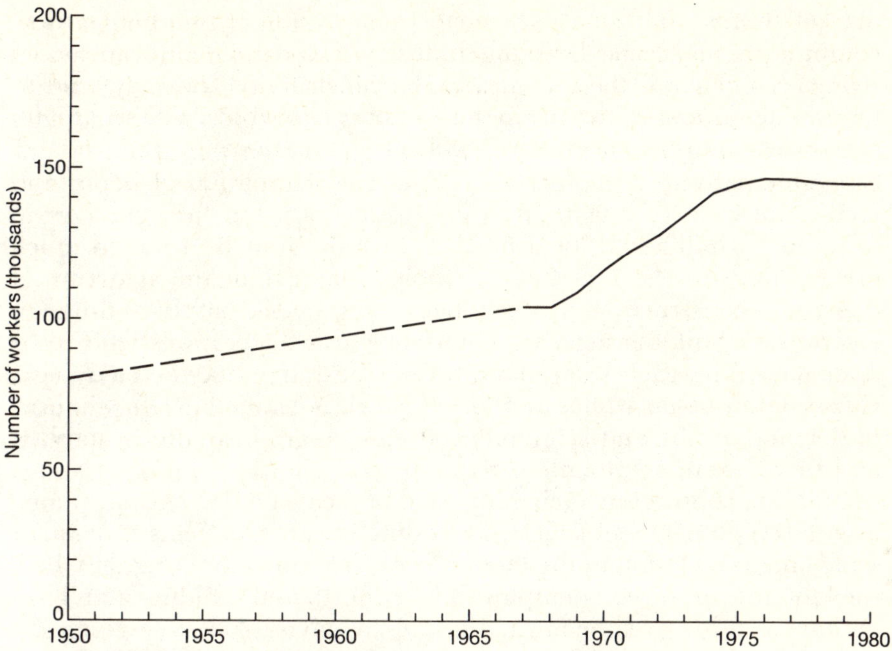

FIG. 2.3 Total employment in the steel industry, 1950–80
Source: ASSIDER data.

The construction industry is closed to international competition. The local monopoly of large contractors ensure control over the price of the whole project, but the subcontractors compete with each other on the basis of price.

Prices are not fixed for a season, for an output, or otherwise administered. Typically, a new price is set on each project for which, given the lack of standardization and the fact that product specifications are complex, completion dates and the quality of services are very significant elements in competition. A tendering procedure[27] is usually used for large projects and for all public projects. Moreover, contractors, in all branches of the sector, are rarely responsible for complete projects. Usually, the main contractor bids for a project and then, under tendering arrangements, subcontracts out parcels of work to specialist trade contractors and to small subcontractors.[28] Pricing and profit policies are therefore pursued in an environment dominated by the tendering system, so that firms at all levels are dependent for their survival upon their success in competing tendering.

Long-term trends in demand tend to be highly regular in the construction industry, and can last for very long periods. An expansion or contraction phase can last for 10 to 15 years.[29] But short-term fluctuations, which tend to be substantial, overlap with these long-term market trends. Frictional, seasonal, cyclical, and legislative factors[30] combine to make the building industry subject to wide and deep swings. In general, the fortunes of the construction industry tend to follow fluctuations occurring in the economy as a whole. The sensitivity of construction to short-term cyclical fluctuations in the level of economic activity is mainly related to the alternation of boom and credit squeeze, leading to stop go sequences.[31] Further, changes in demand by individual local markets and by branch are often much greater than in the sector as a whole. Changes in the structure of demand—construction product being immobile—imply a different location for building activity. Hence, cyclical fluctuations tend to be stronger within each local market. One local area may be enjoying a construction boom while, in another, work is scarce.[32] Thus, changes in demand are by and large reflected in changes in building activity, and therefore in employment requirements.

Building contractors facing a period of recession can choose among a wide range of possibilities: (*a*) a shift towards projects of smaller scale and a reduction in the labour force; (*b*) subcontracting, in which the labour force directly employed is reduced, and building activity is organized through subcontracting; (*c*) inactivity (possible given the little capital equipment in use), where the contractor will dismiss all the workers except very few—that is, those necessary to reorganize the production process in the long term; and (*d*) closure.[33] Thus, whatever the strategy adopted by the single contractor, cyclical fluctuations in building activity are reflected in *fluctuations in employment*. Fluctuations in employment, due to the economic cycle, have to be added to site cycle and seasonal employment changes. As a matter of fact, the workplace is highly variable. Sites of work frequently change, and are not always within the same community. No two projects are identical, so that the workforce on one project may be much smaller or greater than that required by other projects undertaken by the same contractor. The labour force on a single project is highly variable so that, typically, different groups of workers in different numbers are required in the different stages of the site cycle. On-site operations are largely out of doors, with weather playing a role in the possibility of working. As a result, building enterprises are continually expanding or contracting their employment requirements.

2.2 Conclusions

As the preceding description shows, the two industries provide striking contrasts in many aspects of their technological and economic framework. The steel industry is a highly capital-intensive sector in rapid evolution, characterized by large investment, large plants precisely located, and a continuous process of highly mechanized production. The building industry is technologically backward, with extremely fragmented and heterogeneous structure: small enterprises with poor capital equipment are distributed all over the country, and an elastic structure prevails.

The demand in both industries is a demand for durable goods (direct or derived), implying quite wide and deep cyclical fluctuations in their industrial cycle. The steel industry, given the large standardization of the products, the low level of custom barriers, and the existence of steel substitute products, is a highly competitive sector. Moreover, because of the rigidities of the production process, adjustments in quantity are difficult to obtain and expensive, and fluctuations in demand are therefore mainly reflected in the adjustment of steel prices. The building product presents quite opposite characteristics: it is a *one-off* product, highly differentiated, not standardized, immobile, and with no close substitutes; the sector is therefore closed to foreign competition. Fluctuations in demand are reflected in large changes in production, and hence in employment. This implies that, in periods of expansion, total production increases through the entrance of new firms into the market, while in recession these enterprises will cease functioning.

Both industries have experienced a period of very rapid expansion, followed by deep recession in more recent years. While the expansion has stimulated very large investment and technological evolution in the steel industry, the development years show a considerable expansion of employment in the building industry.

To conclude, technical and economic conditions pose different problems in the two industries for the managers, who have to organize the labour process, and the workers, as organized in trade unions for the defence of their interests. *In the building industry* small enterprises with highly elastic productive structures (to cope with changes in demand from site to site) are spread all over the country, and tend to build only one building at a time. After construction the building site vanishes, and the enterprise moves to another area. The result is a demand for a *flexible labour force*, with a high mobility both within the sector (between one area and another and from one enterprise to another) and intersectorally (making it possible to expand and contract employment, according to the general level of demand for building). *In the steel industry* large enterprises, precisely located, with a very rigid productive structure, given the large investment involved and the continuous nature of the production process, face the problem of fully utilizing existing capacity in a product market characterized by wide and deep swings; the result is a tendency to shift excess production onto the foreign market, and towards *a stable labour force* to which the management of the production process and the care of the equipment has to be entrusted.

Notes

1. Over 24 per cent of world steel output is exported (EIU, 1982, p. 2).
2. An integrated steel plant, once the blast-furnace is started up, cannot be stopped, except at the end of its 'campaign'. The blast-furnace works continuously for about 5 to 8 years: then the internal lining has to be demolished and rebuilt.
3. The second process (the open-hearth furnace) is now technically obsolete, and has been increasingly replaced over the last 15 years by the other two (see Appendix A, Fig. A.1).
4. Process departments can include a thermal station, for the production and distribution of steam, oxygen, and blasts of air; an electrical station, for the production and distribution of electricity; and a service in charge of the distribution of fuel.
5. Transport services are usually organized together with a service in charge of transport by sea, by rail and by road; a service in charge of supplying and storing of raw materials; and a service in charge of the storage and delivery of finished products.
6. Such technical and administrative services include laboratories, the testing room and metallurgical services.
7. The use of a combination of techniques for the erection of a building, rather than one technique only, can only be explained by the fact that construction still consists in the manual assembling of different inputs (wood, bricks, mortar, iron, concrete, plaster-panels, and so on). The choice of the technique to be used can differ for each specific part of the building and it will depend on: (*a*) the technical features of the works, (*b*) the cost of the materials involved in the different parts of the works, and (*c*) the industrial design of the works.
8. In the Italian market, the ten largest enterprises produce almost 68 per cent of the total crude steel (Appendix B, Table B.3). In the international market the 47 major companies account for over 70 per cent of the western world's crude steel output in 1981 (EIU, 1982, p. 43).
9. Roughly two to four years are required for a major project.
10. Appendix B presents a brief description of the public and private sectors.
11. These are mainly flat products, such as medium and heavy plates, sheet, coated flat products, strips, and hoops.
12. FINSIDER is the financial holding company that groups all the main steel enterprises in the public sector.
13. In 1978 the mini-steel works produced over 4.5 million tons of hot rolled products, of which about 3.5 millions are reinforcing bars, corresponding to 75 per cent of total national output, and to about 40 per cent of what is

produced in the EEC countries (Ministero dell'Industria, 1979, p. 110, n. 1). There are about 80 steel plants, located either in Brescia or in the valleys around the town (Valtrompia, Valle Camonica, Valle Sabbia). All together, they are equipped with 72 electric furnaces (with a total productive capacity of about 2,500 tons), 53 continuous casting machines and 92 rolling mills (Fantinelli, 1978).

14. Massi and Fumagalli, 1977; Ministero dell'Industria, 1979; *Mondo Economico*, 1976, No. 41, 1978, No. 46, 1979, No. 46; ASSIDER, 1977.
15. See Appendix E. 2.
16. There is a small number of large specialist enterprises in the international constructional engineering tendering market, where they experience extremely close competition. However, there is no competition from foreign firms in the domestic market.
17. According to the data on the capital stock on the Italian industrial sector elaborated by Rosa (1979), the ratio of capital stock per head (K/L) was equal to 10.115 million lira (1970 prices) in 1976 for the manufacturing industry, while it was equal to 1.500 million lira for the construction industry. That is, the capital stock per person employed in the construction industry was almost one seventh of what was required for the manufacturing industry as a whole (Rosa, 1979, p. 39). See Brusco and D'Alessandro, 1979, pp. 26–7.
18. This is a slightly modified categorization of the one proposed by Brusco and D'Alessandro (1979), pp. 46–8.
19. The analysis of Ave and Prizzon (1977, pp. 85–133) of eight of the major real estate companies (on the stock exchange) gives good examples of major real estate companies acting as general contractors.
20. For an analysis of the Italian enterprises working on the international market for civil engineering, see *Mondo Economico*, 1980, No. 8, 1982, Nos. 27–8, pp. 27–45.
21. Indeed, overall, public investment in construction is exiguous, both with respect to public investment in other industrial sectors and to public investment in housing in other western countries. Nevertheless, the role of state intervention in building activity is much higher than the data on direct public investment would suggest. All building activity is strongly affected by the government policy in terms of credit policy, fiscal policy, town planning schemes, renting regulations and, finally, building regulations.
22. *Immobiliari* consist of real estate companies, property trusts, real estate investment trusts, and similar companies speculating in the building market.
23. On the role and development of this group, see Cicconi, 1978; Ave and Prizzon, 1977.
24. The development curve for steel is characterized by a rate of growth, compared with that of the economic system, higher in the initial stage and lower in the final stage.
25. Crude steel production increased from 2,362 thousand tons in 1950, to

23,803 thousand tons in 1974, thus expanding at an annual average rate of growth of 10.11 per cent (ASSIDER data).

26. As a matter of fact, fluctuations in steel consumption are more extreme than fluctuations in capital investment. This can be explained on the basis of three main factors: (*a*) fast growth means a heavy demand for new capacity, but when growth slows down capital investment is concentrated on modernization and replacement, which use relatively less steel; (*b*) fluctuations in demand for steel are always met through the violent movement of consumers' and merchants' steel stocks, thus amplifying the swings due to changes in the consumption of steel; (*c*) finally, indirect trade in steel—i.e. through capital investment imports—have to be taken into account.
27. The usual procedure is for the client to send out drawings and a bill of quantities (a list of numbered items with the quantities needed for each type of work) to contractors, and for the latter to state their prices for all the items of one contract—for supplying the material and labour and doing the work. Tendering may be open (by advertising) or limited (i.e. inviting only a few contractors).
28. The main contractor is responsible for the bulk of the work on site. Specialist firms and subcontractors can be employed to do part of their work, but the main contractor remains responsible for the work, and therefore is paid by the client for it. The subcontractors are then paid by the main contractor.
29. For an analysis of long-term cycles in construction, see Talamona, 1958.
30. Legislative regulations on town planning, building standards, rents, housing prices, etc., are very important in their effect on construction activity, particularly for the housing branch. For a historical excursus on the main economic and legislative acts with respect to construction, see Magnani and Murano, 1978, pp. 15–85.
31. The construction industry, given the high total cost of its products, depends heavily on the credit system. Thus, every credit squeeze is reflected in higher costs, giving rise to contractors' complaints.
32. This is exactly what has happened in the housing branch in Italy over the postwar period. See Chapter 8, section 8.1.
33. The transient nature of many building contractors has to be related to the fact that the sector is a typical labour-intensive sector; this permits the entry (and/or exit) of a large number of small and very small enterprises with a low level of capital equipment in periods of expansion (or periods of contraction).

CHAPTER THREE

Divisions of Labour in Steel and Construction

This chapter discusses the division of labour in the steel and construction industries in the light of the technological and economic characteristics, as discussed in the previous chapter, that define the *realm of possibilities* for the organization of the labour process. The work is based, by and large, on case studies, as explained in section 3.1, but it attempts to give a general description of the main features of the division of labour in the two sectors.

3.1 The case studies

3.1.1 The steel industry

The analysis of the labour market structure in the steel industry is based primarily on case studies of four steel plants: Breda works (Breda Siderurgica), Concordia works (AFL Falck), Dalmine works (Dalmine) and Cornigliano works (Italsider). As already discussed (Chapter 2, Table 2.4), the four enterprises operate in what I classify as separate subsectors of the product market, distinguished by ownership, size of works, location, product specialization, product standardization, technology in use, and degree of automation. In the introductory note to Appendix D, a brief outline of the methodology used is presented. Appendices D. 1 and D. 2 summarize and compare the main characteristics of the enterprises and plants considered.

Breda Siderurgica is a state-controlled enterprise, specializing in the production of special steel. The works, medium-sized and scrap-based, are located in Sesto San Giovanni, an old industrialized area in the Milan conurbation that is characterized by the concentration of quite a few large engineering and metal factories (Ercole Marelli, Magneti Marelli, Breda Termomeccanica, AFL Falck, Breda Siderurgica), and that was subject to large immigration in the post-war period, first from the north-east (in the 1950s) and later from the south (in the late 1950s and early 1960s). Breda has been involved, since the late 1960s in plans for restructuring and in the reorganization of the public special steel sector. But as these plans were never implemented, no major investment has been carried out in the plant in the last decade, and Breda has been going through a period of technological decline.[1] Uncertainty about the future characterizes Breda, given the ups and downs of the various plans for special steel, its very difficult economic position (the losses have been enormous in the second half of the 1970s), and its outdated works.

Concordia is a medium sized, scrap-based steel plant belonging to AFL Falck, a private company specializing in the production of long products, with some specialization in special steel. Concordia is located, together with the other two AFL Falck major steelworks (Vittoria and Unione), in Sesto, divided from the Breda works simply by the railway bridge. The policy of Falck, in the postwar period, has been to update its works continuously, first expanding its productive capacity and then improving the works' performance and the quality of its products, which has required continous and smooth technological innovation. The Concordia works are technologically up-to-date: in the early 1970s a new steel mill, equipped with the UHP electric furnaces and continuous casting, was installed to replace the old steelworks. Moreover, the position of AFL Falck in the product market is very sound, so that it is one of the very few major enterprises in the sector not producing at a loss.

Dalmine is a medium–sized public enterprise grouping of six plants for the production and finishing of large diameter tubes (seamless and welded). The production of steel for the whole enterprise is concentrated in a medium-sized, scrap-based plant located in Dalmine, a village near Bergamo, which has grown up around the steelworks. Despite the development of a certain number of industrial activities in the area, so that it now looks quite different from the small rural village of the postwar period, the Dalmine steelworks still remain the only large factory: the surrounding areas are mainly rural, and the nearest industrialized district is Milan, about 40 miles away. The Dalmine works, after a period of relative technological decline in the 1960s have been involved in large investment plans in the 1970s, with the installation of a new electric furnace, equipped with a vacuum degassing unit and a continuous casting machine, and a new rolling train (PPM–MPM), completely automated, for the production of seamless tubes.

Cornigliano is one of the four large integrated steel plants of Italsider, specializing in the production of flat products. The works, located along the coast near Genoa, were completely rebuilt after the war to expand the public sector steel productive capacity. The plant, equipped with the first continuous rolling mill in Italy, was one of the most up-to-date plants in Europe at that time. Its productive capacity was expanded in the early 1960s with the installation of a new blast-furnace and the expansion of the steel works. It went through a period of relative technological decline (1967–74), when all the efforts of Italsider were concentrated on doubling the size of the Taranto works. In 1975, a plan for the modernization and renewal of the works started with the replacement of the old and outdated open-hearth furnaces with two very large OBM converters, integrated with continuous casting, and the installation of a new cold rolling train.

3.1.2 The construction industry

The analysis of the labour market structure in construction is not based on a sample of enterprises, as with the steel industry, but on a well-defined geographical area. This is for two reasons. First, in the case of construction, the firm is not the relevant unit of aggregation of jobs. On the one hand, production is the outcome of the activity of separate firms, working in close connection (as discussed in the previous chapter); on the other, the possibility of career advancement for workers is related not to their length of service with one employer, but to the acquisition of skills and experience, usually accumulated over a long period in the sector while moving between contractors (as will be discussed in Chapter 5). It follows that in order to explain the labour market structure in construction it is necessary to consider an area, and not a sample of firms, in order to allow for the interaction between firms and the mobility of workers among them.

The second reason for choosing a well-defined geographical area is related to the existence of significant local markets (as discussed in Chapter 2, section 2.1.3) and the wide differences between them. Differences in the quality of the prevailing building activity (category, size of projects, location), techniques in use, the organization of production and labour market conditions, all help to create differences in the labour market structures. Several indicators demonstrate this territorial heterogeneity. First, the importance of construction in total employment varies between geographical areas (Appendix E.3): while in the north-west area of the country construction accounts for 21.2 per cent of total male industrial employment, in the southern area it accounts for over 55.3 per cent, and in some regions over 60 per cent. As a result, in certain districts there exists a variety of job opportunities, while in others construction represents the only job opportunity for a large part of the male labour force, as far as industrial employment is concerned. Second, the importance of irregular and black employment, a well-known feature of the sector—however defined and measured[2]—is quite unequally distributed, being far greater in the less industrialized regions. Finally, labour force characteristics, in terms of skill and age structure, seem to differ widely. Very large differences are recorded in the distribution of the labour force by grade (Appendix E.5): while the main cities and some towns (Milan, Genoa, Rome, Modena, Pistoia) register up to 50 per cent of their labour force as skilled, in the peripheral and in the southern districts most of the workers are recorded as unskilled, and only a much smaller quota (between 10 and 15 per cent) as skilled (for instance Aosta, Sondrio, Padua, Imperia, Frosinone, Palermo, Ragusa, Siracusa, Cagliari). Large differences exist not only between regions, but also within regions: in Lombardia, the urban district of Milan has the largest share of skilled labour for the whole country (50.24 per cent), and the peripheral and mountainous district of Sondrio the smallest (9.88 per cent). A similar picture emerges of the labour force age structure (Appendix E.6): not only are there differences in the average age of the labour force between areas, so that there is a tendency for the northern/urban districts, subject to immigrations, to have a younger labour force, but the career pattern differs too. In some areas age increases with grades, while in others unskilled workers have a higher average age than semiskilled workers (for instance Padua, Venice, Verona, Arezzo, Prato, Rome, l'Acquila, Palermo).

It is clear, then, that the Italian construction industry is very heterogeneous. However, since the purpose of this study is not to describe the Italian construction industry, but to explain how differences in economic and technological situations affect labour market structures, the existence of wide territorial differences suggests the desirability of restricting the analysis of the structuring of the labour market to a homogeneous area, and hence to delimit—geographically—the area of research. The Lombardia region and, within it, the Milan district, is the area chosen. This is an urban metropolitan area where some of the problems and contradictions now typical of the sector first emerged. The aim of the analysis is to explore the structuring of the labour market in this area so as to develop a general framework for the analysis of the construction industry which explains why deep differences exist in the sector.

3.2 Division of labour and characteristics of jobs in the steel industry

Different working situations, in terms of working conditions and skill content, can be singled out in the steel industry. Workers form compact groups with a distinct identity, where the major distinctions can be traced, on the one hand, to the differences between process, maintenance, and ancillary workers and, on the other hand, to the existence of highly differentiated groups among the process workers themselves. The interesting point is that such differences can be taken back to the organization of a steel plant into departments, relating to the *phases* of production, and into maintenance and service sections, relating to the *functions* performed, so that process workers are characterized by the *position they occupy* in the production process, maintenance workers by their *craft-skills* and ancillary workers for their *marginal role*.

(i) *Process workers*. The technical structure of the plant forms the basis for organizing process workers. They are employed by department (pig-iron, steel-making, hot rolling, cold rolling, finishing); within each department the organization of the production process is based on the entrusting of separate stages of the process to separate but interrelated teams, so that each team of workers is in charge of, and fully responsible for, a well delimited phase or subphase of the production process. For example, in the steel–making department the workers are organized in groups according to the furnaces and converters installed. For each furnace there will be a team in charge of the preparation of the burden, another team employed at the furnace for all operations of steel smelting and refining; finally, a third team working in the casting pit for the casting of the molten metal into ingot moulds.

Each single group of workers is distinguished by the position occupied with respect to the production process. Therefore, the distinguishing features of each group within the firm are explained by differences in the characteristics of the capital equipment in use; the chemical, physical, and mechanical features of the stage of the process itself; the nature of the operations and tasks involved; finally, the working conditions and the nature of skills. Within each team, process workers tend again to be characterized by the specific position they occupy in that segment of the production process. It follows that there are some areas, as well as some job posts within each area, that play a crucial role with respect to the process flow.[3] Thus, there is a sort of technological hierarchy of areas and job posts, according to their relevance and impact upon the production process flow. Working conditions, in terms of heat, noise, smoke, danger, dirt, physical exhaustion, and so on, vary widely among departments and, within each, among productive areas. There are some jobs that do not require any particular skill and knowledge but simply the physical ability to stand hard and exhausting working conditions. The number of such jobs has been significantly reduced by technical progress, but some still remain.

(ii) *Maintenance workers*. Maintenance jobs differ from process jobs both in skill content and in division of labour. Here, too, labour is organized, by and large, in small groups, but the work remains largely individual, and what characterizes the maintenance teams is their craft trade.

Maintenance services are organized to support process departments and auxiliary services with the necessary maintenance work. Given the high capital intensity and the complexity of the processes and equipment in use, the role played by maintenance services in the management of the whole factory is quite considerable, and it tends to increase as technical change introduces equipment of increased dimensions, increases integration, and leads to higher mechanization and automation. A rough idea of the role played by maintenance services is given by the share of maintenance workers over the total labour force employed, as shown in Table 3.1. For the plants examined, this ratio varies between 20 and 36 per cent, and the highest ratio is recorded at Cornigliano, the largest and most automated plant.

Maintenance services are organized partly at the department level through the direct intervention of small specialist teams, and partly at the central level in workshops. Maintenance direct intervention is organized to provide (*a*) emergency intervention, by the emergency maintenance teams working on a permanent basis in the process departments, and (*b*) planned intervention, by the department maintenance teams working on a day shift for planned intervention only.

The maintenance emergency teams are organized and structured by department, by trade, and by shift. For each department and for each shift, there is a team of electricians and a team of hydromechanics, plus a team of bricklayers in the steel-making department for brickworks. A team can vary from 6–8 to 8–12 workers, headed by a foreman (as at Breda and Concordia) or a technician (as at Dalmine and Cornigliano). The teams are always the same for shift and department, but the maintenance workers can move to the workshops for a little maintenance work when there is nothing specific to be done in their department.

Planned maintenance work is decided on the basis of regular inspections to the capital equipment. Daily/weekly/yearly programmes, decided in agreement with the process departments, plan for the revision and/or modification of the capital equipment. The work is done mainly in the workshops, on a day shift, by teams of workers specialized by trade, and with some specialization by department.[4] The teams tend to be always the same, but their composition can

TABLE 3.1

Manual workers by occupational group, 1979

	Breda sid. Breda works (31.10.79)		Falck Concordia (31.12.79)		Dalmine Dalmine works (31.1.80)		Italsider Cornigliano (31.12.80)	
	No.	%	No.	%	No.	%	No.	%
process workers	1,533	58.9	688	52.9	3,039	58.6	2,872	41.6
maintenance workers	531	20.4	325	25.0	1,147	22.1	2,521	36.5
service workers	540	20.7	288	22.1	1,003	19.3	1,517	21.9
Total	2,604	100	1,301	100	5,189	100	6,910	100

Source: Data collected from the archives of the enterprises.

vary; the work is more like individual work than team work, despite the fact that workers are organized in small groups. In fact, the most important part of their job consists in the fixing and preparing of their own tools and in the preparation of the necessary spare parts.

The workshops are organized to supply the maintenance service of the departments with the necessary spare parts, when this involves specialist jobs, and to provide for some specialist maintenance work. A variety of workshops is found, such as the engineering workshop, carpentry workshop, electrical workshop, crane maintenance service, motor vehicle service, and building and roads maintenance service. The workers are highly skilled and widely specialized by trade, such as electricians, turners, fitters, metal carpenters, mechanics, and engineers. The work is mainly individual, and takes place in workshops on a day shift; but it is possible for a small team to be organized temporarily in the departments to assemble the spare parts prepared, to test the maintenance work done, and to make the necessary adaptations.

To summarize, when an emergency occurs the emergency maintenance team will provide for immediate and provisional repairs on the shift; the workers employed in planned maintenance, working in the workshops on a day shift, provide for regular repairs on a daily/weekly basis; finally, if and when required, the workers employed in the specialist workshops will intervene to prepare the required spare parts, usually working on specialist jobs only. Moreover, the main maintenance work is usually planned once a year, for the whole factory, when it is possible to stop the major installations. In this case, all maintenance workers are involved and organized on the basis of the general maintenance work planned.

(iii) *Ancillary workers*. The service sections include a large variety of services. Some of them, such as the auxiliary services (thermal station, electrical station), the laboratories, and other technical services, employ skilled workers, whose jobs are similar—in terms of trade, skills, and training—to maintenance jobs. Nevertheless, total employment in these services is either numerically insignificant, as in the case of the auxiliary services, or consists mainly of clerical workers and technicians, as in the case of the technical services. Thus, most of the ancillary workers are employed in unskilled or semiskilled jobs in transport services, administrative services, and personnel services. Most jobs do not require any specific skill and training; and a large number of these jobs—such as messengers, porters, and cleaners—require a very low level of qualification, are completely marginal to the production process, and do not even require any particular physical aptitude.

3.2.1 Differences between process, maintenance, and ancillary workers

Skill, degree of responsibility, working conditions, experience required, and so on, vary widely. Despite existing differences within each group, there are some common features that distinguish process workers from maintenance and from service workers. Table 3.2 summarizes the basic characteristics here discussed.

(i) *Skill*. The process departments employ a large number of unskilled and semiskilled workers whose work is considered tiring, dangerous, heavy, and socially undesirable. They are required to execute simple tasks, with low technical content. Despite that, the steel worker is not merely an executor, relating to precise instructions and to the automation of the machine. Even at a very low level of the hierarchy, the personal responsibilities are numerous. Skilled process workers are distinguished not so much for performing more difficult tasks, but for their higher responsibilities, and greater control and intervention power. Their skills relate to their knowledge about the process and the works, acquired through experience in the same department and, often, at the same works. Thus, these skills are very specific not only to the steel process, but to the particular works and equipment in use. Maintenance workers are all skilled, in the traditional craft sense, and their skills are related to their trade, and are therefore general. Besides electricians, hydromechanics, and metal carpenters, which are by far the largest groups, there is a wide variety of trades employed in the workshops, such as bricklayers, turners, millers, fitters, borers, engineers, and welders. Ancillary workers are employed in unskilled jobs, by and large involving simple manual activities.

(ii) *Training*. Skilled process workers acquire their skills through a long process of on–the–job training within the same department. They are first employed at the lowest grades and then they move up. Skills and knowledge about the process and the works are acquired through temporary mobility on different jobs, within each group, working side by side with experienced workers. Maintenance workers enter the factory with an already completed formal training and possibly some previous working experience in their trade. Once they enter the steel factory they are trained for their specific job through on–the–job training, and this is usually matched with further formal training, organized by the firm, in classes and workshops. As a result, they are characterized by higher school attendence. Finally, no training is required for ancillary workers.

(iii) *The division of labour*. Process workers are mainly organized in teams, where the members of the team are always the same. The

TABLE 3.2

Process, maintenance, and ancillary workers: a comparison

	Process workers	Maintenance workers	Ancillary workers
work	shift work	day work	day work
division of labour	team work (based on cooperation, understanding, team hierarchy)	individual work	individual work
skills	process workers (manual activities of control and regulation on equipment and processes)	craft workers (skills and dexterity based on technical and practical knowledge)	manual workers (no specific skills, simple manual activities)
training	on the job training	formal training and on the job training	no training
position in the production process	direct and high responsibility (for production, machinery, other workers' safety)	indirect responsibility	activities not directly related to the production process
working conditions	hard working conditions (heat, dust, smoke, noise)	normal	normal

continuity in the composition of the labour team is a result of the need for cooperation and understanding in the production process. This leads the workers to know each other very well, but gives them little opportunity to know other workers. Maintenance workers are employed, for the most part, in workshops. Their work is individual, and provides the possibility of moving from one shop to another, or/and to the process departments when required by the maintenance programme. The result is that maintenance workers have a better chance of carrying on discussions with other workers, and of knowing a lot of them.

(iv) *Shift work/day work*. Given the continuous process of production, all process workers are employed on shift work, changing their working times every week. Moreover, in the departments having 21 shifts a week,[5] the workers have to work at the weekend, staying at home in rotation, depending on the shift schedule. The continuous changing of work and life rhythm has a serious effect on their social life.[6] Most of the maintenance and ancillary workers, on the contrary, work a day shift. Only a small number of maintenance workers—those employed in the emergency teams in the process departments—have to work on shift. Nevertheless it is always possible for them to ask to be moved onto a day job. Their contact with the external world (political parties, trade unions, and so on) are therefore much deeper.

(v) *Group/class consciousness*. Finally, the organization of process workers in small groups, the need for cooperation and understanding—even if to different degrees in the various groups—and the nature of collective tasks and operations, can be explained as required in terms of the characteristics of the production process. This, and the fact that workers are always the same in each team, is important in explaining the tendency towards high group consciousness, and group/team solidarity to prevail over trade union/class solidarity (Pizzorno, 1975). The result is that wide differences come to exist between groups, so that workers can be looked at as compact groups with distinct indentities and different interests.

Before concluding, it is important to point out that technological innovation in the steel industry has not only encouraged a change in the composition of the labour force (as the share of maintenance workers tends to increase and that of process workers to decrease), but has affected their characteristics too, so that their differences are becoming less marked.

The increased productive capacity of the works, and new processes, reduces the labour requirements for process workers, while the complexity of the installation increases both the number and the role of maintenance workers within the production process.

The increased mechanization and automation of the processes reduces the need for manual intervention, thereby eliminating some of the heavy, dangerous, and physically exhausting jobs. This process is much more advanced in the rolling and finishing departments, where it has been possible to extend mechanization and automation to the whole rolling process. In the previous stages of the production process flow, automation is less advanced, and there still are some jobs requiring little or no skill but physical strength and capability to stand uncomfortable working conditions (heat, smoke, and noise). At the same time, this reduced need for direct intervention on the process affects the role of the most experienced workers. Rules of thumb and decisions taken simply by sight are now replaced partly (in the steel–making process) or almost completely (in the rolling process) by information conveyed by the process computers installed in the departments, and by the automation of the processes themselves. Process workers are increasingly called upon to control and regulate processes and machinery—through operating stands on the basis of the information given by the computer, rather than through direct intervention based on rule-of-thumb decisions taken by the most experienced workers.

At the same time, the complexity of the equipment calls for continuous maintenance activity, which in the case of highly or completely automated works becomes more like a process of control and regulation. In consequence, some of the existing distinctions between process workers and maintenance workers are becoming looser. This is true, in general, for the large integrated steel plants, producing highly standardized products, where a high degree of mechanization and some automation of the whole process is possible (as in the case of Cornigliano). It is also true, in particular, for the rolling departments, where it has been possible to push for a high/very high degree of automation (as in the case of the new PPM–MPM at Dalmine). It is less true for the medium and small steel plants, producing non-standardized, specialist product, employing smaller and less automated works and equipment (as is the case in all electric furnace departments, at Breda, Concordia and Dalmine).

3.3 The production process and the division of labour in construction

Unlike the case of steel, where technology tends to determine the characteristics of jobs, the division of labour and, more generally, the organization of the labour process is difficult to define in construction. Work organization is extremely flexible, so that the same output can be realised by different combinations of techniques, enterprises, trades, and skills.[7] In the following pages, work organization is discussed according to a typology that does not pretend to be exhaustive, but to give some examples with respect to the prevailing technology in use and to employment relationships.[8] The examples discussed are of improvements, wholesale restructuring, traditional techniques, subcontracting, and industrialized casting methods.

3.3.1 Improvements and restructuring

Improvements to existing buildings, limited to single flats or small houses, consists of brickwork and installations. The work to be done can be complex and quite specific, requiring nonstandardized interventions and some flexibility in adapting to and satisfying all the specific requests of the client, and in allowing for technical, aesthetic, planning, and environmental constraints. A wide range of operations and tasks is involved, including not only different types of brickwork, carried out with a large variety of materials (bricks, solid masonry units, concrete panels, and different qualities of plaster for different coverings—such as paint, cloth, paper, tiles, carpet, linoleum), but also supporting brickwork, decorative brickwork, and the installation of heating and electric systems, eventually in cooperation with non-building workers. The work can be carried out by a craft enterprise or by a small team of a larger enterprise, headed by a skilled worker, fully responsible for both technical and organizational aspects. This is usually a bricklayer, highly skilled, with a good knowledge of the various possible materials and techniques, and also with some ability to handle artistic restoration. He is supposed to work on all the different operations from brickwork, in the proper sense, up to its cladding, plastering, painting, and covering, eventually assisted by a few helpers, and also in the preparation work for the installations. The varied features of every single work require a labour force able to work rapidly in different situations without the intervention of external skilled workers, since, given the fixed nature of the team, such intervention would increase total costs, being not a substitution for, but only an addition to the labour force already employed. Other craft workers are employed occasionally, for the most part plumbers (for the sanitary installations) and carpenters (for the internal and external scaffolding) (ISFOL, 1977, pp. 86–8; Fontanari, 1978, p. 258).

In the case of *wholesale restructuring* (involving the restructuring of an entire building), the work is performed by a relatively larger enterprise, organized according to a division of labour involving not only the distinction of workers by trade (carpenters, bricklayers, plasterers, plumbers, and electricians) but also some forms of rationalization of production (see Appendix C), including the use of prefabricated small components, subcontracting, and the lump. The carpenters prepare and place the scaffolding necessary for the preservation of the internal and external structures; place the supporting timber structures for escalators, ceilings, and lift; fit roof joists, and so on. The bricklayers are required to perform more or less the same tasks as in the previous case, but with a larger amount of standard brickwork. Part of their work is eliminated by employing new inputs (light components), and part is given out to specialist workers, organized in gangs and employed for some very specific tasks only (i.e. plastering, painting, paving, tile-laying, roofing, and so on) and for very limited periods of time. The 'polyvalence'[9] of the bricklayer, typical of the previous situation, is reduced.

3.3.2 New building: traditional techniques

As has been widely acknowledged, the Italin construction industry is quite traditional. Building enterprises, particularly if engaged on small projects, adopt construction methods of the traditional type—i.e. reinforced concrete structure, brickwork for external walls and partitions, and internal installations after the completion of the main structure. The production process is based on the succession, on the same construction site, of a large number of activities, carried out by separate teams of trades, linked one to another, so that one team can start when the previous one has completed its work. There are noticeable differences between contractors in their organization of the labour process—only partly explained by the size of the site, as here discussed, since subcontracting allows for different arrangements, as discussed in the next section.

In the case of *small sites*, i.e. for the construction of an individual house or a three to five–floor building, the production process is organized around the activity of a small and stable group of workers, with a high degree of flexibility and adaptability, to allow the performance of different tasks during the site cycle. Typically, all the workers are employed as labourers at the beginning of the site life, while they are employed by trade as the construction advances: steel fixers for the working and placing of reinforcing bars; carpenters for the preparation of timber shutters, escalators, and trussers; bricklayers for brickwork, plastering, and some finishing. The role of the traditional trades is here exalted, since workers are asked to perform, over the site cycle, a wide variety of operations (ISFOL, 1977, pp. 70–82; Fontanari, 1978, pp. 256–7, 260–1). It is also possible to find a higher degree of division of labour based on (*a*) a small team of workers (five or six), employed with continuity, and (*b*) a larger group of skilled workers, working on the site for short periods only. The first group is in charge of the general management of the site, the direct execution of the operations of their own trade and also the coordination of and cooperation with the specialist workers, employed for specific sequences only. It is frequently the case, if the construction site belongs to a large or medium enterprise, that some of the 'temporary' workers have a stable employment relationship, and rotate among several sites. If the site belongs to a small contractor, it is more likely that the specialist workers are employed for limited periods of time only.

Thus, allowing for possible variations, the organization of the labour process in small construction sites employing traditional techniques tends to show the following features: (*a*) the operative structure of the building site is based on few trades (carpenters, steel fixers, bricklayers, machine drivers, and cement workers), where each of them tends to include other trades whose work content, at least in its basic features, is quite close to theirs; (*b*) labourers are employed to only a small extent (between 20 and 30 per cent, according to the stage of the site cycle), given the use of a variety of cranes, the mechanization of the handling of building materials, the use of prefabricated light components, and the partial mechanization of other operations; (*c*) works which in the past were traditionally considered as builing—such as the installation of heating, electric, and plumbing systems—are increasingly given out to specialist contractors with non-building organizational features; (*d*) finally, the use of all forms of subcontracting, particularly for the final sequences, increases.

The division of labour in *large construction sites* is still based on a few craft trades, broadly defined on the basis of the material handled. But, given the greater use of capital equipment, there is a more numerous group of workers employed in driving and maintenance, such as crane drivers, maintenance workers, electro-mechanics, and engineers (ISFOL, 1977, pp. 82–5). The building site is better structured, and its organizational and technical management is no longer delegated to the most skilled workers. A few technicians and/or clerical workers are employed to supervise not only the technical aspects of construction, but also the division of labour, in terms of the organization and coordination of the sequences and their timing. The division of labour, allowing for possible variations, tends to be more precise and detailed: workers are organized in small teams by trade,[10] each specializing in one sequence of work, and not polyvalent to any great extent. In the central sequences, the teams are hierarchically structured with a team leader and a few skilled workers, possibly helped by one or two labourers. In some cases, the teams are subdivided and distinguished by type of work: for example, carpenters can be organized into one team in charge of horizontal carpentry, one for vertical carpentry, and one for ceilings.[11] In the finishing sequences, the teams are smaller, made up of skilled workers only, and with no hierarchical structure. But the actual organization of labour can vary widely, depending on if—and to what extent—subcontracting is employed.

3.3.3 The use of subcontracting

The labour-only contract and the lump arrangement have always been found in the sector. Subcontracting is found in all sequences of the building cycle and all over the region, but with differences in arrangement, nature, and extent, as summarized in Table 3.3.

Three different arrangements can be found. There is *subcontracting*, in the proper sense, when the main contractor employs a specialist contractor to perform a part of the project, usually a specific work requiring a particular piece of equipment. The subcontractor is, in this case, a separate firm, with its own equipment and employees. There is *labour-only contract* when the workers are not directly employed by the main contractor, or the subcontractor, but make a contract to supply labour, usually through a gang-leader. This can be an employee himself or a self-employed individual who acts as an intermediary between the employer and the workers, organizes the work, gets paid for it, and pays the workers. In the case of *the lump*, a small group of workers (*cottimisti*) can be directly employed by the main contractor and paid for the work done. Payment may take the form of a lump sum for the completion of a specified and particular task, such as a certain sum for every column erected, or a piece rate, i.e. so much money for each square or cubic metre completed.

These three situations are quite distinct according to the law,[12] but the distinction is not so clear in the real world. In fact, apart from the case of subcontractors acting as real enterprises, there is a large area where these different arrangements overlap. As a matter of fact, it is difficult to say if an enterprise is a real subcontractor or simply a gang working on the lump. It can be the case, for example, that a group of workers, actually working on the lump, is formally employed by the main contractor for a minimum number of hours, at the minimum wage, to give some legal appearance to the employment relationship. A contract is negotiated, informally and outside union control, between the main contractor and the gang leader, stating the payment in relation to the quantity of work to be done, generally breaking all union agreements on hours of work, wages, and safety conditions, and also avoiding the payment of social security contributions and taxes.

TABLE 3.3

Subcontracting: arrangements, nature, and extent

Sequence	Arrangement	Nature	Extent
earthworks	subcontract to a specialist contractor with equipment	technical (minimum efficient scale of production larger than other stages)	very extensive
erection of the superstructure	separate firms with no equipment; labour-only contract; the lump	productivity; due times	it exists in some areas and in some enterprises only
finishing and fixing	the lump; labour-only contract; specialist firms	productivity; know-how	very extensive

As pointed out in Table 3.3, subcontracting differs in type of arrangement and extent along with the building process. It is widespread for digging and earthworks, where all operations (ground preparation, digging, earth removal, and piling) are done mechanically by large and powerful machines (excavators, diggers, and power-shovels) driven by skilled workers. It is the high level of capital investment required and the short period for which it is needed that explains the tendency of small and medium enterprises to subcontract this capital-intensive sequence to specialist enterprises and/or to hire from them the equipment—and labour—when required. Only large building contractors, i.e. those able to organize several construction sites, can afford to invest in these machines. Subcontracting is also very widespread in the finishing and fixing operations, where small craft enterprises and gangs are employed, partly to do specialized work (i.e. requiring non-building trades or employing new materials), but increasingly to do some of the traditional building tasks (cladding, plastering, painting, floor covering, and so on). Similarly, subcontracting has begun to be used for the central part of the building process (erection of the superstructure), putting out carpentry, bending and fixing of bars, and concrete casting. The spread of subcontracting into these areas cannot be explained, as in the initial stage, on the basis of capital intensity or economies of scale—apart from a few very specific works. Rather, it is the state of technology, and particularly the fact that the process is still largely manual and craft orientated, that *allows* its de-composition and organization through subcontracting, in a large variety of combinations, as here discussed. Four types of subcontracting are described below.

(i) The first case is that of a general contractor, fully responsible for the execution of a project, who *subcontracts it out, as a whole*, to another building enterprise, defining prices and times of completion. This is the case, for example, of a large building cooperative, La Famiglia, operating at the national level in a large number of projects but only through subcontractors. This enterprise does not own any capital equipment, it employs 60 clerical workers and 20 construction site assistants, but no manual workers. In the construction site examined, the process is organized by subcontracting the whole project to another enterprise, but keeping control and coordination over the building cycle through supervision, in the site, by one assistant. The subcontractor (employing between 20 and 30 manual workers) executes only part of the work directly, and subcontracts parcels of work to small craft enterprises and gang groups to cut costs and meet deadlines (FILCA CISL Lombardia, 1980*b*, pp. 46–53). This subcontractor works almost exclusively for the general contractor and is almost compelled—given the type of tendering arrangements—to organize production through subcontracting.

(ii) A different arrangement is found where a main contractor *subcontracts through a series of contracts* different sequences of the building process, while providing some technical and organizational control through the employment, in the site, of a few employees. This is the case of a large cooperative from Reggio Emilia, which has tendered for a council housing project in Lombardia. While in its own region this cooperative executes most of its projects directly, here it has subcontracted everything 'in order to be competitive with the local building enterprises' (FILCA CISL Lombardia, 1980*b*, p. 67). It employs only a few of its employees[13] (a building surveyor, a work foreman, an aid foreman, a crane driver and a cement-mixer operator) to control and coordinate the building through 'technical assistance', and to control the pace of work of the different subcontractors, by controlling the pace of the machines employed (a crane and a cement-mixer).

(iii) A third type of arrangement exists where a main contractor *limits its activity to a few marginal operations* (such as the preparation of beton and the installation of the scaffolding) *and subcontracts the rest*.[14] The contractor, set within an organizational and technical structure, supervises the site, as in the previous case. At the same time it employs a few workers who are supposed to work as hands assisting the gangs by fetching and transporting materials on a particular floor. These latter tend to be very specialized by trade and by task, and to work very fast, but the work itself is not always very accurate. As a result, the main contractor needs to employ, directly, a few skilled and reliable workers, able to perform different operations, to adjust to different conditions, and to realize what has been done wrong by the gang workers and correct it. But they are also prepared to give them manual assistance (as labourers) when required.[15]

(iv) Finally, the most common arrangement consists of a contractor who *organizes directly the erection of the superstructure but subcontracts all the rest*. The subcontracting of the finishing and fixing operations can be total, when no work at all is done by the main contractor; it can be partial, when only some sequences are given out and others are done directly; or it can involve some cooperation between the workers on the lump and those employed directly by the main contractor.[16] In the last case, the main contractor provides manual labour, while skilled labour is supplied from outside, through subcontracting.

As already pointed out, the phenomenon of subcontracting is not uniform. Nevertheless, it is possible to single out some tendencies, particularly with respect to the final stage of the process, that help to point out the *double nature* of subcontracting: technical specialization on the one hand and fragmentation of old trades on the other. When the work is done by a traditional team, this rotates throughout the building cycle, performing different operations belonging, originally, to a single trade. For example, a team of bricklayers will first do the brickwork, then the cladding and plastering of the external and internal partitions, then prepare floors and floor coverings, and so on. When subcontracting is mainly the result of technical specialization and/or capital intensity, some specific and well-defined sequences are performed by separate specialized teams, while the workers of the main contractor are employed on work in other sequences, integrated in time and complementary to the work of the subcontractors. When subcontracting is mainly the result of the fragmentation of the old trades, the division of labour between the skilled dependent workers and the gangs is peculiar: the *cottimisti* of the gangs do the skilled tasks, while the employees are asked to help and support them, doing all the less skilled and the most tedious operations.

3.3.4 The coffrage tunnel

New methods of production, i.e. industrialized building methods such as prefabricated systems and industrialized casting methods, have been developing, radically affecting the organization of the production process and the trades employed. Such new methods have therefore to be discussed separately, as no continuity with the traditional systems of production is found. Industrialized casting methods are discussed here as an example of the new techniques of production.

When industrialized casting methods, such as the *coffrage tunnel*,[17] are employed, the organization of the production process is completely changed: the erection of the building no longer consists of a succession of distinct sequences, performed by separate teams of trades, but in the repetition over time of the same product cycle. This consists in the dismantling and cleaning of the tunnel; its positioning by means of a crane for the next casting; fixing; the preparation and placing of the electro-weld wire-nettings; the placing of the *negatives* for doors and windows, pipes, and other installations for gas, water, electricity, and heating; and, finally, casting. All these operations are executed by one team of workers, performing simultaneous and not successive tasks, as they have to work in tight relation to each other with a high degree of division of labour within the team. The work is organized, in most cases, in order to make one casting (i.e. one flat) a day, employing a team of 8 to 14 workers, plus a crane driver and a beton machine operator, the size varying according to equipment in use, project design, work organization, and pace of work.

The team is made up of skilled workers, but the work itself is quite simple, mechanical, and repetitive. The only worker with more complex tasks is the work foreman, who has to coordinate the work of the team with that of the crane driver. What is really crucial, when this technique is used, is the role of the technical office. This is supposed to provide for a very detailed and precise definition of the operative cycle. This has to define the sequences and their timing in terms of tasks, workload, time required, and chronological sequence, so as to make it possible to complete the product cycle in one day, to allow the concrete to dry during the night and to restart the process the following day, with no interruptions.[18]

By comparison with traditional building techniques, industrialized casting methods change the division of labour quite dramatically: not only does the management of the production process shift from the skilled workers to the technical office, but the trades themselves are radically affected. Some jobs disappear (such as bricklaying and plastering), others are completely transformed (carpentry), and others greatly simplified (steel fixing). Moreover, the integration of some sequences (which are performed in succession with the traditional building techniques) greatly simplifies the finishing sequences and makes subcontracting more difficult to use.

Thus, the new methods have potentially important implications for (*a*) the internal organization of the production process, as the division of labour changes quite dramatically, and (*b*) the organization of production, in terms of the division of labour between firms, since subcontracting systems—as they are used with the traditional methods of production—become impractical. So far, however, new methods of production, like the coffrage tunnel discussed here, have not been widely used, and should rather be considered as isolated examples of technological innovation—as presented in Appendix C. Their impact in quantitative terms is small, given that the organization of industry still overwhelmingly reflects traditional methods. Because of this, attention in the following chapters will be focused mainly on traditional organization of the production process.

3.4 Conclusions

The labour force in the steel industry is characterized by the *position workers occupy* with respect to the production process flow: process, maintenance, and ancillary workers. In the construction industry, the workers are characterized *by trade* (bricklayers, carpenters, steel fixers, machine operators, plasterers, painters, and so on), but the actual content of each trade is difficult to define, since it depends on the type of project, the techniques in use, and the way in which the production process is organized and subdivided between contractors. Three basic variants are found. The same trade can be employed 'extensively', with flexibility and polyvalence with respect to the workers' abilities and knowledge, when the division of labour is quite traditional and the skilled workers are asked to follow through the various series of stages of the production process; it can be employed 'intensively', therefore with a detailed and strict specialization, when, for example, the division of labour is largely based on subcontracting to different teams of workers, which are very specialized (by trade and task); lastly, trade specialization can be 'marginalized', when the workers' actual skills are under-utilized, as they are asked to perform only those tasks that cannot be subcontracted, because tedious and/or marginal to the building cycle, or because they have to cooperate with the gangs.

Both industries are characterized by the *employment of a considerable number of unskilled workers*, whose work is considered tiring, dangerous, heavy, and socially undesirable. The unskilled workers in the steel industry are required to execute simple tasks, with low technical content. Despite that, the steel worker is not merely a cog, relating only to precise instructions as to the activity of the machine. The tasks and operations are often simple, but at the same time extremely delicate, implying the gravity of the consequences of poorly executed operations. Unskilled workers are employed in the building industry as hodmen or as workers with no specific ability, either for marginal operations (such as loading and unloading materials, or clearing the site), or as hands assisting the skilled workers. Their number may be sharply reduced, not only by the introduction of machinery and equipment, and the pre-packing of materials in small units (pallets) so that they can be lifted and moved around easily by a fork-lift truck, but also by a different organization of labour, based on several specialized teams made up of highly skilled workers only.

Both industries have to *rely on their skilled workers* for the management of the production process. In the steel industry, the technological rigidity of the production process (the high integration and interdependence of the different stages) and the randomness of the steel-making process (i.e. the occurrence of unpredictable events in the chemical/physical transformation process and/or in the performance of the installations) imply a continuous activity of control and regulation of all the variables (process and installations). This activity is mainly performed by the skilled workers, and is based on the ability to notice and to interpret the rise of variances, and to intervene with the required regulating activity. In the building industry, the with the required regulating activity. In the building industry, the production process is the result of a combination of techniques, materials, and trades, where skilled workers are both themselves manually involved in the process and organize the work of the unskilled. In the case of both industries there is a need to secure a skilled labour force with aptitudes specific to the industry. Achieving this poses different types of problems in the two sectors. In fact, as Chapter 2 demonstrated, in the case of steel, there is a need for a *stable* labour force and in the case of construction a demand for a *flexible* (in quantitative terms) labour force.

To conclude, the nature of the product, the technology, its diffusion and use, industrial structure, and market forms, lead to a stable labour force in steel and a flexible one in construction, with both sectors employing a large number of unskilled workers for hard and tiring jobs, and both having to secure the co-operation of the skilled workers for the organization of the production process. However, economic and technological factors alone are not sufficient to define the structure of labour markets. Differences in the economic and technological characteristics in the two cases may be large enough to prevent much overlap between them, but they do not themselves determine the labour market structure; rather they delimit the economic and technological framework within which management, labour, and unions interact. In other words, they can be looked at as constraints on feasible outcomes, determining the *realm of possibilities* for the definition of the labour market structure. Thus, economic and technological factors set different conditions in the two sectors; the following two chapters will try to show how these varying conditions are met.

Notes

1. Breda is one of the very few steelworks still producing steel with open-hearth furnaces.
2. See ISSOCO, 1975; Frey, 1976, pp. 61–8; Frey, 1979, pp. 9–21; Frison, 1979, pp. 86–7; Franciosi, 1979*b*, pp. 79–133.
3. For example, the blast-furnaces (in the case of an integrated steel plant) and the steel-making furnaces.
4. On the weekend, or whenever it is possible to stop the installations, a team of variable composition (depending on the work to be done) dismantles the parts that require repairing; during the week, the work is done in the workshops; finally, when the maintenance work is com-

pleted, the team goes back to the department for the assembling, finishing, and revision of the work done.

5. In the scrap-based steel plants, where the process can be stopped without damaging the installations, it is possible to stop the process during the weekend and work 17 or 18 shifts per week. No such stoppages are possible in integrated plants.
6. At the same time, given the limitation it imposes on social life, shift work creates problems in the recruiting of labour.
7. This has recently found support in a research project on the techniques in use in construction in Lombardia. See FLC Lombardia, 1981, pp. 146–50.
8. This section is based on unpublished material, including (*a*) two large research projects on work organization in construction in Lombardia: FILCA CISL Lombardia, 1980*a*, 1980*b*, based on the analysis of 37 construction sites, and FLC Lombardia, 1981, based on the analysis of 72 construction sites; and (*b*) a research commissioned by ASSIMPREDIL, the building employers' association of the Milan district, to CRESME on subcontracting and division of labour in the Milan district (CRESME, 1976, section 4); this research was based on 22 interviews (6 with employers, and 16 with workers and gang leaders).
9. 'Polyvalence' is the literal translation of the Italian expression (*polivalenza*) currently used in the Italian literature on the division of labour to characterize those qualifications and skills distinguished for their richness and complexity. More precisely, this expression refers not only to the manual ability to perform and combine several tasks, but also to the intellectual grasp of the entire process.
10. That is three to four steel fixers, five to eight carpenters, five to ten bricklayers.
11. See FILCA CISL Lombardia, 1980*b*, pp. 72–3, 82–3.
12. Subcontracting, in the proper sense, is allowed while any other form is explicitly forbidden by law (Legge 23 ottobre 1960, n. 1369) and by the national collective agreement (CCNL Edili, 1979, *Regolamentazione per gli operai*, art. 15, 16).
13. This co-operative is quite large, employing about 260 workers organized in teams of steel fixers, carpenters, bricklayers, floorlayers, plumbers, and so on (FILCA CISL Lombardia, 1980*b*, pp. 68–9).
14. This is the case of Antonioli & C, in FILCA CISL Lombardia, 1980*b*, pp. 103–9.
15. If there are unskilled workers, these are usually employed by the main contractor, and have to give assistance to the teams of steel fixers, bricklayers, carpenters, plasterers, and so on, working on the lump.
16. In the case studies analysed in FILCA CISL Lombardia, 1980*b*, the case of total subcontracting is found at Allegri (pp. 41–4) and Barpero (pp. 95–8); the case of partial subcontracting is found at Nessi Maiocchi (pp. 57–62), CREI (pp. 63–73), CEIM (pp. 76–83), and Italedit (pp. 87–91); and the case of co-operation is found at Edilda (p. 114), and Antonioli (pp. 103–9).

17. See Appendix C for a brief description of this technology.
18. If the process is not completed by the end of the day, then the concrete has to be cast the following day. This creates a one-day delay in the product cycle, since the tunnel cannot be slipped off until the concrete has hardened.

CHAPTER FOUR

The Labour Market Structure in the Steel Industry

The discussion on division of labour in Chapter 3 pointed out the general characteristics of jobs in the steel industry as they are shaped by technological and economic factors. In the process departments, the workers are asked to perform simple operations, in some cases in hard working conditions, but carrying considerable responsibility and requiring lengthy on-the-job training; in the maintenance services, workers who have some skill already in their trade and who are able to improve it are required; in the service departments, most of the jobs are simple, requiring neither skill, job experience, nor physical fitness. This chapter examines how these jobs are internally organized into a system of job clusters: that is, how workers are recruited, allocated to jobs, and organized for work. Section 4.1 examines the classification system in use in terms of the relationship between the characteristics of jobs, workers' skills, and the classification of workers. Section 4.2 analyses how this system of jobs is related to the external market, that is, how workers are recruited, selected, and internally allocated. Section 4.3 discusses how jobs are related to each other and how workers move between them, focusing on the problems of training, internal mobility, career, and turnover.

4.1 The classification system in use

The national agreements for the metal sector, for both the public and the private sector,[1] negotiated in 1973, have introduced a new classification system, known as the *Inquadramento Unico* (IU), which provides for the classification of all employees, clerical workers, foremen and manual workers, on a single grading scale based on seven grades (*livelli professionali*) for the private sector and eight for the public sector, and related to a wage structure based on eight scales. But the IU is not a novelty for the steel industry. In fact, the national collective agreements of 1973 have to be considered as a generalization to all the metal industry of what was settled at Italsider on 24 December 1970, and later negotiated in other large enterprises. The bargaining procedure followed was based on a first agreement (24 December 1970) outlining the principles and the criteria on the basis of which the new classification system had to be singled out, and on a final agreement (26 May 1972), quite long and complex, specifying the implementation of what was previously bargained. A similar procedure (i.e. plant bargaining for the implementation of the principles outlined in the general agreement) was followed by all other enterprises.[2] The result is that, despite the fact that the IU agreements are based on the same general principles, shaped on the Italsider 1970 agreement, their implementation can differ. Therefore, before examining how steel workers are classified and graded, it is necessary to point out the general principles of the IU agreements, taking Italsider as a reference point.

The first point of the new classification system is that it classifies and grades all workers on the same scale, based on the criterion of *professionalità*,[3] which is defined as the capacity to work, to know, and to intervene in the production process.[4] Moreover, it is stated that it should also provide for the valorization of workers' *professionalità*, as above defined. Thus, both the grading of workers (acknowledgement of their level of qualification) and their upward mobility are supposed to be based on this concept of 'new professionalism'.

Secondly, the agreements have worked out *a single grading scale*, for all employees, articulated in eight grades and eight wage scales, to which monthly basic rates are related. The general level of qualification is specified for each grade on the basis of a classification of (*a*) type of activity (manual, technical/manual, administrative); (*b*) knowledge and abilities (general or specific); (*c*) acquisition of knowledge and abilities (procedure and length of time); (*d*) complexity and difficulty of the activity; and finally, (*e*) type of autonomy (execution, guide, control, initiative).[5]

Thirdly, the new classification, despite the fact that it is 'unique' for all workers, maintains the distinction between employees in *three groups*, staff workers, foremen, and manual workers, as far as economic and employment conditions are concerned. In other words, all employees are subject to the same scale of qualification and grading, but this does not affect existing differences, granted to them in the past, in holidays, hours of work, sickness benefits, and so on, even if it established a tendency towards the elimination of any kind of discrimination.

Finally, the agreement is supposed to provide for the *development of workers' qualifications*.[6] A series of mechanisms and instruments, such as job rotation, job enrichment and job enlargement, requalification of workers with diminished psychophysical abilities, and finally mobility of workers from areas and jobs with poor job content and/or hard working conditions, have been suggested, 'in order to promote and evaluate the development and the utilization of the individual workers' professional abilities'.[7]

With respect to the general ideas that have structured the IU agreements, there are two problems that deserve to be discussed: first of all, how this idea of *professionalità* has been translated into practice —i.e. how workers are graded; secondly, how this idea of *professionalità* has been related to the promotion of workers' qualifications—i.e. how workers' careers develop.

4.1.1 The grading of staff workers, foremen, and manual workers

According to the national agreements for the metal sector[8] manual workers should be graded in the first five grades starting from the bottom, foremen in the fourth and fifth, and non-manual workers from the second to the highest. The actual distribution of workers along the classification structure for the four enterprises considered, as shown in Table 4.1, is characterized by (*a*) a considerable interlacing in terms of grades between the three groups of employees, (*b*) a high concentration in the top grades of foremen and manual workers, and (*c*) the grading of a large number of foremen (Breda, Dalmine, and Cornigliano) and a certain number of manual workers (Dalmine and Cornigliano) in grade 6, reserved by collective agreements to non-manual workers.[9] As a result, the majority of employees in all three categories are classified in the same grades (4, 5 and 6). Nevertheless, the four enterprises keep the distinction, set in the national agreements, between employees in three different groups, to which basic differences in terms of status, economic and non-economic privileges, as well as career processes, correspond.[10]

The three groups have different career patterns. In terms of grades, while the careers of staff workers can develop up to the top grade, for foremen and manual workers the highest grade is usually the fifth. Ports of entry are clearly distinguished between manual and non-manual jobs and there is very little mobility between them, so that their career processes are almost completely separated. On the contrary, foremen are precisely the result of a process of internal advancement from the bottom. Despite this, they are considered as a separate and well-distinguished category. Access to it occurs by management discretionary decision on which worker has to be promoted, and it is always reserved for the most experienced and skilled workers, necessarily the oldest and those with the longest length of service. They are usually employed as supervisors, with the role of control and coordination of the workteam. This implies a *technical role* in relation to processes and equipment, in terms of responsibilities and decisions to be taken, and a *hierarchical role* in relation to the workteam, in terms of coordination of their activities and all related problems. But technical change has increasingly reduced and impoverished their technical role, and the development of collective bargaining has progressively eroded their hierarchical role, in terms of decisions over the workers' career, so that the tendency is for a progressive reduction of foremen.[11] The ratio of manual workers to supevisors is quite different between enterprises, so that while at Italsider Cornigliano (49.4 workers per foreman) the tendency is to reduce supervisory staff, Breda (22.8 workers per foreman) still keeps foremen as the basis for the organization of the labour process. This is explained partly by differences in the labour management policies and partly by differences in the technology. In fact, supervisory staff play quite a crucial role, in all processes where the management of the production process is still based on the workers' knowledge acquired through experience, as is the case for the steel-making department.[12]

4.1.2 The grading of manual workers

The system of classification based on the IU, despite the fact that is supposed to be unique for all workers, when applied in the steel industry maintains a distinction in the classification of maintenance and process workers.

Maintenance workers are hired by trade and graded by their skills and abilities. An electrician is an electrician, independent of the fact that a certain job is complex or simple. When a maintenance worker enters the factory he has already a certain skill. This can be improved through experience, and the speed of this process will depend on individual abilities, dexterities, and job experiences. The process of acquisition of grades is, therefore, directly related to the acquisition and improvement of skills on an individual basis. The foreman, or a person in a similar hierarchical position, will verify and decide—usually in agreement with the shop steward—when a worker has improved his degree of skill and deserves a higher grade. Maintenance workers are usually hired at grade 3, being acknowledged as possessing a certain skill, and then upgraded depending on their individual career profiles.[13]

For process and service workers the approach is completely different. Since it is not possible to define process workers' skills in the traditional craft manner, the solution has been, in a sense, the traditional one: the job, and not the worker, is evaluated and graded. Process workers are hired by department and with no skill, since all the training is on the job. Within each department they are allocated to entry jobs (at the lowest grades) and then moved up as vacancies

TABLE 4.1

Grading structure by category of employee

Breda Siderurgica (31.10.79)

	Non-manual workers		Foremen		Manual workers	
	No.	%	No.	%	No.	%
grades						
8	117	25.89		—	—	—
7	115	25.44	—	—	—	—
6	84	18.58	88	77.19	—	—
5	72	15.93	24	21.05	795	30.53
4	36	7.96	2	1.76	1,037	39.82
3	28	6.20	—	—	627	24.08
2	—	—	—	—	137	5.26
1	—	—	—	—	8	0.31
Total	452	100	114	100	2,604	100
average grade	6.27		5.75		3.95	

Falck, Concordia works (31.12.79)

	Non-manual workers		Formen		Manual workers	
	No.	%	No.	%	No.	%
grades						
7	8	5.75	—	—	—	
6	23	16.55	—	—	—	—
5S	39	28.06	—	—	—	—
5	37	26.62	39	100	276	21.21
4	29	20.86	—	—	510	39.20
3	3	2.16	—	—	424	32.59
2	—	—	—	—	91	
1	—	—	—	—	—	—
Total	139	100	39	100	1,301	100
average grade	5.53		5.00		3.75	

Dalmine, Dalmine works (31.12.79)

	Non-manual workers		foremen		Manual workers	
	No.	%	No.	%	No.	%
grades						
8	125	20.70	—	—	—	—
7	145	24.01	—	—	—	—
6	198	32.78	127	72.16	24	0.46
5	66	10.93	43	24.43	2,016	38.85
4	40	6.62	6	3.41	2,395	46.15
3	26	4.30	—	—	609	11.74
2	4	0.66	—	—	142	2.74
1	—	—	—	—	3	0.06
Total	604	100	176	100	5,189	100
average grade	6.26		5.69		4.22	

Italsider, Cornigliano works (31.12.79)

	Non-manual workers		Foremen		Manual workers	
	No.	%	No.	%	No.	%
grades						
8	268	16.60	—	—	—	—
7	507	31.41	2	1.14	—	—
6	593	36.74	126	72.00	294	4.30
5	171	10.60	46	26.29	4,192	61.26
4	71	4.40	1	0.57	1,711	25.00
4	4	0.25	—	—	520	7.60
2	—	—	—	—	125	1.83
1	—	—	—	—	1	0.01
Total	1,614	100	175	100	6,843	100
average grade	6.44		5.73		4.59	

Source: My own collection from the archives of the enterprises.

occur in better-graded jobs. The grading of jobs is crucial in defining the grading of workers even if, as will be discussed later on, workers can be graded differently from the jobs they hold. And the grading of jobs seems to reflect (*a*) *the position of the job* with respect to the production process flow, so that the 'key' departments and the 'key' job posts tend to be better graded than the marginal departments and jobs, (*b*) *the responsibilities* involved in such positions, with respect to both processes and equipment, so that higher responsibility is rewarded with higher grades, (*c*) finally, *the working conditions*, so that heavy and dirty jobs are better graded than others.

Tables 4.2 and 4.3 show the grading of jobs by department in two plants, and the grading of jobs within the steel-making department.

On the basis of the average grade by department, and within departments by section, it is possible to work out a hierarchy of departments and a hierarchy of sections: (*a*) maintenance jobs[14] are better graded than process department jobs, and the latter better than service section jobs; (*b*) the ranking of process departments in terms of grades is very clear, and reflects the production process flow, so that the steel-making department is better graded than the rolling department, which is better graded than the treatment and finishing departments; (*c*) finally, also within the process departments, it is possible to single out a ranking of sections and jobs, where higher grades correspond, basically, to the key sections and to the key jobs with respect to the production process flow. In this respect, the steel-making department provides a clearcut example: all jobs directly related to the smelting, refining, and casting of steel are better graded than the others.

4.1.3 The development of workers' occupational qualifications

As already pointed out, the general and preliminary agreements on the IU have claimed that the development of the workers' qualification has to be promoted. The mechanisms and procedures introduced through plant collective bargaining for the implementation of what is stated in the preliminary agreements can be seen as the result of trade union pressure to assure *all* process workers some internal advancement, either as the result of a process of job-climbing or, at least, in terms of grades. The basic principle on which workers' qualifications are measured, and therefore on which workers are graded and upgraded, is their mobility and availability to move and rotate between different jobs. More precisely, the Italsider agreement (which can be taken as a reference point for all the others) states that the promotion of workers from one grade to another should refer not to what the workers do but to what they *can* do:

Upgrading takes place according to the workers' abilities, concretely shown, to perform job activities of a higher grade. . . . The evaluation of a worker's abilities to perform job activities of a higher grade takes place through the employment of the worker, either temporarily or permanently, on a job post of a higher grade. (Italsider agreement, 26.5.72, art. 4)

The procedures that have been singled out for upgrading are substantially the same for all steel plants, and they can be grouped as follows: (*a*) upgrading by vertical mobility on a vacant job, better graded, as job holder (i.e. upward mobility); (*b*) upgrading by rotation, on job posts of higher grade (vertical rotation) and/or on several job posts of the same grade (horizontal rotation); (*c*) upgrading by substitution on a temporarily vacant job post for continuing periods of time (substitution of temporary vacancies); (*d*) upgrading as the result of the creation of new job positions from the recomposition of tasks previously associated to distinct job positions of a lower grade (i.e. job enrichment).

Despite the fact that the case of job enrichment (case (*d*)) was included in the agreements as a means of promoting workers' qualifications, it has been applied very little (and only for very specific jobs, so that the division of labour, in terms of the definition of job posts and job content, has not been substantially affected by the IU agreements. On the contrary, the introduction of formal rules for upgrading related to internal mobility (cases (*a*), (*b*), and (*c*)) allows workers to be better graded with respect to the jobs they hold, continuing to perform the same activities.

The procedures introduced for upgrading are subject to some time constraints expressed in terms of minimum length of service in the new grade (case (*a*)) or in the previous grades (cases (*b*) and (*c*)) and a minimum number of rotations and substitution, as shown in Table 4.4. In the case of upgrading by promotion, the time constraint (expressed in terms of months of service required in the new job) has to be interpreted as the time required to be trained into the new job, before being acknowledged at the grade associated with the job held. In the case of promotion by rotation and by substitution, time constraints are higher, and depend not only on the number of days for which the worker has been employed on a different job, but on his length of service, per grade.[15]

These agreements have therefore introduced some mechanisms for the upgrading of workers which depend basically on their internal mobility. As a result, it is possible that a worker is graded differently from the job he holds. At the same time, the acknowledgement of a higher grade by rotation, either vertical or horizontal, does not change the worker's job position, so that he can still be asked to rotate on the

TABLE 4.2

Manual jobs by grade and department (% distribution)

Breda Siderurgica (31.10.79)

Grades	Steel dept. (%)	Rolling dept. (%)	Finish. dept. (%)	Main-tenance (%)	Quality control (%)	Transp. service (%)	Other services (%)	Total (%)	(No.)
5	38.98	19.97	12.42	57.29	34.66	5.22	4.65	26.55	(685)
4	30.11	31.93	32.63	29.14	43.56	11.74	6.05	27.75	(716)
3	20.70	41.98	36.84	8.98	16.83	54.78	45.12	31.98	(825)
2	8.33	4.52	13.69	1.80	0.99	25.22	7.95	8.22	(212)
1	1.88	1.60	4.42	2.79	3.96	3.04	36.23	5.50	(142)
Total	100	100	100	100	100	100	100	100	
(No.)	(372)	(686)	(475)	(501)	(101)	(230)	(215)		(2,580)
Average grade	3.96	3.64	3.35	4.36	4.04	2.91	2.35	3.62	
ranking	3	4	5	1	2	6	7		

Dalmine, Dalmine works (1.1.80)

Grades	Steel dept. (%)	Rolling dept. (%)	Main-tenance (%)	Services (%)	Total (%)	(No.)
5	39.78	19.30	60.00	14.02	30.65	(168)
4	41.94	25.00	24.17	29.90	28.65	(157)
3	16.13	50.44	14.16	40.16	34.67	(190)
2	2.15	4.38	1.67	4.67	3.47	(19)
1	—	0.88	—	11.22	2.56	(14)
Total	100	100	100	100	100	
(No.)	(93)	(228)	(120)	(107)		(548)
Average grade	4.20	3.55	4.43	3.33	3.81	
ranking	2	3	1	4		

Note: Figures for Dalmine are based on a sample of jobs, 1 every 10, for all departments.

Source: My own collection from the archives of the enterprises.

TABLE 4.3
Manual jobs in the steel-making department by grade
Breda Siderurgica (31.10.79)

Sections	1	2	3	4	5	Total	Average grade
cleaning	7	—	—	—	—	7	1.0
scrap area	—	9	30	1	—	40	
charge preparation	—	22	28	—	—	50	2.68
tapping	—	—	5	—	—	5	
1st furnace (electric)	—	—	—	7	20	27	
2nd furnace (electric)	—	—	2	4	17	23	
3rd furnace (open-hearth)	—	—	2	2	15	19	4.73
4th furnace (open-hearth)	—	—	—	3	16	19	
slag skimming	—	—	—	1	3	4	
casting and stripping	—	—	5	88	56	149	4.37
vacuum casting	—	—	—	2	7	9	
steel works workshop	—	—	2	7	11	20	4.45
Total	7	31	74	115	145	372	3.97

Dalmine, Dalmine works (1.1.80)

sections	1	2	3	4	5	Total	Average grade
scrap area	—	—	—	3	—	3	4.00
scrap selection, charge prep.	—	—	1	6	1	8	
furnaces:							
steel making and casting	—	1	2	18	15	36	
furnace operators	—	—	—	—	4	4	4.48
maintenance	—	—	2	1	6	9	
continuous casting	—	—	—	—	9	9	
conditioning/1	—	—	5	3	—	8	
conditioning/2	—	—	—	4	—	4	3.50
ingot turning	—	1	5	6	—	12	
Total	—	1	15	41	35	93	4.17

Note: Figures for Dalmine are a sample, 1 every 10, of the total jobs in the steel department.

Source: My own collection from the archives of the enterprises.

TABLE 4.4

Upgrading constraints bargained by grade and process

	(1) Upgrading by vertical mobility	(2) Upgrading by rotation		(3) Upgrading by substitution	
	No. of months required in the new job before upgrading	Minimum length of service (years)	Minimum no. of days of rotations	Minimum length of service (years)	Minimum no. of days of substitution
grade:					
to 2nd	1	2	50	2	22
to 3rd	2	2	60	2	44
to 4th	2	3	90	3	44
to 5th	2	4	110	4	44
to 6th	3	6	130	5	66
to 7th	3	7	150	5	66
to 8th	3	7	150	5	66

Source: Italsider agreement, 26.5.73, art. 4.

same jobs, even if of a lower grade; similarly, in the case of promotion by substitution, the worker will be asked to move back to his previous job post, of a lower grade, when the job holder is back.

4.1.4 Workers' grading and workers' skills

From the previous discussion it should be clear that there is little relation between workers' grading and workers' skill level, as this term is usually understood. First of all, the nature of skill is basically different in process and in maintenance jobs. Secondly, the relation between skill and grade is different for the two groups of workers, so that, while maintenance workers are graded by their skill level in their trade, process workers are graded depending on the grade associated with the job held and the possibility of movement. Thirdly, despite the fact that it is possible for process and service workers to be better graded than their jobs, maintenance workers are always graded higher than process and service workers. Thus, traditional craft skills are still better rewarded than process workers' abilities. Technology affects strongly the grading of process and service workers, and their ranking tends to be the same between plants and over time: process departments are better graded than services, and process departments concerned with the earlier stages are better graded than those concerned with the later stages. Thus, the ranking of workers by grade and department, as shown in Table 4.5 (pp. 92–3) is basically the same as the ranking of jobs by grade, as shown in Table 4.2 (see pp. 86–7). Fourthly, differences in the general grading level are noticeable between the enterprises, with Cornigliano recording the highest average grade (4.63) and Falck Concordia the lowest (3.75).

To summarize, even if the classification system in use is based on the grading of jobs, at least for process and ancillary workers, it allows a classification of workers different from that of the jobs held, with considerable variations between the steel enterprises. The existing differences, as shown in Table 4.5, have to be related to (*a*) differences in the grading of jobs between departments, (*b*) differences in the grading of jobs between enterprises, and (*c*) differences in the internal organization of workers' careers. The previous discussion has shown that the grading of jobs, in relative terms, is strongly shaped by the technological features of the production process. Nevertheless, the actual grading of jobs within each enterprise is the result of a complex bargaining process that took place in the early 1970s, reflecting differences in the power relationship between labour and management, and between groups of workers (as will be discussed in Chapter 7, section 7.4.3). The next two sections will examine how a certain structure of jobs is related to the external market, i.e. how workers are hired and allocated there, and how their careers then develop.

4.2 Entry

4.2.1 Demand for labour and hiring policies

Process workers are employed to fill manual jobs characterized by hard working conditions. The management of the production process involves a continuous activity of control and regulation of all the variables, where the tasks to be performed are often simple, but carry considerable responsibilities for materials and equipment. All this calls for a *responsible and reliable* labour force, physically able to handle heavy work and a big factory, willing to be employed in uncomfortable jobs and to work on shifts. Maintenance workers are asked to fill highly skilled jobs, for which previous formal training is required for the acquisition of the basic theoretical and practical knowledge—within their trade. Demand for maintenance workers is orientated towards *workers with some skill already*, in their trade, and able to improve it through further formal and on-the-job training, implying both the study of advanced subjects, such as electronics and oleodynamics, and specific on-the-job training on the capital equipment in use. The service sections tend not to generate a demand for labour from the *external* labour market. Most of the service jobs are simple, do not involve any specific skill or physical fitness, and tend to be filled internally by workers who are aged and/or with health problems, and therefore no longer are able to handle the hard work of the process departments. Vacancies are filled with external recruitment only for those jobs which cannot be filled internally with 'downgraded' workers, either because they require some skills (as is the case for few jobs in the laboratories, quality control sections, thermal station, and electric station) or because they require physical fitness (as is the case for the internal transport services). On the whole, ancillary jobs have to be considered as a residual section, to which workers from all process departments are confined when they can no longer be employed elsewhere.

Thus recruitment occurs for process departments and maintenance sections, while vacancies in the services are filled, by and large, through internal mobility. A general goal is followed by all the steel enterprises in the recruitment of their labour force: they look for a *stable and loyal labour force* to which to entrust the management of the production process and the care of the equipment. If, on the one hand, they look for process workers in good physical condition and for maintenance workers with some skill already, they look, on the other hand, for a responsible labour force which intends to stay and to develop its working career there. These characteristics refer neither to technical, professional, physical nor attitudinal features, but to social behaviour. And this explains the screening devices singled out in

TABLE 4.5

Manual workers by grade and department

Breda Siderurgica (31.10.79)

Grades	Steel dept.	Rolling dept.	Finish. dept.	Main-tenance	Quality control	Transp. service	Other services	Total	(No.)
6	—	—	—	—	—	—	—	—	—
5	44.89	28.28	16.00	59.08	45.55	6.52	9.30	31.55	(814)
4	35.48	39.94	55.16	31.14	47.52	23.91	32.09	38.60	(996)
3	14.52	29.88	18.95	9.18	6.93	52.18	39.54	23.53	(607)
2	5.11	1.90	9.89	0.60	—	17.39	19.07	6.32	(163)
1	—	—	—	—	—	—	—	—	(—)
Total	100	100	100	100	100	100	100	100	
(No.)	(372)	(686)	(475)	(501)	(101)	(230)	(215)		(2,580)
Average grade	4.20	3.95	3.77	4.49	4.39	3.20	3.32	3.95	
Ranking	3	4	5	1	2	7	6		

AFL Falck, Concordia works (31.12.79)

Grades	Steel dept.	Rolling dept.	Maintenance	Services	Total	(No.)
5S	—	—	—	—	—	(—)
5	19.12	11.78	35.38	19.11	21.22	(276)
4	39.70	45.98	40.31	29.17	39.20	(510)
3	36.18	33.05	20.62	41.32	32.59	(424)
2	5.00	9.19	3.69	10.40	6.99	(91)
1	—	—	—	—	—	(—)
Total	100	100	100	100	100	
(No.)	(340)	(348)	(325)	(288)		(1,301)
Average grade	3.76	3.60	4.07	3.57	3.75	
Ranking	2	3	1	4		

TABLE 4.5 (cont.)

Dalmine, Dalmine works (1.1.80)

Grades	Steel dept.	Rolling dept.	Main-tenance	Services	Total	(No.)
6	—	—	2.50	—	0.55	(3)
5	62.36	29.82	57.50	29.91	41.42	(227)
4	27.97	57.02	26.67	52.34	44.52	(244)
3	6.45	10.09	9.16	13.08	9.86	(54)
2	3.22	3.07	4.17	4.67	3.65	(20)
1	—	—	—	—	—	(—)
Total	100	100	100	100	100	
(No.)	(93)	(228)	(120)	(107)		(548)
Average grade	4.49	4.14	4.45	4.07	4.25	
Ranking	1	3	2	4		

Italsider, Cornigliano works (1.12.80)

Grades	Pig-iron iron	Steel dept.	Hot roll.	Cold roll.	Main-tenance	Quality cont.	Auxiliary serv.	Transport services	Other Services	Total	(No.)
6	1.82	1.12	0.44	2.56	9.76	—	5.36	1.93	1.12	4.66	(322)
5	56.36	77.35	67.35	57.73	69.69	93.84	82.14	52.76	51.84	64.07	(4,427)
4	25.76	16.37	25.22	20.99	18.21	4.62	8.93	24.73	34.88	21.75	(1,503)
3	15.45	5.16	6.56	16.26	2.26	1.54	3.57	13.95	11.36	8.26	(571)
2	0.61	—	0.43	2.46	0.08	—	—	6.63	0.80	1.26	(87)
1	—	—	—	—	—	—	—	—	—	—	(—)
Total	100	100	100	100	100	100	100	100	100	100	
(No.)	(660)	(446)	(686)	(1,015)	(2,521)	(65)	(168)	(724)	(625)		(6,910)
Average grade	4.43	4.74	4.61	4.42	4.87	4.92	4.89	4.29	4.41	4.63	
Ranking	6	4	5	7	2	1	3	9	8		

Note: Figures for Dalmine are based on a sample of jobs, 1 every 10, for all departments.

Source: My own collection from the archives of the enterprises.

terms of sex, age, and place of origin. All the workers recruited are male, neither too young nor too old, and not southern—or at least not too recently immigrated.

4.2.2 Screening devices

(i) *Sex*. Apart from the case of Breda, which has in recent years had to hire a few women, steel is a traditionally male sector and has never recruited women, so that even amongst non-manual workers the proportion of women is very low.

(ii) *Age (Appendices D. 3 and D. 4)*. The policy followed is to recruit workers who are neither so young as to pose problems of reliability, nor so old as to pose problems of adaptability. Most of the workers recruited are between 21 and 30 years old. This policy is more stressed at Dalmine (79.3 per cent) and Cornigliano (77.5 per cent), Breda and Falck recruiting a higher proportion of both younger and older workers, but still covering most of the vacancies with workers of the same age group (59.7 and 51.8 per cent, respectively).

(iii) *Place of origin (Appendices D. 10, D. 11, D. 12)*. The tendency is to prefer workers socially integrated with the area where they live. Given the location of the plants examined in the 'northern triangle', and subject in the past to large immigrations, this has implied not recruiting southern people, particularly if they are recent immigrants. At Dalmine, almost all the workers (92.9 per cent) are from the Dalmine village or from the numerous villages in the Bergamo district. Similarly, at Cornigliano the labour force is by and large locally recruited (77.2 per cent), either from the Genova district or from the inland (Val Polcevera, Val Bisagno, Levante) and the Savona district, even if there is a certain proportion of southern workers. In the case of Falck and Breda, given their location in a highly industrialized area, characterized by considerable immigration in the past, it is no longer possible to recruit, locally, non-southern workers. A large proportion of the labour force at Falck is originally from the nearby valleys and mountain areas (Bergamasco, Bresciano, Valtellina) and a quite considerable proportion (42.7 per cent) still lives in the villages, therefore commuting to work every day. Falck prefers to hire Lombard commuters rather than southern workers living in Sesto or in the environs, so that almost no southern people are employed there. Breda has succeeded in following a similar policy only up to the early 1960s; with the economic expansion and the relative shortage of labour, they had to start to recruit southern workers, and by 1979 about 70 per cent of the new recruits were not from Lombardia. From Table 4.6, showing

TABLE 4.6

Breda Siderurgica, manual workers by year of hiring and place of origin (1974 and 1979)

	Before 1951	1952/ 1957	1958/ 1963	1964/ 1969	1970/ 1971	1972/ 1974	Total LF in 1974	New LF hired in 1979
Milan district	47.3	27.3	6.1	7.6	8.1	8.4	11.8	17.1
rest of Lombardia	32.0	45.3	44.1	32.2	23.4	19.7	30.9	11.0
rest of north Italy	12.1	16.2	6.8	7.8	8.8	6.8	8.5	2.4
Total north Italy	91.4	88.8	57.0	47.6	40.3	34.9	51.2	30.5
central Italy	1.8	2.5	10.4	6.5	4.6	4.8	5.9	3.7
south Italy	5.4	8.7	32.1	45.4	54.2	60.0	42.3	65.8
abroad	1.4	—	0.5	0.5	0.9	0.3	0.6	—
Total central–south Italy	8.6	11.2	43.0	52.4	59.7	65.1	48.8	69.5
Total	100	100	100	100	100	100	100	100
(No.)	(222)	(161)	(511)	(831)	(638)	(497)	(2,860)	(164)

Note: LF = labour force.

Source: 1974, elaboration on Facchini and Umidi, 1980, p. 8; 1979, Breda Siderurgica archive.

the structure of the labour force by place of origin and period of entry, it can be seen clearly how this process has been taking place progressively, and with a certain delay with respect to the immigration waves.[16] Up to 1957 most of the workers were from the rest of the region, mainly Bergamo and Brescia districts. Later on, when this flow started to dry up, Breda began to recruit southern workers in increasing proportions. Now that this source too has started to diminish, some women have been hired.

(iv) *Schooling and work experience (Appendices D. 5, D. 6, D. 7).* There are precise differences between process and maintenance workers with respect to both schooling and previous experience. These factors are not considered significant for jobs in the process departments: most of the tasks are manual and all the training is on the job, and it is therefore sufficient if workers can read and count. Their formal education level is in fact very low: between 70 and 90 per cent have no more or less than 5 years of education (Appendix D. 7 (*a*) and (*b*)). All process workers had some previous working experience, but never related to steel jobs: a large number of them have been employed as bricklayers and labourers in the building industry, as apprentices or general manual workers in other industries, and in marginal jobs in the service sector.

Process workers are hired and allocated within the factory on the basis of the labour turnover requirements, independent of their previous job experience. This is also the case for a few workers recruited by Dalmine and previously employed at Falck and Breda:[17] they have been allocated to jobs without taking into account their previous steel experience—for example, a worker previously in the steel department has been allocated to the rolling department, and one previously employed as a crane driver has been employed at the continuous casting machine. Within the process departments, there is a clear tendency to allocate workers with the lowest education to the initial stages of the process, i.e. to those departments with more manual and physically tiring tasks; while workers with more education are allocated to the final stages, i.e. to those departments where jobs involve control and regulation, and require mental concentration. This is even more stressed in the case of new works, as in the case of the rolling department at Dalmine: the workers with eight or more years of schooling are allocated preferably to the new rolling train (PPM—MPM), as shown in the Table 4.7.

Maintenance workers' formal education and previous experience are important for their screening, since they are required to have good theoretical knowledge of their trade and some practical knowledge as

TABLE 4.7
Dalmine works, workers hired in the rolling mills by educational level (1979)

	1st and 2nd rolling mills	New rolling mill (PPM–MPM)	Total rolling dept.
Licenza Scuola Superiore	2	4	6
Licenza Media	23	122	145
Licenza Elementare	22	39	61
less than *Lic. Elem.*	1	—	1
Total	48	165	213

Note: Five years of education are required for *Licenza Elementare*, a further three for *Licenza Media*, and a further five for *Licenza Scuola Superiore*.

Source: Dalmine archive.

well. They have, on the whole, a much higher level of education, and most of them have had some significant work experience. They are hired and allocated according to their previous career pattern, so that there is some continuity between their formal education, their previous experience, and their jobs in the steel plants.

4.2.3 Recruitment methods and ports of entry

According to Italian law, hiring can take place either *directly* between an enterprise and the labour force already employed, or *indirectly* through the local Labour Office (*Ufficio di Collocamento*) where the unemployed and workers looking for a job are registered. If an enterprise recruits through the Labour Office, it is allowed to screen among registered workers only for highly skilled or confidential jobs, as far as manual jobs are concerned. This is necessarily the case for only very few jobs in the steel industry since, in the first case, most skills, both for process and maintenance workers, are industry and firm-specific, therefore acquired on the job, and in the second case they are numerically not significant. For all other types of manual jobs, hiring which takes place through the Labour Office does not allow for any screening: the enterprise has to specify for each type of job the number of workers to be hired, and the Labour Office, on the basis of the ranking (established by law) of the unemployed registered there, will send to the enterprise the number of workers required. Workers can either accept or refuse—and this will affect their ranking positon—but not the enterprise. The fact that to hire through the Labour Office means not to have the possibility of screening explains the firms' preference for direct hiring from other enterprises. This implies, for the worker, mobility from one job to another without being unemployed, and, for the firm, the possibility of screening on the basis of the job applicants. In this case, the possibility of following a precise screening policy depends, basically, on the inflow of applications to the enterprise, given its labour force turnover.

Data, both on the flow and the stock of applications and on the relation between workers examined and hired, are not easily available. The steel enterprises examined regard this information as confidential. Nevertheless, their general strategy is quite clear: they all recruit their labour usually *only* through direct hiring (Appendix D. 13) and through screening among workers already employed and applying there for a job, and carefully avoid hiring through the Labour Office, since this would not allow for any selection. And this implies that neither the unemployed nor school leavers are recruited (Appendix D. 14), with Cornigliano being the only exception, since in recent years a certain number of school leavers has been hired for maintenance jobs. This policy has to rely on a sufficient inflow of applications from workers employed elsewhere. Job applications are the result of both spontaneous decisions of workers willing to be employed there and of the invitation of management, to foremen, supervisory staff, and the workers themselves, to propose and present workers to be hired. In this respect, the case of Breda, which has been recently forced by the lack of applications to recruit through the Labour Office—and consequently to hire women—is an exception, and shows the general deterioration of its position both in the product market and in the labour market.

4.2.4 Differences in hiring policies

The problem of recruiting labour seems to be an old problem for Breda. The first difficulties arose in the early 1960s, and were expressed by management as follows:

> It happened between 1960 and 1963, at the peak of the economic expansion. At that time, Breda Siderurgica started to record a certain number of voluntary quits. The traditional labour force, from the Bergamo and the Brescia districts and the Brianza, conscious of the fact of being trained in a highly prestigious firm, found 'promotion', or at least a nearer and more convenient job, in one of the many small machine workshops that the economic boom gave rise to in their place of origin. Lacking what was considered by the industries of Milan as the local labour supply (even if . . . mostly commuters) we had to start looking further away. (*Dal ferro all' acciaio*, 1967, p. 195.)

Table 4.6 (p. 97) shows very clearly how this process of progressive substitution took place, with the firm at first hiring workers from the rest of the region and later on workers from other regions. But difficulties in recruiting manual workers for the process departments persisted and became more severe in the 1970s. In 1974 Breda decided to expand its capacity by increasing the number of working days per year, arranging for workers' summer holidays over several months in order to avoid closing the factory. But this project was not easy to realize because of the difficulties in recruiting the necessary labour, as reported by the Breda management:

> The project provided for the recruitment and the hiring of about 100 workers by the end of April, so as to allow for their training, side by side with the skilled workers. This was in a particularly delicate period for the local labour market, since there was little labour supply and with no skills. Despite the attempts to advertise the planned hiring, both within the enterprise and outside it, the results in terms of job applicants were relatively low. In order to meet the labour requirements, the enterprise had to extend recruitment to very recently immigrated workers, non-conscription free [i.e. still liable to military service], over 40 years old; there was essentially a lack of real screening and workers had to be selected almost exclusively on the basis of their physical requirements. What has been said is supported by the comparison of the ratio workers hired/workers examined in the periods April–July 1973 and 1974: while in 1973 this ratio was 1/4.8, in 1974 it was 1/2.7. (Zanetti Polzi *et al.*, 1975, pp. 82–3.)

In the second half of the 1970s, given the economic difficulties and the uncertainty about the future of Breda (in terms of restructuring, closing down, and reconversion), its position in the local labour market, i.e. the workers' image of the enterprise in terms of the certainty and stability of jobs, started to deteriorate. The inflow of applications has been falling rapidly, so that now it is sufficient only to cover between 30 and 40 per cent of the turnover, and labour requirements have to be met partly through the local Labour Office.[18]

Thus, the relative shortage of job applicants with required characteristics (male, northern or not too recently immigrated, neither too young nor too old) has caused first the lowering of the traditional hiring standards, and then recruitment through the local Labour Office with no possibility of screening. And this has implied the hiring of male workers with a temporary attitude (i.e. accepting employment at Breda but willing to leave as soon as they find a 'better' job) and the hiring of women. To understand this, it is important to know that up to 1977, when the law providing for equal rights for women at work was enacted, it was possible to recruit labour for manual unskilled jobs through the local Labour Offices specifying the sex. But after the 1977 law, discrimination against women—at least directly—is no longer possible (Cremonesi *et al.*, 1981). And given the structure of unemployment (see Table 4.8) to recruit through the Labour Office

TABLE 4.8
Registered unemployment, Sesto San Giovanni (September 1980)

	Men	Women	Total
1st class	188	585	773
2nd class A	65	113	178
2nd class B	401	692	1,093
other classes	149	133	282
Total	803	1,523	2,326
of which:			
willing to be employed now	550	1,352	1,902
of which:			
as labourers	19	269	287
as skilled workers	403	558	962
as non-manual workers	128	525	653

Note: 1st class includes adult unemployed; 2nd class A, young unemployed (between 15 and 21 years); 2nd class B, school leavers and people looking for their first employment; other classes, house-workers and retired workers.

Source: Ufficio di Collocamento, Sesto San Giovanni.

means to hire women.[19] Data on registered unemployment at Sesto, at the time of the case study, show that out of 2,326 unemployed only 803 are men, out of these only 550 are willing to be employed now, and out of them only 19 for manual/unskilled jobs.

Immediately after the equal rights law, Breda asked the Labour Office of Sesto for ten labourers to employ in the steel-making department. This request was met with the offer of ten women, whom Breda refused to hire. The local trade unions sued the enterprise for discriminatory practices; Breda lost the case, but continued in its position and appealed against the labour court sentence. The appeal was lost, too, and Breda had to hire the women. From that time on, about 60 women have been hired, and only very few of them (four or five) have left the factory. They are all unskilled, and mostly house-workers with no previous industrial experience. They have been employed, not in the steel-making department, but in the finishing department. The management has preferred to move some workers—male—from this to the steel-making department, and to concentrate all the women in the finishing department, characterized by a higher turnover and a lower average grading.[20]

The position of Falck with respect to hiring is quite opposite to that of Breda, despite the fact that they are only few miles apart.[21] The inflow of applications, given the relatively low labour turnover, is still considered quite good, and sufficient to isolate the enterprise from problems of shortage of labour with the required characteristics. To understand this, it is important to take into account that (*a*) the position of AFL Falck in the product market, even in periods of deep recession, has been quite sound—and thus its image in the labour market too—and so a job at Falck is still considered a good and secure industrial job, and (*b*) the policy followed by Falck in recruiting its labour is based on very tight links with some areas in the region (the Bergamo and Brescia districts and, partly, the Valtellina) and the personal relations of its employees (managers, foremen, workers). The mountain valleys, relatively poor and with little employment opportunities, have been considered for a long time as typical areas of recruitment for the steel industry.[22] Over the last 30 years, their economy has changed considerably, but they continue to supply labourers for the process departments of Falck. Hiring is almost exclusively based on applications to the enterprise, in most cases presented with a letter of reference from an employee of Falck; the enterprise, in the screening, always follows the policy of first hiring (whenever it is possible) the relatives, the people of the same village and the friends of its employees, so that all the workers hired are directly or indirectly known; moreover, workers of the same village tend to be allocated to the same team and shift. This procedure is perceived by the workers as a privilege, as they have some power to affect hiring: this has reinforced, over the past, the links between certain villages and the enterprise and, at the same time, it has built a strong sense of loyalty towards Falck.

Dalmine has a similar recruitment policy, taking advantage of its geographical position. The plant is located in a village, from which the enterprise took the name, a few miles from Bergamo. At the time of its construction, in 1908, the large supply of cheap labour in the rural areas surrounding the village was among the reasons for the choice of the location of the steel works (Hertner, 1978, p. 111). The economy of the village has grown considerably in the postwar period, as new enterprises have developed in engineering, knitting, and garments; the area no longer depends completely on the steelworks, as it did in the past,[23] but Dalmine continues to be the main large factory, and it still represents a privileged point of reference for the labour force of the surrounding villages. Given the very low turnover of the labour force, the inflow of applications is large enough to allow an accurate screening. The policy followed is similar at that of Falck: all the workers recruited are directly or indirectly known, and the employees themselves constitute a network of contacts and information, as they all come from the same villages. Most of the hirings are direct hirings, even if in the last few years a certain number of unemployed have been recruited. This reflects, not a lack of screening, but the low level of unemployment in the area and the good relationship between the local Labour Office and the firm: the practice is first to screen the workers, with an interview and a medical test, and then to ask them to register at the Labour Office; these workers are then sent 'officially' by the Labour Office to the firm on the basis of its 'numerical' request, and hired.

The Cornigliano works are located in an area dominated by some very large enterprises all belonging to the public sector; there are only a few medium enterprises, while the small firms sector is very large but characterized by more uncertain prospects. A job in the public sector is still looked at as a stable and secure job; in particular, as the Italsider plant has never had redundancies, up to the time of the case study, for reduced activity or restructuring, there is a large inflow of applications for direct hire. Thus, the steelworks still act as a point of attraction for the labour force of Genoa and the inland. Traditionally, the steelworks have employed unskilled labour, therefore recruiting among workers with a very low educational level. In fact, 73 per cent of the labour force has less than eight years of schooling (compulsory education) (Appendix D. 6), and workers with a higher average level of education are concentrated in maintenance jobs. Moreover, until very recently, the recruitment policy preferred workers neither too young, nor too old, but with quite a wide range of age groups among which workers were recruited. Most recently, and especially after 1977, a change in the hiring policy has been noticeable. The average educational level of the newly recruited is considerably higher: in 1974, only 20 per cent of the workers recruited had eight or more years of education, while in 1980 this ratio was 67 per cent (Appendix D. 8). Similarly, the average age of the newly recruited is lower, with a remarkable concentration in the 21–5 age group: in 1974, 27 per cent of the total workers hired were in this age group, and in 1980, 54 per cent (Appendix D. 9). The change in the recruitment policy has to be associated with the changes introduced in work organization:[24] experimentation on division of labour had been carried on since the early 1960s, but it was in 1978 that, through an agreement with the unions, based on work groups (referred to as 'operative units'), management decided to extend the innovations systematically, with their gradual introduction, department by department. The decision to extend, gradually, to all departments the new forms of division of labour was motivated, on the management side, by the need to regain efficiency. The introduction of work groups was supposed to improve the technical and economic performance of the enterprise, i.e. better output quality and lower costs.

To conclude, there are noticeable differences in the recruitment policies of the four enterprises, and therefore in the characteristics of the labour force employed. Falck and Dalmine continue to pursue their traditional hiring policies, and they still manage to recruit labour of the required characteristics, all from Lombardia, all male, in a large proportion from the same villages and valleys, with the difference that in the case of Falck a large number of these workers commutes to Sesto every working day, while in the case of Dalmine the labour force employed lives in the area surrounding the factory.

Breda and Cornigliano have changed their hiring policies, but in two different directions: on the one hand, Breda has been lowering its hiring standards as its position in the product market, and hence in the labour market, has been deteriorating; on the other hand, Cornigliano has been setting higher standards, as a way of recovering efficiency. Lacking the traditional chains of recruitment of Falck and Dalmine, being located in an industrial area with a shortage of male labourers, and having experienced—in the most recent years—financial difficulties, so that its image has deteriorated, Breda has been facing difficulties in recruiting labour, and the policy followed has been to lower its hiring standards. This is reflected in its labour force structure: (*a*) over 50 per cent of the workers employed are originally from the south (Appendix D. 11);[25] (*b*) there is a considerable number of commuters, about 30 per cent (Appendix D. 12), from the valleys and villages in the poor and mountainous areas of Bergamo and Brescia, but increasing difficulties have emerged in recruiting from these areas as their economic development has made available better employment opportunities, at least in terms of work distance; (*c*) since it has not been possible to pursue a precise screening policy, given the insufficient number of job applicants, a considerable number of workers accept employment at Breda as a temporary solution, until they find a better job;[26] (*d*) finally, as a last resort, women have started to be recruited.

The change in the recruitment policy at Cornigliano is not motivated by difficulties in the labour market, but by problems with respect to the internal market, i.e. in the organization of the labour process, and with respect to its economic and financial position. The management goal of regaining efficiency has been pursued, on the one hand, by improving the technical control over processes and works through the use of process computers on real time and, on the other hand, by delegating the organization of work to the group itself, where work groups have been introduced. This has involved the elimination of individual differences, the elimination of hierarchical levels, and the grading of all workers at the same grading level, the fifth, the highest for manual workers. Hierarchy does not exist any longer, neither career nor promotion, and all the workers are acknowledged as possessing the same qualifications. In this respect, the change in the hiring policy seems to be a way to eliminate possible conflicts, within each group, between workers who had to develop their internal career step by step in a long process, and the newly recruited. Cooperation within the group is essential, and a change in the social composition of the labour force, in terms of higher education levels, seems a way to legitimize the same level of qualification for both the old and experienced workers, who had to work hard for their internal advancement, and the young and inexperienced workers. The conditions in the labour market, e.g. high unemployment among school leavers, have allowed this change of policy.

4.3 Career and internal mobility

The next point to be investigated is how workers, having entered the steel works, are organized to work. The nature of the internal career process results in a grading structure highly concentrated in the upper grades, as was shown in section 4.1. This section examines how workers move within and between the job clusters, as defined by the technical features of the production process. That is, it focuses on the process of internal career, in terms of entry jobs, training, internal mobility, and turnover, pointing out the differences between enterprises and among different groups of workers (process, ancillary, and maintenance workers).

4.3.1 Differences in work organization between the plants

Given that the position in the production process, activities involved, skill content, working conditions, and training requirements of jobs vary widely between process, maintenance, and service jobs, the actual way in which labour is organized, i.e. which worker is asked to do which activity, differs among steel plants.

Breda Siderurgica is characterized by a fairly rigid and traditional division of labour based on: (*a*) a precise job description, defining the tasks of every job post; (*b*) the definition of the 'technological' and 'necessary' manpower requirments by department and section, i.e. the number of workers required for the functioning of the production process on the basis of the job posts, and taking into account average absenteeism and breaks; (*c*) the allocation of workers to job posts on individual and permanent bases (job-holding system); (*d*) internal mobility to cover temporary vacancies and to substitute workers with reduced productive capacity. Despite this precise job description and definition of individual job posts, there is a certain degree of *informal polyvalence*: within a team, workers tend to be quite flexible about the actual division of labour, for they substitute for each other, cooperating and interchanging informally when required. Over the last decade Breda has not experienced any major change in work organization, partly due to the lack of technical change, and partly due to the workers' resistance to innovation. Labour tends to be very traditional, and all the efforts of the unions have been directed towards (*a*) the defence of employment, bargaining over the 'necessary' manpower requirements, and (*b*) the control over issues previously handled by management (i.e. promotion, upgrading, mobility).

Work organization at Falck is quite similar: very traditional, with no major innovation. It is based on the definition of the job posts, technologically determined, by department and section; in each department there is a pool of workers allocated as a 'reserve' to fill vacancies (both temporary and permanent) in all its sections, through mobility from the bottom; finally, workers are allocated by section through a job-holding system, defining for each worker his own individual job post. Every job post involves a well-defined series of tasks and operations but, unlike in Breda, they are not formalized in a precise job description, so that the definition of individual jobs still allows for some *cooperation and interchangeability* within the teams. Substantial technical innovation has been introduced over the last ten years, including the complete renewal of the steel department with the installation of a continuous slab casting machine in 1970, but work organization has not changed: both labour and management tend to be very traditional, and the bargaining activity has been concerned basically with the definition of the mobility paths for each department and section, simply formalizing the internal mobility already in use and relating it to the workers' upgrading, without affecting the actual division of labour.

At Dalmine, some changes were introduced when the steelworks were completely renewed in 1976, and a new rolling train (PPM–MPM) was installed in 1978 (Ciborra and Colombo, 1981, pp. 112–34). The traditional division of labour, similar to that of Breda and Falck, has been partially modified by making it more flexible and reducing manpower requirements. Very schematically, when a worker is temporarily absent, this does not call for any substitution through temporary mobility from the bottom, but—within certain limits and for certain sections—the workers of the team will substitute for the absent worker by cooperating in sharing his tasks.

More precisely, (*a*) there is a precise definition of 'sub-areas' (sections), in terms of skills and processes, characterized by specific process goals; (*b*) the workers employed in a sub-area have at their disposal the resources and the information necessary to pursue the sub-area goals and to cope with the emergence of changes and unforseen events; (*c*) this involves some job integration, *partial operative polyvalence*,[27] but not the constitution of 'homogeneous groups' with complete intechangeability between the team workers, such as at Italsider; (*d*) moreover, small maintenance work, such as fitting, has been integrated in the process work to increase the feedback on damages, repairs, and malfunctioning, between process and maintenance work of that sub-area; (*e*) finally, although the hierarchical structure still exists, it is reduced to one hierarchical level per shift: a white-collar employee responsible for the work of the teams of a certain area. Higher-level roles do not involve the management of the sub-area, but the solution of planning problems and technical/specialist consultancy, to provide all required information, and limit intervention to exceptional circumstances. These innovations were introduced at Dalmine after a period of relative economic and technological decline (1965–75) and an upsurge of internal conflicts.[28] The management changed policy by following an innovative strategy, involving not only its technical but also its organizational structure, with the goals of increased efficiency and a relative reduction in manpower requirements. Given the very traditional labour force employed, it has been easier to introduce changes in work organization through technical changes. Moreover, these innovations are the result of a long process of consultation and negotiation with the unions, involving both process and maintenance workers, but limited to the areas and sub-areas affected by technical innovation, even if with the idea of extending the changes to the whole factory.

At Cornigliano, management and trade unions started talking about innovations on work organization in the mid–1970s, and they were first introduced—at an experimental level—in 1978. The story is quite similar to the previous one, but the process is far more advanced, at least in qualitative terms, since the experiment of work groups ('homogeneous groups') has implied the *complete interchangeability* of the workers within each sub-area. That is, (*a*) the plant is organized in areas (departments) and sub-areas (sections), where the operative unit (OU) is in charge of a well-delimited phase of the process (a sub-area), defined in terms of productive goals and resources; (*b*) within each sub-area the job posts, technologically determined, are precisely defined; (*c*) workers are not any more allocated to individual job posts but to the OU in general, with the common aim of reaching the goals identified for that sub-area; (*d*) it is the OU, as a whole, that is responsible, on the one hand, for the processes and works and, on the other hand, for the organization of work within the group, including training, rotations, vacancies, and interchangeability between job posts; (*e*) as at Dalmine, the hierarchy is highly reduced, so that there is only one level (*capoturno*) above the OU, and the tendency is to eliminate completely the role of the foreman. The new division of labour based on the OU has been introduced by management, through collective bargaining, at an experimental level in those departments (sintering, OBM converters, continuous casting) that have experienced radical technological innovation. Therefore, it is not (at the time of the case study) generalized to the whole factory, so that there are some departments (rolling, finishing, transport, and storage) that are still based on a more rigid division of labour, with individual job posts and high internal mobility between job posts of the same section.

4.3.2 Entry jobs

Process workers are hired by department, with no possibility of choice for workers but according to labour requirements. Vacancies are filled through internal mobility, and recruitment occurs only at the bottom of the hierarchical structure, for the most unpleasant jobs. Since internal mobility occurs from the hot departments towards more comfortable jobs in the finishing departments and services—while the opposite is impossible (or impracticable) for some sorts of traditionally established practices—turnover is higher in the backward sections of the production process, and entry occurs there to a large extent.[29] Within each department, the new workers are allocated to the most marginal jobs, involving the handling and transport of inputs and outputs. For example, in the steel-making department they are usually allocated in the scrap section, where they work on the discharge of steel scrap and other materials, or they are allocated to the preparation of the furnace charge; in the rolling department, they are employed as slingers (*imbragatori*) for the slinging and handling of ingots and finished products.

There are some differences between steel plants. At Breda and Dalmine, entry jobs are precisely defined within each department; when a worker enters a factory, he is allocated in an entry job *as a job holder*, and from there he can move up according to the mobility paths negotiated by department and section. That is, the entry jobs are the first step in the workers' internal career. At Falck and Cornigliano, workers entering the factory are first allocated to a department as a *reserve pool of labour*, not holding any individual job, but employed there for general work and to replace temporary vacancies in all different sections of that department. When a vacancy occurs, the worker with the longest length of service in the reserve pool is permanently allocated to the section and moved as a job holder to the vacant job, finally starting his internal career. These differences in the allocation of the newly recruited is related to existing differences in the organization of temporary vacancies.

At Breda, the manpower requirements are fixed by department and by section, on the basis of the job posts technologically determined, taking into account the average rate of absenteeism and work breaks; when a temporary vacancy occurs in a section, the workers are temporarily moved up along the mobility paths—established through collective bargaining—and according to the workers' length of service, both in the section and in their jobs. The determination of the manpower requirements necessary to cover the technological requirements has been one of the main bargaining issues of the 1970s at Breda. The unions have demanded an increase in the labour force employed as a way to redistribute the workload and lighten the unpleasant working conditions resulting from the obsolescence of the works and lack of new investment.[30] The position of the unions over this issue is quite rigid: when a temporary vacancy occurs, and the labour force employed is not sufficient to cover it (i.e. the necessary labour requirements have not been satisfied through hiring) the workers refuse to share the tasks of the absent worker, and stop working. Given the stop/go hiring policies over the last decade, quite a few stoppages have occured for this reason in the last few years.

At Dalmine, the procedure is apparently similar, but with a much more flexible attitude towards the problem. In particular, where work groups have been introduced, workers are asked to fill temporary vacancies through internal rotation and interchangeability, allowing for a reduction in manpower requirements. At Cornigliano and Falck, the problem of temporary vacancy is met by allocating workers individually to job posts within each section, and by having in each department a reserve pool of workers with no individual jobs, and ready to be moved to any section when a temporary vacancy occurs. In this case, mobility between sections of the same department is high, and workers from the reserve can be asked to move to any job, but always at the bottom of the job ladder of any section of the department.

At Cornigliano, in those areas where homogeneous groups have been introduced, the solution is different: the reserve of labour does not exist, and the homogeneous group is responsible itself for temporary vacancies; no job post is individually held, and the workers have to organize themselves with respect to both production and division of labour. Similarly at Dalmine, there is a more flexible solution to the problem of internal mobility, based on the workers' acceptance of a higher interchangeability and the sharing of tasks, thereby reducing labour requirements.

In all cases, the entry positions for process workers are only very few, precisely determined, always at the bottom of the job ladder, and therefore low-graded, usually implying hard physical work but marginal to the production process. Process workers are usually graded at the second grade (considered as an entry grade), and then upgraded after a period of training and adaptation to the work environment.

Maintenance workers, as already pointed out, are hired by trade and allocated into the maintenance services, according to their previous formal training and work experience. They are graded more highly than process workers, since some skill is already acknowledged to them. Most of them start their career at grade 3 (Breda, Falck, Dalmine) or 4 (Cornigliano), and they are upgraded according to their single career profiles; but sometimes maintenance workers directly hired from other enterprises are acknowledged a higher grade, at the time they enter a steel factory, as is the case for a small number of maintenance workers at Breda (Appendix D. 15) and Falck. Cornigliano and Dalmine do not allow for any difference in entry: all maintenance workers are hired at the same entry grade, but it is possible for the workers with a high skill already to make a faster career.

4.3.3 Training

Given the considerable power of process workers with respect to both production and works, and the consequences that can result from the incorrect execution of particular tasks, their training is very important. This is not only for theoretical and practical knowledge of the manual and intellectual operations involved, but for adaptation to the work environment. This helps to explain why all the workers recruited for the process departments are selected with some previous work experience. Their required pre-entry training is not 'technical' (i.e. industry or firm-specific), as is the case for maintenance workers, but 'social': the large factory can benefit from the effects of the workers' previous socialization to the manufacturing activity, not with respect to direct experience in the specific job, but in the sense of having a certain familiarity with know-how and factory behaviour.

When process workers enter a steel factory, they receive some very general training in a short course (20–40 hours) in which they are not trained for any specific job, but are acquainted with such general aspects as the characteristics of the enterprise, its regulations, the main characteristics of the production process, and the structure of the plant, safety and accidents prevention, and finally the social security systems. Their technical training is almost all carried out entirely on the job: new workers are placed side by side with a skilled and experienced worker, until they perform the jobs effectively. The time required varies according to the tasks involved, but since most of the entry jobs are very simple (consisting mostly of manual jobs for the handling of the materials) the time required is always very short. Further training, i.e. the acquisition of the necessary practical knowledge and experience, is always acquired on the job, in an informal way, by imitation, working side by side with the other workers of the team. This process is very much related to the process of internal mobility: process workers are hired at the bottom of the job ladder, within each department, and they have the opportunity to learn and acquire experience and manual dexterities when they are allowed to work in a different job position. Therefore, they can acquire further skills only if they have the opportunity to move on to different jobs, and this is possible when vacancies occur, as internal mobility from the bottom is largely used to fill temporarily vacant jobs. Thus, their career and training processes are strictly related to their internal mobility (horizontal and vertical mobility) within a department and within a section. All the skills acquired are industry-specific and, to a very large extent, work-specific, so that exit, not just from the industry, but even from the plant, would imply a whole new process of training. The difficulties that a worker faces in looking for an alternative job, without a loss of status, in terms of both total earnings and qualification, have to be emphasized and taken into account when considering labour turnover.

Quite a different training and career profile characterizes maintenance workers. They enter the factory when they have already acquired some skill in their trade, they receive—as process workers do—some general training in an introductory course of 20–40 hours, and they are then put to work side by side with an experienced worker. When the number of maintenance workers recruited is regarded as significant, the steel enterprise may organize some short but specific introductory training courses in their trade.[31] All four enterprises concentrate most of their efforts on the formal training of labour for maintenance workers: specific and advanced courses are regularly organized by groups of trades, and maintenance workers are asked to attend them in their working hours.

4.3.4 Vacancies and internal mobility

The career process differs for process and maintenance workers. Maintenance workers improve their skills through experience and further formal training. Their upgrading is therefore related to their skills, within the *famiglia professionale* to which their trade belongs. That is, for each trade (mechanics, electricians, fitters, metal carpenters, turners, welders), a professional development profile—what a worker should be able to do at different skill levels (A, B, C)—has been defined, through plant collective bargaining. Maintenance workers' internal careers become simply a problem of verifying the skill level and acknowledging the corresponding grade (5th, 4th, and 3rd). And this is quite straightforward: a maintenance worker either can or cannot do a certain complex task, so that the process of upgrading depends exclusively on the acknowledgement of a single worker's personal abilities and dexterities. The practice is that, at regular intervals, the foremen or the superior in charge will verify the skill level of the maintenance workers under his control. This process can be accelerated through formal training, and it is in the interest of the enterprise to organize the training of their maintenance workers.

For process workers, as was pointed out earlier, the problem of career (in terms of upgrading) is directly related to internal mobility, and this is related to the specific features of the technology in use. The discussion on technology (Chapter 2) has pointed out the *rigidity* of the technology in use (i.e. a continuous process, in a rigid sequence, with high integration and interdependence among the different stages) and a certain *variability* in the chemical and physical transformation processes, and in the performance of the installations. The discussion on work organization (Chapter 3) has shown that management of the production process implies continuous control and regulation of all the variables, and that this activity is mainly performed by the workers, who are asked to notice and to interpret the rise of variations, and to intervene with the required regulating activity. This implies a large use of internal mobility to allow for a certain degree of flexibility and adaptability to the production process and its variations. In fact, internal mobility is largely used in the steel industry as (*a*) an instrument for the organization of the production process, given the technological rigidity, to allow for unpredictable events and temporary vacancies, (*b*) an instrument for training, since all the training is on the job, and a worker can learn a different job only when he is given the opportunity to move, temporarily, to another job, and (*c*) a way to reallocate workers who are not able any longer to stand heavy working conditions. In this respect, it is important to note that while cases (*a*) and (*b*) imply mobility within a department and are both related to a process of internal career, case (*c*) implies mobility between departments, and is usually associated with the end of the workers' internal careers.

(i) *Mobility within the process departments.* A considerable degree of internal mobility has always been common in the steel industry. Process workers can be asked to move from one job post to another, either permanently, to a better job, or temporarily, to a different job in the same section. The first case occurs when there is a vacancy within the team: the worker with the longest length of service in the grade immediately below (and in the factory) will be promoted as a job holder and upgraded; all the workers after him—in terms of jobs held and length of service—will be moved up too and upgraded. In the second case, horizontal and vertical mobility is employed to fill temporary vacancies, so as to fill all the technologically determined job posts in that section. This involves a process of rotation of different job posts (of either the same grade or different grades) and of substitution of temporary absent workers.

This process of internal mobility, filling vacancies, temporary substitution and interchangeability in emergency situations, tends to develop almost exclusively by department and by section, according to the mobility chains, defining the sequence of job posts a worker has to perform to get to the top positions. It is possible that there are some common positions at the bottom of these mobility chains between sections of the same department; but internal mobility—in terms of the development of careers—occurs only within each section of the process departments (and never between departments). The workers rotating on different jobs and/or substituting temporary absent workers, acquire the right—after a certain length of service in their previous grade and a certain number of hours of rotation of substitution (as indicated in Table 4.4 (p. 89))—to gain a grade higher than that of the job held. For example, if the first melter is temporary absent, the second melter substitutes the first melter, and the worker employed at the charge substitutes for the second melter. They all get, for the time of substitution, the pay of the job for which they have substituted. When the first melter is back to work, they all return to the jobs they individually held, at the corresponding wage rate. But, at the same time, they accumulate a certain number of hours of substitution that gives them the right to be upgraded, after a certain length of service in the previous grade and a certain number of hours of substitution. Similarly, they can be upgraded if they are willing to rotate, when required, to different job posts classified at the same level. That is, a worker employed at a job post of grade 3 can be upgraded to grade 4 after a certain number of hours of rotation on different job posts of the same grade. Everything related to internal mobility and the related upgrading process, as here discussed, has been precisely defined through collective bargaining at the plant level: *mobility paths*, defining by department and section the direction of mobility for promotions, substitutions and rotations; *priorities for promotions* in terms of length of service in the job, in the department, and in the plant, and abilities; and *rules for upgrading* for rotation and substitution (number of hours of rotation/substition and length of service).

The combination of high internal mobility, due to the features of the production process, and the acknowledgement of the associated right to be upgraded have resulted, over time, in a continuous and progressive upgrading process,[32] so that now a considerable number of workers are graded higher than the jobs held. For example, at Dalmine 36.7 per cent of the total labour force is graded more highly than the jobs they fill, and this percentage increases up to 44.3 per cent if one excludes maintenance workers, for whom the distinction between job grades and workers' grades does not hold. At Breda these ratios are lower (26.8 per cent for the total labour force and 31.6 per cent excluding maintenance workers)[33] but with an increasing tendency, over the last few years, to upgrade through rotations (see Appendix D. 29). Job rotations and substitutions are used in all four plants, mainly to allow workers allocated in dead–end jobs or sections, with little possibility of upward internal mobility, to have some career, in terms of grades. In fact, the extent of upgrading by rotation and substituion is higher in the low-graded departments, such as finishing and rolling. The case of services is different: workers are moved there, in low–graded jobs, for health problems, keeping their original grade, but with no further possibility of career (Appendix D. 28).

The general principles for the development of workers' careers are similar, but differences in management and union strategies over the issues of manpower requirements, internal mobility, and upgrading have produced differences in the grading structure of the labour force, as shown in Table 4.5. At Breda, the trade unions have been concerned, first of all, with employment issues; their negative attitude towards an extensive use of internal mobility means that they have not been willing to exchange harder work (increasing the workload per worker, saving manpower requirements) for a little improvement in the grading of workers. At Cornigliano the strategy of the unions has been quite different: they have tried to guarantee all workers some career, therefore encouraging job rotations and substitutions. Within each department the workers have been asking to rotate, even when this was not necessary for the process, to get higher grades. And management has allowed this kind of 'warranted' policy to absorb internal conflicts. At Dalmine, the unions have followed a very similar policy, encouraged at the beginning by group conflicts over grading, and management has adapted to it, as it allows greater internal flexibility and less labour requirements. At Falck, the effects of the agreements on internal mobility have been less stressed than in the other plants; this is the combined result of (*a*) a traditional labour force, attached to the traditional hierarchy and not willing to modify it substantially, (*b*) a trade union concerned with avoiding internal sectional conflicts, and (*c*) a traditional management, which has tried to minimize the impact of the agreements keeping a control over the actual internal mobility of workers. The final result is a considerably higher general grading of workers at Cornigliano and Dalmine than at Breda and Falck.

To summarize, it is possible to say that collective bargaining has created a set of rules which make the process of upgrading clearer and more certain, with the aim of reducing to a minimum the discretionary power of management. The time that must be spent in a grade is not simply a function of seniority (i.e. related to the length of service in a certain job and in a certain department), but is related to the processes of internal mobility and to the mechanisms of job rotation and job substitution. Differences in management and union strategies over these issues have resulted in different grading structures, so that the length of time that must be spent in a grade varies by department and enterprise. Certainly, demand for labour plays a role in this process, since where demand is higher—either because labour turnover is higher or because employment is expanding—upgrading through promotion is quicker. But the unions do not object to this, since their main concern is to guarantee *all* workers—and in particular those in dead-end jobs and departments—some career. For example, the data for Cornigliano (Appendices D. 25 and D. 26) show that all workers employed have been progressively assured some prospects of career advancement. In fact, both the average length of service per grade and the average age per grade have been considerably reduced for the lower grades (i.e. grades 2, 3, and 4), so that it is possible to say that union control over internal mobility and upgrading now makes it impossible for workers to be stuck in the bottom grades. Nevertheless, this does not preclude the possibility of some workers enjoying much faster career advancement than the average. The distribution of workers by length of service in the top grades (i.e. grades 5 and 6; see Appendix D. 25) clearly shows that upgrading is not simply the result of automatic processes related to the length of service, but that other factors have to be considered. The demand for labour is certainly one important factor in speeding up career advancement. This is certainly the case at Breda. Among the process departments, the steel-making department is the one with the highest average grade (see Appendix D. 27), with 69.1 per cent of the labour force in grades 4 and 5. This is also the department which shows the highest labour turnover (Appendix D. 35) and which registers the highest number of upgradings (Appendix D. 28), where this is due by and large to promotions, i.e. upward mobility created by vacancies.

Before concluding, it is important to note that where (in a few departments at Dalmine and at Cornigliano) and when (starting in 1978) work groups have been introduced, the problem of vacancies, internal mobility, career, and upgrading are solved by delegating them to the work group itself. Possible vacancies are filled by the interchangeability and work sharing among the other workers within the group, giving to all workers the possibility of getting to the top grade simply as a result of a training process taking place on the job through time.

(ii) *Mobility between departments*. There is a constant flow of workers from the departments at the beginning of the process towards those at the end. In the integrated plant of Cornigliano, a considerable number of workers move from the coke area, blast-furnaces and steel plant towards the rolling and finishing departments and services. Similarly, in the other plants the flow is from the 'hot' towards the 'cold' areas, and not the other way round. Mobility between departments is always voluntary, either because workers cannot any longer tolerate an uncomfortable working environment, for problems of health or age, or because they do not want to. It is almost impossible for the enterprises to move workers between departments, even when this would be required, as vacancies occur in some departments and excess labour in others. The policy followed is to plan carefully for the hiring in the 'hot' areas, and to let workers move down the production process. This explains the very few hirings in the services where there is a large inflow of workers from the other departments.[34] Involuntary mobility between departments might occur, to use workers made free by technical evolution or by a drastic fall in product demand. In both cases, the final solution—which workers are affected and where are they going to be moved—is negotiated with the unions, whose general strategy is to share the burden among all the workers.

In all cases, when a worker is moved from one department to another he has to start his career again from the bottom, as internal mobility, in terms of climbing up the job ladder, is possible only within each department, by section and team. This is due to the workers' resistance within each team to accepting a newcomer: he is considered an outsider, and therefore has to re-climb the job ladder (but keeping the grade previously confirmed). This is the case of workers moved from the coke area to the hot rolling department, or from the steel to the finishing department. The situation is different when they are moved—in most cases for health problems—to the service sections. Here, most of the jobs are simple, low-graded, and with very little possibility of advancement. It is frequently the case that highly skilled workers, with long experience in the process departments, are moved to the services as cleaners or watchmen, implying the end of their working careers.

(iii) *Promotion to a different employment category*.[35] As has been already pointed out, the position of foreman is the result of a long internal career process. Foremen are never hired from outside, but internally recruited through promotion of the oldest and most experienced workers. Given the tendency to reduce supervisory staff, this role is, numerically, progressively less significant. In any case, it is up to the management to decide which workers are to be promoted as foremen.

Non-manual workers have a very distinct career pattern, even if it is possible for some manual workers to be promoted to white-collar jobs. But this is more like a process of internal screening among workers with a high level of education than a process of internal career progression from the bottom. This explains the very low hiring of staff workers at Cornigliano, and the policy of filling vacancies in the white-collar jobs through internal promotion (see Appendix D. 33). And this has been possible given the relatively high number of manual workers recruited with a high school attendance. It is amongst them that the enterprise performs its screening for white-collar jobs. In the other enterprises the situation is more traditional, and almost all non-manual workers are recruited from outside.

4.3.5 Turnover

All careers are internal to the steel plants: when workers enter as unskilled they are guaranteed some career, at least in terms of grades, if they are willing to stay. Upgrading and promotions are strongly related to the workers' length of service, and quite independent of their previous experience. For example, at Cornigliano, the career profile is to enter the factory at around 30 years of age and to be classified in grade 2; within two years workers are upgraded to grade 3, and within 10 to 14 years to grades 4 or 5; grade 6 is reserved for the most skilled workers, those who have spent a very long part of their working life (over 20 years) in the steel plant.[36] On the contrary, if they decided to leave the factory, their specific skill is lost and they have to start a new career process. This explains why steel workers either leave soon after entering or stay. As a result, turnover rates are very low, and the bulk of the labour force is composed of workers with long service.[37]

Turnover rates are in fact low with respect to both the other categories of employees and the manufacturing industry.[38] But differences are noticeable between plants, with Breda and Falck Concordia recording relatively higher rates. This seems to be explained, by and large, by the higher voluntary quit rates of their new recruits. In the case of Concordia this is due to the higher proportion of young workers in the total labour force recruited; in the case of Breda, to the difficulties met in recruiting labour, the lowering of the hiring standards, and the hiring of workers with a 'temporary' attitude. Despite these differences, turnover rates at Breda and Concordia are not considerably higher,[39] and, in general, it is still true that those who stay are likely to remain until the end of their working life.[40] Thus, on the whole, a considerable number of workers leave their jobs in the steel industry at the end of their working lives.[41] Differences in the turnover rates by department are not very significant, and they reflect differences in the internal mobility flows between departments more than actual differences in the workers' behaviour.[42]

4.4 Conclusions

To conclude, differences in division of work and internal organization of the labour process are found between the steel plants: and the tendency seems to be away from a hierarchical and structured division of labour towards a collective and cooperative organization, where technical reorganization offers the opportunity. But these differences cannot be explained purely on technological terms—as would appear at first glance, since the two plants with the major technical changes are those now experiencing the innovations in work organization. In fact, Falck Concordia was the first to renew completely its steelworks, but without changing the organization of work. Moreover, the research done on work organization in the steel industry has pointed out that, despite the existence of a 'formal' work organization based, by and large, on individual job tasks, hierarchically and rigidly defined, the 'actual' organization is based on group behaviour with a high interchangeability of tasks.[43] In this respect, an organization solution, such as the OU, with the changes involved in hierarchical structure, grading structure, division of labour, training, career, and mobility, seems to be a feasible solution, extendable to other departments and plants and therefore not exclusive of certain technical innovations. Technology can explain *what* type of solution is adopted, in the sense that it defines the problems that have to be solved in organizing production, but not *when and why* a change is introduced, as the interaction with the social relations of production has to be taken into account. The problem of why there are such differences will be discussed in Chapter 7.

Notes

1. There are two separate national collective agreements in the metal industry, one for the private and one for the public sector. The national agreements, renewed every three years for the whole sector, are in fact very much alike and are negotiated almost at the same time.
2. Breda Siderurgica agreement 7.5.72, 2.10.73; Dalmine agreement 25.2.72, 11.7.73; AFL Falck agreement 1.3.75.
3. Italsider agreement 24.12.70, art. 3.
4. Lettieri, 1971, pp. 115–16.
5. A series of practical examples (i.e. exemplification of some professional job profiles) is suggested, on the basis of which all employees should be graded. Italsider agreement 25.5.72, *Allegato* 1, *declaratorie*.
6. Italsider agreement 24.12.70, art. 3, and agreement 26.5.72, art. 2.
7. Italsider agreement 26.5.72, art. 1.
8. CCNL Industria Metalmeccanica Privata, 1973, table D.
9. This is the outcome of the upgrading process that took place in the 1970s in all industrial sectors, and that has been particularly rapid and intense in the steel industry, as will be discussed in Chapter 7, section 7.4.
10. The three groups are clearly set apart, so that both national collective agreements and plant agreements provide for different treatment in matters such as probation, controls on working hours and pay deduction for delays, salary and wage payment, seniority wage increases, and so on. That is, employees with the same level of qualification (i.e. at the same grade) are not granted the same economic and employment conditions.
11. For example, at Cornigliano (and in general in all the Italsider steel plants) the tendency is to eliminate the role of foremen (*a*) by incorporating part of their 'technical role' (knowledge, experience, ability to take decisions about processes and works) into the new automated systems (i.e. process computers on real time), and introducing technical staff for the management of the information through the computer, and (*b*) by eliminating their 'hierarchical role' be delegating to the workers themselves all decisions concerning the coordination of their activities. This will be discussed in more detail in Chapter 7, section 7.4.3, (v).
12. Appendix D. 2 gives details of the structure of employment by department and category of employment for the four enterprises; Appendix D. 49 shows the tendency to reduce this role for Cornigliano.

13. The maintenance workers' degree of skill is classified into three levels: C, in training, B, skilled, and A, highly skilled and experienced, corresponding to grades 3, 4, and 5 respectively.
14. And also similar jobs, in terms of skill content, such as the quality control service at Breda or the auxiliary services at Italsider Cornigliano.
15. Similar constraints are found in the other plant agreements. Breda Siderurgica agreement 2.10.73; Dalmine agreement, 11.7.73; AFL Falck agreement 1.3.79, point 3.
16. Immigration from the south into the Milan district was extremely high up to 1963 (*Assessorato al Lavoro della Regione Lombardia*, 1974, p. 376), since when it has progressively declined. Breda started to recruit southern workers at the turn of the 1960s, and since then has done so increasingly.
17. Sixteen workers have moved from other steel factories to Dalmine, in 1979; they all are from the Bergamo district, and employment at Dalmine implies getting nearer to the workplace.
18. Given the stop go recruitment policy followed—depending on Breda's economic and financial position—the problem is greater in periods of high recruitment.
19. Now, when an enterprise makes a numerical request to the Labour Office, specifying the jobs available, it cannot refuse to employ a worker who happens to be a woman willing to accept the job.
20. See Tables 4.2 and 4.5 and Appendix D. 44.
21. At AFL Falck, hirings are planned by department, quarterly, on the basis of the average turnover and on the available data on possible retirements (workers' age and length of employment). The recruitment and the screening of the labour force occurs at the central level for all the factories of Sesto on the basis of the applications available, submitted directly to the single plant or to the central office.
22. At the beginning of the century the working class of these valleys was made up of peasants, used to very hard working conditions and poor living standards; moreover, since there was a certain number of puddling furnaces and ironworks in these valleys, they were used to work there when needed. Until the late 1950s there was still a quite considerable number of these peasant workers, commuting to Sesto to work in the steel plants and working their land in their spare time. See Chapter 7, section 7.2.
23. Up to the early 1960s the steel plant had a major role in the economic and social life of the surrounding area. The *comune* where the plant was located contained about 8,000 inhabitatnts, about 1,800 of whom were employed in the steelworks, while the rest were made up of building workers, tradesmen, and a large number of peasants and small farmers, in large part working the land belonging to the firm. The other 5,000 employees were generally commuters from 220 small villages in the district (out of 232), within an average range of 16 miles (Ancona *et al.*, 1957).
24. The changes introduced to work organization and their effects on the

organization of the labour process are further examined in Chapter 7, section 7.5.

25. But they have been living in Sesto for quite a few years, so that only a very small proportion have only recently arrived in the north.
26. In fact, turnover among the newly recruited is much higher than for the labour force as a whole (Appendix D. 47), and this helps to explain the higher turnover at Breda with respect to the other steel enterprises, as discussed in the next section.
27. That is, the workers have to rotate—to a certain extent—between job posts within their sub-area, so as to cooperate and to acquire the knowledge of the technical features of the sub-area, the goals of the sub-area, and its interdependence with other sub-areas. And this involves, also, the partial substitution of temporarily absent workers.
28. See Abbatecola, 1975; Collettivo Dalmine, 1972.
29. See entry rates by department, Appendices D. 35, D. 37, D. 39, D. 41.
30. Breda Siderurgica agreement 1973, art. 32.
31. Falck, for example, periodically organizes—when the number of new recruits is regarded as worthwhile—one-week courses in electronics and technical drawing.
32. See Appendices D. 19, D. 20, D. 21 and D. 23.
33. For Dalmine, the data are based on the system of acquisition of the grade, as shown in Appendix D. 30. The figures at the bottom of the table, referring to the total labour force, show that 36.7 per cent (column 3) are workers temporarily moved to a lower grade job for personal reasons (e.g. illness) and keeping their original grade; 24.8 per cent (column 4) are workers upgraded through rotation and substitution; and 5.5 per cent (column 5) are workers permanently moved to a lower grade job for age or health reasons, but keeping their original grade. Thus, excluding figures for maintenance workers, the percentage of workers graded higher than the jobs rises to 44.6 per cent, which is the sum of the three components: 8.2, 29.9 and 6.5 per cent respectively.

    For Breda Siderurgica, the data are based on a direct comparison between the grade of jobs and the grade of workers, as shown in Appendix D. 27. The figures along the diagonal in each section of the table refer to the workers who have the grade of the job they hold; the figures at the left of the diagonal refer to workers in training who have not yet been given the grade of the job they are doing; and the figures at the right of the diagonal refer to workers graded higher than the jobs they do. The percentages have been calculated taking the data at the right of the diagonal: (i) for the total labour force, the data considered are those in part (*h*) of Appendix D. 27; (ii) to calculate the percentages with the exclusion of maintenance workers, figures in part (*d*) of the table (referring to maintenance workers) have been subtracted from figures in part (*h*) of the table (referring to the whole labour force).
34. See Appendices D. 35, D. 37, D. 39, D. 41.
35. See Appendices D. 31, D. 32, D. 33.

36. See Appendices D. 25, D. 26.
37. The percentage of workers with more than ten years of service is 48.93 at Breda, 51.61 at Falck Concordia, 49.82 at Dalmine, and 46.21 at Italsider Cornigliano. See Appendices D. 16, D. 17.
38. See Appendices D.31, D.32, D.33, D.34.
39. For the manufacturing industry the annual average rate of departure for manual workers for the period 1978–80 was 13.53 per cent; for Breda Siderurgica for the period 1972–9, was 7.23 per cent; for AFL Falck, Concordia works, for the period 1973–9, it was 6.78 per cent; for Dalmine, Dalmine works, for the period 1970–9, it was 6.26 per cent; and for Italsider, Cornigliano works, for the period 1976–80, it was 5.33 per cent. See Appendix D.34.
40. See Appendices D. 47, D. 48. For a discussion on labour turnover at Breda see Coletti *et al*., 1977.
41. Between 25 per cent and 43 per cent leave for retirements or death; see Appendix D. 43.
42. See Appendices D.35, D.37, D.39, D.41, D.44, D.45, D.46.
43. See D'Andrea, 1976; Del Lungo, 1976; Butera, 1977, 1979; Uccelli and Amatori, 1978.

CHAPTER FIVE

The Labour Market Structure in Construction

Chapters 2 and 3 have pointed out two apparently conflicting characteristics of the demand for labour in construction. On the one hand, the process of production is still, by and large, the result of the manual assembling of different inputs; technical innovation has reduced the number of unskilled workers, but the process continues to be organized around the manual activity of different craft trades, with skills largely related to the materials handled. Therefore, building contractors have to rely on the activity of their skilled workers; and their problem is to secure them when required. On the other hand, given the economic and technological features of the sector, building contractors tend to have a structure as flexible as possible, both in terms of capital equipment and in terms of labour force, thereby minimizing the costs of possible inactivity. The problem that the sector, in general, has to face, with respect to the organization of the labour process, is to secure a skilled labour force willing to be employed in a sector characterized by uncertainty. This chapter analyses how this problem has been solved in the Milan district. The first two sections present a further analysis of the concept of skill, in order better to show the nature of skill and the position of skilled workers in the labour market, and of the concept of flexibility, in order to point out the impact of flexibility on employment for different groups of workers. The following three sections try to shed light on the problem of securing a skilled labour force in an unstable market, discussing three separate but interrelated questions: (*a*) who are the workers entering construction? (*b*) how are they trained? (*c*) what is their career pattern?

5.1 Skills

Chapter 3 made clear that it is not possible to define skills and trades precisely, as the division of labour varies widely in construction. The same sequence of the production process can be executed employing different building methods: some tasks may disappear, the content of others can be drastically modified, and new operations can be introduced. Also, the work content implied by each single technique can be subdivided among trades and skills in different ways, so that it is possible to find a division of labour based on a precise, detailed, and minute definition of tasks, or a division of labour where only a few specific tasks are rigidly fixed, the rest being done without differentiation by the large majority of the workers. Moreover, the diffusion of subcontracting as well as the introduction of new building components have induced a further division of labour and the emergence of new specialized trades. Thus, the definition of skills in construction has to take into account, on the one hand, the *division of labour by trade*, basically referring to the organization of the production process in sequences, characterized by the working of different materials; and, on the other hand, the *division of labour between contractors* (main contractor, subcontractors and self-employed), referring to the type of employment relationship and to the payment system in use (hourly wage, piece rates, and the lump).

5.1.1 Skills and trades

A large variety of crafts and trades is found in the sector. This is partly reflected in the national collective agreement that specifies over 50 trades.[1] Data are available only by grade, not by trade, but evidence from other sources[2] shows that, of this large number of trades, only a few are numerically significant, the most traditional and the most flexible performing a wide variety of operations over different sequences of the process (bricklayers, carpenters, steel fixers, and plant operators), while there is a relatively small number of workers spread over a large number of very specialized trades (scaffolders, plasterers, pavers, roof slaters, floor tilers, and so on) performing some very specific operations. Thus, a precise definition of building trades, given their large number and all the possible variations in the definition of their work content, is difficult. Instead, I propose a categorization of trades that points out existing differences in the *nature* of their skill.

(i) Bricklayers, carpenters and steel fixers remain the basic trades employed in construction. They are craft-skilled trades, implying not only some manual dexterity and technical knowledge about the materials used, but also some concept of physics, ability to read a project design and to execute it, and the ability to make adjustments and solve unforeseen problems, and therefore enjoying a certain autonomy of work. These traditional trades are the most flexible, since they may perform different tasks during the site cycle, adapting to its changing needs. Such is the case of the carpenter, who first prepares the internal and external scaffolding, adapting its structures to the weight requirements and to the nature and displacement of the fulcrums; later, he builds and places the timber shutters within which the concrete is cast, undertakes preparatory work for escalators and lifts, and, finally, is employed in the joining work needed for finishes. Similarly, the bricklayer is employed first in the erection of foundations and superstructure; then on brickwork for the erection of internal and external walls; later for the preparation and pulling of plastering; and finally in covering and paving. Thus, what distinguishes traditional building trades from industrial trades is the workers' ability to perform different operations—throughout the process—with a general knowledge of the production process and a large degree of autonomy in the organization of their work. This peculiar feature is significantly weakened when a more precise division of labour is employed, subcontracting is introduced, or small new components are used, as part of the workers' tasks and knowledge is either transferred to other trades or incorporated into the new materials produced outside construction. But still these traditional craft skills continue to be based on *the acquisition of experience and knowledge* in on-site activities through a long on-the-job training process.

(ii) A secondary category of trades, such as plasterers, painters, pavers, tile layers, and terrace workers, arises from a division of the traditional craft trades. A strict specialization is implied, as these tasks are the result of a high division of labour, but their skill content is—in most cases—quite low.[3] Skill here is no longer related to the traditional craft skill, but depends basically on the dexterity needed to do a *repetitive and simple task at speed*, and this depends more on the strength of the worker (implying physical strength and ability to stand uncomfortable and tiring positions) than on a high level of general skills. The case of tile layers is a typical example: it is the strict specialization (i.e. definition of one narrow task) that allows them to do the work at a high speed.

(iii) Another group of trades can be defined by the *equipment in use* on the site (cranes, digging and earthworking equipment, engines, and electrical systems). Here, the skill content is related to the ability to drive, use, and maintain machines. Thus, the skill content, and hence the training required, are directly related to the power and complexity of the equipment.

(iv) Finally, there is a group of trades whose skills are *craft orientated, but less specific to construction*, than others. Electricians and plumbers are the most common trades, but there is also a large variety of very specific trades defined according to the installations and services for which they are employed (heating and gas engineers, tinsmiths, and so on).

The first two categories of trades, by far the largest, are employed by both general and specialist contractors, main contractors, and subcontractors; plant operators are employed by specialist contractors, equipped for the capital-intensive sequence of the building process, or by large building contractors; while the last group of trades is increasingly employed by the non-building enterprises that manufacture installations and non-building materials,[4] that are installed on the site by their skilled workers.

5.1.2 Division of labour, subcontracting, and skills

The widespread use of subcontracting means a variation between trades as well as within trades. The organization of the labour process in terms of a division of labour between a main contractor, supplying equipment, materials, and the auxiliary labour force, and subcontractors, supplying the specialized workers required for the execution of specific stages of the project, means that the same trade may be employed in quite different ways by contractors and subcontractors.

Building contractors tend to employ (*a*) a small number of permanent highly skilled workers, performing general supervisory functions over the entire building cycle, (*b*) a relatively small group of unskilled workers with temporary employment relationships,[5] performing a large variety of unskilled operations to support the work of the first group and to assist the subcontracting gangs, and (*c*) some skilled and semiskilled workers required for those specific sequences that the main contractor decides to execute itself.

The whole process is organized around the activity of the first group of workers. They are, for the most part, quite old and very well experienced in construction site life, so that they can follow and control most of the sequences, cooperating with the other workers when necessary. They constitute a sort of polyvalent structure, but above all secure and trustworthy, that can be employed in a series of tasks as the construction site advances. They should not be considered as specialized workers, since their skill reflects their general knowledge about the process and is not the result of strict specialization. The evolution of the organization of the construction site through the use of subcontracting has made this group of workers very important: they can be considered as a complement to the gangs, allowing the technical staff to plan better and to follow the activity of the site. But these workers' skills are the result of a very long and hard on-the-job training process that took place spontaneously and started at a very early age. They are therefore becoming more and more rare.

Other skilled workers can be employed by trade, depending on the policy followed in subcontracting. It is possible that some trades are not employed at all by the main contractor, while others are employed but the workers are asked to perform only some operations, and not all the tasks they are able to perform, so that their skills are not fully utilized. In general, gang groups are used for specialist and skilled sequences, while the skilled workers of the main contractor tend to work for the nonstandardized and most tedious jobs, including general services, assistance to the gangs, and nonspecialist tasks. The case of Gadola[6] is a typical example of this type of division of labour:

> In the years 1976–7 the ratio of work performed by the subcontractors was around 50 per cent, but up to 70–80 per cent in some building sites. Looking more carefully at the data, it can be seen that since all the general services (storage, maintenance, cranes, and technical assistance) were performed by Gadola's labour force and given that these activities employed about 60 per cent of the workers, the actual ratio of the building operations (carpentry work, iron work, brickwork, cladding, and so on) performed by the external workers was much higher (80 per cent of these operations) and the 20 per cent that was left to the workers of Gadola was concerned, essentially, with the most complex and tedious tasks, and for this reason difficult to subcontract. (From a minute of the *Consiglio dei Delegati*, in FLC and C. d. D. Gadola, 1980, pp. 19–20.)

Subcontractors tend to have common organizational features: (*a*) they are autonomous in relation to the main contractor; (*b*) they basically supply skilled labour, while equipment and materials are in most cases supplied by the main contractor; (*c*) they are paid on the basis of the work done (piece-work or lump); (*d*) they perform specific and specialist sequences of the process, including the auxiliary work required. Given these common characteristics, it is possible to single out two main types of organization within which skills are employed differently. The first is based on a small team, two to five workers, all skilled, as defined at point (ii) in section 5.1.1 above, and performing one specific sequence only (such as steel bending and fixing, cladding, tile laying). This type of team has no hierarchical structure, but it is based on some sort of internal democracy, so that decisions with respect to the work to be done, pace of work, and payment are taken by the team mates together (and the salary takes the form of sharing in the profits). They are, for the most part, relatively young, northern, and almost exclusively from the villages near Bergamo and Brescia, either friends or relatives, commuting together in a small van from their villages every morning. They are well known to each other, used to working together, and motivated to work at speed.

When workers belonging to the same trade are employed by both the contractor and the subcontractors, not only do the employees of the main contractor have to do all the tedious and unskilled tasks, but they must also work at the pace established by the gangs:

> A rational organization of labour would suggest that the teams of specialist workers (gangs) should perform the most skilled jobs and the employees perform a subordinate role with the times and methods set by the *cottimisti* . . . . The dependent workers do not at all like this type of relationship, which can be said to be one of subordination, and they often boycott the work of the others, and these, in their turn, don't fail to react. (From an interview with an employer, in CRESME, 1976, Section IV, p. 12.)

And it is precisely this peculiar division of labour between contractors and subcontractors, and particularly the very difficult relationship between the employees and the gangs, that helps to explain the appearance in recent years of a second type of gang organized to provide all the labour force required for an entire sequence of the process—such as, for example, the erection of the superstructure. The employers have, in these cases, preferred to give everything out to the subcontractors, to solve the difficult problem of co-operation between dependent workers and *cottimisti*. This second type of gang is characterized by a relatively larger size (from five to ten workers) and a hierarchical structure (gang-leader, skilled workers, and labourers), where the gang-leader (*capoccia*) has a prominent and crucial role in recruiting, making the contract with the main contractor, organizing the work of the gang, and paying the workers, and the unskilled workers are employed for marginal and auxiliary jobs, with little or no possibility of interfering with decision-making, including those affecting their pay.[7]

5.1.3 The structure of the labour force by skill

The average skill level of the sector has never been very high,[8] construction activity being largely manual and therefore calling for the employment of a large number of workers as hodmen and labourers, to lift and move materials. The number of unskilled workers employed can be drastically reduced with the introduction of equipment for vertical and horizontal transport, as well as for loading and unloading operations; the mechanization of some simple operations with the introduction of hand power-tools and machines (cement gun, plastering machine, electric hammer, electric screwdriver, electric drill); the use of prefabricated small components (such as fibreboard ceiling panels, plastic sheeting, and tubular scaffoldings); and, finally, the purchase of beton from specialized enterprises rather than producing it at the site. Moreover, the organization of the production process through subcontracting to specialist contractors and gang groups tends to reduce the number of unskilled workers, since among subcontractors skilled workers are mainly employed to ensure a fast pace of work. And it is precisely the large use of subcontracting in all its forms that helps to explain the high ratio of skilled workers in the Milan district (52.86 per cent in 1981), with respect to both the rest of the region (Appendices E. 21 and E. 23) and the country (Appendix E. 5).

5.2 Employment flexibility

The main elements of the technical and economic conditions of the industry have been discussed above. They can be summarized briefly. The existence of a very large number of building contractors, whose average size is small, means that building employment is geographically scattered; the nature of the product, one-off and immobile, calls for a mobile labour force; the technology is use, relatively simple and requiring little capital equipment, makes entry into and exit from the sector, and shifts to and from other branches or other geographical areas, relatively easy, so that the turnover of building enterprises in any one area is quite high; finally, the nature of demand and the features of the output means that building activity is subject to wide fluctuations (site cycle, economic cycle, and seasonal fluctuations). Thus, construction, because of its economic and technological conditions, has a flexible productive and organizational structure. And this implies flexibility with respect both to capital equipment, with the aim of limiting total expenditure, and to the labour force, to cut down the numbers of permanently employed workers.[9] This latter point refers not only to the policy of hiring and firing, made possible by the specific legal regulations that are applied to construction only,[10] but also to the employment of all the various forms of subcontracting and to the recruitment of workers with a 'temporary' and provisional attitude towards the sector.

Building contractors are continuously expanding and contracting their labour force. The high territorial mobility and the wide cyclical fluctuations combine to make building employment intermittent, so that a considerable pool of workers is employed discontinuously and on the basis of high mobility. If this is true for the country as a whole, employment fluctuations appear even deeper at the local level, given the changes in the structure of demand. Over the last two decades, construction activity has shifted from the urban and northern districts towards the peripheral and southern districts (Appendix E. 38). While in the period 1961–71 the urban districts of north and central Italy counted for 31.27 per cent of the new houses built, and the peripheral areas of the south for 12.79 per cent, in the following decade their shares were 11.63 and 31.69 per cent respectively. The Milan district, in particular, experienced a high boom in the late 1950s and early 1960s followed by a declining trend, particularly marked in the city, where the total number of houses built in the period 1971–81 has been less than one-fifth of that of the previous decade (see Appendix E. 39), only partly compensated for by the building activity in the rest of the district. Employment increased rapidly during the boom years, and the number of workers registered at the local *Cassa Edile*[11] rose to 97,346 in 1963. But since then there has been a declining trend, with fluctuations around it, so that only 38,623 workers were registered as employed in the district in 1981 (see Figure 8.5, Chapter 8).

But the actual number of workers affected by these fluctuations is even greater, since the *total* number of workers employed locally over the year in the sector is always considerably greater than *average* employment, given that a considerable number of workers are only temporarily in the district. Figure 5.1 gives an approximate idea of this phenomenon: in 1981, the number of workers employed on average per quarter was 38,623; but the total number of workers employed

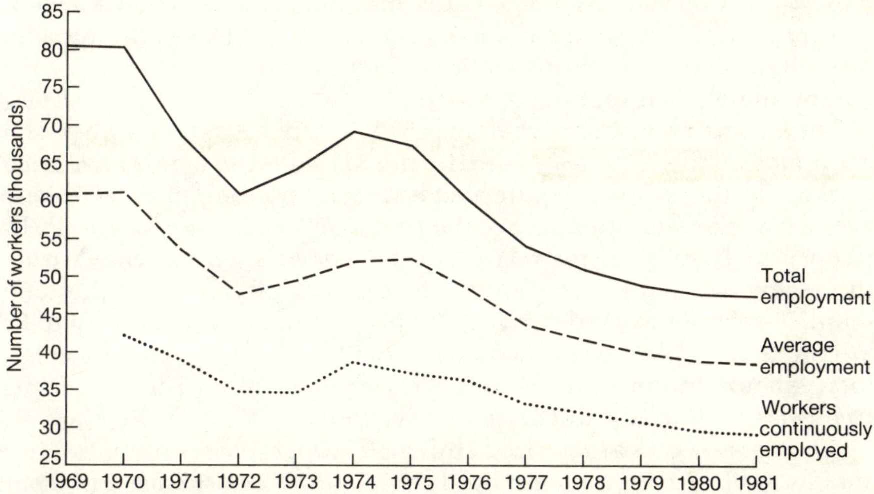

FIG. 5.1 Number of workers employed in construction in the Milan district, 1969–81

Notes:

1. 'Total employment' refers to the total number of workers registered as employed in the course of the year.
2. 'Average employment' refers to the average employment per quarter, i.e. the number of workers registered as employed in the course of the quarterly registrations.
3. 'Workers continuously employed' refers to the total number of workers who have been recorded as employed in the district in all four quarters.

Source: Compiled from *Cassa Edile* data; see Appendix E. 7.

over the year to cover the existing jobs was equal to 47,568 and out of them only 29,183 were employed in the district with some continuity.[12] The rest of the labour force was employed for only part of the year (i.e. recorded as having been employed during one, two, or three quarters only) because they either entered the sector, left the sector, moved in and out of the district, or were discontinuously employed. So that, on the whole, for every 'non-full-time' job about two workers were employed.

Geographical mobility, seasonal fluctuations and contractors' turnover cause a considerable number of workers to have some sort of 'temporary' employment relation to the sector in the district. But the phenomena of mobility, temporary employment, and discontinuity affect members of the labour force differently. It is possible to single out five different types of relation to employment within the sector: (*a*) workers with a stable and continuous employment relationship, (*b*) workers with high territorial mobility, (*c*) workers entering the sector, (*d*) workers leaving the sector, and (*e*) casual workers, employed only occasionally and with discontinuity. Available data are not categorized in this way;[13] nevertheless it is possible, on the basis of other data and information, to give an approximate estimate of the magnitude of each group.

The group of workers characterized by some sort of stable and continuous employment[14] in the district are all skilled, and have been working in the sector for quite a considerable number of years. These are the workers entitled to get the *premio di professionalità edile* (PPE) (Appendix E. 8), a bonus related to the worker's permanence within the sector and paid according to the number of years and the total number of hours worked per year.[15] This group can be estimated to be around 20 to 25,000 workers (accounting for about 45–50 per cent of total labour employed in the district over the year), with a declining trend but with minor fluctuations over time.

The workers characterized by high geographical mobility are mainly skilled; they are employed on the lump or organized in small craft enterprises, moving around the region to exploit the product market conditions. This group is not numerically very stable: they may move to larger enterprises, organize themselves as self-employed, or move out of the sector, when the conditions of the product market and/or their own physical condition no longer allow them good earnings. For 1981, this group can be estimated at around 9,500 workers (20 per cent), but allowing for wide fluctuations over time, according to product market conditions and to their shifts in and out of the dependent/independent employment relationship.

The workers entering the sector are, for the most part, very young, with no work experience and no skill (see next section). They enter the sector with the intention of staying only until they find a better job, and they are therefore not interested in learning a trade. It is possible that some of them have some kind of permanent employment relationship, but they are more likely to work intermittently. From the data on the new workers registered at the *Cassa Edile* of Milan, given by age structure (Appendix E. 10) and by classification grade (Appendix E. 9), this group can be estimated at around 5,000 workers (10–12 per cent) for 1981.

The workers leaving the sector can be either old—at the end of their career—or in their prime (between 25 and 40), both skilled and unskilled, and therefore leaving the sector because they have found a better job. The approximate number in this group should be around 5,500 workers (12–14 per cent).

Finally, there is the group of workers with an unstable and intermittent relationship with the sector. It is not possible to give a reliable estimate for them, since it is among these workers that the largest rate of non-registration and other irregularities are to be found. A considerable number of workers have been employed in construction for some part of their working life, and some of them keep a temporary link to construction either as *moonlighters*, with a stable non-building occupation and a job in construction at weekends, during their holidays, or when they are off the shift in their regular job, or in *Cassa Integrazione*;[16] or as *occasional workers*, working in an unstable non-building job and occasionally in construction, when they are compelled to by their economic conditions. These irregular and occasional workers are very likely to be found on small improvement jobs, where controls are almost impossible to apply and the unions have no contacts.

Table 5.1 takes the data on the number of workers employed for four terms as an indicator of the trend in 'continuous' employment; the number of workers employed for less than four quarters but with continuity as indicators of the trends of entry into and exit from the sector in the district; and the number of workers employed with discontinuity as an indicator of the trend for casual workers. A clear tendency towards a degree of stability in the labour force is found, as the number of workers employed with continuity over the year tends to increase.[17] But, given the rapid and continuous decline in employment, the increased stability seems to be more the direct effect of the shrinking of construction in the district, and of the difficulties in finding a labour force willing to be employed there (as will be discussed later), rather than the result of a change in the organization of the labour market.

TABLE 5.1

Stable and unstable employment in the construction industry, Milan district 1973–81

	Continuously employed (1)	Leavers (2)	New entrants (3)	Discontin. employed (4)	Total employmt. (5)	Average employmt. (6)
No. of workers:						
1973	34,588	10,037	13,615	5,917	64,157	49,438
1974	35,563	12,031	14,092	7,472	69,158	51,913
1975	37,238	11,786	11,725	6,621	67,370	52,262
1976	36,113	11,577	8,190	4,281	60,161	48,314
1977	33,167	9,778	8,030	3,099	54,074	43,601
1978	31,919	8,913	7,210	2,896	50,938	41,621
1979	30,786	8,130	7,105	2,850	48,871	39,931
1980	29,682	8,210	7,247	2,711	47,850	38,942
1981	29,183	7,838	7,537	3,010	47,568	28,623
Δ 73–81	−5,405	−2,199	−6,078	−2,907	−16,589	−20,815
Δ% 73–81	−15.6	−21.9	−44.6	−49.1	−25.9	−21.9

% distribution:					
1973	53.9	15.7	21.2	9.2	100
1974	51.4	17.4	20.4	10.8	100
1975	55.3	17.5	17.4	9.8	100
1976	60.0	19.3	13.6	7.1	100
1977	61.3	18.1	14.9	5.7	100
1978	62.7	17.5	14.1	5.7	100
1979	63.0	16.6	14.6	5.8	100
1980	62.0	17.2	15.1	5.7	100
1981	61.4	16.5	15.8	6.3	100

Notes: Δ = absolute variation; $\Delta\%$ = percentage variation.
For the definition of (1) see note 12.
For the definition of (2), (3), and (4) see note 13.
For the definition of (5) and (6) see notes to Figure 5.1, p. 131.

Source: Compiled from *Cassa Edile* data.

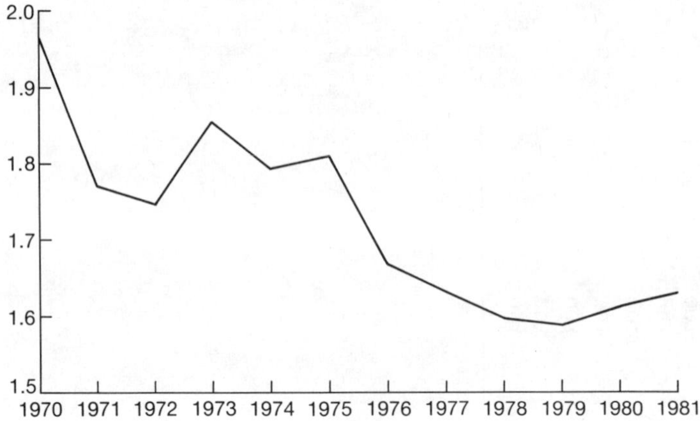

FIG. 5.2 The ratio 'total employment/workers continuously employed' in construction as an indicator of temporary employment, 1970–81

Source: Compiled from *Cassa Edile* data; see Appendix E. 7.

Overall, 'total' employment shows wider swings than 'average' employment, which in turn shows more than 'continuous' employment. Figure 5.2 shows that taking the ratio of total workers employed over 'continuous' employment as an indicator of the phenomenon of temporary employment, this tends to rise when employment is expanding (as in 1973–5), and to decrease when it is contracting (as in the following years). It follows that employment in construction can be increased only if there is a sufficient number of workers willing to be employed on a temporary basis; also, employment can rapidly be reduced by making these 'temporary' workers redundant, i.e. they are the first not to be employed and to leave the sector in a slump.

As already pointed out, there is no information available on the continuity of the employment relationship, or on the type of employment arrangement in the sector (contractor employee, subcontractor employee, self-employed, labour gang). The previous discussion, sustained by data on the number of quarters the workers have been working (see Table 5.1), even if it does not allow us to evaluate precisely the balance between permanent and temporary employment, provides an estimate of trends. A more difficult question to answer is that of the balance of employment between permanent contractors and permanent subcontractors, as well as between temporary contractors and temporary subcontractors. This is made difficult by the fact that labour working in all the various forms of subcontracting (that is, employed by real firms acting as subcontractors or by fictitious firms acting as labour-only subcontractors, the self-employed, and those organized in labour gangs) may be registered at the *Cassa Edile*, or may be working as 'black labour', without any kind of formal employment relationship. To understand the quantitative aspects of this pehnomenon, it has to be said that at the beginning of the 1970s it was estimated[18] that the various forms of subcontracting were employing roughly 15 to 20,000 workers in the Milan district; most of these workers were not registered at the *Cassa Edile*, and therefore by and large were employed as 'black labour'. At that time (1973), there were 49,438 workers (average employment) registered at the *Cassa Edile* (see Appendix E. 7). Since then, the situation has changed because of three main tendencies: (*a*) subcontracting has been expanding, as the data on the fragmentation of the sector show (see Tables 8.3, 8.4, Chapter 8); (*b*) total employment in the Milan district has been contracting, with temporary employment recording a more pronounced decline, so that on the whole the employment relationship in the sector tends to be more permanent than in the past (as above discussed), and this is the case for both contract and subcontract workers; (*c*) the 'illegal' aspects of the subcontracting phenomenon have been noticeably reduced, as an increasing number of firms have been registering with the *Cassa Edile*.[19]

To summarize, subcontracting has been expanding throughout the 1970s, so that now the weight of subcontracted employment is certainly higher than it was at the beginning of the period examined. It is also possible to say that a considerable number of workers employed by subcontractors have a 'permanent' employment relationship (as defined above, p. 132) at least in the sense of a certain continuity of employment within the sector. Moreover, given the situation of a shortage of skilled labour in the district, these workers tend to have—on the whole—relatively good prospects of employment, whether as employees, as self-employed workers or as members of gang groups. And this explains the tendency for a considerable number of workers to follow individual strategies which aim to take advantage of market conditions through the combination, over time, of (*a*) regular waged employment, (*b*) non-regular waged employment (either as a first or as a second job), (*c*) self-employment. Finally, 'temporary' employment (as defined above, p. 133) has been decreasing both among contractors and subcontractors, as total employment in the sector has been contracting. Nevertheless, in both cases it represents, necessarily, the type of employment that the sector can offer to new entrants, as these are necessarily unskilled. Thus, it still plays a crucial role with respect to the problem of recruiting labour.

To conclude, the problem for building contractors is not how to screen workers, but how to find a labour force willing to be employed on a temporary basis, i.e. up to the end of the site life or for shorter periods, with no certainty about the future. In fact, unlike the steel enterprises, building contractors do not follow any precise or predetermined recruitment policy: instead, hirings reflect who is willing to be employed in construction in any one period, given a demand for labour with certain job characteristics and distinguished by instability, high territorial mobility, and uncertainty about the immediate future, as well as about career prospects in general.

5.3 Workers entering construction

People entering the building industry have always been characterized as those who are *compelled to work in the sector*, either for lack of better alternatives or as a result of compelling real conditions. This was the case at the turn of the century, when employment in construction increased with the entry of a large number of seasonal labourers from nearby rural areas. Similarly, during the upturn of the late 1950s and early 1960s, the expansion of the sector provided first jobs for most of the rural/southern immigrants arriving in the urban/industrial districts to look for work. Induced by the need to earn some money immediately, they found it relatively easy to get a casual job in construction, even if this often meant illegal, underpaid employment, with no social security, and uncertain prospects. Moreover, immigrants with no money and no house could find their first place to live in the site shanties.[20]

Nowadays, even if both demand and supply conditions have changed considerably, the sector continues to recruit those workers who are constrained or compelled to work in construction. This is the main conclusion of two case studies on the attitude of building workers towards the sector:[21]

> In the course of the interviews . . . it emerged clearly that the building sector is considered one of the worst employment options, one that workers accept only if pushed by unequivocal necessity or by a precise economic advantage. (CRESME, 1976, Section V, p. 10.)

None of the workers interviewed had started work in construction as a result of a precise personal choice, based on the evaluation of other real alternatives. Most of the workers said they had been compelled to work in construction because there was no possible alternative job open to them and/or because of compelling objective conditions, such as the need to support a very poor family (i.e. one with a very low family income or no income at all); by lack of education or of any skill; and by their own situation—and that of their families—as immigrants. In the Milan district, most of the workers employed in construction are from the lowest social strata; they are originally from the poorest areas of the country and therefore involved in problems of adapting to a new social environment; they have a very low level of formal education; and they entered the sector at a very young age, with no previous work experience—or only in very marginal and secondary type of jobs.

(i) *Age and skill.* In the ISFOL case study,[22] 84.3 per cent of the workers interviewed had started working at the age of 18 years or younger. The few workers who entered the sector at a relatively older age are, for the most part, skilled and employed to install heating or lighting or as machine operators by specialist building contractors, and are therefore characterized by a non-building career pattern, due to the industrial nature of their skill.

Data from the *Cassa Edile* of the Milan district seem to confirm the tendency for young and very young workers to enter the sector. Data available refer to all those newly registered, and they therefore do not allow us to distinguish between new workers entering construction and construction workers entering the Milan district from other districts. Nevertheless, from the data on their age and classification grade structure, it is possible to argue that the inflow of workers entering the sector is made up of very young and unskilled workers. In 1981, 9,191 workers entered the district: 57.54 per cent were 25 years old or younger (Appendix E. 10) and 54.33 per cent were registered as unskilled or apprentices (Appendix E. 9) (and similar figures are found for the previous years). It is possible that there are some skilled workers among those entering construction for the first time. This may be true of workers who have acquired their skill through formal training or on the job in other sectors, or who have moved to construction from other sectors related to construction but in decline, such as quarries and mines, or joiner's shops. But this applies to only very few workers, given that in construction the vast majority acquire their skills on the job. It is also possible that there are some workers who are no longer young but still unskilled, who have been working in construction in other districts, and who have moved to the Milan district. But this is likely to be the case only for a small group of workers, since the tendency is for building contractors to keep the most skilled and loyal workers tied to the enterprise, moving them from one site to another, and hiring labourers locally when required.

Therefore, on the basis of the information available, it is possible to argue that about half of the inflow of workers registered at the *Cassa Edile* consists of young and very young unskilled workers entering the sector for the first time. It is also likely that a quite considerable number of them have already had some experience in construction on an irregular and unstable basis, so that their actual age of entry is lower than the *Cassa Edile* data would suggest. But the inflow of these very young, unskilled, and inexperienced workers is not sufficient to cover the demand for labour in the district. And the sector has to depend partly on mobility from other districts. These workers are mainly skilled, they are either employed by their contractors on a continuous basis, and therefore follow the enterprise from one site to another, or are organized in gangs or small craft enterprises, moving around the region, according to the product market conditions.

(ii) *Previous work experience*. Most of the construction workers had entered the sector either as their first work experience or after having been employed in marginal jobs. The ISFOL case study (Appendix E. 13) shows that 39.5 per cent of the workers interviewed began their work experience in construction, and the figure is higher for the most traditional trades (bricklayers, tile layers) and lower for the industrial type trades (machine operators). The workers with some previous work experience had been employed, mostly, as peasants in the rural and poorest areas of the country or in non-industrial, secondary-type jobs, such as helpers in small craft shops, costers, pedlars, shop boys or seasonal waiters: that is, in temporary, unstable, and low-paid jobs.[23]

(iii) *Geographical origin* (Appendix E. 14). What has been previously said about age, skill, and work experience tends to be true for all workers entering construction, all over the country. With respect to their geographical origin, there are wide diffences, so that while in the rest of the country most of the construction workers are locally recruited, in the north-west part of the country, and particularly in the cities, the vast majority of the workers are of migrant origin. This includes both workers recently arrived, from the south and in general from poor agricultural or mountainous districts, and the second generation of migrant labour, living in the suburbs and employed in unstable and temporary jobs. The case study by CRESME (1975) showed that in the north-west part of the country only 33 per cent of the workers employed were originally from the same regions, while 16 per cent came from the north-east, 9 per cent from the centre and 42 per cent from the south.[24 25]

(iv) *Schooling* (Appendix E. 16). Given their family and social background, construction workers have, in general, a very low level of education, so that, it is still possible to find a high percentage of illiterates or semiliterates among them (between 20 and 30 per cent)—considerably higher than in manufacturing industry (12.5 per cent).

To conclude, both with respect to the workers' places of origin and to their labour market experience, workers entering the sector come from those areas and activities which tend to be abandoned, because of their low income, instability, and uncertainty. In the past, this implied, particularly for the peasants leaving the fields for good and not being able to find a job in another sector immediately, that they accepted employment in construction in order to survive while waiting for a better job opportunity. Now the sector is no longer a parking area in which migrant labour from the north-east and the south finds temporary employment, but it still continues to absorb workers from the lowest ranks, economically and socially, and the problem for the Milan district is that this inflow is no longer as plentiful as it was in the past. But if the number of workers in this position is becoming smaller and smaller, those entering construction are still those that, in their own words, 'have been compelled' by their situation to seek employment in the sector, as no better jobs were available. Entry into the sector is the result of objective circumstances, acting as constraints, or at most the result of a choice of the 'least bad', i.e. when the alternatives available are to work in the fields or as an apprentice in a small craft shop. This is crucial in explaining the workers' attitude towards the sector, and therefore their lack of interest in learning a trade and their determination to stay only temporarily, as discussed in the next two sections.

5.4 Training

As previously pointed out, employment in construction is less unstable than it used to be.[26] Nevertheless, employment instability remains a feature of the sector, compared with the manufacturing industry, albeit with considerable differences between groups of workers. Below is the evidence from a survey on days worked in construction in 1976:

> Working days per worker vary from 23.1 to over 120 per quarter, with an average of 61 days for total employment. And these data do not take into account the problem of the underemployment of dependent workers, related to contingent situations. Apart from territorial differences, the data seem to suggest the tendency of some groups of workers to secure work to the disadvantage of the others. This phenomenon is clearly related to the evolution of the division of labour, which is particularly advanced in the Milan district, with the tendency to decentralize the different sequences of construction to specialty contractors or gang groups. These focus on the trade of their skilled workers and on their high pace of work in order to secure a share of work more than proportional to the number of their employees. (From the talk by Dr. Mostacci, Director of CRESME, at a conference on the division

of labour, skill and training requirements, in *Regione Lombardia*, 1978, pp. 35–6.)

In the building industry a worker has the possibility of securing good and certain prospects of employment if he can acquire the necessary skill. Skilled workers have a more stable relationship to the sector, both in terms of continuity of employment with the same contractor and in terms of days of work per year, than unskilled workers. In the research carried out by CRESME (1975), 72.8 per cent of the skilled workers had been employed with the same contractor for at least a year or more, while only 28.2 per cent of the unskilled workers had the same length of service (Appendix E. 20). Moreover, even within the group of workers with a length of service of one year or more, the number of days of work per year was higher, on average, for foremen (219) and skilled workers (206), than for unskilled workers (195) and labourers (194); similarly, differences were found between the 'modern' trades, such as mechanics (222) and machine operators (221), and the 'traditional' trades, such as bricklayers (201) and carpenters (178).[27]

The process of the acquisition of skill is, in the vast majority of cases, and particularly for the traditional trades, the result of a long on-the-job training process. The data of the ISFOL case study (Appendix E. 17) are very precise in this respect: 72.8 per cent of the workers interviewed (for the most part skilled) acquired their skill on the job, simply learning by working side by side with a skilled worker. But this figure is much higher in the traditional trades—bricklayers (96.8 per cent), carpenters (84.3 per cent), and pavers (88.6 per cent). By contrast, a considerable number of workers employed in the so-called 'modern' trades, such as machine operators and installation engineers, have acquired their skill through formal training (81.8 and 50.8 per cent respectively) or on the job but in other sectors (10.6 per cent and 13.1 per cent), so that their training pattern is very different from that of the traditional trades.

Vocational training exists in construction, but it is both inefficient, with respect to the type of training required, and quantitatively insufficient, since only a very small number of workers receive it. National agreements provide for building schools, financially supported by a contribution from the contractors paid according to the number of workers they employ.[28] There are 35 building schools in Italy, but only very few of them are considered as efficient. The training courses of EFMEC, the vocational training organization for the Milan district, are considered adequate, in terms of the structure of training, but their role is minimal compared with the total number of workers entering the sector. Formal training suffers from several problems. First of all, the number of workers trained is too low, and their training inefficient with respect to the needs of the sector. Secondly, most of the courses are for workers already employed, not for new entrants, and they therefore do not help to solve the problem of a shortage of labour willing to stay in construction. The courses are also poorly attended, because of the social and economic costs of attending evening classes, often far away from the place of work.[29] Then, too, the fall-out rate is very high, so that only a few workers complete the courses. Fifthly, the courses for young workers entering the sector are few and, in most cases, they act more as recruiting agencies than as a source of training, and there is a lack of continuity between the school and the yards, so that young workers are often not asked to perform the trade for which they have been trained at the school. Finally, there is a general tendency among these young workers to abandon the school, or to abandon the sector once the course is completed. The difficulties in which formal training finds itself have been considered by both employers and trade unions in the Lombardia region. They all agreed that vocational training is inadequate, with respect to the needs of both employers and workers, and varies widely within the region, in terms of the type of courses offered, training orientation and type of training, as well as the structure of the courses, their length and times.[30]

It follows that training, for the vast majority of the workers, is the result of an informal process taking place on the site through direct contact with a skilled and experienced worker, well versed in the complexities of construction site life, and with the technical knowledge specific to his trade. This learning process can be looked at as the *spontaneous result of building activity*, and consequently depends on the way the production process is organized (i.e. the building enterprise structure) and labour is employed within it (i.e. the division of labour). In fact, training is made easier in the case of an enterprise which itself carries out all the main sequences of the process, as is the case with a general contractor that organizes its labour force by teams of trades. Within each team, unskilled workers are employed in a subordinate role, but training can still take place, since they work closely with the skilled workers. By contrast, both a strict specialization by contractor and an accentuated division of labour tend to make the training process more uncertain. This is the case when unskilled and semiskilled workers are employed in jobs that are not only subordinate but also marginal within the building process.

On the whole, the time recorded for the acquisition of skills is quite long. The ISFOL (1977) case study showed that over half the skilled workers interviewed (53.6 per cent) acquired their skills after ten years or more of apprenticeship. A similar figure (51.3 per cent) was found by the CRESME (1975) case study (Appendix E. 18). This can be explained not only in terms of the large variety of tasks to be learned and their difficulty, but also in terms of the uncertainty of the training process, due to the economic and technological features of the sector. Work tends to be temporary at any site, so that very high mobility characterizes the labour force, particularly if unskilled. Given the technology in use and the organization of production by a succession of different teams of trades, workers may be hired for different jobs over time, so that their training tends to be casual, especially when they first enter the sector, and their career path is neither linear nor clear. This explains both the very long average time for training and the large number of workers still employed as unskilled, despite several years in the sector.[31]

A situation of rapid expansion of employment or a shortage of skilled labour can reduce the time required for training. This helps to explain differences (by location, age, and period of entry into the sector) in the training times recorded. The differences recorded between the south and the north of the country and, in particular, the relatively short training times recorded in the Milan district, where the shortage of skilled labour first showed up, make it possible to conclude that, when demand for labour requires it, the length of time needed for training and upgrading can be reduced (ISFOL, 1977, p. 53). But, on the whole, training remains a long and uncertain process. And it is precisely this lack of certainty about career and the length of training that makes it more and more difficult for young workers to accept employment in construction with the intention of staying.

5.4.1 Subcontracting and training

It is widely acknowledged, by employers, trade unions, and students of the sector, that the traditional process of training has been interrupted, and that this has to be related to the changes that have occurred in the organization of the labour process, particularly the increasing use of subcontracting.[32]

On a traditional construction site, where the bulk of the activities are performed by the employees of the main contractor, on-the-job training is based, essentially, on observation and imitation. Unskilled workers can learn by looking at the work of the most experienced workers, in the slack times between helping them with one or another task. This is possible if they are asked to assist one or, at most, two skilled workers, preparing and supplying them with the material they need. But where and when subcontracting is used, there is little opportunity to learn a trade, since the skilled workers, employed directly by the main contractor, are asked to perform auxiliary tasks and general supervision on the site, while labourers are employed as hands to the gangs in a large variety of unskilled and marginal operations, therefore eliminating all their slack periods. The training of unskilled workers is also very difficult, if not almost impossible, in the case of the main contractor which executes some sequences itself but tries to keep the number of unskilled workers very low, and asks them to perform a great variety of tasks. This was the case at Gadola (see note 6), after the trade unions had asked the employer to reintegrate some operations that had previously been subcontracted:

> On the problem of recovery of skill, it is necessary to point out that with the reintegration of some sequences in a situation where the relation of skilled/semiskilled workers to unskilled is 3 or 4 to 1, if it allows the former to improve their skills, this achievement becomes almost impossible for the labourers. (FLC and C. d. D. Gadola, 1980, p. 26).

Moreover, the use of subcontracting over a long period can have some negative effects on the skill level of the craft workers employed directly by the main contractor, since their skills tend to be under-utilized.[33] In fact, at Gadola, serious difficulties arose when the enterprise started to organize some sequences directly: some trades (i.e. steel fixers) were hardly employed at all and it was difficult to recruit them in the market; other skills were found to be seriously damaged by the practice of subcontracting, since Gadola's skilled workers were no longer able to perform properly what was supposed to be part of their trade (cladding and plastering); and other trades were almost completely lost (tile laying and paving).[34]

The subcontractors, in their turn, relying on the trade and dexterity of their specialist/skilled workers, make the entry and training of young workers very difficult. In fact, young workers tend to join a gang *when they have some skill* already, and not the other way round. The splitting up of building contractors, whatever form it takes, hampers the process of training both with respect to the main contractor and with respect to the subcontractors. The gangs tend to supply their work in a sort of set package, on the basis of some standardized operations, and employing the minimum of unskilled labour. This has been made possible by proposing a division of labour in some respects less detailed than on a traditional site: the workers of the gang perform *all the tasks* necessary for the sequence to be done, including those previously performed by the young and unskilled workers. Moreover, this externally imposed division of labour, which is both very well-defined and standardized, means that the organization of the gang tends to reproduce itself over time, avoiding the recruitment of young unskilled workers—since this would disrupt its organization, which is necessarily based on an extremely fast pace of work.[35] The picture is not substantially different for the larger gangs, in charge of complete sequences of the building process: they employ very few unskilled workers, and these are given marginal and completely unskilled tasks, making their training very difficult. One young *cottimista* interviewed complained that:

> Here we have to do everything in a hurry. There is not even time to stand looking, because we have to be quick. I am here to carry bricks, to do this and that, but I haven't got a trade yet. If I don't get out of this gang I will have to go on working as a donkey for tuppences. (In CRESME, 1976, Section 4, p. 46.)

It has just been said that little or almost no training takes place inside labour gangs and subcontract groups. Thus, it has to be explained how subcontract groups reproduce, given that they employ skilled labour but do not provide for their training. Here, a distinction should be made between those craft skills based on the acquisition of experience and knowledge (as defined at point (i), p. 125), and those skills based on the dexterity to do a repetitive and simple task at speed (as defined at point (ii), p. 126). This second group includes trades such as pavers, tile layers, and terrace workers, for which the problem of training is a minor one, as the skill content— in the traditional sense—is extremely low and can be acquired in a few months. In such tasks, the crucial element is physical strength, in the sense of the ability to stand a very high pace of work in uncomfortable and tiring positions. For this group of trades, the gang acts as a channel of recruitment to the industry: the gang-leader or members of the gang who organize the work take in young workers, if they are willing to learn the trade quickly and work fast. As a result, these subcontract groups tend to consist of family clans, groups of relatives, and groups of fellow villagers (who either commute from the districts of Brescia and Bergamo, or are immigrants organized on the basis of their area of origin). For the first group of trades, by contrast—those based on craft skills—the problem of training is crucial, but the subcontract groups do not and cannot (given their organizational structure) provide it. Instead, they are obliged to recruit among those working for the contractors who have already acquired some skill in their trade or, better, are the workers themselves who try to become self-employed or work in a subcontract group, as soon as they have got the necessary skill through some work experience with a main contractor:

> Even if the young workers come to work as employees in our firms, it is not difficult to notice sooner or later an attitude of substantial reservation about their employment position as dependent workers. In general, they try to learn their trade, if they are not yet well experienced, always aiming at the target of a non-dependent employment relationship. (From an interview with an employer, in CRESME, 1976, Section 4, p. 18.)

It is precisely the increasing use of subcontracting for the execution of works requiring the employment of traditional craft skills—such as carpenters and steel fixers—that has continually reduced the supply of these trades in the district. To conclude, the situation can be described as a vicious circle. Almost no training takes place in the subcontract groups; fewer and fewer contractors organize these sequences of the construction cycle directly or in their entirety, and a smaller and smaller number of workers is therefore properly trained. Moreover, a relatively large number of these skilled workers prefer to have an independent employment relationship, at least until they are strong enough to stand the work; and this in turn makes it difficult, even for those contractors who would prefer to organize the work directly, to find and keep the necessary skilled labour force. Thus, a larger and larger number of contractors prefer to give out part of the work in order to solve the problem of recruiting skilled labour. All this has led to a serious shortage of skilled labour in the district, and the problem will become more acute in the near future.

5.5 Internal and external mobility

The discussion up to now has drawn attention to the fact that the career process in the construction industry is mainly external rather than internal to the enterprise. Skills are acquired through the accumulation of experience by moving around between enterprises, geographical areas, and subsectors. Permanence within the sector, and even within the same enterprise, does not necessarily imply career advancement. Data on the average age of workers per classification grade bring this out very clearly. In some districts of the country (10 out of 27), the average age of unskilled workers is higher than that of semiskilled, and in a few cases even higher than that of skilled workers (Appendix E. 6). Thus, for a large part of the labour force, permanence within the sector does not allow the worker to gain qualifications or to establish a career. The fact that in some districts, for example, in Piemonte and Lombardia, skill increases with age is more a reflection of the better job opportunities open to unskilled and semiskilled workers, and therefore their higher turnover in terms of intersectoral mobility, than of a smooth career pattern in construction.

Stability and good prospects of employment are possible *after* a skill has been acquired. A worker has better employment opportunities as he acquires a trade: contractors compete to attract skilled workers, and they try to tie them to their enterprises with extra bonuses or other forms of payment. Employment fluctuations are, in fact, much more marked for semiskilled and unskilled workers than for skilled workers, as shown in Table 5.2. Using the coefficient of variation as a measure for instability, this is over five times higher for unskilled than for skilled workers. Moreover, despite the fact that skilled workers, within each different type of enterprise, are more stable than semiskilled and unskilled workers, they tend to move, in general, from craft to industrial enterprises, and from very small enterprises to large ones. This must be related to the higher risk of inactivity and lay-offs in small and craft enterprises. As a result, these enterprises are characterized by a higher labour force turnover, by comparison with industrial and large enterprises (Appendices E. 12, E. 11).[36]

But building workers are not only attracted by stability, continuity of employment, and certainty about wage payment. It is quite common for craft-skilled workers to move between different types of employment relationship in their career. These stages include: the *regular dependent job*, with various types of insurance and benefits (social security, pension, unemployment benefits, and so on); the *irregular dependent job*, as the first or the second job, in small enterprises, acting as subcontractors, or in gangs working on the lump; the *independent job*, as a self-employed person, a small employer, or a gang-leader (Pichierri, 1982, pp. 55, 57–8). In fact, most of the small entrepreneurs in construction are ex-craft workers; similarly, in the co-operatives most of the partners are skilled workers. This suggests, on the one hand, a

TABLE 5.2

Instability of employment by classification grade, Milan district, 1972–81

	Annual average	Standard deviation	Coefficient of variation
skilled	26,197	1,331.59	5.08
semiskilled	11,223	1,971.24	17.57
unskilled	19,187	5,250.20	27.36
Total*	57,085	7,837.85	13.73

*This includes apprentices, site watchmen, and workers with no grade.

Source: See Appendix E. 21.

peculiar relationship between craft skills and entrepreneurship and, on the other hand, that workers employ a very independent and individual strategy in the labour market, resulting in a quite complex work career. This process is, in many respects, favoured by the characteristics of the sector itself. The cyclical and seasonal nature of construction work and the high territorial mobility induce workers to organize themselves in such a way as to exploit the instability of the sector; the characteristics of the production process—and the need to rely on the skilled workers—permits this type of individual entrepreneurial strategy (and also makes possible its reverse), and encourages a form of small business mentality, where the idea of progress and advancement is related to individual sacrifice and endeavour. Thus, employment stability, good employment prospects, and good earnings are not only limited to the skilled sections of the labour force, but also depend on workers' individual strategies and on their ability to take advantage of product market and labour market conditions, relying on their knowledge of the product market and their connections in the labour market.

Allowing for possible differences in employment stability, prospects and rewards, three main groups of workers can be singled out. *Skilled workers directly employed by building contractors* (industrial and medium-sized enterprises) enjoy stable and secure jobs, but their earnings tend to be low, basically at the level agreed through collective bargaining. *Skilled workers employed by subcontractors, or self-employed, or organized in gangs*, experience high job mobility (rotating among sites and firms) and very high earnings, and that basically depends on their ability to work very fast. Nevertheless, employment for this group is not secure, and is contingent on product market conditions and on the workers' ability to get in and out, accordingly. Finally, *unskilled and semiskilled workers* are characterized by a more unstable and intermittent employment relationship. They are hired when required and dismissed when work on the site ends; their earnings are unstable and relatively low, given the higher risk of unemployment and the relatively low earnings in construction with respect to the manufacturing sector (Appendix E. 29).

Not only is the career process uncertain in construction, so that permanent employment in the sector does not necessarily lead to the acquisition of a trade, but, even when workers do acquire skills, this is not sufficient to keep them in the sector. All workers show a high propensity to leave. This was the main result of the CRESME (1976) case studies on workers' attitudes towards the sector. Their willingness to leave as soon as they had the possibility of a more suitable job outside construction, was common to all workers—skilled and unskilled, young and old alike. Similarly, when the young students of the *Scuola Edile* (building school) of the Milan district were interviewed, not a single young worker said he intended to stay in construction. The formal training they were receiving was considered a way of surviving for a few years, until they could find a job in the manufacturing industry, or simply as way of getting some higher education in the hope that this might serve as a sort of 'passport for the civilized world of work' (Sabbatini, 1972). This negative attitude towards the sector finds support at the national level in the data on the turnover of the labour force: construction shows a sort of anomalous behaviour with respect to the general trends in the manufacturing industries.[37] A drop for labour turnover rates is found in the 1970s, and this is explained, on the demand side, by the constraints imposed through the *Workers' Statute* on the dismissals of workers[38] and, on the supply side, by the tendency to stay in a job. Entry and departure rates had dropped quite substantially both in manufacturing and construction. But while, in the case of manufacturing, the fall in the departures rates was due to a fall both in dismissals *and* in resignations, in construction a rise in the resignation rate was recorded, as shown in Table 5.3.

TABLE 5.3
Annual average labour turnover rates in manufacturing and construction (% per year)

	Total entries		Total departures		Resignations	
	1965–70	1970–7	1965–70	1970–7	1965–70	1970–7
construction	90.6	65.1	88.5	70.7	20.7	24.8
manufacturing	29.1	20.6	26.0	20.7	13.4	10.6

Source: See Appendix E. 30.

Thus, while in the manufacturing industry the labour force tends to remain and improve its working position from inside the factories through collective bargaining, in the construction industry the labour force tends to move out, looking for a good and stable job outside the sector. Some workers leave when they are offered a *secure job*, in many cases even if at a lower wage; some when they find a *better job* in terms of working conditions, social prestige, career prospects, earnings, and so on; some after they have *earned sufficient money* to start an independent activity, like opening a cafe or a small shop in their own village.

Propensity to move is high among all construction workers, but ability to move is unequal among them, and exit from the sector largely depends on the demand for labour in the other sectors of the economy. Table 5.4, on the changes in the employment structure by age group, shows this. In the expansionary years, 1973–4, total employment showed an increase by about 5,000 units; the increase is mainly due to the inflow of young and very young workers (15–25 years). At the same time, there was a decrease in the middle age groups (31–40 years), compensated for by an expansion in the upper age groups (41 years and over). The following period, 1974–9, was distinguished by a rapid and marked contration: total employment fell by over 20,000 units. Practically all age groups showed a contraction, but in the middle age groups (31–40 years) this took the form of a major decline and in the upper age groups only a very modest one (the 56–60 years age group even recording an increase). In the last few years, the sector seems to have reached a more stable situation: the labour force employed has continued to contract, but by only 1,300 units. Again, however, the trends vary widely by age group: the youngest (15–20 years) and the oldest (51 years and over) age groups

TABLE 5.4
Employment fluctuations by age group, Milan district, 1973–81 (total variation)

	Δ 1973–4	Δ 1974–9	Δ 1979–81
15–18	+1,514	−2,022	+1,036
19–20	+1,066	−1,503	+206
21–5	+1,122	−2,189	+599
26–30	+650	−2,652	−273
31–5	−333	−3,636	−202
36–40	−110	−3,541	−1,426
41–5	+98	−2,530	−826
46–50	+139	−645	−516
51–5	+686	−191	+51
56–60	−674	+148	+140
>60	+185	−786	+52
Total	+4,343 (+5,001)	−19,542 (−20,287)	−1,159 (−1,303)

Notes: Δ = absolute variation.
Data refer to absolute changes in the employment structure by age group, as data on inflows and outflows of workers are not made available.
Data in brackets refer to the total variation, including the numbers for which data on age are not available.
Source: See Appendix E. 26.

recorded an increase, while those in between showed a further decline, particularly marked in the 36–46 years age group. Young workers show considerable mobility in and out of the sector; in particular, when there is an expansion in job opportunities they enter the sector in quite substantial numbers. The workers in their prime are those recording continuous and heavy reductions, both in periods of expansion and of recession. They are also those with the strongest need to move into secure and stable jobs, given their increasing family responsibilities, and are those with the best job opportunities in other sectors of the economy. The oldest workers tend to stay until retirement age, some having reached a stable position in construction, others because they are trapped there. The changes that have occurred in these mobility patterns over the last ten years have resulted in a substantial change in the structure of the labour force by age: the middle groups have been progressively shrinking (so that the ratio of workers between 26 and 41 years old has fallen from 40.9 per cent in 1971 to 27.3 per cent in 1981) while the oldest and youngest age groups have been expanding, leading to a progressive ageing of the core of the labour force (Appendix E. 26).

The mobility patterns just discussed must be taken into account when considering the problems of recruiting labour to construction. It is well known to people dealing with the industry that there is a shortage of labour in the sector.[39] The data just examined clearly show that this cannot simply be attributed to a lack of young workers coming into the sector. Of course, the increase in school attendance, the increase in the average income per dependent worker, and the end of the migrations have certainly reduced the flow of labour willing to be employed in the sector, and data on the structure of unemployment support the view that there is indeed a relative shortage of manual labour. The unemployment rate for male workers in the Milan district (Appendix E. 27) is relatively low, and the number of manual workers registered as unemployed in construction (Appendix E. 28) is small compared to the total number of manual workers registered as unemployed in the district. However, data on the structure of the labour force by age (Appendix E. 26) and on the age structure of newly registered workers (Appendix E. 10) discussed above suggest that the crucial problem is not the lack of a sufficient inflow of labour into the sector, but rather the outflow of workers between 25 and 40 years of age. Thus, it is not that young workers do not enter, but that they do not stay.

Employers have repeatedly complained that it is almost impossible to recruit workers willing to be regularly employed as dependent workers.[40] But while they admit that the problem of recruiting labourers is relatively easy to solve, the problem of how to find young skilled workers is extremely serious (and they tend to solve it by recruiting gangs). Thus, the shortage of labour is mainly a problem of lack of skilled workers. This can be explained as the result partly of the outflow from the sector of workers in their prime and partly of the reluctance of young skilled workers to be employed by building contractors—preferring, as they do, an independent employment relationship, either self-employed or working in gangs. It is the possibility of immediate access to large sums of money, compared to what they would earn as dependent workers in construction or outside the sector, that attracts all the best skilled young workers to the area of subcontracting, thus taking labour away from the established building contractors.[41] But they tend to stay only while their physique allows them to work extremely hard and make good money. As they get older, they either try to move back as dependent workers or they move out.

The possibility of high earnings in subcontracting is not, however, enough to keep labour in the sector. All workers, skilled and unskilled, dependent workers and *cottimisti*, have a negative image of the sector when they enter, and this image is worsened by their work experience in the sector, so that they all share an intention to leave the sector. The reasons for this are related to the physical, economic, and social costs of work in construction. The physical costs are a product both of the work itself and of the general working conditions. Building work is hard, whatever technology is used, and it is the heaviness of building work which presents a real threat to the worker's health. But physical exhaustion follows not just from the constant hard work, fatigue, and bodily discomfort, but also from exposure to unpleasant weather conditions—heat in summer and cold in winter—exposure to the hot and humid steam from the cement, the ubiquitous dirt (mud, cement, lime, and soil), the danger, and the inadequate measures for accident prevention. The discomfort caused by high and continuous geographical mobility, which often means long commuting distances or long periods away from home in uncomfortable conditions, and the lack of decent services such as changing rooms, showers, sanitary facilities, a canteen or a place to eat and cook, are also a common source of complaint. The economic costs of working in construction are the product of uncertainty about continuing employment, about future monthly and yearly earnings, as well as the threat of earnings dwindling with age. As discussed above, a certain degree of stability and good earnings are possible for workers with the required skill and the necessary physical strength to stand hard work. Actual earnings can be substantial, but future earnings are always made uncertain by the possibility of accidents, illness, and ageing itself. Construction workers are well aware of this, and they look on the idea of remaining in construction with anxiety. This in turn produces psycho-sociological costs. These are in part related to in terms of uncertainty and insecurity about the future as previously discussed, and in part to the workers' low opinion of the industry, and consequent lack of self-respect.

To conclude, many of the sources of dislike for and alienation from work in construction cannot simply be overcome through higher wages, since they are deeply rooted in the nature of construction work itself. The crucial problem for the sector is not merely, therefore, that of increasing the wages of dependent workers, but—given the product market structure, the technology in use, and the organization of the production process—of increasing to a considerable extent the share of stable, secure, and decent jobs, with good training and career prospects, and high stable earnings.

Notes

1. See *CCNL Edili*, 1979, art. 87, pp. 73–85.
2. ISFOL, 1977; FLC and C. d. D. Gadola, 1980; FILCA CISL Lombardia, 1980*b*.
3. See ISFOL, 1977, pp. 79–81; Fontanari, 1978, pp. 260–1.
4. This includes non-traditional materials produced by other industrial sectors, for example the textile (producing carpets) and rubber (producing linoleum) industries.
5. This group tends to be laid off when the site is closed.
6. This is a large building enterprise in the Milan district, acting at the regional and—for some projects—national level, employing 250–350 employees (FLC and C. d. D. Gadola, 1980, p. 13).
7. This can take the form of a day rate, instead of a piece rate, as for the skilled and semiskilled workers.
8. See Pichierri, 1982, p. 54; Franciosi, 1979*b*, pp. 67–9.
9. See ISFOL, 1977, pp. 25, 30–7; Cipollini and Frison, 1980, pp. 3–4.
10. It is on the basis of the specific features of the sector that regulations defining the employment relationship in construction are related to the lifetime of the building site, instead of the lifetime of the enterprise. See *Legge* Aug. 6 1975, art. 9, reprinted in *CCNL Edili*, 1979, pp. 171–2; Brusco and D'Alessandro, 1979, p. 25; ISFOL, 1977, p. 34.
11. The *Cassa Edile* is a welfare institution for the construction industry, set up on a district basis to collect contributions (from employers and manual workers) and to pay them to the workers registered there as delayed wages in cases of unemployment or illness, and as holiday payments, Christmas bonuses, and so on. For a detailed discussion, see the introductory note to Appendix E.

12. That is, they were registered as employed in the district in all four quarters of the year; but this does not imply that they were working for all of each quarter, so that it is possible that they have experienced some inactivity within each period considered. Data on the number of weeks worked per worker (Appendix E. 15) show this.
13. Available data from the *Cassa Edile* of Milan (see Table 5.1, p. 134) allows one to distinguish employment on the basis of the quarters in which workers are recorded as having been employed. In 1981, 61.35 per cent of the total number of workers registered over the year were recorded in the four quarters considered (*continuously employed* as discussed in note 12 above). Of employment which has been recorded for less than four quarters it is possible to distinguish several groups: 16.48 per cent *entered* the district and/or the sector during the year (i.e. they had been working continuously from the second, third, or fourth quarter); 15.84 per cent *left* the district and/or the sector (i.e. they worked continuously in the first, or up to the second, or up to the third quarter); while 6.33 per cent have been employed *discontinuously*.
14. This does not imply that these workers have had no spell of unemployment, but simply that they have been employed, including temporary unemployment spells, in the district during the period considered.
15. The PPE was first introduced through national collective bargaining in 1976 and then changed in 1979. The first agreement granted the right to the PPE to all workers that had been employed in the sector for three years with a minimum of 3,000 hours work; the subsequent agreement set the rule at 2,100 hours worked per biennium. See *CCNL Edili*, 1976, *Regolamentazione per gli operai*, art. 32, p. 37, and *Allegato C*, pp. 88–91; *CCNL Edili*, 1979, *Regolamentazione per gli operai*, art. 32, p. 42 and *Allegato C*, pp. 98–101.
16. These are workers temporarily laid off or put on short time (less than 40 hours per week) and who are entitled to wage supplement payments paid by the Wage Supplement Fund (*Cassa Integrazione Guadagni*).
17. This is also reflected in the tendency towards a lower labour turnover (Appendix E. 19).
18. This information has been given by Mr Bianchini, Director of the *Cassa Edile* of Milan.
19. With respect to this last point, it has to be said that the 1973 and 1976 national collective agreements for construction introduced some constraints on subcontracting. In particular, they have established the 'solidary responsibility' of the main contractor towards his subcontractors (i.e. the former's joint responsibility, in law, with the latter), in all matters related to the employment relationship. In fact, the interest of the main contractor in the regularization—at least to a minimum extent—of subcontractors has pushed a growing number of small firms to register with the *Cassa Edile*. But this does not imply that all the workers registered are 'regular' workers: in many cases the registration hides the phenomenon of labour-only subcontracting and gang groups, as workers are registered only for a minimum number of hours of work,

to give some sort of legal cover to the employment relationship. And this makes it impossible to distinguish between contractor-employees, subcontractor-employees, labour-only subcontractor workers, and labour gang workers.

20. See Chapter 8 p. 231.
21. CRESME, 1976, Sections 2 and 3 respectively. The first analyses the experience of 55 workers employed in two large urban areas (Milan and Rome); the second is based on 29 interviews with Italian emigrants employed in construction abroad (Lugano and Monaco).
22. This is a case study of the career profiles (focusing on the training process) of a stratified sample of 519 workers, mostly skilled. 35.6 per cent of the workers interviewed started working in construction at the age of 14 or younger; 48.7 per cent between 15 and 18; 13.5 per cent between 19 and 24; and 2.1 per cent over 24 (ISFOL, 1977, Appendix, Table 6, pp. 136–7).
23. Franciosi (1979*b*, pp. 38–9) reports the results of the CRESME (1975) case study on 4,400 workers employed by 15 large building contractors: 40 per cent of the labour force, rising to 60 per cent for labourers, had been working in agriculture. Similar results are found by CRESME (1976, Sections 1 and 2) and ISFOL (1977, pp. 47–9).
24. Franciosi (1979*b*, p. 72), in reporting the results of the CRESME (1975) case study, pointed out that the situation is quite different in the rest of the country: in the north-east 94 per cent of the labour force employed in construction is from the same regions, 75 per cent in the centre, and 98 per cent in the south.
25. At Gadola (see note 6 above), 60 per cent of the manual workers are originally from the south (FLC and C. d. D. Gadola, 1980, p. 15).
26. Bruni (1979*a*, pp. 64–113) showed that this is the case also for the country as a whole.
27. Reported in Franciosi, 1979*a*, p. 43 and 1979*b*, pp. 43–4, 125.
28. See *CCNL Edili*, 1979, *Regolamentazione per gli operai*, art. 42, pp. 46–8.
29. Vocational training for workers already employed is organized by EFMEC through two-year evening courses, taking place from October to April, for a total of 10–14 hours per week (on four evenings and on Saturday morning). The courses include training for bricklayers/pavers, carpenters/steel fixers, assemblers for prefabricated components and painters/paperhangers, for which no previous school-leaving certificate is required; and training for plant operators (crane/digger drivers) and electro-mechanics, for which the school-leaving certificate is required.
30. The fact that training is neither sufficient nor efficient does not imply that it is not regarded as important. On the contrary, the unions have been proposing and discussing possible changes in the system and structure of vocational training in the region as a way of overcoming the problem of the shortage of labour. See Sabbatini, 1972; Carlino, 1973*a*, 1973*b*; Riccardi, 1977; FLC Lombardia, 1976, 1977; FLC Milano, 1979*a*, 1979*b*; *Regione Lombardia*, 1978.

31. 41.7 per cent of the unskilled workers interviewed for the ISFOL (1977) case study had been employed in the sector for over 10 years without being promoted to a higher grade. Similar figures were found by the CRESME case study (1975) for unskilled workers (49.1 per cent) and labourers (31.9 per cent) (Appendix E. 18).
32. ISFOL, 1977, pp. 55–6; Gruttaduria, 1976, pp. 14–6; Gruttaduria, in *Regione Lombardia*, 1978, pp. 61–3; CRESME, 1981, in FILCA CISL Lombardia, 1981, p. 63; FLC Milano, 1979*b*.
33. See Mostacci, in *Regione Lombardia*, 1978, p. 35.
34. See FLC and C. d. D. Gadola, 1980, pp. 25–6.
35. See Gruttaduria, in *Regione Lombardia*, 1978, pp. 59–61.
36. It is interesting to notice that labour turnover decreases with size of firm, with the exception of very large enterprises (over 250 employees). These employ a relatively large share of unskilled and semiskilled workers (Appendix E. 22) and they record a relatively high labour force turnover (Appendix E. 11). This can be explained by the fact that they operate at the national level, moving over long distances, recruiting locally most of the labour force required, with the exception of technicians and a few very skilled workers.
37. Industrial firms showed a marked slowing down in total departures and entries in the 1970s, compared with the 1960s. Several studies have analysed the change in the labour turnover rates, pointing out the progressive internalization of the Italian labour market. See Garonna, 1979, p. 156; Dell'Aringa, 1974; Modigliani and Tarantelli, 1979.
38. The principal legislation concerning dismissals is Law No. 604 of 15.7.66 and Law No. 300 of 30.5.70 (known as the 'workers' statute'). Under this latter law no worker may be dismissed without 'just cause' or 'justified reasons'.
39. See CRESME, 1976, and 1981, pp. 59–61; ISFOL, 1977, pp. 41–3; Mostacci, in *Regione Lombardia*, 1978, pp. 35–6; Gruttaduria, 1980, pp. 9–10; FLC Milano, 1981, pp. 9–15.
40. In fact, it was on this account that ASSIMPREDIL, the construction-employer association for the Milan district, commissioned two research projects from CRESME (1976 and 1981).
41. See CRESME, 1981, in FILCA CISL Lombardia, 1981, pp. 59–61; FLC Milano, 1981, pp. 9–15.

CHAPTER SIX

Preliminary Conclusions

The empirical work on the steel and construction industries in Italy presented in the previous chapters attempted to shed light on the functioning of the labour markets, focusing attention on their structure. This chapter brings together the main points of the argument discussing, first, existing differences between labour market structures and, secondly, the factors shaping these differences. The main conclusion is that labour markets are shaped by a long process of interaction between a number of factors—product market conditions, technological evolution, labour market conditions, and social relations of production. To understand the present, therefore, it is essential to look at historical developments with an awareness of the interrelations between these factors.

6.1 Labour market structures differ

The hypothesis underlining this work, as discussed in Chapter 1, is that the labour market is better analysed as a segmented market, whose segments are distinguished by the fact that they treat workers differently, independent of their own characteristics. The steel and the construction industries are two clearcut examples. Both industries recruit a large proportion of manual workers, with little or no skill, no previous training, and little formal education. They are employed in hard and tiring jobs, with no prestige but with the possibility of high earnings. Despite these similarities, quite opposite labour market structures distinguish the two sectors. In the steel industry, large plants employ a well-structured labour force; workers are hired according to a precise screening policy and employed in jobs that are stable, secure, well-structured, and with possibilities for advancement. Once a worker is hired, he is considered part of the internal market, independent of his skill, qualification, and allocation. If he decides to stay, he has the opportunity to acquire experience and skill, and to be moved up, in time. A set of well-established rules defines ports of entry, mobility, and career patterns, so that jobs are secure and the career process is clear and well structured.[1] In contrast, in the building industry, only the very skilled workers have secure jobs, their stability depending mainly on their scarcity in the labour market and on the employers' tendency to tie them to the enterprise; the majority of the workers have no secure job and no defined career, with uncertainty about future earnings and prospects of employment. A large number of workers are employed on casual jobs, with instability and uncertainty about the future; stability and continuity of employment are possible only after they acquire the necessary skill. Thus, what distinguishes construction from steel is not only that *good and stable jobs* are lacking, but that there are different mechanisms allowing for the acquisition of stable jobs with prospects of continuity. While in the steel industry this is assured *when a worker enters the steel factory*, by his permanence within the plant, in the construction industry this is associated with the *acquisition of the required trade and skill*, and this is possible only if he is willing to undergo a very long and uncertain training process.

According to the categorization suggested by the LMS debate, the steel industry is a very good example of an internal labour market and the construction industry of a secondary market. Some qualification is, nevertheless, required. In the steel industry, very well-structured rules govern all aspects of labour; but this does not imply that the same set of rules is applied to all groups of workers. Instead, divisions exist between process, maintenance, and ancillary workers. For the first group, the possibility of advancement is directly related to their physical condition and depends on their mobility patterns at the works where they are employed; for the second group, the possibility of advancement is the result of individual working experience and ability; for the last group, there is no possibility of a career. Not only is there a clearcut distinction between the three groups of workers, so that there is no mobility at all between maintenance and process departments, while the mobility between process departments and service sections—when it happens—implies the end of the worker's career; but also, within the process departments, careers develop only by department, and mobility between departments implies the beginning of a new career process. Thus, the internal market is segmented in its turn.

The construction industry can be described as a secondary sector, both because many disadvantaged workers are confined to it and because it is characterized by job instability, poor and uncertain career prospects, unstable earnings, and uncertainty about future income. Nevertheless, it would be wrong to classify all segments of the labour force as secondary in the classic sense. Construction draws its unskilled workers from a general labour market and even its most skilled workers often move between industries. The skilled segment, however, acts more like a traditional craft organization under conditions of uncertainty, where a high proportion of the risk is borne by the workers in the form of temporary employment and high inter-industry mobility. It is the labour market for unskilled workers in the construction industry which seems to fit more closely into the standard secondary classification. But even here some qualification is needed. In particular, in so far as the industry serves to channel workers from rural to urban occupations, it also plays a part in transforming some 'secondary' workers into 'primary' workers.

6.2 Why do labour market structures differ?

It has been seen that workers who are apparently similar are treated differently as they end up in different segments of the labour market. Differences in the labour market structures imply differences in the way in which labour is recruited, allocated, trained, organized to work, promoted, and paid—as discussed in relation to the steel and construction industries in the previous chapters. And this has to be directly related to the way in which the labour process is organized within each sector.

To make this point clear, it is necessary to refer to the debate that followed the publication of Braverman's (1974) study. Following Marx's analysis of the labour process (1976, Vol. I, Part 4), subsequent studies have focussed on the role of employers in organizing the labour process.[2] This involves not only material relations between inputs and outputs, as suggested by the orthodox economic theory of the firm, but also social relations of production. This is based on the fundamental fact that workers sell their labour power for a specific period of time at a given price, not their labour. And it is the inability of employers to purchase labour, and the necessity of purchasing labour power to perform labour, that explains their crucial role in taking charge of the work process, so as to guarantee the production of profits. The labour process debate has examined the employers' strategic concern in increasing their control over the workplace, giving a historical account of how work has been transformed over the last century. Different approaches have led to different accounts of the transformation of work and its effects. The analysis has shifted from a rigid determinism that appears to draw much of its inspiration from the stages theory of capitalist development in Marx's work, emphasizing the issues of control and deskilling (Stone, 1975; Edwards, 1979; Gordon *et al.*, 1982), to a more dialectic and integrated approach that takes into account the specific economic conditions for the firm's economic development, which constrain employers' labour management strategies, and the role of workers' organization, resistance, and internal conflicts in countering employers' control over the workplace (Kahn, 1976; Elbaum *et al.*, 1979; Littler, 1982; Lorenz, 1983).

With respect to the problem of the structuring of labour markets, the labour process debate has made clear that the firm cannot be considered as the 'black' box within which inputs are transformed into outputs, since production is the result of both material and social relations. And this implies a need for the firm to secure labour of the required characteristics, to secure its cooperation at the minimum cost in the organization of production, and to sell its products for the realization of a profit. These three aspects of the activity of the firm are clearly interconnected: the type of labour recruited (in terms of skill, necessary training, behaviour) affects the way in which production can be organized. This determines the costs of production, and therefore the realization of profits. In order to guarantee the realization of profits, various means are employed by the firm to control work organization. It follows that the processes of recruitment, allocation, training, division of labour, promotion, and payment, can be considered as the set of interrelated mechanisms through which the labour process is organized. The labour market structure is the product of the interaction between these processes. From this perspective differences in labour market structures have to be analysed as the result of differences in the organization of the labour process, and therefore they have to be taken back, as suggested by the developments of the labour process debate, both to the material conditions, i.e. what I would call *the economic and technological constraints*, and to the social relations, i.e. *worker/employer interactions*.

The work done on the steel and construction industries supports this perspective, in showing clearly that the structure of the labour markets in these sectors in terms of job structure, hiring, training, promotion, and payment can be understood fully only in the light of their economic and technological characteristics.

In the building industry small enterprises, spread all over the country, with very flexible structures in order to adjust quickly to changes in demand, tend to build only one building at a time, so that after its construction the yard will vanish and the enterprise will move to another area; the result is a demand for a flexible labour force, with high mobility both within the sector and inter-sectorally. The steel industry is characterized by a small number of very large and precisely located enterprises, where the large investments involved raise the problem of full utilization of existing capacity. Correspondingly, a stable labour force seems necessary. These differences in the economic and technological conditions are crucial in two respects: first, in defining the *realm of possibilities* with respect to the way in which the labour process has to be organized; second, in defining the *problems* employers have to solve in organising the labour process and trade unions have to face in organizing labour, and in taking the necessary action to defend their workers.

The economic and technological factors can be looked at as constraints on feasible outcomes, defining the framework within which the power relationship between labour and management operates. Given the social relations of production, competition in the product market and the pattern of demand shape the economic structure of industrial sectors and define the technology in use. It has been argued (Piore, 1975*b*) that there exists a precise and clear relationship between technology in use and the labour market structure. This is correct if it means the definition of the realm of possibilities, but it is not if it implies a one-to-one relationship between technology in use and the structure of the labour market. Given the same technology, different systems of production—and thus various organizations of the labour process—are feasible. This is true for all kinds of techniques, even if the range differs according to the characteristics of the technology in use. For example, the relation between technology and the labour market structure seems to be better defined and more rigid as we move from low capital-intensive techniques, such as those employed in the building industry where the possibilities in terms of organization of the labour process look wider, to high capital–intensive techniques, such as those employed in the steel industry. In this last case, a given technique of production (such as, for example, the electric steel-making process) corresponds to a certain production process in terms of installations, layout, physical/chemical characteristics of the process, and the operations involved. This leads to the definition of some general features in the organization of work (as discussed in Chapter 3) for that stage of the production process, defining globally (not invidually) the operations and tasks to be performed, the knowledge and skills required, the necessary physical fitness, etc. But who does what and how, i.e. how the labour process is organized, depends—as argued earlier—on the social relations of production. Thus, the economic and technological conditions define the framework within which labour and management interact.

At the same time, the economic and technological conditions define the problems that management and labour have to face, with respect to their own strategies: employers in the organization of the labour process and unions in the organization of workers for the defence of their interests.

For employers, the crucial problem in the building industry is to organize the labour process so as to meet the great variability in product demand, at the minimum cost, and at the same time to secure the skilled labour required to erect the building. In the steel industry, the central problem for management is to organize the labour process so as to secure a regular and continuous flow of production, given the high costs and damages that can occur in case of interruptions or mismanagement of either the production process or the equipment; therefore, management has to secure a cooperative and responsible labour force willing to intervene to avoid discontinuities and interruptions.

For the trade unions organizing labour in the building industry, the main problem is that they cannot rely on a stable organization at the workplace. The peculiarities of the building industry raise difficulties both in trade union organization and in the formation of a class consciousness. Given a fragmented industrial structure and the dispersion of workers in a large number of construction yards, which close down and move to different places when the construction is completed, the trade unions are organized mainly outside the yards. Their strength is constrained by product market conditions, and their policy is extremely defensive, aiming to minimize the uncertainty of employment and to assure a certain continuity in wage payments. In the steel factories, trade union organization is facilitated by the gathering together of a large number of workers in a single factory, and by the existence of a well-structured labour force within the factory. The integrated nature of the process of production and the organization of labour in small and compact teams of workers, with distinct identities, affect not only the strength of union organization—much greater than in construction—but also the power of single groups of workers with respect to the production process, since small groups can stop the entire production. And the tendency is for group interest to prevail over class interest. The problem of uncertainty and instability does not exist; once inside a steel plant, the workers tend to stay, since the experience and qualification they acquire there do not usually give them better chances outside. The possibilities of training, upward mobility, and career are therefore all internal to the plant. Thus, the trade unions' main problem is to control these processes according to their own strategies, on the one hand limiting the discretionary power of management, and on the other hand minimizing internal conflicts.

Thus, trade unions organize themselves on the basis of the existing conditions of production. That is, the economic and technological conditions under which unions act constitute the basis for the development of labour organization and industrial relations, affecting their organization, power, and strategy. Product market conditions, technology in use, and industrial organization can have either a negative or a positive effect: they can weaken the union organization and limit the impact of the actions taken, as in the case of construction; or they can favour their organizations and strengthen and amplify the effects of their actions, as in the case of steel.

Finally, the social relations of production can have a feedback effect: product market conditions, industrial structure, and technology in use can change as a result of trade union organization and the existing divisions between groups of workers; as the outcome of trade union action and their impact upon the organization of the labour process and managers' responses to such actions; or as the indirect result of trade union action which affects the conditions of competition between employers in the product market.[3]

Before concluding, it has to be said that the realm of possibilities defined by the economic and technological framework which is relevant for the determination of the labour market structure is what is *perceived as such* by employers, workers and unions. Hence, given the economic and technological constraints, the balance between employer, worker, and union strategies, with respect to what they perceive as feasible, defines the labour market structure; and this has a feedback effect by setting new and different problems, modifying the realm of possibilities perceived by the other side, and thus giving rise to a continuous process of change in labour market structure. In fact, every time a strategy is set out, by whichever side, the *fact* of its being a strategy modifies the environment, and thus the realm of possibilities for the other side. And this calls—sooner or later—for an adjustment in the strategy of the other side, thus leading to a continuous and iterative process.

6.3 The dynamics of the labour market structure

The main conclusion from what has been previously discussed is that the labour market structure, in terms of wage structure, grading structure, working conditions, turnover, and composition of the labour force, is the result of a complex interplay of factors. The problem of the structuring of the labour market has to be regarded as an *iterative process*, where the nature of product market competition, industrial structure, and technology in use, as well as labour/management relations, are seen to be the main determinants. The process of the structuring of the labour market is a dynamic one: hence it should be analysed as the result of the interrelations between the variables singled out. Therefore, the analysis should not be in static descriptive terms but in a *historical perspective*. Thus, not only does the labour market structure *differ* as we move from one segment to another; but the labour market structure *changes* over time. And in order to understand why labour markets differ in their structures, it is necessary to discuss how they change over time, taking into account both the economic and technological framework within which management and labour interact, and the institutional framework which affects their motivations and strategies.

The need for a dynamic analysis has been underlined by different hypotheses, even if with different emphases. The dual labour market hypothesis[4] has emphasized the interaction between developments in the economic structure, the development in technology, and the pattern of labour market behaviour. In the radical approach,[5] the segmentation of the labour force is analysed as the result of a historical process in which class conflict plays a central role. The segmentation of labour is seen as a product of the postwar period, when the USA economy was characterized by a period of rapid capital accumulation. The large corporations began to explore new mechanisms for more effective and reliable labour control at the same time that workers succeeded in forming large and powerful industrial labour unions. New systems of control in the labour process became consolidated in the USA, and this produced a segmentation of labour. A different approach has stressed the active role of workers[6] within a situation of developing capitalism. It is argued that the process of segmentation is not simply reducible to the management strategy to 'divide and rule' labour; workers play an active role through collective bargaining, as they organize themselves in trade unions.[7]

Following this last approach, we could say that the development of capitalism is a process of continuous change. New industries, new techniques, new markets, and new institutions are created, while others are destroyed. The continuous changes in labour processes, in technology, and in methods of work organization have quite a large and complex impact on the employment structure. The result of this historical process involves changes in the distribution of labour between occupations and industries, in the skills required, and in the composition of the labour force. This process creates problems for both the capitalists and the workers. The need for capitalists is not only to prevent the development of working-class consciousness, as argued by the radical approach, but to organize the production process for the realization of profit. The introduction of new techniques of production and of new methods of work organization may interrupt the existing social relations of production and create situations of conflict because of trade union opposition. At the same time, the disruption of jobs, skills, and occupations due to the evolution of the capitalist system creates problems for workers, their bargaining power being reduced as competition for jobs is created. Thus, workers are continuously threatened by changes caused by the evolution of capitalism, and this may induce defensive action on their part.

Because of the development of capitalism there is a continuous threat of displacement of labour and redundancy of skills. Workers' organizations adapt and restructure themselves in order to face changes in the economic structure and to act defensively. And conditions of production constitute the basis for the development of workers' organizations. Trade union action takes the form of defence against the competition in the labour market that the capitalist system generates with its evolution. Employers have to pursue their goals (profit maximization, firm expansion, increase in market power) in economic terms; and their decisions (change in technique of production, closure of plants, subcontracting, dismissals, etc.) can create conflict situations. Employers take action in order to minimize their total costs, but their action is constrained (both socially and economically) by the action of workers' organization and workers themselves. The problem is, therefore, to analyse the changes in the economic system taking into account the interplay between employers and workers.

To conclude, the labour market structure is defined by the way in which employers, workers, and unions, though their social relations, try to develop strategies to resolve the problems posed by the economic and technological conditions; and it is this process that gives rise to the segmentation of the labour market into qualitatively non-uniform segments. Moreover, within a changing economic and technological environment, the interaction of the social relations of production with the development of the forces of production makes segmentation a continuous and iterative process, where this iteration is not directed towards some equilibrium, but rather reflects the dynamics of economic evolution.

The next two chapters will explore how the changes in the economic and technological conditions in the steel and construction industries have interacted with management/labour strategies in shaping the labour market structure.

Notes

1. There are no established rules for redundancies, as is for example the case in the UK, where lay-offs by seniority have been in use for a long time. This has to be related to the economic conditions of the sector in the postwar period (characterized by continuous expansion and the non-occurrence, until now, of major redundancies) and the lack of collective

bargaining at the plant level until the late 1960s. In most recent years, redundancies have been negotiated with the unions. This is the case with redundancies resulting from technical change in a certain department, or with temporary redundancies due to lack of demand or slow-downs in production. In such cases, the unions will negotiate on how many and which workers are going to be affected, following the general strategy of (*d*) minimizing the total burden, and (*b*) minimizing the burden per worker, therefore aiming to distributing the burden over the largest possible number of workers. The final solution will depend, given the general strategy of unions, on the specific situation.

2. See Friedman, 1977; *Politics and Society*, 1978; Zimbalist, 1979; Nichols, 1980; Littler, 1982.
3. These relations have been recently explored by Elbaum and Wilkinson, 1979; Lazonich, 1979; and Zeitlin, 1979. As they demonstrated, the social relations of production and the development of the forces of production interact in a dialectical manner. It is the continual process of conflict, compromise, and cooperation between capitalists and workers, the process of competition between employers, and the existing divisions between the working class, that lead to changes in the labour process.
4. Doeringer and Piore, 1971; Piore, 1975*a*; Berger and Piore, 1980, pp. 64–5.
5. Gordon, 1972; Stone, 1975; Reich *et al*., 1973; Edwards *et al*., 1975; Edwards, 1979; Gordon *et al*., 1982.
6. Kahn, 1976; Wilkinson, 1977; Friedman, 1977; Rubery, 1978.
7. In this attempt, workers and workers' organization have been assigned an active role, and changes in the employment structure have been taken into account. It is within this approach that Rubery (1978) has extended Braverman's (1974) thesis of the development of labour market stratification.

CHAPTER SEVEN

The Dynamics of the Labour Market Structure in the Steel Industry

7.1 The evolution of the steel industry

During the postwar period the Italian steel industry has considerably expanded its productive capacity and introduced very significant technological innovations. The new processes and equipment have been characterized by a much higher level of productivity. Only a small increase in the labour force was needed to create a dramatic growth in production. The changes in technology resulted in a shift in the composition of the labour force, as the number of manual workers decreased and that of technical staff increased, and in job content, with fewer direct manual operations and more activities of control and regulation on equipment and processes. These changes run parallel to a transformation of the social organization of the industry, from a hierarchical and 'individualistic' system to a non-hierarchical and 'collective' system of organization.

This chapter focuses on the evolution of the social organization of production, and begins with a discussion of the evolution in the economic and technological framework.

7.1.1 Economic development

The modern Italian steel industry came into being only at the beginning of this century, when pig-iron started to be produced on an industrial scale in blast-furnaces. By the early 1930s, the sector was already settled in terms both of techniques of production and of industrial structure. There were a few integrated plants using OH furnaces to refine pig-iron, and a large number of steelworks employing electric furnaces to smelt and refine scrap. The public sector concentrated on the production of pig-iron and the private sector on electric steel.[1]

After the second world war, the steel industry was left in a difficult situation. Its productive structure was technically backward and economically inefficient, with excess capacity spawned by its fragmented and uncoordinated development; and the plants were deeply damaged by bombing, with over two-thirds of total damages in the main public sector plants (Ilva, 1948). A heated debate broke out on whether or not the industry should be maintained and developed

(Daneo, 1975, pp. 306–18). Some claimed that it should be limited to the modernization and strengthening of the existing scrap-using mills; others argued that the coastal steel works should be reconstructed, in view of the sharp rise in steel consumption and the fact that it was cheaper to transport raw materials by sea. Despite the apparent clash between these two solutions, both were realized, each playing a part in that kind of multiple development which is one of the most remarkable aspects of the Italian iron and steel industry. The public sector developed on the basis of an ambitious plan of reconstruction and expansion, known as the *Piano Sinigaglia* (Sinigaglia, 1948; FINSIDER, 1948). This took up an earlier plan[2] for the expansion of the country's productive capacity, concentrating the production of pig-iron and the bulk of steel in a few very large, integrated coastal works. It involved the closing down, in the 1950s, of a large number of small steelworks; the construction of two new, large, integrated plants (Cornigliano in 1951–3 and Taranto in 1960–4); and the modernization of the other two integrated plants (Piombino and Bagnoli). The realization of this plan ran parallel to the modernization and development of the private sector, where medium-sized and small scrap-based steelworks predominated. These plants concentrated on quality steels and special steels—to which the dimensions and greater flexibility of smaller steelworks were better suited—with particular product specializations, in which they quickly reached a leading position in the national market.

Throughout the postwar period, the industry developed steadily and rapidly to meet the continuous rise in steel consumption (Table 7.1).[3] Cyclical fluctuations were met by shifting them to the foreign trade balance: in periods of recession, imports decreased and exports increased; in periods of boom the trends were reversed, leaving domestic production almost unchanged. This was made easy by the fact that steel production was lower than consumption until the early 1970s. In 1974, for the first time, the long–sought goal of meeting consumption through domestic production was achieved. But, as the investment plans were reaching completion,[4] a major recession hit the world steel market, following the oil crisis, and the Italian economy entered a period of stagnation. The long upward trend was reversed, and steel consumption did not reach its 1973 level again until 1979. Thus, demand slumped while new capacity continued to expand. Steel consumption forecasts, on which the investment plans had been based, turned out to have been greatly overestimated, so that the investment completed by the public sector produced a substantial surplus capacity, followed by heavy losses (see Chapter 2, Figure 2.2).

TABLE 7.1

Crude steel production and apparent consumption in Italy
('000 tons and annual compound rate of growth)

	Crude steel production		Apparent consumption	
	Tons	%	Tons	%
1952	3,635		4,040	
		+9.8		+11.7
1963	10,157		13,586	
		+8.3		+6.2
1969	16,428		19,543	
		+7.7		+3.1
1974	23,803		22,797	
		+0.4		+0.4
1979	24,250		23,237	
		+1.1		−4.8
1981	24,777		21,177	

Source: Elaboration on ASSIDER data.

7.1.2 Technical innovation

The considerable expansion in steel production in the post-war period was realized partly through the expansion of productive capacity, with the building of new plants, and partly through the replacement and modernization of existing plants.

Starting from the mid-1950s, the manual and semi-continuous rolling trains were progressively replaced with continuous rolling trains of increased dimension. These were highly mechanized and partly automated, and incorporated very substantial technological improvements, such as sophisticated electronic controls, considerably greater speeds of operation, larger slab furnaces, automatic roll changing, and automatic speed changing.[5] Starting from the mid-1960s, oxygen basic processes, such as LD and OBM converters, were introduced to replace the old OH furnaces and to expand total steel production. Steel productive capacity per furnace was increased dramatically as a result of the larger dimension of the furnaces and the extreme rapidity of the new processes (from a few hundreds to over seven thousand tons per day per furnace, as shown in Appendix A, Table A. 1). The old electric furnaces were replaced with larger, ultra-high-power (UHP) furnaces, able to melt and to refine larger quantities of steel of better quality in shorter times. In the 1970s, continuous casting machines started to be introduced, speeding up the process by eliminating some sequences completely. In the integrated steel plants, to match the increased productive capacity of the steelworks, larger and larger blast furnaces were installed throughout the period; their productive capacity was considerably increased not only by increasing the diameter of the blast furnaces,[6] but also by improving their lining, and by better controlling the charge, the temperature, the blast of air, and its heating.

The technical changes introduced have led to higher productivity, higher speeds, the elimination of some operations, and a higher degree of coordination between the different installations. Innovations introduced at one stage of the process have often created bottlenecks in the following stages, leading to the introduction of other modifications, including economies in transport and heating achieved by further integration, so as to reduce discontinuities. All these changes, by increasing the integration of the works, have led to greater rigidity in the production process. Moreover, the instrumentation and automation introduced, by increasing the degree of scientific control of production, have improved the works performance, i.e., they have resulted in better quality of output and lower costs.

With the increase in plant and works dimensions, associated with extensive technical transformation of the production process, there has been a considerable increase in total productive capacity, with only a minor expansion in total employment.[7] The marked evolution from manual or scarcely mechanized processes to highly mechanized and, in some cases, automated processes have reduced manpower requirements, by eliminating or reducing the need for the direct intervention of manual labour, and have changed the structure of employment: a relatively smaller number of process workers and a larger number of maintenance workers is now required.

7.2 The social organization of the steel industry in the 1950s and 1960s

In the early postwar period, the industry was characterized by technologically outdated works, with little mechanization, and involving a large amount of direct manual labour. The production of steel was based on OH furnaces and electric furnaces, the first used mainly in integrated steel plants and the latter in scrap-based mills only. In both cases the process was slow, as eight to nine hours were required between one casting and another. A series of collective manual tasks was involved (such as the addition of lime, ferro-minerals and other additives by means of shovels; the skimming of the slag; the closing and the taking off of the furnace pouring tap; and the cleaning of the ladle). All this was performed under the supervision of the first melter (*maestro forno*), who took decisions throughout the process on the timing of the charges and the quantities and timing of the additives, simply by rule of thumb, for example, by looking at the molten metal itself. Mechanization and instrumentation were little developed, so that both the quality and quantity of steel produced depended on the workers' performance. In the rolling mills, all the trains were manual or semi-mechanized, and a large number of workers were employed for moving, transferring, and manipulating the hot metal during the rolling process. The work involved was extremely heavy, requiring the simultaneous cooperation of small teams of workers to catch the hot metal from one stand, reversing it, and feeding it into another stand with the aid of large, heavy tongs. Two teams were employed for each stand. The workers of each team would work both simultaneously, to handle the hot metal through the stands, and intermittently, with one team working and the other resting. The tasks involved required remarkable effort, physical strength, manual dexterity, and quick reflexes.

As demand for steel started growing, the sector expanded by installing new OH and electric furnaces of increased productive capacity, and by replacing the old manual rolling trains with highly mechanized ones (Ancona *et al*. 1957; Scortecci, 1961). In a situation of rapid growth and rapid technological evolution, the shaping of the labour market structure[8] was influenced by a mixture of union weakness, particularly at the workplace, and the managerial authoritarianism/ paternalism that characterized the Italian industrial relations system at that time.

The principal manifestations of trade union weakness were the division of unions along ideological lines, the centralization of their organizational structure, the centralization of the level of decision-making (both in conflicts and in bargaining processes), their organizational absence at the workplace, and the low level of membership.[9] Collective bargaining was highly centralized, and based on national, inter–industry and industrial sector agreements, negotiated by the national general unions (the three general confederations, CGIL, CISL, and UIL) and by the national industrial unions (federations by category), respectively. All aspects related to the management, deployment, and application of labour power were negotiated at the national level. National collective agreements, renewed by industry every three years, were concerned with an array of issues such as piece-work, working times, payment systems, and overtime. Plant bargaining was not very common, and was limited to the application or implementation of what had been agreed at national level. Moreover, after 1962–3, efforts to establish a system of plant bargaining met with great difficulties. Thus, up to the late 1960s, any form of control on the workers' side over the workplace and the labour process was either indirect and mediated through general agreements bargained outside the workplace, or very informal and not very effective. Trade unions were organized outside the factories, and the body representing the workers within the plant, the *Commissione Interna*, was not a formal trade union body, even if all its members were unionized.[10]

Management's discretionary power was as a result quite boundless within the factories. The change in the political climate after the 1948 elections had allowed the entrepreneurs to regain control over the factories, a control that was pursued, both by the private and by the public sector, through the combination of apparently contradictory mechanisms, which were all designed to discipline the working class: paternalism, discipline, discretionary and discriminatory practices. These measures included experiments with social assistance to steel workers and their families for the provision of houses, resort colonies for their children, and the creation of a fund for their education.[11] This welfare policy was matched by a toughening of factory discipline. Fines, punishments, lay-offs, suspensions from work, and the allocation of workers to 'confine departments' were used to discourage trade union activity, to control the labour force, and to organize the labour process. For example, when a maintenance worker was found to be a union activist he was removed from his job in the process departments and allocated to a single workshop, thus limiting his contacts with the other workers.[12] In the process departments, temporary contracts were used to employ labour for the process departments, thereby breaking the unity of the working class, as these so-called 'seasonal workers' were continually threatened with the possibility of not having their contract renewed if they went on strike or did not respect the discipline of the factory.[13] Moreover, unilateral and discretionary policies were used for all issues related to the allocation, promotion, and payment of workers. These policies included (*a*) favouring the internal career of the 'loyal workers', through internal mobility and promotions, and extending to them a large variety of monetary incentives and personal bonuses, and (*b*) discriminating against the others with the threat of lay-offs, temporary contracts, or allocation to the 'confine department'.

To understand the management's boundless power within the factories, the characteristics of the labour force have to be considered, too. Most of the manual labour was done by process workers, since maintenance and service workers counted for no more than 25 to 30 per cent of total employment. The vast majority of process workers were peasant workers, not living in the area surrounding the factory, but in the countryside or mountainous areas nearby, and working the land in their spare time.[14] A large number of them were from the same villages, not only commuting together but also working in the same department, team, and shift. Their poor education (many of them were illiterate), the fact that they had spent most of their working life in the same department, and their attachment to their peasant origin contributed to make their links with the external world very weak. Moreover, process workers' skills were industry- and firm-specific, and therefore the possibilities of career advancement were necessarily related to the worker's permanence within the steel plant. All this helps to explain the workers' acceptance of the paternalistic authoritarianism of management, as well as the tendency to develop small-group interests. Maintenance workers were craft skilled, usually with some previous industrial experience, and better educated. They also lived in the area around the factory, and were well-integrated into the social milieu. They represented the aristocracy of the steel workers, and it was among them that trade union activists were found. But given, on the one hand, the political climate of those years and, on the other hand, the sociocultural origin of the majority of the labour force, their efforts to counter internal management policies had very little impact.

7.2.1 The labour market structure

(i) *The division of labour and hierarchical structure*. Given the state of technology, little mechanized and quite empiricist, the management of the production process required a large amount of labour, implying both manual work and experience. In the process departments, the majority of workers were employed in jobs requiring almost no skill in the traditional sense, but physical integrity, strength, resistance to fatigue, the ability to withstand very uncomfortable working conditions, and courage to face unforeseen and dangerous situations. The number of skilled workers was small among process workers, but their role was crucial with respect both to production and to the organization of the other workers.[15]

The labour process was organized around the features of the technological cycle: small teams of workers were in charge of complete sections of the production process. Within each work team, the division of labour was based on a long and well-structured hierarchical and pyramidal structure, founded on informal job ladders, established by tradition on the basis of the job posts technologically determined. The workers in the top positions (*maestro forno*, *capocolata*, *capotreno*) were the most experienced, i.e. those with the longest length of service within the same department and the same work team. The use of technology was still quite empiricist, and the management of the production process was, in a sense, delegated to these senior workers. They controlled, regulated, and supervised the production process by rule of thumb, taking decisions when needed, and coordinating the activities of the work team. This gave them considerable discretionary power over the other workers, not only in the carrying out of the production process, but also in the organization of the labour process itself, i.e. taking decisions over job allocation, mobility, careers, promotions, personal bonuses, and discipline.[16]

The basic principles for the social organization of maintenance workers (as well as all other workers employed in non-productive activities) were not very different from those found in other industrial sectors where the labour force employed was craft skilled. In the steel industry, maintenance workers were craftsmen, specialized by trade (such as electricians, engineers, and fitters), with their level of skill varying according to their individual abilities and experience. They were organized—as is still the case today—by trade, either in the process departments or in workshops. In all cases, they acted more as individuals than as a team, and the actual division of labour among maintenance workers depended on their individual skill and ability to do complex work.

(ii) *The career structure*. The workers' career, as far as process workers were concerned, was related to the possibility of climbing up the hierarchical structure. The career was very long, as 15–20 years of service were required to get to the highest positions, and quite uncertain, since it depended on where the worker was allocated (department, team, job), when he entered the steel plant, the opportunities available in terms of vacancies, and the worker's physical condition. In any case, career advancement was at the foreman's discretion and in no way controlled by the workers, least of all by the unions. The foreman, usually the oldest and most experienced worker, had a wide measure of control over other workers' career. This control was based on a mixture of 'prizes' (promotions, mobility, upgrading, personal bonuses, incentives) and 'punishments' (downgrading, obstacles to career development, fines), which were used by management to reinforce the workings of the factory system and to organize the production process, securing the necessary cooperation and consent of the labour force. All mechanisms for the organization of the internal labour market (mobility, training, promotions, and rewards for loyalty and good behaviour) were presented in the context of career advancement. And the idea of career and the hierarchical structure was internalized by the workers themselves, particularly by the most experienced ones.[17]

The maintenance worker's career was directly related to the acquisition and improvement of his craft skill. It was therefore linked more directly with innate abilities, individual training, and the demonstration of aptitude and skills.

(iii) *Internal mobility*. In this system of social organization, internal mobility was used to resolve the problems posed by the technology in use and, at the same time, to discipline the labour force. Given the need to maintain continuity in production, a certain flexibility in the utilization of the labour force was required to secure a continuous flow of production. This was achieved by making considerable use of internal mobility, which consisted in the movement of process workers between different job posts, within each department, and within each team.[18] Mobility could be either permanent or temporary, horizontal or vertical, upward or downward.

Temporary mobility was used to fill temporary vacancies, according to the needs of the production process. Upward temporary mobility was also used as a form of on-the-job training. The worker, after having moved to a certain position for some time, was trained and therefore ready to be upgraded when that particular job post was permanently vacant. Permanent mobility could take place either upward or downward. The worker with the longest length of service would be moved up on the job ladder when a job post in a higher grade became permanently vacant. The worker's career pattern consisted of climbing up the hierarchical structure, step by step, according to the vacancies and at the foreman's discretion. But since many jobs implied considerable physical effort and exposure to hard working conditions, it was often the case that workers no longer fit for certain jobs were downgraded to marginal and secondary jobs, involving a loss of wages, status, and hierarchical position (Vallini, 1957, pp. 20–1; Pozzobon and Mari, 1978, p. 188).

Maintenance workers were not affected by such a system. They were hired by trade, and graded and paid according to their craft skills. They had to perform their job within a particular trade, and their career was linked to their individual abilities, and to the improvement and demonstration of aptitude and skills. It was a sort of individual process of learning by doing, rewarded with higher grades and higher wages.

(iv) *'Job ranking'*. The formalization of this organization was based on a classification system, *paghe di posto*, peculiar to the steel industry, according to which process workers were graded and paid according to the job posts they were filling. It was a sort of job ranking, according to which each job post (*piazza*) of the process departments had an associated wage rate, established not through collective bargaining but by tradition. A process worker's skill was defined by—and dependent on—the position he occupied in the production process. In other words, it was the job, and not the worker, that was classified and graded. Process workers were supposed to move both temporary and/or permanently between job posts, with their earnings changing according to their mobility patterns.

Maintenance workers and all other workers employed in non-productive activities were classified, graded, and paid according to the prevailing system in use in Italy, *sistema delle qualifiche*.[19] That is, they were hired by trade and, within each trade, graded and paid according to the skill acknowledged to them by the employer or the foreman.

The existence of two different systems of classification for process and maintenance workers was related, on the one hand, to the need to meet technological rigidities through a high flexibility in the use of labour, expressed in terms of a high internal mobility; and, on the other hand, on the fact that the *sistema delle qualifiche* made it impossible to ask workers to perform a job different from the one they were hired for, unless they were promoted. The principle on which the system of job ranking was based was that both the job and the wage could vary, with no limit being set by the job 'category', as was the case for maintenance and service workers. In this respect, the distinguishing feature of the job ranking system was precisely the different mobility pattern associated with it. The underlying idea was one of complete interchangeability: process workers could move upward or downward according to the needs of the production process, earning higher or lower wages, according to the job posts filled.

(v) *Wage system and wage structure*. A worker's pay was calculated, by and large, on the basis of three main elements: basic rate, piece rate, and allowances. The basic rate consisted of the wage rate associated with each single job post. In this respect, the structure of wages (basic rates) reflected not only the hierarchical structure of jobs within each department, so that job posts involving greater responsibility with respect to both equipment and other workers were better paid, but also the role played by every single job post in the production flow.

The 'key job posts', i.e. those affecting production more directly, were in fact better paid.[20] The result was that workers' earnings depended on their individual position in the production process and on their internal mobility patterns. Piece-work, extensively used in the process departments, was directly related to output (tons produced), usually taking the form of team piece-work. Given the state of technology, actual production (number of tons per casting, of castings per shift, and of tons of steel rolled), depended to a large extent on the direct intervention of the labour force. This implied the need for collaboration, understanding, and joint effort in a work team, developing, on the one hand, a quite remarkable team spirit within each team and, on the other hand, strong competition between teams. As the division of labour was based on tasks that had to be carried out jointly by small work teams, this contributed a sort of stimulus to do better, to produce more than the other teams, and represented a sort of control on the workers' side. Management was well aware of this, and used it, through team piece rates, to increase control within each team and competition between teams (Botta, 1978, pp. 378–82). Piece rates accounted for over 30 per cent of total earnings, but as technical change led to greater mechanization, the tendency was to reduce their significance. Finally, there was a large number of allowances, directly related to the individual job filled and to the conditions in which the job was performed. Most of these allowances were related to conditions prejudicial to the worker's health, such as heat, noise, exposure to smoke and fumes, and risks. The fact that wages depended on many different elements, and the fact that mobility was high, produced a very fragmented and differentiated wage structure.[21]

7.3 The job analysis and job evaluation system

This double system, based on the job ranking for process workers and on the *sistema delle qualifiche* for maintenance workers, was employed up to the early 1970s throughout the private sector and in some public sector steel enterprises. Italsider replaced this double system with a job analysis and job evaluation system (JA and JE), at the time of its creation in 1960;[22] management decided to extend the JA and JE system, in use at Cornigliano since its construction, to all its plants.

The integrated plant of Cornigliano was built by the public sector in 1951–3 as the starting point of a very ambitious project for the development and modernization of the Italian steel industry. The steel works at Cornigliano were considered at that time the most up-to-date plant in Italy and one of the most modern in Europe, equipped with the first example in Italy of a continuous rolling mill for the production of plates, sheets, and strips.

The technical innovation introduced in the pig-iron and steel-making departments consisted mainly in an increase in the dimension of blast-furnaces and OH furnaces installed; an increase in the speed of the processes, allowing for higher productivity; and improved instrumentation, allowing for better control of production. This did not involve a substantial change in the mechanization of these processes, and therefore did not substantially affect the way in which the production process was organized. By contrast, the new continuous rolling train was distinguished by a remarkable increase in the level of mechanization of the rolling process, involving not only much higher productivity, but also a radical change in the organization of the production process. Manpower requirements were reduced; the manual and direct intervention of labour in the rolling process was reduced quite substantially; while activities of control and regulation, as well as maintenance work, were considerably increased. Table 7.2 summarizes the main changes brought about by continuous rolling by making a comparison with a manual and a semi-mechanized rolling train.

Public managers introduced at Cornigliano not only the best available installations and techniques for the production of steel, but also what they thought to be the best techniques in use for the organization of the enterprise as a whole and, particularly, for the management of the labour force (Cai, 1976, pp. 29–31). The management policy was to build a sort of ideal factory, based on up-to-date, highly productive equipment with the possibility of further enlargement, and also on the most advanced techniques available for the management of the production process, the control of output, the division of labour, and labour relations. The purpose was the creation of a rational and efficient organization capable of solving *all* sorts of problems, including those related to labour. The solution proposed, for the management of labour, was a combination of four main policies: (*a*) a very detailed description of division of labour (job analysis); (*b*) a precise definition of the criteria for the determination of wages (job evaluation); (*c*) wide use of internal mobility to allow for the increased rigidity and integration of the processes; and (*d*) the recruitment of a 'new working class'.

A job analysis was carried out in full. This formalized the division of labour, specifying the tasks and operations involved for each job. Some changes were introduced in the division of labour, due partly to the technical innovations introduced, and hence to changes in job content, and partly to the formalization of the division of labour, hence to the higher rigidity implied by very detailed job descriptions.

TABLE 7.2
A comparison of a manual, a semi-mechanized, and a continuous rolling train, 1959

	Manual	Semi-mechanized	Continuous
(*a*) *Productivity and costs of rolling:*			
tons produced per total hours worked*	100	340	1100
total costs per ton*	100	76	64
rolling cost per ton*	100	59	30
kilowatt per worker	26	94	135
kilowatt per ton	59	82	200
time required for maintenance work*	100	180	560
No. of workers per shift	43	37	37
(*b*) *Degree of mechanization of working activities (Bright's scale) (% distribution):*			
manual activities	44	15	6
mechanized activities	24	32	15
automated activities	32	53	79
total activities	100	100	100
(*c*) *Job posts by type of work autonomy towards the process*† *(% distribution):*			
manual work	79	57	34
mechanized work	16	33	46
supervisory work	5	10	20
total job posts	100	100	100
(*d*) *Job posts by type of team work (% distribution):*			
individual work	—	12	10
simultaneous work	88	42	26
integrated work	12	46	64
total job posts	100	100	100

Notes: * Index numbers.
†'Manual work' refers to activities involving energy given by labour; 'mechanized work' refers to activities involving the control of energy by the equipment; 'supervisory work' refers to activities in which the intervention of labour occurs in cases of necessity on auto-regulated equipment.
Source: Scortecci, 1961, pp. 318, 324.

The job analysis was used to define the wage structure: each job was classified on the basis of certain characteristics, and these were evaluated on the basis of defined criteria, thus determining the evaluation of wage rates, job by job. In this way some of the previous formal distinctions between maintenance and process workers were eliminated; however, these two groups of workers were still differentiated by type of division of labour, by training process, by skill, by level of education, by degree of internal mobility, and by pattern of advancement. Therefore, the labour force was still made up of numerous groups of workers with distinct characteristics and differentiated interests. In fact, the main innovation of the JA and JE system was that the criteria on the basis of which each single job was analysed and evaluated were now formalized, and therefore clearer and more certain. But this did not change the basic principles used, so that it is possible to describe the JA and JE system introduced at Cornigliano in 1953 (and then extended at Italsider) as a rationalization of the job ranking system: workers were classified, graded, and paid by the job, and thus it was the jobs, and not the workers, which were classified and paid.[23] In particular, as far as process workers were concerned, production continued to be characterized by technological rigidity—now even greater because of the higher automation of the processes—and by the collective nature of work activities: team work continued, in fact, to be required in most departments. This, and the very detailed division of labour introduced with the job analysis, called for large internal mobility, as with the job ranking system, and this high mobility was related to on-the-job training and to career structure. Finally, a new working class, i.e. one with no steel tradition, was recruited.

In order to understand the recruitment policy followed by Cornigliano SpA, it is crucial to realize that, at the time the steel works were constructed, the restructuring plan for the public sector steel industry was also being carried out, involving the closing down of several out-dated steel works. In the Liguria region, where the works were located, three steel plants belonging to the Ilva holding (Savona, Voltri, and Bolzaneto) were closed down, making 2,901 workers redundant. By 1959, only 421 were found reemployed in the steel industry, and 824 were still unemployed (D'Alamo, in Vento, 1981, p. 152). Management did not hire the workers freed by the restructuring of the other factories, preferring to hire young workers (25–30 years old), with no previous experience in steel factories, with the most heterogeneous and non-industrial working experience (as peasants, craft workers, pedlars, barbers, and so on), originating in the rural areas nearby. The argument put forward by management was 'technical': as the works, the processes, and the organization of the factory were new, then the structure of the labour force had to be new too.[24] But the underlying reasons were more 'social': management wanted a working class willing to cooperate with the new project, which consisted in the construction and organization of a factory without conflict, where everything could be predetermined on the basis of 'objective' criteria. The working class of the steelworks closed down in the region was not suited for such a project: 95 per cent of them were members of CGIL, 60–70 per cent communist, and about 20 per cent socialist. They all had a very strong trade union tradition, characterized by a an allegiance to the communist party.[25] Thus, hirings took place with the aid of careful 'political' screening, carried out through parish churches, as well as political and personal connections. It was only for the top grades (foremen, supervisors, and engineers), and for the highest manual positions in the process departments, that employees freed from restructuring in the other steel plants were hired. In this last case, the experienced and older workers were employed only for a few years, until their retirement age, in order to allow for the training of the labour force. As they retired, they were replaced with technicians, and as a result the jobs that belonged to the most experienced manual workers were transformed into white-collar jobs.

When, in 1960, Cornigliano S.p.A. and Ilva, the two largest companies of the public sector, merged into a new corporation, Italsider, management decided to extend the JA and JE system in use at Cornigliano to all its plants, thereby adopting a uniform policy all over the enterprise. An agreement was reached with the unions, some changes were introduced, but they were irrelevant to the principles on which the system itself was based (Cai, 1976, pp. 35–8).[26 27] All the other steel enterprises, both in the public sector and in the private sector, continued to organize the labour process around the job ranking system inherited from the past.[28]

7.4 The impact of changes in the Italian labour movement on the organization of the labour process

The technical innovation that took place in the 1960s in the integrated steel plants brought out some of the contradictions implicit in the JA and JE system. At the same time, changes in the social context allowed workers to develop a critique of the division of labour based on the JA and JE system, and to start fighting against it.

In the large integrated plants, the impact of technical innovation was greater, as the standardization of output and economies of scale typical of these works allowed for higher levels of mechanization and the introduction of some forms of computer control. First, the steady increase in productivity due to technical innovation led, on the one hand, to continuous attempts by management to readjust incentives to coincide with what they saw as 'objective efficiency criteria', and, on the other hand, to trade union opposition to the system of incentives in use, as the unions became aware that all the factors determining piece rates were directly decided by management (the features of the equipment, their production plans, and manpower requirements) (Cai, 1976, pp. 40–1). Secondly, technical change progressively modified the division of labour, eliminating some tasks, creating new ones, and modifying the skill content of jobs; this necessarily called for modifications in the evaluation system. Because, however, of the principles on which it was based, the JA and JE system turned out to be very rigid, so that the modifications required by technical change were introduced only with great difficulty. Finally, as increased automation brought with it a progressive deskilling of labour, in terms of the traditional skills, different qualifications were required and the concept of skill itself, as perceived by the workers, began to change.

Meanwhile, in the scrap-based steel plants, the mechanization of the rolling mills and the modernization of the electric furnaces had been set in train. But given the different technological features of the scrap-based plant, the process of mechanization was less advanced, and technical changes were easily and smoothly absorbed.

7.4.1 Changes in the Italian labour movement

The intense labour conflicts which developed from 1967 onwards, with the emergence of labour organization at the workplace and the rapid spread of plant bargaining, changed the pattern of the industrial relations system. The struggles of this period overturned the power relations within the factories, and succeeded in bringing some constraints to bear on the discretionary power of management, thereby reducing flexibility in the use of labour. The acknowledgement of workers' rights[29] and the establishment of trade union organization within the factories (through the development of new plant-level structures—shop delegates, factory councils, and general factory meetings) gave rise to a process of decentralization of decision-making and negotiating activity that changed the prevailing pattern of industrial relations. Particularly, the right to negotiate at the workplace (no longer regulated by general centralized agreements) profoundly changed power relations within the factories, giving the trade union movement considerable control over the organization of the labour process.

The intense labour conflicts which began to develop in the factories from 1967 onwards gave rise to the emergence of a plethora of new demands from the rank-and-file: generalized upgrading, flat wage increases, abolition of strict limitation of incentives and piece-work system, reduction of the pace of work and the workload, complete refusal to accept dangerous and risky jobs in return for money, refusal or limitation of overtime, and finally, reduction in working hours. These demands, for the most part the spontaneous result of the needs of certain groups of workers, were not part of the unions' overall strategy. In fact, they stood in marked contrast to the tradition of trade union bargaining, which tied wages to skill level (i.e. to professional qualifications) and to the growth of productivity. The trade unions faced the problem of developing a policy that could link different rank-and-file demands into a more general and non-sectional strategy. The unions translated these demands into an overall, long-term strategy centring on two issues: equality and control over the organization of production. The demands for greater equality, identified as a sign of the crisis of the prevailing system of classification, and the demands for greater control over work organization, identified as a critique of the traditional system of the organization of production (based on a division of labour unilaterally imposed by management), were reflected in a variety of solutions within the factories. Gradually, new common ground emerged from the initially differing positions, with the union proposal of the so-called *Inquadramento Unico* (IU)—a single grading scale for manual workers, foremen and non-manual workers. The new classification system integrated the wage structure of the three categories of employees; it reduced the number of grades; it reduced wage differentials between the highest and lowest grades; and, finally, it introduced some dynamics with respect to the problem of career and qualifications.

The IU was first introduced at Italsider, in 1970, after a very long and hard struggle started at the Cornigliano works to replace the JA and JE system, which had been in use since 1960 and was highly criticized, particularly by the less skilled workers. But the idea of the new scale developed at Italsider rapidly became an arena of common debate in the Italian trade union movement, and the IU began to be negotiated in other steel enterprises, including Dalmine and Breda, and in other industrial sectors. From 1973 onwards it was introduced in all major national collective agreements, starting with the metal sector.

Intense bargaining activity, at plant and shop-floor level, followed the introduction of the new classification. Struggles around the IU became battles for the control of the organization of production. And, as a result of the bargaining activity that followed, the workers increased their control over a large number of issues.

7.4.2 Changes in the steel industry

The idea of the IU was first developed by trade union officials at Italsider in 1970, following the campaign mounted by the workers to do away with the JA and JE system. The system was heavily criticized for its pseudo-objectivity: the workers saw it as a way of artificially dividing workers and immobilizing them in 54 classes (Lettieri, 1971, p. 114; Coppola, 1971, p. 257). They criticized the career structure implicit in the system itself, since it was only for a small number of workers that the idea of a career had a real meaning. In fact, over 60 per cent of manual workers were graded in the ten lowest classes, out of 24, and less than two per cent in the seven highest classes (Pesce, 1970, p. 5; Torneo, 1970, p. 254). Finally, the system was criticized for its rigidity in terms of wage negotiations: it did not allow for the upgrading of workers in the less skilled jobs, in spite of the fact that this was happening in all the major enterprises at that time. With its fixed criteria on the basis of which each job post was analysed and evaluated with respect to the others, the system prevented wage demands from serving as a rallying point for any large group of workers, since each demand had to be justified on the grounds of specific job conditions, and these differed between the various sections of the labour force (Cai, 1976, p. 39).

The proposed new system was intended to express the ideas and the demands of the workers. Its explicit aim was to unify the pressure generated by different groups, by amalgamating the wage rates (previously organized in three completely separate wage structures) and reducing existing differentials (both in wages and in employment conditions). The new classification was a way of grouping all employees in a very small number of categories, based on professional qualifications and work experience. At the same time it introduced a new dynamic, in direct conflict with the JA and JE, which was related directly to the workers' personal experience. The central idea on which the new system was based was the concept of *professionalità*, as it was explained by one of the leaders of the struggles at Italsider:[30]

> New professionalism means turning the principle of the job evaluation system upside down. The achievement of this new criterion is perceived by the workers as an overturning of the old practice of de-skilling, as a collective fact that helps to unify the workers, to assure mobility outside the cages created by the job evaluation. The new professionalism, moreover, takes as its point of reference, in broad terms, the capacity to work: capacity to know the production cycle and to intervene in it. In this sense, the new professionalism is identified as a collective fact, and it tends towards homogeneity, even if this homogeneity is not immediate, but is realized through the development of experience that springs from a concrete socialization of work. (Lettieri, 1971, pp. 115–16.)

The general strategy underlying this concept of a new professionalism was quite radical, and the struggles for the IU soon became a battle for control over the organization of production, decisively shaped by intellectual and overtly ideological influences:

> A new classification policy cannot, however, be limited solely to the question of wages. It must be integrated into the general strategy that aims to extend the scope of social control by the workers over the conditions of work . . . . Fundamentally, the problem of classification is the problem of the organization of work . . . . This situation is not a technical necessity. It is open to collective transformation. That is why the problem cannot be reduced to a demand for a 'fair' system of classification . . . . It is the transformation of the organization of work that workers must insist on, their potential abilities which in fact they will never be allowed to bring into play at work. (Lettieri, 1970, pp. 148–9.)

The idea originally underlying trade union strategy at Italsider was based on a critique of the existing division of labour, unilaterally imposed by management, and was orientated towards the development of a different division of labour. To this end, the unions pursued two different but parallel approaches. As well as attempting to control the production process by imposing a series of constraints on the organization of production, which resulted in a system of formalized guarantees preventing any unilateral decision on important issues, the unions began to work in the somewhat ambiguous direction of an alternative and different type of division of labour. The starting point for the latter approach was the concept of the new professionalism. The impact of the changes introduced through plant and shop-floor bargaining was profound and far-reaching. But the results achieved were contradictory, with respect to the initial ideas and purposes.[31] The next section will discuss the main changes that occurred in the organization of the labour process in the steel industry after the introduction of the IU.

7.4.3 Changes in the organization of the labour process in the steel industry

(i) *The division of labour*. The final agreements on the implementation of the new classification system (see Chapter 4, note 2, did not produce substantial changes in the division of labour. Both process and maintenance workers continued to perform the same jobs they were performing before, albeit with real differences in their classification and payment, so that the wage structure became very flat and many differences were abolished. The production process was still organized in terms of the definition of job posts that needed to be filled, and process workers were still supposed to move between posts, when required. The new classification system called for a reclassification of all manual job posts, within each shop-floor, from the previous 1–24 classes of the JA and JE, at Italsider, and the large number of *paghe di posto* of the other steel factories, to the 1–5 levels of the IU, with the result that very different jobs could now be classified at the same level. Wages were still related to the job posts process workers filled, with the difference that now workers acquired the right to a higher grade after a certain number of rotations and replacements, though continuing to be employed in a job classified at a lower grade. For maintenance workers the IU implied their grading according to their level of qualification. And since technical innovation had led to more complex equipment, both the number of maintenance workers and the significance of their role had increased; as a result, they tended to be better graded than process workers.

(ii) *The classification system and the grading structure*. After the settlement of the Italsider agreement, on 26 May 1972, and of agreements in the following couple of years in the other steel enterprises, a quite complex process of classification was carried out. The workers had to define, through a process of collective discussion, their own scale of classification for each shop-floor, on the basis of what had been settled in the general agreement. This process involved all employees, and it took place first at the level of the work team and the workshop, and then at the factory level. But the discussion over the grading structure soon became a discussion over job posts and job tasks, with a tendency to continue to evaluate the job rather than the worker, and therefore in conflict with the trade union policy itself. Difficulties and conflicts between process and maintenance workers, as well as among different groups of process workers, and between the trade union officials and the workers, started to appear when the new classification had to be implemented. The process of discussion ended, in many cases, with the re-emergence of sectional pressures, a weakening of working class unity, and a return to group claims.[32] In other words, the discussion among workers, instead of eliminating differences, produced a continuous process of comparison based on existing differences, and as a result destined to reestablish them. The new classification system was then introduced after a very long and diffuse bargaining process,[33] implying a direct confrontation not only between workers and management but between groups of workers as well, with the trade union officials in the position of mediating the conflict in an effort to devise some general strategy. The distribution of workers across the new grading structure was therefore the result of several different forces at work: the balance of forces between the many groups of workers, as well as between management and workers, management policy, and trade union policy within the factory. This explains the differences found in the distribution of workers throughout the grading structure, both between different steel plants and, within the same plant, between different departments (see Chapter 4, Table 4.5).

(iii) *The wage structure*. In the years that followed the introduction of the IU, the wage structure became flatter and flatter. All the differences that had existed with the previous systems—both job ranking and job evaluation—were eliminated, and wage differentials were widely reduced. A large number of wage elements previously related to individual and/or specific conditions (such as personal bonuses, premiums, individual incentives, and rewards for dangerous and heavy work) were abolished. Wages depended now by and large on the 'professional level' attributed to the workers employed in certain jobs. At the same time, as a result of automatic mechanisms introduced for the workers' 'professional development', the distribution of the labour force within the grading structure changed over time, emptying the lowest grades (1, 2, 3). That is, the acknowledgement of higher grades after a certain number of rotations and replacements, in recognition of increased qualifications expressed in terms of the ability to work and the experience acquired through temporary mobility on different jobs, allowed workers to be graded at a level higher than that attached to their jobs. Moreover, as a consequence of the struggles and the demands of single groups of workers, higher grades were granted through shop-floor collective bargaining. This process took place in the first years after the introduction of the IU. Demands for higher grades were advanced by several groups of workers, and this process tended to regenerate itself by imitation. A general tendency toward upgrading developed, replacing wage bargaining. Appendices D. 19, D. 20, D. 21, and D. 23 show the effect of this tendency upon the distribution of workers along the grading structure, for the four enterprises considered. Taking Breda as an example, while, in 1972, over 67 per cent manual workers were classified in the three lowest grades, these grades were progressively emptied, so that, by the end of 1979, they accounted for only 29 per cent.[34] The result of this tendency, given the upper limit for the grading of manual workers established at the fith level, was a very flat wage structure. In most of the large steel enterprises, the grade 1 level is never used; grades 2 and 3 are entry levels for process workers and maintenance workers, respectively; blue-collar workers are, by and large, concentrated in two grades only: 4 and 5 (see Chapter 4, Table 4.1).

(iv) *Mobility, skill, career*. As has already been said, agreements on the IU reversed the criteria for classification: it was the worker and not the job that had to be graded. And the basic concept for workers' grading was their *professionalità*. Moreover, this system was supposed to introduce some devices to account for the development of individual professional abilities, and this modified quite drastically the upgrading system in use for process workers. The mechanisms introduced through collective bargaining (job rotations, job enrichment, job enlargement, training and re-training) were supposed both to increase individual abilities and to take better account of them. Therefore, criteria for upgrading were associated with such mechanisms. The general agreements, at the enterprise level, determined the basic rules for upgrading by establishing, for example, the minimum length of service, the number of rotations, and the number of days of replacement required to get to a higher level. Decentralized bargaining, by plant and by shop-floor, singled out the different solutions for each department. The outcome of this decentralized bargaining activity was a large number of minute agreements, defining detailed career patterns for all sections of the steel factory, and for all jobs. This implied: (*a*) the definition of mobility paths, within each subsection of the production process, in terms of the jobs to which a worker, hired and allocated to a certain position, is supposed to move, both vertically and horizontally; (*b*) the definition of the rewards of that mobility, in terms of the acknowledgement of a higher grade after a specified number of rotations and replacements; (*c*) the definition of criteria for a permanent move to a higher graded job.

To conclude, mobility, skill, and career were still interrelated, as they had been previously. But collective bargaining limited the almost absolute discretionary power of the foremen over mobility and career by establishing procedures and criteria for promotions. As a result, the career process became *clearer and more certain*, because of the introduction of negotiated criteria and procedures for the regulation of career processes; *flatter*, because of the reduced number of grades and therefore the flattening of the hierarchical structure within each team; and finally, *quicker*, because of the automatic mechanisms introduced, and because upgrading was no longer restricted by the availability of vacancies. At the same time, career as such lost most of its original meaning, not only in terms of wage differentials, but also in terms of the worker's position within the hierarchical structure and the power relationship attached to that position.

(v) *Hierarchical structure*. The extensive and well-defined hierarchical structure inherited from the past, on the basis of which the whole labour process had been organized, became subject to substantial changes both in its pattern and in its function. Now that all job posts had been compressed into no more than three or four grades, the hierarchical structure was considerably simplified by the reduction in the number of grades and steps. Figure 7.1 shows the changes that occurred in the hierarchical structure for Cornigliano when the JE system was replaced by the IU.

Moreover, the role of the hierarchy, and particularly the role played by foremen and supervisors, was considerably reduced. The ligitimization of this role had previously been based on a detailed division of labour, expressed in terms of a precise separation of tasks, knowledge, and responsibilities, and thus based on the authority granted to the hierarchy from such an organizational structure. The hierarchy and the authority associated with it were accepted by the workers as they accepted the career structure, the promotion system associated with it, and the right of the foreman to choose. The introduction and spread of automation, through the installation of process computers on real time in the process departments, partly reduced the role of the foremen: some of their role in controlling and coordinating the production process was incorporated into the new equipment. In fact, in

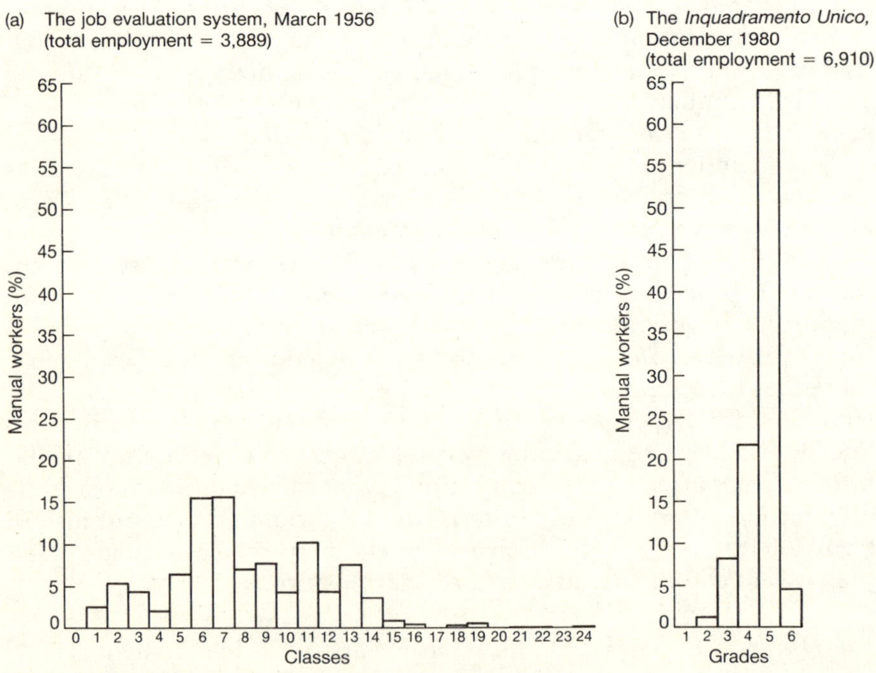

FIG. 7.1 Manual workers by classification grade at Italsider, Cornigliano works, in 1956 and 1980 (% distribution)

an emergency, or in cases where the control system run by the computer was in error, the workers now preferred to ask for the intervention of the computer technicians rather than for the decision of the foreman (*Collettivo Tecnici Italsider*, 1979, p. 38). This change in technology occurred at the same time as the struggles of 1968–73, rejecting the foreman's authority. The foreman's power in terms of decision over workers' careers, mobility, promotion, and downgrading, as well as disciplinary actions (fines, suspensions, dismissals), was restricted by a number of factors: (*a*) the replacement of their discretionary power with clear rules and procedures negotiated with management, and (*b*) the replacement of their discretionary power with decentralized bargaining between shop-floor delegates, on the one hand, and managers responsible for labour relations, on the other.[35]

7.5 Problems of rigidity and the need for flexibility

The changes imposed by this new level of labour organization upon the labour market structure raised major problems for management, and its responses to this challenge have been quite varied, though some similarities are found. The innovations in the division of labour, introduced at Italsider, represent the most advanced answer, on the management side, to the workers' challenge. This section discusses the problems management had to face, the different solutions advanced—particularly the innovations introduced at Italsider—and finally, the effects of those solutions upon the labour process.

7.5.1 The problems

As a result of the bargaining activity that took place in the early 1970s, orientated toward the control of the labour process and the limitation of management's discretionary power, managers faced three main problems.

(i) *Higher labour costs*. The replacement of the previous systems with the IU resulted in a general upgrading of the labour force. This was the combined result of the different criteria used to classify workers and of the processes introduced to guarantee them some 'professional development' (i.e. job rotation, job enrichment, and job enlargement). Given the widespread use of internal mobility, typical of the steel industry, the acknowledgement of these processes as indicators of the acquisition of a certain level of qualifications, and as a basis on which to award higher grades, produced a general tendency towards upgrading (with a limit of grade 5 for manual workers) and an upward flattening of the wage structure.

Upgrading was a general tendency of the 1970s, but it is particularly noticeable in the steel industry. Appendix D. 18 compares the grading structure of five large steel enterprises with a sample of large engineering enterprises. Despite the differences, all steel enterprises show a much higher concentration of workers in the two highest grades (4 and 5). This, of course, produced higher labour costs per head, and therefore higher total labour costs.

Moreover, with the new classification, there was no longer a stable relationship between the job performed and the worker's grade, since this depended not only on the job post filled, but on his own experience. Thus, management could no longer control productivity and labour costs through control of the division of labour. This was quite clearly perceived by the Italsider management:[36]

> The relationship between skill/division of labour/productivity, which in the past was assured by the stable relationship between the classification system and the rewards, represented by the job evaluation and the analytical incentive system in use, has become now quite critical. (Fantoli, 1980, p. 201.)

(ii) *Rigidities in the employment of labour.* The idea underlying the struggles of the late 1960s was that the organization of production, at the factory level, was the expression of a power relationship between management and workers, and that as a result everything was open to negotiation. The intense and widespread bargaining activity that followed imposed a system of control over a large number of issues, such as the classification system, grading structure, wages policy, internal mobility, upgrading and promotions, overtime, pace of work, workload, and resting times. This in turn produced a new series of rigidities in the use of labour.

As far as mobility in particular was concerned, the bargaining activity which followed the introduction of the new classification system changed its procedures quite considerably. The new link between mobility and upgrading produced a contradictory situation. On the one hand was the workers' demand for higher internal mobility, as it is here expressed by a foreman and a worker:

> suddenly, everybody wanted to rotate and we have been accused of not producing opportunities for professional development. . . . (foreman)

> the oldest workers act as a brake on us; if they don't rotate, they restrict our career prospects: the foreman should give us other ways out. . . . (worker) (Segatori and Torresini, 1979, p. 45.)

On the other hand, these new attitudes sometimes produced an impasse, where workers were not willing to move, to rotate, or to replace a fellow worker, when required, if this did not count towards or result in a higher grade:

> workers rotate only to get the grade, not to learn (foreman)
>
> if I have the fifth grade, why should I work in job posts with less professional content? (worker) (Segatori and Torresini, 1979, p. 45.)

This situation was quite general to all enterprises examined, but the problem was far more acute where the workings of the IU did not leave any space for manoeuvre, either on the management or on the trade union side. And this was the case at Italsider and Dalmine, where the upgrading process was very far advanced, with over 89.1 and 87.9 per cent of workers respectively classified in the highest grades, in 1977 (Appendix D. 18).

(iii) *Inefficiency*. The traditional management techniques for the organization of the labour process were based on a complex and informal system of meritocratic premiums and punishments, and were assigned in a discretionary fashion through the hierarchical structure. On this basis, management was able to assure the collaboration of the labour force. All mechanisms for the organization of the internal labour market (on-the-job training, mobility, replacements, rewards for loyalty and responsible behaviour, promotions, and upgrading) were related to the idea of career advancement. The idea of career lost much of its original meaning with the changes introduced via the IU and its automatic mechanisms. At the same time, the hierarchy at the workplace lost control over career processes. All this rendered inefficient and worthless what was left of the traditional techniques: (*a*) a detailed division of labour; (*b*) the organization of the production process into a large number of jobs, positions, and grades; finally, (*c*) a hierarchical structure emptied of its previous role.[37]

7.5.2 The possible solutions

The problem of rigidity imposed by the increased power of the workers at the workplace was perceived from the very beginning by the entrepreneurs. The responses have been quite varied, but it is possible to single out two main solutions in the steel industry.

In some industrial sectors, the enterprises have regained flexibility by subcontracting to smaller firms, where in general unions are weaker.[38] But, given the characteristics of the technology in use (continuous and integrated process), and the economies of scale typical of the steel industry, decentralization was not a feasible solution. Instead, some steel enterprises tried to minimize the impact of workers' demands, adopting a sort of 'defensive policy', in which mobility, promotions, and grades were still used to organize the labour process. This seems to be clearly the case for AFL Falck and Breda Siderurgica, where the distribution of the labour force along the grading structure is far less concentrated and, particularly, the upward flattening process is not yet as marked as in the other steel companies (see Chapter 4, Table 4.1). On the other hand, the policy pursued by other steel companies, such as Italsider and Dalmine, has been quite different: they tried to anticipate new solutions in terms of the division of labour and the organization of the labour process in general. In this way, the initiative was taken by employers as a way of reaffirming their prestige and position[39] over the issue of the organization of the labour process.

As management did not have an alternative model of work organization, research projects and experimentation were started from the very beginning. At Italsider some innovations were introduced in specific areas and in a few plants, after 1972, in order to single out possible solutions. Experiments continued in a large number of plants, but always carried out in small and well-delimited areas of the production process.[40] In 1978, a company agreement was made to carry out new forms of work organization, plant by plant and department by department, outlining the main criteria and principles on the basis of which innovations should be introduced. Other public sector steel companies (Dalmine, Terni) have carried out similar experiments in work organization, introducing innovations gradually and then generalizing them through plant collective bargaining. Both the content of the agreements and the tendencies in work organization are quite similar among steel firms: they all focus upon the utilization of work groups. In this respect, it is important to say that the changes introduced into the steel factories are quite distinct from those introduced in other enterprises over the same period: the steel industry was the first to introduce experimentation, reacting directly to the challenge of the trade union movement; also, the diffusion of research and experimental activity was much wider than in any other sector;[41] further, the results of the innovations had a real impact upon the division of labour and the organization of the labour process;[42] finally, the innovations introduced, based on the diffusion of work groups, were not a complete novelty, since some forms of collective work had always operated, though in an informal way.[43]

7.5.3 The work group

Research activities and experimentation on work organization were carried out in the public sector steel industry in the 1970s with the aim of singling out possible ways of re-planning the division of labour.

Despite the large differences in the methodology adopted, all the projects are quite homogeneous in their underlying ideas, with a common trend, typical of the steel industry, towards the use of work groups. The re-planning of work organization, based on work groups, has two implications: one *technical* and one *social*, the first referring to the *installations*, the second to the *workers* there employed. Installations and workers are considered as a whole, in their interaction, giving rise to the so-called 'Operative Unit' (OU), and this has a technical and a social implication. The technical implication refers to the fact that the OU only refers to complete sections of the production cycle; within each section the work group is responsible for all the functions of analysis, control, and regulation of the process and the output, including also some maintenance work, emergency interventions, service activities, care of equipment, and so on. Thus, the OU should be technically autonomous, with no external technical interference in the management of the process of that specific segment of the production cycle. The social implication refers to the fact that the operative unit is responsible for the organization of the labour process within it. That is, the distribution of jobs, tasks and operations, shifts and planned absences from work, holidays, training and on-the-job training, and so on are all delegated to the work group as a whole.

All the interventions and experiments around work organization put forward by Italsider and other steel enterprises in the 1970s were without doubt induced by the problems posed by the increased rigidity of labour both for the production process and for the management of the labour force itself.[44] It was, therefore, necessary to find new forms of work organization that would permit a form of control over the production process no longer based on an individual and capillary control of the labour force. The management needed a form of control of the labour process based on the workers' consent, and therefore in line with the demands advanced by the workers' struggles. At the same time, Italsider was facing a critical situation both financially and in terms of its position in the product market.[45] Therefore, there was an urgent need to regain technical and economic efficiency. And the innovations introduced in work organization through collective bargaining were, in the first instance, motivated by the need to recover and/or improve efficiency and productivity and to develop a better use of workers' qualifications (experience, knowledge, capacity to learn).[46] Thus, the main and explicit target for management, pursued through the innovations introduced, was the improvement of production, both in quantitative and qualitative terms.

This was not something new, and it could not have been otherwise: it is the usual aim of management. What *was* new was the way in which this aim was pursued. More precisely, what changed is indicated in the relationship between 'control' and 'output', for the realization of profits. Control is no longer exercised through a detailed and diffuse system of directives and supervision over the labour process—based on a very detailed division of labour and on an individual hierarchical form of control through foremen and supervisors. With the changes introduced through the new classification, such a system has become useless, costly, and difficult to implement, given the changes in the social relations within the factory (Del Lungo, 1976, pp. 250–3). In this context, the redesign of work organization around the idea of the operative unit is intended to regain economic and technical efficiency through a more general and global system of control, more directly related to output.

The solution itself—that is, the operative unit which is relatively autonomous for the organization of the labour process but acts within a well-defined segment of the production cycle—is suggested by the technology, and it is made possible, or easier, by the recent technical innovations introduced. The fact that the production process is continuous and organized in integrated but distinguished stages, where each stage is assigned to small groups of workers, would seem to suggest the possibility of some form of collective work. Moreoever, the empirical work done on the division of labour in the steel industry (D'Andrea, 1976; Butera, 1979) has noted that, in fact, despite the precise division of labour within each team, and the definition of tasks and operations for each single job post, a tendency to transcend this strict division of labour was already in existence: a large degree of cooperation and understanding, mutual assistance, and interchangeability between jobs were already employed by process workers, producing—informally—some forms of 'autoregulated cooperation'. As a result, the new form of organization, based on work groups, has incorporated, expanded, and formalized some of the concepts and ideas already established. The existence of forms of cooperation within the teams has made it easier to overcome a strict division of labour, and this helps to explain the development and the diffusion of forms of work organization based on work groups in the steel industry.

At the same time, technical changes introduced in the 1970s, and particularly the employment of process computers on real time[47] in the main process departments, have made possible and facilitated the shift from the old form of work organization to the new one. The mechanization and the partial automation introduced into the production process have reduced considerably the direct intervention of manual labour, compared with the postwar situation. The production flow is tied to the time required by the installations to complete the processes of chemical/physical transformation. It cannot, therefore, be speeded up or slowed down, as in the past, by the pace of work imposed by thc team employed there. Nevertheless, the intervention of the team is still crucial in assuring that all operations are properly executed, and that they are on time, so as to allow for a regular flow of production. The main problem for management, in the organization of the production process, is therefore related to the achievement of a regular flow of production. With the previous system of work organization, based on a detailed division of labour, a hierarchical structure, and an internal labour market structure linking mobility, training, promotions, and careers, workers were induced to conform with a certain type of behaviour in order to assure a regular flow of production. The struggles of the late 1960s, and the bargaining activity which followed, rejected that system and imposed several constraints on it. As a result, the division of labour which had given rise to many separate jobs survived, and with it some part of the hierarchy (foremen and supervisors), though these had little control over the labour process. There was, therefore, a contradiction between the formal system of control and the actual mechanism of control itself. The diffusion of process computers in all the main stages of the production process, and the automatic control of production in all its variables effected through them, suggested the solution. The idea was that the role previously played by the hierarchical structure within the labour process could be played by technology itself, mainly through the diffusion of process computers. In this respect it is interesting to turn to the speech given by Mr Sette, president of Italsider at that time, and therefore immediately after the introduction of the new classification system, when entrepreneurs started to consider possible responses to the workers' challenge:

> . . . in an integrated steel plant, where coal and iron ore are shipped, discharged, and treated by sintering, the coke plant transforms coal for the blast furnaces which produce pig-iron, that is refined into steel, that is then rolled, giving finished products: in a production process of this type, I would say that the possibility that output is produced regularly and integrally is given by the cycle and production flow. . . . In such a productive organization capital could regain control, from the point of view of production, could recover what will be lost in terms of individual piece-work through an organization of the production flow more correct and more precise, more timed, more controlled, more synchronized . . . And today, one of the elements that can make this possible in a more rational way is the introduction . . . of data management computers and process computers on all installations. Once the production flow has been determined and organized in a certain way, the computer can assure the time optimization of the production flow:

the computer with its terminals can reach the departments and determine, fix, clock the times and the methods that optimize, and reduce the time losses for the whole production flow from the store of raw materials and semi-finished products, to the store of the finished products and forwarding. (Sette, 1973, p. 233.)[48]

7.5.4 Effects on the labour process

I will briefly discuss the main effects of the innovations introduced through work groups upon the labour process, on the basis of the preliminary experimentation at Italsider Cornigliano, after 1978.[49]

(i) *The division of labour*. The workers in a defined and complete segment of the production cycle (such as, for the steel-making department, raw materials, the converter, anti-pollution, and auxiliary installations) are collectively responsible for its management. That is, within it, the operative unit overcomes the logic of the division of labour into individual jobs. Within the work group, *the whole group of workers and activities* are 'taken back to a unity' from two aggregative factors: targets and operative autonomy.

The OU targets are negotiated at the department level, and they refer to production, safety, and workers' qualifications. The crucial target is the productive one, and this is agreed as the concrete and measurable result of a complete segment of the production cycle, involving the work of the whole operative unit. For example, for the converter operative unit the productive target is defined in terms of tons of liquid steel produced in a defined period of time.

The OU operative autonomy refers to the group's freedom to allocate the work activities given to it, in order to achieve predetermined targets. With respect to the organizational superstructure, this implies non-interference; with respect to the work group itself, it implies the distribution of tasks and operations among the members of the OU. And all this implies, in turn, cooperation between workers and interchangeability between posts.

To conclude, plant collective agreements determine and specify by department (*a*) the production targets (both in quantitative and qualitative terms), (*b*) the activities that have to be performed by the operative unit, as a whole, (*c*) the working conditions, and (*d*) the manning requirements, per OU and per shift. Then, the group of workers within each OU is responsible for the management of that section of the production cycle. Therefore, within that segment of the cycle the workers have complete autonomy over all issues related to the division of labour, mobility, vacancies, shifts, holidays, training, and so on.

(ii) *The division of labour, skill, mobility.* With the overcoming of the division of labour based on detailed individual positions and jobs, the concept of skill itself can no longer be related to the individual worker. Instead, it becomes more like a collective concept, related to the totality of the technical requirements of that part of the production process under the control of the work group. As a result, the idea of mobility (i.e. shifts, rotation, and even promotion from one single job to another) becomes obsolete as well. Within the single work group there are no differences between the workers with respect to the posts: they are all defined simply with reference to the OU within which they are employed: *operatori* (operators).

(iii) *Grading system and structure.* Differentiated activities and posts are still defined and outlined within each OU, but this definition of the work performed by the OU is not reflected in a distinction between separate individual jobs.Therefore, the distinction of jobs by grade disappears too. The same grade, the fifth (the highest for blue-collar workers), is granted to all workers within the same operative unit. Grades are used only with reference to training: the newly hired worker is graded at the third level. The work group itself is in charge of its on-the-job training, and within a limited period of time (precisely four-and-a-half years), the worker will be upgraded to the fifth level, that is, when his training process is completed. Now, the distribution of workers along the grading structure depends only on hirings and the training process (Carlini, 1981). Moreover, within each OU the agreements have singled out the possibility of grading some workers at a higher level, the sixth, previously precluded for manual workers. But this is only available for a limited number of cases within each OU. This possibility has been introduced where the activities of the unit itself call for a more experienced worker; it also allows the older and more skilled workers to get better treatment.

(iv) *Hierarchical structure and career.* The most remarkable result, if compared with the work organization system in use in the postwar period, is the vertical disintegration process within each work team, so that no hierarchical structure is left within the OU. The 'first operator', that is the worker graded at the sixth level, is distinguished from the other workers of the group by the fulfilment of some specific tasks and operations, usually involving higher responsibility and experience; but he plays no role in the coordination or control of the work group, since this is the task of the OU itself. The roles of foreman and supervisor disappear, and are replaced by a new hierarchical position: *assistente.* This is a white-collar position, with the specific functions of planning, coordinating and controlling the productive results of the OU. The *assistente* is therefore responsible for the correct conduct of the process, and his functions of control are related to the technology in use and its correct management, and not to the labour process. Career is meaningless, as far as manual workers are concerned: the acquisition of grades is simply a matter of training and time, and is collectively negotiated. The possibility of having a career would remain only if promotion to a white-collar position were possible, but a clear distinction between blue-collar and white-collar jobs still holds.

(v) *Wage system and wage structure*. Wages are basically related to grades: therefore the wage structure is almost completely flat within the group. But differences are possible between work groups, since the 1981 agreement has introduced a bonus system related to the achievement of productive targets, and this is settled in the shop-floor agreements.

(vi) *Flexibility*. With the work organization based on the OU, all the problems of worker flexibility, with respect to the needs of the production process, are completely shifted onto the group itself. Training, mobility, replacements, vacancies, the division of labour, holidays, overtime, everything is decided by the work group. On the one hand, this seems to reflect a positive judgement on the new work organization system, particularly with reference to the original demands advanced in the early struggles. It overcomes the idea of individual skill[50] and it gives autonomy to the workers, in the sense of real determination of the distribution of tasks and jobs. At the same time, it can be looked at more criticially.[51] The new form of work organization overcomes the problem of rigidity, particularly with respect to the problem of internal mobility. This is no longer imposed, but autonomously determined within the OU by the workers themselves. In other words, what is left in the workers' hands is the management of their own internal mobility between posts, tasks, roles, and functions—which means, in turn, delegating to the workers the responsibility for their own flexibility. The separation between control and execution still holds: this is also formalized by keeping the distinction between manual and non-manual workers, technicians and workers, and it is made possible by technical changes.[52]

7.6 Conclusions

The rapid diffusion of workers' representatives at the factory level, the process of trade union decentralization, and the diffusion of plant and shop-floor bargaining have had a particular influence on the labour process in two ways. First, the changes introduced imposed a system of control, either unilaterally or through negotiations, over the various aspects of the labour process, while in the past managers' power was both extremely extensive and discretionary. This allowed, for the first time, workers' direct control over the organization of production, thus representing a drastic change of direction. Secondly, the intense labour conflicts which developed from 1967 onwards, and the decentralized negotiations which followed, were concerned with a highly innovative array of issues, with respect to traditional trade union bargaining policy. The focus of contention became the organization of the labour process itself, thus shifting the arena of the class struggle, and increasingly imposing limits and constraints on management's prerogative in the organization of the labour process.

Workers began to claim that everything could be negotiated, since everything was the outcome of power relationships. In the early 1970s, workers' power was extremely high within the steel factories; and workers succeeded in increasing wages, in increasing control over the labour process, and in reversing some of the mechanisms in use for the organization of the labour process. The outcome of the struggles was not only higher labour costs and a drastic reduction in management discretionary power, but also the fact that discipline, supervision, hierarchical structure, the relationship between mobility/skill/career, and the other processes used to organize the labour process became redundant, since they could not, as before, be used to push for greater effort, that is, for increased output through increased labour input. Thus, workers' actions rendered inefficient some traditional forms of organization: the old mechanisms could no longer reach the targets they were designed for, in the sense that they could not induce workers to follow a certain behavioural pattern within the factory.

But the result of trade union action has been, on the whole, more negative than positive. That is, it has served to obstruct the old system of the division of labour rather than suggest anything different, and this despite the ambitious original idea of overcoming the actual division of labour. Management has regained control of the labour process by introducing changes in the organization of work. It has regained flexibility within the labour process by switching from a very detailed division of labour, based on a minute system of control implemented through the hierarchical structure, to a form of work organization based on a global system of control. Here the work group is responsible for the organization of the labour process, and what is controlled are not the activities of the work group but the result of those activities. What is interesting to note is the fact that, even with this new system of work organization, what remains crucial is the distinction between control and execution. In fact, the new work organization introduced at Italsider is based on a very precise and clear distinction between the control structure and the executive structure, as clearly stated by management:

> The control structure is related to the coordination, planning, improvement, and control of the productive results through which the enterprise ensures that the whole range of executive activities are effectually and efficiently orientated toward the achievement of the targets planned. The executive structure is related to the whole range of activities orientated toward the realization of the targets planned. (Fantoli, 1980, p. 208.)

Notes

1. The development of the industry was the combined result of (*a*) the speculative intervention of certain powerful financial groups, headed by the banks (Confalonieri, 1976, Ch. 2, pp. 262–333) and indirectly supported by the central government, which guaranteed large defence contracts, and (*b*) various private initiatives, favoured by the technological developments in electro-metallurgy that made it possible to use scrap, instead of iron ore. The recession of the late 1920s had hit the sector heavily, and had put the banks involved with it in deep financial difficulties. As a result of a major bank salvage operation, a large number of equity shares of the major steel enterprises had passed from the banks into public hands, with the creation of IRI, in 1933, and FINSIDER, in 1937.
2. A national plan (*piano autarchico per la siderurgia*) for the reorganization and restructuring of the public sector steel industry was devised in the 1930s, but its fulfilment was interrupted by the war (Castronovo, 1978, pp. 166–71).
3. Productive capacity developed steadily over the period 1950–69, with an overall rate of growth that is second only to that of Japan (Cockerill, 1974, p. 9).
4. The doubling of the size of the Taranto works (the fourth integrated plant) increased the country's productive capacity in steel by about 12,000 thousand tons between the end of the 1960s and the mid-1970s.
5. The complexity of the operations, their automatic nature and integration, have made them well suited to computer control. For this reason the rolling mills were the first equipment to be automated when process computers on real time were introduced in the 1960s. See Filippi, 1972; Colatto, 1978; Belgrano, 1979.
6. The first blast-furnace installed in Italy at Portoferraio in 1902 had a diameter of 3 metres. The last blast-furnace installed at Taranto in 1970 has a diameter of over 10 metres (Nicodemi and Zoia, 1980, p. 9).

7. Total employment was estimated to be 70–80,000 units, in the immediate postwar period (Sinigaglia, 1948), and it is now estimated to be up to 146,520 units (ASSIDER, 1980); see Chapter 2, Figures 2.1 and 2.2.
8. There has been almost no work done on the labour history of the Italian steel industry. This section draws most of its information from the oral history available. This includes Vallini, 1957, collecting ten autobiographies of steel workers (pp. 9–25, 62–72, 89–113, 131–7, 145–70, 236–59, 269–76); Manzini, 1976, on the working life of a trade union activist employed at Falck Unione since 1937; Botta, 1978, based on fifteen interviews with retired steel workers from Ilva Novi, focusing on the period 1930–55; Crespi, 1979, containing nine autobiographies of steel workers at Falck and Breda (pp. 41–104, 119–80, 263–74); and Contini, 1980, based on a long interview with a retired steel worker employed at Ilva Piombino, focusing on the period 1935–60. Other relevant works are Broglia and Galbo, 1962; Cervetto, 1954; Ilardi, 1973; Leonardi, 1956.
9. Regalia *et al*., 1978, pp. 137–9; Beccalli Salvati, 1972, p. 199.
10. Members of the *Commissione Interna* were elected by all workers employed in a given plant from political lists of candidates, supported by the unions. On the many limitations of this body see Treu, 1971, Ch. 2; Regalia, 1978; Accornero, 1974.
11. See Pozzobon and Mari, 1978, pp. 115–25, and Neufeld, 1954, pp. 42–9, on the paternalistic policies of Falck.
12. These workshops were called 'confine departments' by the workers, as they were used mainly to prevent union activists moving around the plant.
13. On the experience of these temporary workers, see Vallini, 1957, pp. 93–4, 131–4, 158.
14. On the peasant origin of the labour force at Falck, see Pozzobon and Mari, 1978, pp. 132–9; for Breda, see *Dal Ferro all'Acciaio* (1967), pp. 192–4; and for Dalmine see Ancona *et al*. 1957.
15. According to the data of the *Ministero del Lavoro* (Appendix D. 50), in 1963 the total number of skilled workers employed in the steel industry was lower (12.9 per cent) than in manufacturing (17.0 per cent). Moreover, the total number of skilled workers was unevenly distributed, so that while 20 to 30 per cent of maintenance workers were skilled, the percentage was much lower among process workers (2 to 5 per cent). See Pozzobon and Mari, 1978, pp. 220–1, on the structure of the labour force by classification grade at Falck.
16. Behind this hierarchical structure, there also lay the need to prevent industrial accidents; a team discipline ruled by the oldest and most experienced worker facilitated the smooth management of the production process, and also made it possible to avoid the much tougher punishments of the department supervisor in cases, for example, where the casting of the steel was defective. The foreman was not excluded from the punishment, and it was therefore in his own interest to discipline his subordinates (Pozzobon and Mari, 1978, p. 136).

17. See Botta, 1978, pp. 380–3; Vallini, 1957, pp. 93, 147; Pozzobon and Mari, 1978, p. 136; Mantero, 1961.
18. Giugni (1964, pp. 18, 87, 98–9), in his analysis of the industrial relations system in the iron and steel industry, acknowledged a very high level of internal mobility.
19. The traditional classification system in use, the so-called *sistema delle qualifiche*—developed in the early part of this century from earlier classification systems based on trade—was the combined result of two major changes: the development of collective bargaining, and the development of the factory system. All trades were divided into skilled, semiskilled, and unskilled sectors (*operaio specializzato*, *operaio comune*, *manovale specializzato*, *manovale comune*).
20. A comparison of wage structure of job posts in three steel plants of the public enterprise, Ilva, showed a quite clear relation between the structure of wages by job post and the role of job posts in production. See Parenti, 1958, Part V, Tables V.2, V.3, V.4.
21. For instance, at Dalmine there were over 1,200 job wages for about 7,000 process workers, out of 12,000 employees in total.
22. In 1960, Cornigliano SpA and Ilva, the two largest public sector steel enterprises, merged into a new corporation, Italsider. This included ten steel plants, five of which were integrated, employing over 30,000 employees (see De Rosa, 1978, pp. 269–72; Castronovo, 1980, pp. 290–4).
23. The principle was the same, while the factors of evaluation and their weight were different (Bonel, 1967, p. 201). Given the changes in technology, what was required was not to induce workers to work harder, but to assure a regular flow of production, given the increased mechanization of the works. This explains the importance given to factors of responsibility and the small role played by piece-work.
24. See the interview with a technician of the Cornigliano works, in Botta, 1981, pp. 107–10.
25. See Botta, 1981, pp. 78–91, and his interview (p. 120) with the secretary of FIOM at Sestri Ponente between 1951 and 1957.
26. An agreement (9.12.60) was signed for the introduction of three separate systems: one for manual workers (30.4.61), one for foremen (6.6.62), and one for non-manual workers (9.5.63). They differed both in terms of the factors considered for evaluation and in the weight given to them. Blue-collar jobs were evaluated on the basis of 12 factors (previous experience, training, intellectual abilities, manual dexterity, responsibilities for goods, equipment, production process, and other workers' safety, mental and visual effort, working conditions, risks) and classified in 24 categories. For all employees there were, in all, 54 different categories.
27. The replacement of the job ranking system with the JA and JE system in the ex-Ilva steel factories was quite smooth and provoked no conflicts. This can be explained partly by the fact that—at least for process workers—the JA and JE represented a sort of rationalization of the existing job ranking system, and partly by the fact that the level of wages was

higher than with the old job ranking systems (Giugni, 1964, p. 87).

28. JA and JE systems have not received much attention in Italy. They represent a quite limited experiment within the overall Italian context (Broglia, 1962), with the most significant examples in the steel industry, at Italsider, and in the petro-chemical industry, at ENI.
29. The Act passed in 1970, known as the *Statuto dei Lavoratori*, was a workers's charter, establishing principles for the regulation of both industrial disputes and trade union organization within factories and workshops, as well as for the protection of workers' rights at the workplace. The charter was the direct result of the upheavals of 1968–9 (see Regalia *et al.*, 1978, p. 152).
30. Antonio Lettieri, a national union official of the FIOM CGIL, was responsible for drawing up the demands made by the rank-and-file.
31. This has been widely acknowledged by many authors (see for example Della Rocca, 1982, pp. 160–1; Chiaromonte *et al.*, 1982, pp. 15–8), and by the unions themselves. See on this the papers discussed at the Conference organized by IRES CGIL on 'The division of labour and collective bargaining', in *Quaderni di Rassegna Sindacale* (1982).
32. The tendency for conflict and group claims to arise has always been a characteristic of the steel industry. This was the case in the years immediately after the Liberation, when the trade union movement was strengthened by the political events; plant representative structures were being reorganized, and plant bargaining was taking place in several large factories in the north. Similarly, an upsurge of group and sectional conflicts arose when plant bargaining began again in the late 1960s. For an analysis of sectional conflicts in the 1940s, see Pozzobon and Mari, 1978, pp. 150–98. For the following period, see Abbatecola, 1975, for Dalmine; Carabelli, 1975, for AFL Falck; Beccalli, 1975, for Redaelli; and Vento, 1981, for Cornigliano Italsider.
33. This process has been relatively easy for all workers previously graded according to the *sistema delle qualifiche*, as it was necessary simply to reclassify the old grades into the new levels of classification; but it has been particularly complex in the case of process workers, involving the conversion of a system based on a job-by-job analysis into a new one based on the classification of workers into five grades only. This explains also why the introduction of the IU has been much more complex in the steel industry than in any other industrial sector.
34. This was not the direct result of trade union bargaining for upgrading, but the indirect result of their search for mechanisms (job rotation, job enrichment, job enlargement, replacement) that could guarantee the possibility of 'professional growth' for all workers. Workers continued to perform by and large the same jobs, and the mechanisms introduced to improve qualifications became an automatic upgrading process.
35. This has become very common for all decisions related to disciplinary action. See on this Veneto, 1974, pp. 102–5, 249–57.
36. Mr Fantoli is general personnel manager at Italsider.
37. This, too, was quite clearly perceived by management in the public

sector: 'In fact, the pattern of the division of labour in the steel industry is not only a direct outcome of the layout of the installations, but it is also an instrument to direct and manage the labour force. The division of labour into job tasks and the consequent system of classification—JA and JE—were in fact, above all, a direct derivation from the hierarchical and organizational structure of the enterprise, a method for managing careers and for the control of productivity, an industrial relations system functional to the type of stratification of skills prevailing in the labour market.' (Fantoli, 1980, p. 201.)

38. In fact, the role of the trade unions is quite important in understanding the recent developments in the area of small industry in Italy. See Brusco and Sabel, 1981; Sabel, 1982; Brusco, 1982.
39. See on this the document prepared by the participants of an experimentation group at Italsider, in Della Rocca, 1974.
40. On the experimentation with work organization in the public sector steel industry see Della Rocca, 1974; Micheli *et al.*, 1976; Del Lungo, 1976; Uccelli and Amatori, 1978; Butera, 1977; Fantoli, 1980.
41. Del Lungo (1976, pp. 245–51) made a survey of all the major changes that occurred in the Italian large enterprises in the public sector, up to 1976. Out of 24 observed cases of innovations introduced in work organization, 22 were found in steel plants.
42. In the 1970s, experimentation with new forms of work organization was carried out in several large enterprises, in many industrial sectors, but with few results, either in terms of their diffusion and relevance, or in terms of their impact upon the division of labour. For the most part, experimentation and research tended to be limited to a few large enterprises and, within them, to a very few experimental cases. Moreover, they mainly consisted of a sort of job design, orientated toward the recomposition of job tasks, but without real substantial changes in workers' qualifications and skill. This seems to suggest that, in a large number of cases, the research done and the innovations introduced were more like an attempt to recapture workers' consent, than a significant and positive change in the division of labour. On the research and the experimentation carried out on work organization in Italy in the last decade, see Del Lungo, 1976; Segatori and Torresini, 1979, pp. 85–106; Graziosi, 1979, pp. 129–54; Butera, 1980; Della Rocca, 1982, pp. 160–6.
43. The work done by D'Andrea (1976) and Butera (1979) at the Terni steel works pointed out how cooperation, understanding, and collective work is in fact an essential feature of the 'actual organization of the labour process', typical of the steel industry.
44. This point was quite clear to all parties involved; see Della Rocca, 1974, pp. 179–80; Fantoli, 1980, p. 201.
45. See *Ministero dell'Industria*, 1979; *Mondo Economico*, 1981, 18 March, p. 49.
46. Italsider agreement, 21.3.78, *Premessa*, point 2, and Part I, point 1.
47. For a discussion of the development of computerized planning and control systems for production at Italsider, see *Collettivo Tecnici Italsider*, 1979.
48. From the contribution given by Sette at the conference on 'Science

and the division of labour' organized by the *Istituto Gramsci* in Turin in 1973.

49. The company agreement of 1978 decided to experiment, through collective bargaining, with new forms of work organization for the achievement of better efficiency, increased productivity and development of workers' qualifications. On the basis of the experiments carried out since 1978, a new company agreement was settled in 1981, which decided on the extension (but not the generalization) of the 'operative unit' to all its steel plants. The effects of this last agreement were yet to be fully worked out, at the time of this case study.
50. This was, originally, the idea underlying the workers' demands for a new classification system. See Lettieri, 1970, 1971; Surrenti and Treu, 1971; Regalia *et al.*, 1978; Veneto, 1974.
51. For different evaluations of the 1981 Italsider agreement, see Carlini, 1981; Italia, 1981.
52. See Italsider agreement, July 1981.

CHAPTER EIGHT

The Dynamics of the Labour Market Structure in the Construction Industry

8.1 The evolution of the construction industry

The construction industry is characterized by the repetition over time of long and asymmetrical cyclical waves, of 15–20 years, distinguished by smooth growth and a sharp and deep decline. The Italian construction industry has experienced, over the last century, five major phases: three in the prewar and two in the postwar period, as shown in Figure 8.1. These long cyclical fluctuations tend to follow, in general, the economic development of the economy and, in particular, the processes of inurbation of the population. The 1875–97 phase followed the process of unification of the country; the 1897–1918 phase occurred with early industrialization and the rapid process of inurbation in the first decade of this century; the 1918–45 phase saw a rapid expansion of construction activity up to the beginning of the 1930s, as the result of a new process of inurbation that followed the first postwar period, and a period of instability and stagnation due, partly, to restrictions imposed by fascism on the use of inputs useful for military materials.

The two postwar phases are distinguished by their shorter cycle and their less marked instability, with respect to the previous period, but are still characterized by deep fluctuations by comparison with the rest of the economy.

The 'first phase', 1949–64, ws characterized in general by very rapid expansion, checked only by a brief downturn in 1956. The exceptional expansion of the construction industry in this period was encouraged, at first, by the reconstruction of the country and, in particular, by the reconstruction of the housing stock damaged by war bombing (over 25 per cent of housing was damaged) and by the very low level of construction activity in the prewar period (as shown in Figure 8.1), which had left an outstanding demand for new houses; and, in the following years, by the process of industrialization and urbanization. The rapid economic development of the period up to 1964 was centred on the 'northern triangle', and strengthened even further the dualism of the Italian economic structure: large migrations

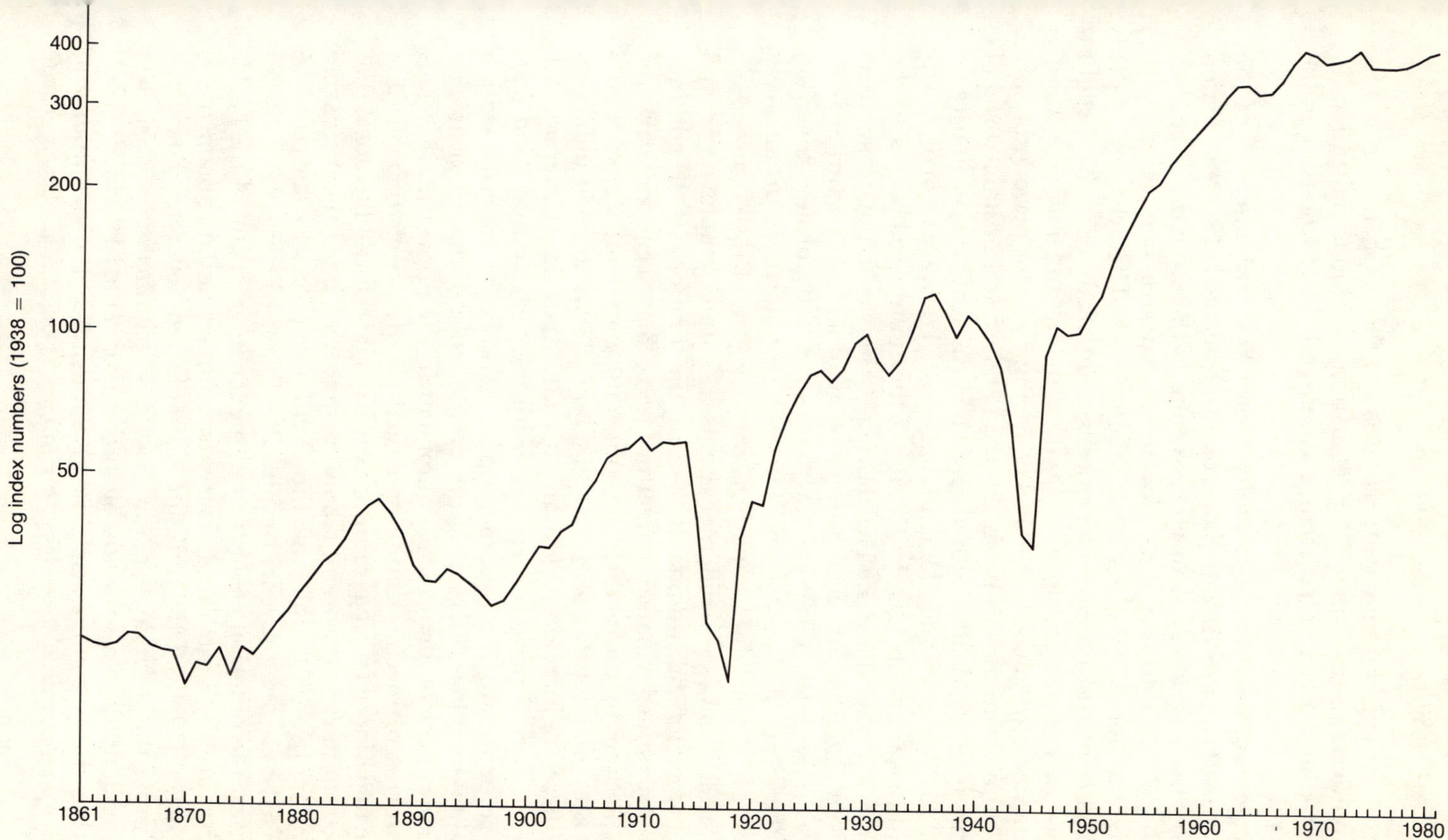

FIG. 8.1 Value added at constant factor costs in the construction industry, 1861–1981 (semi-log scale based on index numbers, 1938 = 100)

Source: ISTAT, *Annuario di contabilità nazionale*, 1982, Tables 12, 74.

from the agricultural and southern areas to the northern and industrial communities took place. Urbanization and industrialization, in turn, produced a large increase in the demand for new housing in the developing urban areas.

The general recession of the mid–1960s, however, interrupted the rapid growth of the Italian economy, and affected the construction industry more seriously than other sectors of the economy. The 'second phase', 1964–81, saw a very low level of construction activity with wide fluctuations around its trend (Figure 8.2). This was due to the low level of construction in new houses, only partly offset by a slight increase in general construction and in repair and modernization. Demand for construction has been changing over this period not only in magnitude but also in its structure. The low and unstable level of demand has drastically limited the construction of new houses in the urban districts and demand has shifted towards small towns and tourist areas, that is, from the northern/industrial areas to the southern/peripheral areas.[1] The shortage of houses in the urban areas has given rise to an upsurge in improvement and restructuring,[2] but this has only partly offset the low level of activity in new construction, therefore making the downturn in the northern/urban areas remarkably deeper, by comparison with the rest of the country.

Figure 8.2 shows the different trends in output, employment, and capital stock for the two phases. During the 'first phase' the continuous and sustained expansion in output (+ 8.23 per cent per year) was made possible by an increase in both total employment and capital stock. Employment rose from 1,108 million in 1951 to 2,157 million in 1964, therefore increasing substantially but at a smaller average rate of growth (+6.23 per cent per year) with respect to output, and with great responses to changes in output. A process of mechanization started taking place, increasing the capital stock of the sector, from a situation of lack of almost any equipment in the prewar period. This first process of mechanization consisted in the acquisition of quite simple machinery (such as cranes, exavators, and fork-lift trucks) that reduced, in part, the work of labourers, and contained the increasing demand for labour. At the same time, reinforced concrete started to be employed to a large extent. Despite the delay, with respect to other countries, the diffusion of this technique for the erection of the building structure was quite rapid. The extraordinary building boom of the 'first phase' favoured the diffusion of reinforced concrete and, at the same time, this technique made possible a significant expansion in building activity in a situation of shortage of skilled labour.

During the 'second phase', the relationship between output and employment is much less clear: output increased at a very low rate

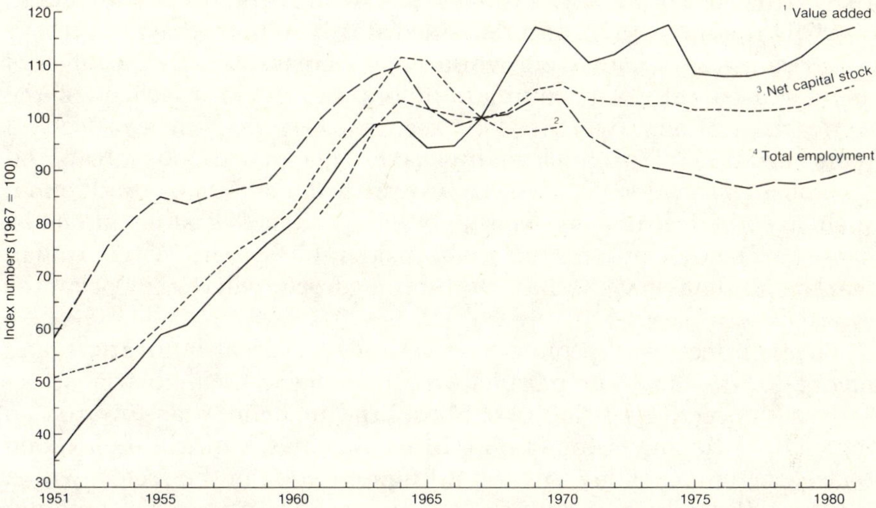

FIG. 8.2 Value added, net capital stock, and total employment in the construction industry, 1951–81 (index numbers, 1967 = 100)

Notes:

1. Value added, index numbers at constant factor cost.
2. Net capital stock, at constant prices, at the mid-year.
3. Net capital stock, at constant prices, at the end of the year.
4. Total employment (*occupati presenti*), estimate for national accounting.

Source: For 1, 2, and 4: ISTAT, *Annuario di contabilità nazionale*, 1982; for 3, data made available by Rosa, *Ufficio Studi, Confindustria*, Rome.

Additional note: Value added, net capital stock, and total employment in construction, annual compound rate of growth, 1951–64 and 1964–81 (%):

	VA construction	Net capital stock construction	Employment construction	VA economy
1951–64	+8.23	+6.23	+5.00	+5.35
1964–81	+0.99	+0.16	−1.17	+3.78

(+0.99 per cent per year), with substantial fluctuations around it; employment has been on a marked declining trend (−1.17 per cent per year), and with very depressed responses—particularly after 1970—to cyclical fluctuations in output; while capital stock increased only slightly up to 1970, and remained steady in the following decade. As a result, capital stock per worker has increased not as the effect of an increased rate of accumulation, but simply as an effect of the contraction of employment. This seems to suggest that a process of reorganization of production has taken place with no substantial technical innovation. In fact, industrialized methods of production, such as prefabricated systems and industrialized casting methods, have never been applied to any considerable extent in the Italian market, so that they still have to be considered, where they occur, as isolated examples.[3]

These processes of economic evolution, technical innovation, and mechanization have run parallel with a change in the industrial structure of the sector. In the 'first phase' the tendency was towards an increase in the dimension of both firms and sites, while in the 'second phase' the tendency lay towards a fragmentation of the sector, with a substantial decrease in both firms and sites dimension.[4] This chapter will explore how these changes in economic and technological conditions have interacted with management/labour strategies in the shaping of the labour market structure.

8.2 The traditional building enterprise

In the Italian construction industry, the craft/traditional enterprises survived till the early 1950s, that is, until reinforced concrete was introduced on a large scale. Their organizational structure was inherited from the craft enterprises of the turn of the century, as no major change in the economic and technological conditions of the sector occurred.

8.2.1 Technology in use

In the traditional craft enterprises of the turn of the century, buildings were largely brick-built, particularly in the towns. Construction was organized in a continuous and progressive process, starting with the foundations (when required by the characteristics of the building) and then erecting, floor by floor, brick walls as load-bearers, and subsequently floors, external walls, and the roof, with no technical variation.[5] The technology in use was completely manual, requiring a massive input of labour. The work was performed by a group of highly skilled bricklayers, with a wide and complete knowledge of the construction process, and able to solve all the problems that occurred during the building cycle.

Building activity, particularly for housing, took place in the private sector, and building contractors worked, for the most part, on commission. At the head of the craft enterprise there was the 'master mason', a craft bricklayer with a complete knowledge of the 'art of building', and who himself participated in the production process. With the development of the credit system at the beginning of the century, and the increased possibility of self-financing, some building contractors started to produce for sale or rent. At the same time, shareholding companies and industrial enterprises started to develop, headed by an entrepreneur rather than a master mason. In these cases, the entrepreneur did not participate in the actual production process, but hired some assistants (in some cases, engineers or architects) to direct and control the works (De Vecchi and Treu, 1979, p. 23).

8.2.2 Division of labour

At the beginning of the century, 552,497 workers were recorded as employed in construction, accounting, with the textile and garment industries, for over 60 per cent of total waged industrial labour.[6] The sector included workers employed in construction works (building, roadworks, railways, and reclamation works) and those employed in the production of building materials (brickmakers and kilnmen). Within it there existed a large number of trades, with building workers grouped under one trade only: bricklayers. This was by far the largest group, and the other trades, all very specific, therefore accounted for only a limited number of workers.[7] Within each trade, the workers were classified according to the skill acquired in their trade, as shown for building workers in Table 8.1. There are no available data on the structure of employment by skill, but given the state of technology—completely manual and very traditional—it is possible to argue that the general skill level was low, as a large number of unskilled labourers had to be employed for operations of internal transport.[8]

All workers, skilled and unskilled, including the master mason himself, took part directly in the building process. The organization of production was based on the model of the *corporazioni di mestiere* (guilds of trades), that is, with a precise hierarchy of skills and roles, with at the top the master mason and at the bottom labourers (*manovali*—unskilled workers employed for simple and manual tasks, involving no skills, in support of bricklayers' work), navvies

TABLE 8.1
The wage structure in construction, Milan district, 1901–26 (Italian lira)

	Minimum hourly wage		Gross average daily wage	
	1901	1910	1921	1926
bricklayers	0.36	0 .38	27.17	31.28
apprentice bricklayers	0.28	0.37	24.77	28.48
navvies	0.26	0.34	22.37	26.08
labourers	0.24	0.32	17.40	20.40
boys	0.15	0.22	13.40	17.20

Source: for 1901: Convenzione, 1901, art. 3, reprinted in De Vecchi and Treu, 1979, p. 216;
for 1910: Convenzione, 1910, art. 5, reprinted in De Vecchi and Treu, 1979, p. 221;
for 1921 and 1926: Rossi, 1926, p. 557.

(*badilanti*—unskilled workers employed mainly for digging up), and boys (*garzoni*).

The master mason had the responsibility for the execution of the entire project, and directed the works, helped by one or two assistants. The master mason assistant was his factotum: he recruited the labour force, supervised the building activities and set the pay-rolls. The work was carried out entirely by bricklayers, who executed directly and manually all phases of the building process with the cooperation of a large number of service workers (labourers, navvies, and boys), whose distinction and organization in terms of tasks was related to experience acquired in a unique and long on-the-job training process. The bricklayers were personally in charge of most operations necessary for the construction of the building, and participated in all the subsequent different operations taking place on the site (foundations, brickwork, cladding, and plastering), in this way 'being able to retain a unitary outlook of their own work' (Paci, 1962, p. 167). Given the lack of any mechanization, the bricklayers required a large number of unskilled workers, whose job was partly to bring all the materials and tools required to the catwalk, and partly to assist in the actual production process.[9] The work was usually organized in small teams (*quadriglia*) (Schiavi, 1910, p. 375) made up of one or two skilled bricklayers, one or two apprentices, and a few hodmen. This meant, for example, that while the skilled bricklayers were in charge of the external sides of the walls, paying attention to their perpendicularity, the apprentice bricklayers had to fill the internal part of the wall, and the hodmen had to hand them the bricks, as required. Similarly, apprentice bricklayers were in charge of the first plastering and bricklayers of the finishing coat.

Hodmen and boys were employed for all transport of materials within the site and to the catwalk where the bricklayers were working. The boys, in particular, were supposed to take mortar and water to the bricklayers, and to keep their tools clean. The navvies were labourers employed for digging, and thus mainly employed in the first sequences only.

8.2.3 Hierarchy, training, and career

As previously said, the organization of work was highly hierarchical, with deep differences in craft skill, hierarchical status, and wage. Career patterns were related to the acquisition and improvement of one's trade, acquired working side by side with more experienced workers. This process of training and career was unique, as the distinction between different working positions was related to the different degrees of skill in their trade, and also very long, as the technical and practical knowledge required was very broad. Building workers were first employed as boys at a very early age, for general services and the internal transport of materials.[10] Getting older, and physically stronger, they were promoted to hodmen, and employed in a small team of bricklayers to help the skilled workers. Watching closely the work of the bricklayers, they could start learning the trade and later working themselves as apprentice bricklayers. Their further training and advancement was related to the acquisition of further experience, and to their individual dexterity in the trade.

The confirmation of a grade was the responsibility of the master mason: he decided when to confirm it. But the process of training and career progress was in fact controlled by the skilled bricklayers. Thus, they had a sort of 'informal' control of the other workers: they led and regulated the training process, and they basically decided—or suggested to the master mason—which workers in their service should be promoted. Thus, this hierarchical organization implied, within each team, a strong dependence on the bricklayer by his subordinates.

But career opportunities were not the same for all workers. In this respect, two groups have to be singled out: the 'permanent' and the 'casual' construction workers (see Figure 8.3). The first group included the bricklayers and the apprentice bricklayers, that is, those who began employment in the sector at a very early age and were willing to stay; their training and career pattern was neither quick nor

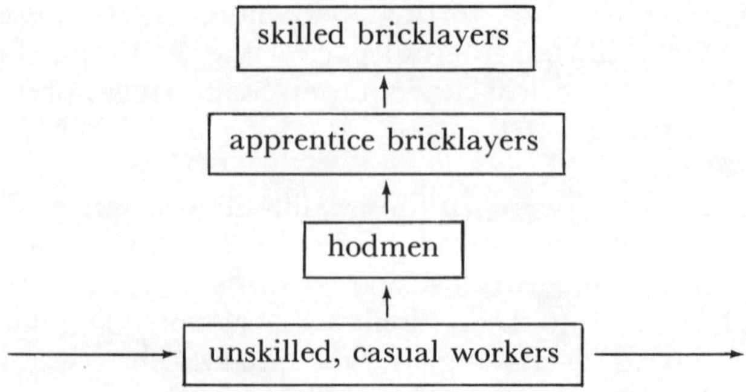

FIG. 8.3 The traditional pattern of career in the construction industry

easy, but they had the possibility of learning and improving their trade in the long run. The second group of workers consisted of peasant workers, employed only temporarily in construction as navvies or hodmen, and with very little possibility of making a career. They were subject to employment fluctuations in relation to, on the one hand, the economic conditions in construction and, on the other, the seasonal character of agricultural work and the cyclical fluctuations affecting it. Given the casual nature of their employment relationship in the sector, they had little chance of being properly trained, and therefore few career prospects. This horizontal segmentation between the group of permanent workers—those with a long career within the sector—and the group of casual workers—those with almost no prospects of career—can only be explained by taking into account the characteristics of the technology in use and the general economic and social conditions of the country.

Technology was completely manual, so that expansions in demand could be faced only if it was possible to expand employment considerably. As fluctuations in building production were quite substantial, this was reflected in the level of employment. And it was the nearby rural areas that supplied the construction industry of the towns with this fluctuating mass of casual and unskilled labour.

8.2.4 Labour market conditions

At the beginning of the century the industrial structure of the country was extremely underdeveloped—scarcely mechanized, and based on small craft enterprises, employing an improvised labour force with few qualifications and with a very large turnover. A large supply of labour was made available partly by the migration flows from the agricultural areas towards the towns, but mainly by temporary seasonal migrations, related to both industrial and agricultural activities.

The most common type of people employed in the industrial sectors were not the immigrants but the peasant workers and worker peasants, alternating work in the factories with that in the fields. In most of the cases they were peasants who took on the role of industrial workers for part of the year. This osmosis between industry and agriculture was particularly marked in the areas where the textile industry had developed, and for those industrial activities, like construction, with strong seasonal features.[11] The peasants would move to the town looking for a job in periods of agricultural recession or during the low season; similarly, in case of unemployment, they would return to the fields where they could survive on products from the land.

This was also the case in Lombardia, the most developed and dynamic region of the country. Here, in the low and well-irrigated part of the plain, where large industrial farms prevailed, wage workers and day labourers were employed, integrating the work in the fields with cattle breeding and the manufacturing of dairy products, and therefore able to find employment throughout the year. In the hilly and dry part of the plain, where the small farms were rented or run on a *métayage* system, growing corn and maize and breeding silk worms, the peasants were employed intensively during the spring and the summer, leaving many of them unemployed during the autumn and the winter. A large number of women could find temporary employment in the textile industry (particularly in the silk industry), while the men moved to town looking for jobs in construction (De Vecchi and Treu, 1979, pp. 15–16, 33). Thus, as the result partly of seasonal fluctuations and partly of the recessions in agriculture, manual labour was freed from the fields and willing to move temporarily into town looking for employment. This phenomenon was very pronounced in periods of rapid urban expansion, as in the 1880s and in the first decade of this century, but it has continued to characterize the construction industry.

These peasant workers were, for the most part, originally from the agricultural areas north of Milan (the villages of Brianza and, later on, Bergamo and Brescia) and from the surroundings of the town. They would move to town very early in the morning, gathering at *Il Ponte*, a place in town where the master masons or their assistents would go to look for cheap labour to hire (*Libro Ricordo Storico*, 1906, pp. 140–1). Here they showed themselves and their tools, waiting to be asked to work. In winter, or when the rural areas were hit by a recession, an even larger number of peasants would pour into town offering themselves at very low wages. This labour force, ambivalent, fluctuating, and unskilled, kept tight links with the rural environment, not only in economic terms but also in social terms, preserving their customs of working times, dressing, eating, style of life, and attitude towards the employer (De Vecchi and Treu, 1979, pp. 33–6).

The group of permanent construction workers was made, for the most part, of bricklayers that had acquired their trade after a long and hard apprenticeship. Due to the craft features of the sector, they had retained a series of attitudes typical of the old guilds of trades: they were very proud and jealous of their 'art', attached to and respectful of the hierarchy and craft traditions. This produced a very precise and rigid chain of command between master, bricklayers, and boys.[12] A large number of them were originally from the districts of Varese and Como (*Libro Ricordo Storico*, 1906, pp. 139–40)—towns with very old building traditions—and commuted to Milan weekly, living in town. They often knew how to read and write, and they had their own culture. In many cases they were organized in the first forms of labour organization to develop in the country (De Vecchi and Treu, 1979, pp. 33–4).

8.2.5 Trade union organization and labour market structure

The first forms of labour organization began to develop in Italy towards the end of the nineteenth century. The construction workers were among the first to get organized, mainly as members of the *Società di Mutuo Soccorso*, a structure organizing workers of different trades but all belonging to the same geographical area, in many cases including both employees and employers.[13] With the development of the first struggles, this form of organization revealed its structural weaknesses. A radical change in these organizations occurred *simultaneously* with the foundation of the political party, *Partito Operaio Italiano*, in 1885, and was strongly affected by the spreading of socialist ideas and by changes in the political climate of the country. The old *Società di Mutuo Soccorso* were transformed into *Società di Mutuo Soccorso e Resistenza* and a new form of organization, *Leghe di Resistenza*, basically organizing workers by trade, developed. They restricted membership to waged labour only, and they were set up both for the defence of workers and for the improvement of their employment conditions, creating funds for mutual assistance in the face of unemployment and lack of earnings due to lay-offs and strikes. These labour organizations, locally based, developed first in the construction industry in the major towns of the north. But they did not develop on this craft trade basis alone, as they soon perceived the need, for their survival and growth, to look for unity with other craft trade organizations with similar goals. For this reason, the *Federazione Muraria* was created in 1889 on the initiative of several associations of constructions workers in Milan, Bologna, and Turin (De Vecchi and Treu, 1979, p. 57). Ten years later it was renamed the *Federazione Italiana Operai Edili* (FIOE), proposing itself as (*a*) a federation of a whole category of trades unified by type of production process—construction—and organizing all sections of waged labour (skilled, apprentices, unskilled), and (*b*) a class organization having as its main goal the generalization of resistance. In a very short time. FIOE became the major national federation of the industrial sector, with 43,220 members (11,875 in the Milan district alone) by 1909 (see Table 8.2).[14] The main goal of FIOE was a coordinated system of support and resistance, through its intervention with subsidies in cases of strikes, while collective bargaining, in the forms in which it was taking place, was carried on by the individual associations at the local level.

The local associations did not achieve a real bargaining position until 1919, the main obstacle being the hostile attitude of employers, who refused to acknowledge in these organizations the legitimate representatives of categories of trades. In fact, until the first world war there was no collective bargaining in the proper sense, but simply *concordati di tariffa* (i.e. agreements on wages, including the definition of the maximum number of working hours and general disciplinary conditions), involving simply a moral commitment of the subscribers, with no collective and legal obligation to respect what was agreed. Looking at the agreements concluded in this period, it is interesting to notice that from the very beginning the efforts of the union organizations in construction were directed not only towards the definition of minimum basic rates and maximum working hours, but also towards the abolition of piece rates and all forms of labour-only subcontracting.

TABLE 8.2
Federazione Italiana Operai Edili *membership, 1899–1920*

Year	Sections	Members
1899	10	532
1907	520	45,858
1909	430	43,220
1914	450	45,000
1920	1,050	175,000

Source: for 1899, 907, and 1909, De Vecchi and Treu, 1979, p. 59; for 1914 and 1920, Cipollini, 1979, p. 17.

Until the beginning of the century, payment by results was the norm in the sector. This allowed skilled bricklayers to get earnings higher than those set in the *concordati*, which were in many cases not sufficient to meet the workers' family needs. The system allowed master masons to reduce total labour costs, and hence to bid for contracts at a low price, while still making a profit. As construction workers began to get organized, one of their goals was the limitation and regulation of piece-work. In particular, it was the early craft organization of the bricklayers (*Società Muratori*) which manifested its opposition towards individual piece-work (*a*) for technical reasons, as it led to badly executed tasks, and therefore to a degradation of the craft trade, (*b*) for economic reasons, as it led to conflicts over work between different groups of workers, and to unemployment for some of them, and (*c*) for social reasons, as it led to a higher rate of work accidents (see Schiavi, 1910, p. 379).

To understand better the opposition of the early movement towards individual piece work by bricklayers,[15] it has to be said that at that time brickwork was organized in small teams. The skilled bricklayer was in some cases given a little extra money, by the contractor, with the task of speeding up the pace of work, in order to force the other three members of the team to follow him in the erection of the brick wall.[16] This system was considered by the unions as fictitious piece work:

> In this case one or two workers, at the most, pretend to be piece-workers or subcontractors, but in fact they are only special waged workers employed to exercise tyranny over their fellows. The master mason who wants to avoid the trouble of constantly supervising the labour force resorts to this strategy of creating fictitious piece-workers; and they, in turn, apart from getting some extra money, also know how to 'fix' wage rates for their improvised subordinates. (from a document of the *Confederazione Generale del Lavoro*, quoted in Schiavi, 1910, p. 381.)

According to the unions, individual piece-rate systems were not technically possible in brickwork, given (*a*) the impossibility of setting a price for all the different parts of the building, and (*b*) the fact that the work was not individual, but the result of the work of the team. Master masons, in order to induce workers to work harder, thereby lowering the labour cost per unit of output, could either use 'fictitious piece-work', or could subcontract a task to one or more skilled workers. In this last case, the workers acted as self-employed, working on a subcontract basis: they would recruit the necessary labour and set the wage rates, bargain the price with the employer, and get the difference between the price of the task and the total labour cost. In both cases, these workers acted as labour-only subcontractors, who could earn extra money by inducing their fellow workers to work harder with no corresponding increase in wages. Collective piece-work (team piece-work), even if allowed by the unions, was rarely used, as the employers themselves found it difficult to establish rights and duties for all members of the team, and in particular with respect to the relation between skilled and unskilled workers.

When, in 1907, for the first time, two *concordati* were signed, one in the Milan district and one in the Turin district, they proclaimed the abolition of individual piece-work and labour-only subcontracting in brickwork.[17] And later, after the first world war, when FIOE—strong in its increased membership (see Table 8.2)—succeeded in negotiating the first collective agreement for the construction workers of Milan (25 March 1919) and in getting recognition for its collective bargaining position, it restated its strong opposition towards individual piece-work and labour-only subcontracting (Andreasi, 1968, p. 247). Moreover, the agreement covered (*a*) the official acknowledgement of FIOE, (*b*) the institution of an organization (*Cassa Edile*) for the creation of a fund to subsidize the unemployed, financed by a contribution calculated on the basis of workers' wages and paid by both employers (0.7) per cent of wages) and workers (0.6 per cent of wages), (*c*) the acknowledgement of the workers' councils and their responsibility for the correct implementation of the agreements, and (*d*) the reduction of normal working hours per day to eight (Andreasi, 1968, p. 247; Cipollini, 1979, pp. 17–18).

To conclude, the unions began developing in construction on a *local basis* and grouping workers *by trade*, being primarily concerned with the interest of the trade as a whole, and therefore opposed to piece-work and subcontracting, as both led to exploitation. Thus, the attitude of the early union organization in Italy towards piece-work and lumping did not differ from what has been considered a general tendency of the sector. As Dunlop (1958, Ch. 6) has shown in his comparative analysis of industrial relations in building, union organizations, as they began to emerge in this sector, opposed piece-work and lumping, and sought to limit remuneration to the time method of payment. This was also the case for those countries—like Sweden and the UK—which came to accept some forms of payment by result. Thus, the Italian construction unions were similar both in their general targets and in their organizational structure to the early unions of other countries. The distinguishing feature of Italian experience was the social basis of the unions, as no restrictions on entry and no apprentice training was enforced. Instead, they encouraged education through the establishment of trade schools, and they created the basis, through the creation of the *Cassa Edile*, of a social welfare system designed to defend all workers against the instability and uncertainty of the sector.

With the upsurge of fascism, the newborn trade union organizations were dismantled and the worker's councils (the union organizations at the workplace) abolished. National bargaining was set by 'federation of categories'. The fascist unions bargained at the central level with the employers' associations, so as to avoid direct confrontation between employers and workers. And, in this way, employers managed to overcome the limits and restrictions imposed by the early union movement. In particular, they managed to get round the achievement of the eight-hour day (settled in the 1919 agreement) when a law was passed in 1923. This introduced the possibility of exceeding the normal eight hours per day (48 per week) for those sectors, like construction, which were subject to seasonal fluctuations, with the only limitation that the yearly average per worker should not be more than normal working hours. Also, the restrictions imposed on individual pieced-work and lumping were abolished, allowing contractors to use different forms of payment by results, without any kind of regulation. In other words, the very few restrictions that had been imposed by the unions were weakened or eliminated. And this resulted in increased working hours, a reduction in wages, the implementation of rigid discipline inside the sites, and the re-establishment of individual piece-work and lumping as a means of increasing productivity without having to pay for it (Cipollini, 1979, pp. 18–24). Moreover, these gains were clearly perceived by the contractors, who pushed for and welcomed the changes introduced by the fascist government:

> . . . the hourly wage rate has replaced the day wage rate. More recently, legislation and union organizations have increasingly regimented wages by setting a limit for working hours (to eight per day), fixing wage rates for different groups of workers, hiring of labour through the labour offices, . . . creating special wage rates for overtime, and other similar measures. Our government can boast that it has coordinated and tempered all these measures for the expansion of our economy; in fact, it is easy to understand the earlier embarrassment of contractors faced with the crude application of these concepts, as this was done by the working-class organizations, whose aim was to limit production, in order to paralyse the entrepreneurs' profits. Nevertheless, it would be naive to think that the tendency among the workers to adopt a 'don't care' attitude has been completely overcome. (Astorri, in Cipollini, 1979, p. 21.)

In fact, it was made explicit that payment by results could easily be used to induce workers to work harder for a small increase in wages.

8.3 The rise of the large industrial building enterprise

The traditional craft industrial structure survived till the beginning of the 1950s. In Italy, erecting techniques based on reinforced concrete were accepted with difficulty and resistance from their first introduction at the beginning of the century.[18] Even the limited use made of reinforced concrete for the erection of houses and public buildings in the 1920s and 1930s was almost completely removed by the economic policy of the fascist government. An autarchic economic plan began in the early 1930s, with a campaign against the use of reinforced concrete. In 1936 its use was forbidden for all residential buildings up to five floors, and later on it was prohibited for all types of construction.

The slow diffusion of reinforced concrete, first, and its prohibition, later on, brought about—in the prewar period—an extension over time of the traditional technical and organizational structure. Up to the early 1950s the industry was still based on a traditional and fragmented structure, with building activity organized chiefly on brickworks with very little or no mechanization (Bianchi, 1952, p. 316). The central role in the production process was played by the bricklayers, organizing and supervising the work of the unskilled. The division of labour was vertical and hierarchical, based on differences in skill and experience, and was reflected in differences in status and wages. The distinction between workers of different grades was based on their skill level with respect to a unique training pattern: unskilled workers, apprentice bricklayers, skilled bricklayers. The classification grades in use were therefore supposed to reflect the different steps of a long but unique career. The traditional organization of production, and its breakdown into trades, including both skilled and unskilled workers, was still structured to produce the necessary training and upward mobility for those staying in the sector.

Nevertheless, the lack of building activity during the war had made the training process uncertain. In fact, since 1941, any building activity stopped, and all the labour force available was employed in war works, that is, digging and large masonry works, not requiring any specific skill and often directed and supervised by improvised technical and supervisory staff, who had little concern for quality and the cost of the works. In the early postwar period, construction workers were employed in large reconstruction projects on the road and rail systems, in clearing rubble, and in some projects to rebuild existing housing. The first group of works required a large number of workers for manual and unskilled tasks. The second group of works, even if requiring a larger number of skilled workers, had to be completed in such a hurry that there was no time to give the necessary attention to the quality of the works and thus to the training of the young workers (Bianchi, 1952, p. 315; Cipollini, 1979, p. 26). The recovery of the sector, largely based on unskilled activities, resulted in an expansion of employment, and served as an immediate source of relief for large numbers of unemployed in the early postwar period. Workers with no previous experience in the sector could be employed immediately in construction without requiring any training. At the same time, the low level of building activity in the prewar period, and the lack of construction activity in housing for almost a decade (see Figure 8.1, p. 209, had interrupted the process of training, and had left the sector with a shortage of skilled labour.

8.3.1 The introduction of reinforced concrete

Major changes in the structure of the labour market in the construction industry can be traced first and foremost to technical changes brought into play by the postwar boom, which had far-reaching effects on the organization of the industry.

The postwar economic slump was overcome by a long and tumultuous period of economic expansion. The phase of rapid industrial development centred in the northern triangle was matched by the really exceptional growth of the urban areas, largely based on speculative private activity. During the boom, building projects increased in number and in size, and the overall demand for labour increased substantially. It was then that reinforced concrete came into its own. In a situation of shortage of skilled labour, the huge expansion in building activity was made possible by the introduction of this new technique of construction. In traditional construction technology, where very large brick-built walls carry the weight of the building, the production process is unique and continuous. The new methods employed concrete beams and columns for load-bearing, splitting the unitary building cycle into a series of separate stages. And this speeded up the building process, allowed more precision, cut costs and, at the same time, made it possible to organize the work of a growing number of workers with no previous experience in construction. A large number of semiskilled workers, who were available in large numbers and whose training was minimal, were employed to support the skilled labour, of which there was a real shortage. Large, powerful capital equipment began to be used for digging and earth removal, thereby introducing a high degree of mechanization into all the operations involved in the initial sequences; while cranes, tower cranes and fork-lift trucks started to be employed in the later sequences to reduce the problems of moving materials and to speed up the process. The diffusion of the use of reinforced concrete and the process of mechanization were quite rapid, and, though most firms remained small and labour-intensive and continued to employ largely unskilled labour, some large industrial firms developed, especially in the urban areas.

8.3.2 Division of labour

Industrial building techniques had a major impact on the labour process. Within quite a short period of time, the traditional building process, based on brickwork, was transformed by the widespread use of reinforced concrete. As a result, the building process itself was split. The erection of the load-bearing structure (columns and beams) was separated from the construction of external walls and partitions, and carried out with a completely new technique, using different materials and employing different skills.

The building process was organized by different teams of workers (carpenters, steel fixers, bricklayers, plasterers), each using specific inputs and particular techniques, and each performing only one part of the entire process. Within each team work was organized in a hierarchical way, and the distribution of tasks within the team largely depended on skill and experience. The original bricklayer craft was broken up and divided into specific jobs:

(i) carpenters were employed to build and dismantle timber shutters;
(ii) steel fixers worked on the steel necessary to reinforce the shutters internally;
(iii) cement workers prepared and cast concrete;
(iv) bricklayers were in charge of all brickwork and plastering, and this trade then became a specialization in itself.

The different teams rotated inside the building site in rigid succession. Each team was headed by a skilled worker, helped by a few apprentices, but in addition quite a large number of semiskilled and unskilled workers were involved, mainly in moving and lifting whatever was necessary for the work to be done. Indeed, with the exception of the first sequences of the production process—the excavation—and most of the transport operations, a large part of the building activity still consisted of manual tasks, and a large number of unskilled and semiskilled workers were still employed in the sector.[19] By giving supervisory roles to experienced workers, the new division of labour on site made the best use of skilled labour, which was in crucially short supply.[20]

The division of labour brought about by the introduction of reinforced concrete was also affected by the introduction of some quite simple mechanical equipment. At the beginning of the 1950s the mechanization of the sector was extremely underdeveloped: about 75 per cent of total labour costs were attributable to operations of transport inside the site (Bianchi, 1953*b*, pp. 886–7). The slow but progressive process of mechanization of the sites, that took place from the early 1950s onwards, not only reduced manpower requirements, but also helped to force and regulate the pace of the entire site, greatly simplifing the problems of control over the labour process:

> . . . while the internal transport of a construction site is organized on the ground through wheelbarrow and vertically through skip hoists, which function discontinuously, nothing will show, for example, if the team of bricklayers or the team of labourers serving them have started, as they say, being sluggish. But, it is enough for a crane or a continuous skip hoist to be installed on a site for this to operate as a metronome for all the activities: if the material is not provided from the ground the machine will start making empty trips; if the bricklayers or the cement workers are slowing down their pace of work, the machine will start accumulating, at their side, the materials that have not yet been used. (Bianchi, 1952, p. 317.)

Moreover, the intensified division of labour, brought about by the introduction of new equipment, was carried even further, not for technical reasons, but in order to speed up the pace of work. In a report on the problems of industrialization in the sector, it was pointed out that the innovations introduced through the 1950s and early 1960s were of modest proportion, and in no case such as to determine a radical transformation of the production process:

> It has to be underlined that the innovation carried out in the sphere of machinery and equipment, if it has not contributed substantial changes in execution times, costs, and quality, precisely because the production process remains, largely, at a pre-industrial level, it has, nevertheless, helped to give rise to a new entrepreneurial frame of mind, more open and more interested in a rational organization of the site, compelled by the locking up of capital stock
>
> The first impact has been on the technical/organizational structure of the enterprise (particularly the most modern ones), and it has led to the employment of labour according to a higher division of labour, and according to more rational criteria and principles; while the role of the bricklayer 'able to do everything' has become of secondary importance, employers prefer to use teams of specialists, like carpenters, steel fixers, bricklayers expert in casting, bricklayers expert in plastering, and so on. Moreover, we have seen the rise of a new type of labour force, previously non-existent, . . . the maintenance workers of the site, the scaffolders, the workers employed to assemble metal parts, and those employed to drive the equipment (cranes, dumpers, hoists) and so on.

The mechanization of the site has also led to some changes in the sequence of the building phases. . . . While, before, it was usual to start the works of the main structure after having completed that of internal walls, now it is usual to start the internal partitions and the external walls as soon as the main structure allows it, . . . The tendency is to execute different works at the same time, not only to shorten the times of execution, but also to reduce general costs and to employ to the fullest extent both the equipment and the skilled workers. (Pinchera and Veneziani, 1965, pp. 153–4.)

8.3.3 Hierarchy, training, and career

This combination of developments, however, could not leave the training and career structure of the industry untouched. The introduction of reinforced concrete, and the process of mechanization and rationalization of the site, by interrupting the unitary building process, also interrupted the unitary mobility and career patterns within the industry. The workers entering the sector could no longer expect to follow a linear path in their training or in their career. They could be hired at different times for different jobs, and their training was therefore more casual and longer than in the old traditional building enterprise, especially when they first started working in the industry. At first, they were employed as labourers to serve the skilled workers (as they were in the traditional craft enterprises). But, given the high site and firm mobility and the increased division of labour, the process of training and upward mobility became much less clear thereafter. Nevertheless, it has been acknowledged that the training process was still working, even if in a more casual way (see Figure 8.4).[21] Building contractors were not interested in keeping a stable labour force. Given the large supply of seasonal immigrant workers, the construction sites

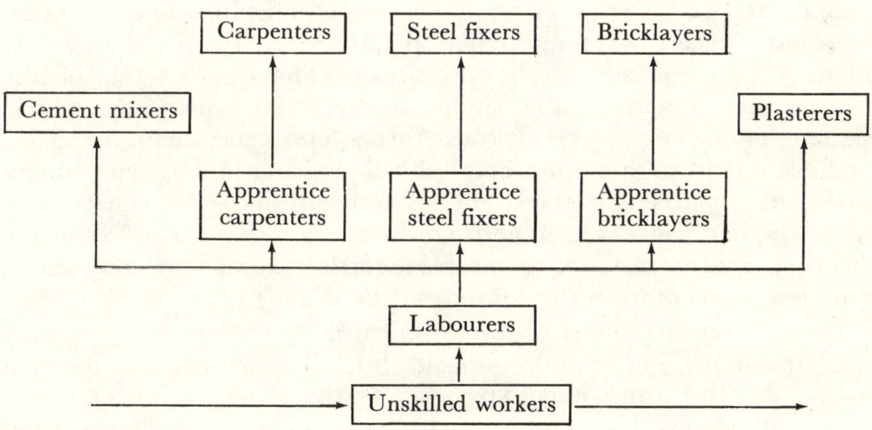

FIG. 8.4 The career pattern in large industrial building enterprises

of the Milan district were organized in terms of a stable group of skilled workers, while groups of labourers were hired and dismissed, during the site cycle, according to the specific needs of the site. Pelicciari (1963, pp. 25–64), in his analysis of a medium-size construction site in the district, pointed to the existence of two distinct groups of workers: the stable workers (*fedelissimi*) and the general labourers.[22] The first group was made up of 10–12 workers (out of about 50 workers employed in that site over the year), all skilled, having experienced the same career pattern (that is, having started working in the sector at a very early age and having being employed in construction for very many years), all northern and mostly from the same regions (Friuli, Veneto, and some districts in Lombardia, such as Como and Bergamo). The stable, skilled workers were crucial in the organization of the site: it was on them that the superintendent of the site had to rely not only for the execution but also for the organization of the construction site. They were distributed between the different activities of the site by craft specialization. Within their craft trade they were completely responsible for both the execution and the organization of work, including the supervision (and training) of the other workers. The organizational structure was necessarily highly hierarchical, with, at the top, the site superintendent and his assistant; but as the projects increased in dimension and involved both administrative and technical work in the site office, they had to rely on a group of experienced and stable workers they could trust.[23]

The second group of workers consisted of (*a*) a small group of skilled and semiskilled workers with a rather intermittent and discontinuous employment relationship with the enterprise ('regular' seasonal workers), and (*b*) a larger group of unskilled labourers with a casual and occasional employment relationship. The 'regular' seasonal workers were hired periodically when required, therefore moving between sites and enterprises. They had some of the characteristics of the stable skilled workers (*fedelissimi*), i.e. mostly skilled, having acquired their trade through long service in the sector, and roughly from the same geographical areas, but relatively younger and with a relatively shorter time of service in the sector. These were men who had succeeded in getting some training, but who could not yet be considerd as part of the trustworthy workers. Among them, only few workers from the south and the islands could be found.

On the contrary, most of the unskilled labourers were immigrants from the south, both young and old, but all unskilled, and the vast majority with no previous experience in the sector. They were employed at the lowest level in the organization of the site, for general and unskilled activities. They were hired in variable numbers, according to the project under construction and the stage of the work, and employed for a few months only and then laid off. For those of them with previous working experience in construction, in their own villages, employment in the north meant a considerable increase in their earnings. Consequently, if they did not have a trade already, they were little interested in learning one, as this would have involved a loss in present earnings (associated with the loss of overtime work in order to be able to follow the evening training courses),[24] for a relatively small increase in their future earnings. This explains also their willingness to tolerate very high mobility between construction sites and enterprises, sometimes moving between as many as three or four sites in a month (Pellicciari, 1963, p. 15), in order to best exploit the conditions of the market.

Among the workers employed with no continuity, a considerable number were willing to move out of construction, either because they wanted to return to their villages (as was the case for some older workers), or because they wanted to move into a different industrial sector with a stable and secure job (as was the case with the young workers). For a large number of immigrants, employment in construction was the first step in their career in the industrial world. Thus, the construction industry experienced high inter-sectoral mobility, particularly in the years 1959–63, at the peak of the economic boom, when employment in the manufacturing industry was rapidly expanding, and the construction industry began to experience problems of labour shortage.[25]

To conclude, the new organization of labour, besides introducing and strengthening a segmentation of the labour force *between* trades, reproduced *within* each trade a vertical and hierarchical division between skilled and unskilled workers. As a result, in a situation characterized by a rapid increase in the demand for labour and a large inflow of immigrants, two different patterns of labour mobility developed, so that the labour force itself came to form two main groups: the skilled workers and the labourers. For the first group, the upward mobility pattern was still working; for the second, career prospects were quite uncertain. Paci, in the analysis of a large building enterprise located in the Milan district in the 1960s, concluded:

> Two distinct professional hierarchies overlap at the workplace: on the one hand, there are the older workers, divided roughly into two levels: semi-skilled . . . and skilled workers (bricklayers, carpenters, steel fixers); on the other hand, there are the younger workers, mainly hodmen and labourers (equipment operators, apprentice bricklayers, apprentice carpenters). . . . a clear crystallization of building employment into two groups identifying two different migration waves: the first (Lombardo–Veneta) took place before

the industrialization of the sector, and experienced a traditional training process at the workplace; the second (southern migration), taking place in more recent times, has found the traditional mechanisms of apprenticeship and upward mobility to the skilled jobs partly blocked. (Paci, 1963*b*, pp. 42, 44.)

Given job instability, low career prospects, and the need for immediate earnings, horizontal mobility and overtime work were preferred to the long queues for vertical mobility.

8.3.4 The labour market conditions

The building boom depended on finding a new source of supply for unskilled (and potentially variable) labour. Employment in construction increased considerably and was particularly concentrated in the northern and urban districts.[26] The supply of construction workers was provided by the massive migrations of rural workers from the north-east, the south, and the islands. Over one million people moved into the northern triangle in the decade 1946–56, most of them concentrated in the major cities.[27] An even higher inflow of immigrants characterized the following years (Paci, 1973, pp. 53–5, 129), until the phenomenon was interrupted by the economic recession of the mid 1960s.

For the construction industry of northern cities, it was nothing new to draw its labour from among the immigrants. The Milan district, in particular, had seen large and continuous migrations into the sector in the prewar period as well. But some substantial features distinguished these from the postwar migrations. In the prewar period, and for part of the migrations up to the late 1940s, the phenomenon had an organic feature: workers were moving either seasonally or permanently in relation to their work experience and to the development in the economic structure, and as a result were quickly integrated into the productive and social structure (Alasia and Montaldi, 1975, pp. 64–6). For the construction industry, this involved traditional migrations from certain areas of the country, characterized by a precise relation between the workers' place of origin and their jobs in the construction industry.[28] In other words, for the immigrants of the early period there was a sort of predefined mobility pattern, both professional and geographical, through which they could find employment and develop their careers in the sector.

The immigrants of the postwar period, particularly those from the south, could feel no sense of continuity, either economic or social, when they came north. They were, for the most part, unskilled workers, with no previous industrial experience, and had left their villages because they had no job and no prospects of getting one. In the vast majority of cases, they were either unemployed or employed in secondary and marginal jobs, as their irregular administrative position put them out of the 'regular' labour market. To understand this, it has to be pointed out that a law, passed under the fascist regime to halt inurbation, was in force until the late 1950s. According to this law, the vast majority of immigrants were irregular (a sort of 'illegal' immigration within the country) from the point of view of their employment relationship. This law had two major implications for them: (*a*) if they were not resident in the *comune* (the administrative local unit) where they wished to be employed, they were not entitled to a regular work permit (i..e. the local labour office would not issue them an employment card); and (*b*) if they did not have a permanent job, the *comune* would not give them a residence permit. But the law, on the one hand, could not limit these large migrations inside the country and, on the other, necessarily placed these workers in an irregular administrative position. Because of that, they were willing to adapt, and to accept any secondary, irregular, and low-paid job.

Given the characteristics of the construction industry, a large number of these immigrants found a job in the sector as their first employment. Their low level of qualifications, their general conditions of need, and their immediate need to earn some money, as well as their inability to object and lack of bargaining power, made it possible to create a sort of 'black market' for cheap labour. They were often exposed to exploitation and illegal working conditions by the building contractors, employed at wages below the minimum bargained with the unions, and with no social insurance. In some cases, they were also employed during strikes and in times of labour unrest, so that conflicts exploded between northern and southern workers (Alasia and Montaldi, 1975, pp. 32–3).

For a large number of immigrants, employment in the construction industry was a solution not only to the problem of earning a living but also, temporarily, to the problem of accommodation. The small savings they had brought from their villages were never enough to allow them to find proper accommodation, as they also had to survive for long periods before finding a job. They often took as a place to sleep houses that were being demolished, cellars, attics, or the first floors of the houses being built.[29]

To conclude, the building industry, given its economic and technological conditions and the excess of labour supply in the market, consequently assumed a subsidiary and complementary role with respect to the leading industries. On the one hand, it allowed for the absorption of the workers expelled from the rural area (thereby mitigating the burden of unemployment), and, on the other hand, it thereby provided temporary jobs for recent migrants, thus constituting a reservoir of nonskilled labour for developing industries. In this period of rapid evolution and expansion of the sector, trade union action succeeded in defending only the strongest sections of the construction labour market.

8.3.5 Trade union action and the labour market structure

In the postwar period the unions had to reorganize themselves after a long period of inactivity. The entire organization was reconstructed 'from above' on the basis of a highly *centralized structure* and *national agreements* (inter-industry and industrial sector agreements), in contrast to what had happened when the unions first emerged.[30]

In the construction industry, the difficulties of reorganization were increased by the specific features of the sector (which was fragmented into a large number of small enterprises, scattered over the country, and with no fixed location) and by the characteristics of the labour force employed (i.e. besides a small group of stable workers, there was a large number of temporary and unstable workers, mainly immigrants employed in construction for short periods only).

Until the mid–1960s, the sector was organized by the 'horizontal unions', that is, the general union confederations (CGIL, CISL, and UIL), with CGIL being by far the strongest among construction workers. This can be explained partly in terms of the centralized bargaining policy pursued by the general unions, and partly by the lack of a pre-existing official organizational structure and the costs associated with its reestablishment. Trade union representatives were formally excluded from the building site, and there were limits imposed on the powers of the 'internal commission',[31] a structure set up to represent workers' interests on the building site. In this period, both trade union organization and the activity of collective bargaining were located outside the site. The very marked ideological division between the general unions after 1948 implied no unity of action, therefore weakening even further the union movement. CGIL, the major general confederation among construction workers, centred the workers' organization round the *Lega* re-establishing the traditional structure of the pre-fascist period. The *Lega* was a place in each village where all the building workers of the community would gather for discussions and meetings, and to glean news of trade union activity, collective agreements, and so on. The entire organization of the *Lega* was based on the voluntarism of its activists: they would produce trade union propaganda, collect subscriptions, organize strikes, circulate the news, and sell the trade union magazine. The *senatore* was the typical representative of the local organization in construction: a volunteer militant activist who, because of his personality, personal prestige and experience in the trade union movement, was the historical leader of the *Lega*, with his presence felt both on the site and in the *Lega* of the village where he was living. The *senatori* were for the most part members of the communist party, with a strong political commitment, and were all skilled craftsmen.

The difference between the general unions and the *Leghe* can better be understood in terms of their main activity. The unions gave assistance to the local organizations, presented demands for the renewal of the national collective agreement and the district collective agreements, and bargained for them, while the *Leghe* had to unionize the workers and organize the strikes.

There were only very few trade union officials at the local level, and for the most part with non-building origin.[32] This was due to the low level of union membership in the sector, and to the low and uncertain earnings of construction workers. In fact, until towards the end of the 1960s, the level of unionization was low: out of 60,000 workers registered at the *Cassa Edile* of Milan, no more than 10,000 were unionized.[33] Most of the union members were skilled workers, originally from the district and the nearby area, or who had arrived in the district with the prewar migrations. Unionization among the new immigrants was difficult, both because of their lack of a trade union tradition, and because of their irregular position in the labour market, which made them afraid of losing their jobs.

National collective bargaining was the central point of trade union activity. The general theme underlying trade union policy was the defence of construction workers against uncertainty (redundancies, seasonal fluctuations, unemployment, illness, and accidents) through the strengthening of the *Cassa Edile*, acting as a wage reserve fund for a labour force characterized by high labour turnover, instability, and mobility. The issues related to the actual organization of the production process (the division of labour, promotion, upgrading, pace of work, and so on) were scarcely tackled, with the noticeable exception of labour-only subcontracting, as this was prohibited in all its forms. Despite the fact that union contracts specifically forbade labour-only subcontracting, this was widely used in the sector during the whole period, as a way of recruiting cheap labour and controlling its productivity (Cipollini, 1979, pp. 49–70).

It was quite common for a skilled worker, who was directly employed by a contractor, to be given a task to complete for a stated price (i.e. a sort of lumping), for which he would recruit and pay a number of workers. Given the state of technology, a considerable number of unskilled workers were needed to support the work of skilled workers, and this system became a channel for the recruitment of cheap labour, in a period characterized by an expansion in building activity and an increase in total employment, which resulted in a high total labour turnover. Usually, the workers were paid on the basis of a day rate, established by the *capocottimista*, and at the completion of the task they were given a bonus related to the difference between the price set by the contractor and the total day wages. By increasing the pace of work, the time required to complete the task was reduced, and this led to a higher difference, and it was the *capocottimista* who decided by how much and how to distribute this to the team workers. The system inevitably resulted in the violation of subcontracting agreements, employment standard conditions, hiring regulations, internal migration norms, and safety regulations, as well as the non-payment of family allowances, unemployment benefits, social security contributions, and so on. The wage rates varied with the bargaining power of the teams as well as with that of the individual workers, and in accordance with the seasonal and trade cycle of building activity, as well as with the conditions of the labour market. For example, in periods of contraction, competition between subcontractors and between teams of workers led to a contraction of task payments. And in order to get enough money to live, the workers had to increase considerably their pace of work. The unions strongly criticized the phenomenon, as it resulted in the exploitation of some workers by others, the violation of all union agreements, the breaking down of class solidarity, and the division of the working class at the place of work. The unions therefore tried to oppose labour-only subcontracting and the lump, not just by banning them in collective agreements, but also by taking certain positive actions, for example, reintroducing and regulating piecework. Nevertheless, subcontracting and lumping arrangements continued to be used to recruit new entrants, and to evade collective agreements. Throughout the 1950s until the mid-1960s, a considerable number of workers were employed on an irregular basis, evading the payment of social security contributions and taxation, at wages lower than those negotiated with the unions.[34] The features of the sector and the lack of organization inside construction sites created, in fact, enormous difficulties in the control and implementation of national agreements. And it was the general weakness of the unions and their lack of control at the workplace that led this phenomenon to become widespread.

At the same time, a dichotomization in trade union activity emerged as some medium and large enterprises started developing, in the early 1960s, in the urban districts of the north. The large size of both enterprises and sites, and their industrial features, allowed for the establishment of a strong local organization and the enforcement of national collective agreements. In some cases, for example in the enterprises involved with the construction of the underground in Milan, this also involved the achievement of decentralized collective bargaining. It was on the basis of these experiences that 'unions of category' were developed in the mid–1960s, and began developing a unitary policy and unitary actions, progressively increasing trade union power in the sector.

8.4 Changes in the industrial structure

In the 'second phase', 1964–81, new multi-purpose equipment was made available. The tendency was to replace equipment of the first generation (such as huge tower cranes) with more flexible ones (such as crane trucks), but without increasing significantly the degree of mechanization of the sector. The main innovation introduced consisted in the employment of hand power-tools, which speeded up the work, and the use of a large variety of small prefabricated building components, thereby reducing site work. Small components were increasingly employed in finishing, with the tendency to 'rationalize' the production process, reducing to the minimum the interdependence between the different sequences of work. Thus, there was a move from a process of production consisting of a series of integrated and interconnected operations to a process consisting of a series of separate and non-integrated operations (FLC Lombardia, 1981).

The technical changes introduced throughout the 1970s led to a further fragmentation of an already fragmented industrial structure. In fact, despite their impact on building methods, the changes introduced in technology in the previous phase had had only a limited impact on the industry's organization. Although a number of large industrial building enterprises developed, especially in the urban areas, the market structure remained fragmented, with many small contractors. At the end of the 1960s and in the early 1970s, a process of further fragmentation took place, when the industrial building contractors began to break up into small, specialized enterprises. The industrial census shows a decline in the size of both building enterprises and sites from the 1960s onwards for the country as a whole, and in the Milan district this is true of the whole postwar period (see Table 8.3).

Annual data from the *Cassa Edile* of Milan presented in Table 8.4 allow a closer examination of the trend in the size of building enterprises for the period up to 1981. The latter survey has a different coverage to that of the industrial census, and this explains differences

TABLE 8.3
Average employment per construction enterprise and site, 1951–81

	1951		1961		1971		1981	
	Ent.	Site	Ent.	Site	Ent.	Site	Ent.	Site
Italy	15.4	11.7	17.0	13.1	7.5	6.2	n.a.	3.68
Milan district	31.3	19.6	29.4	19.1	16.0	11.3	n.a.	4.28

Note: Data refer to total construction, including installation; the 1981 data are provisional, and are based on the total productive units classified as building productive units (independently of the main activity of the enterprise to which they belong), while the data for the previous years refer to all enterprises classified as building enterprises and their productive units.
Source: ISTAT, *Censimento generale dell'industria e del commercio*, 1951, 1961, 1971, 1981.

in the absolute size of enterprises given by the two sources. Nevertheless, both sources show a significant decline in firm size, and Table 8.4 suggests that the decline accelerated during the 1970s, when the average employment in building enterprises in Milan was halved.

Figures for Milan suggest that the decline in the average size of enterprises is the combined effect of two different trends: (*a*) the

TABLE 8.4
Average employment per enterprise in construction, Milan district, 1955–81

Year	Average employment per enterprise	Year	Average employment per enterprise
1955	25.5	1968	17.3
1956	25.4	1969	22.6
1957	23.9	1970	22.9
1958	23.9	1971	28.4
1959	24.8	1972	19.0
1960	26.0	1973	19.0
1961	26.3	1974	18.4
1962	25.6	1975	17.8
1963	25.6	1976	16.3
1964	23.2	1977	14.1
1965	18.6	1978	11.6
1966	16.4	1979	10.8
1967	16.6	1980	10.3
		1981	9.9

Source: Compiled from *Cassa Edile* data.

decline of total employment, and (*b*) the increasing number of small contractors operating in the district (see Figure 8.5).

In the previous cycle, both employment and enterprises had increased during the boom and decreased during the slump. But, from the end of the 1960s, when total employment in construction was continuously declining, the number of enterprises increased. This change in the industrial structure is partly explained by the fact that building contractors adapted to the persistent recession by reducing direct employment and resorting to subcontracting, but partly too by the decision of increasing numbers of workers to become self-employed and/or to organize themselves into small, usually specialized, craft enterprises. This development was particularly marked in the years 1976–81, and was also found at a national level. Tables 8.5 and 8.6 show the significant change in the distribution of contractors and employment in more detail, setting out the percentage share of employment for each type of enterprise.

The degree of specialization of contractors operating in the Milan district has also increased. General building contractors are still by far the largest group, but their importance compared with specialized contractors has declined. In 1970, general building contractors were

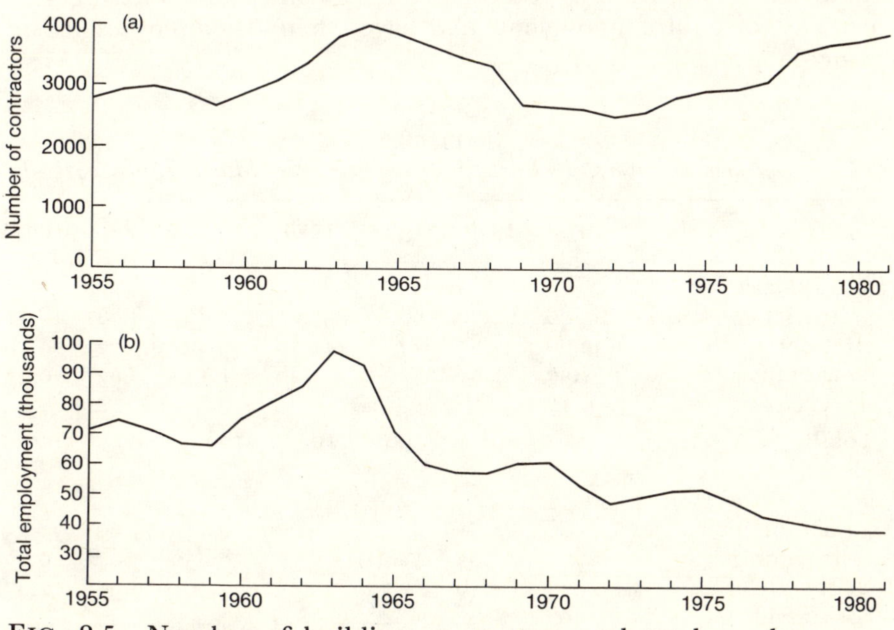

FIG. 8.5 Number of building contractors and total employment, Milan district, 1951–81.

Source: *Cassa Edile* data.

TABLE 8.5
Building contractors by type of enterprise, Milan district, 1975–81

	1975	1976	1977	1978	1979	1980	1981
industrial enterprises	1,927	1,908	1,887	1,858	1,812	1,811	1,879
craft enterprises	965	1,032	1,166	1,673	1,852	1,922	1,966
co-operatives	45	53	47	45	42	35	36
not classified	5	—	—	—	—	—	—
Total	2,942	2,993	3,110	3,576	3,706	3,768	3,881

Source: Compiled from *Cassa Edile* data.

85.7 per cent of all contractors, employing 88.6 per cent of building workers; in 1981 the corresponding figures are 77.1 and 79.9 per cent (*Cassa Edile* data).

Finally, large contractors have either drastically reduced their labour force or have disappeared. In 1969–70, there were 20 building contractors with over 250 employees; by 1981, there were only 3. As a result, the small and very small contractors have grown in relative importance and, by 1981, 88.8 per cent of contractors, offering 49.9 per cent of total employment, had fewer than 20 employees (*Cassa Edile* data).

TABLE 8.6
Contractors and employment by legal position of enterprise, Milan district, 1975–81

	1975	1976	1977	1978	1979	1980	1981
(*a*) *Contractors* (%):							
industrial enterprises	65.50	64.39	60.87	51.96	48.89	48.06	48.41
craft enterprises	32.80	33.85	37.61	46.78	49.97	51.02	50.66
co-operatives	1.53	1.76	1.52	1.26	1.14	0.92	0.93
not classified	0.17	—	—	—	—	—	—
Total	100	100	100	100	100	100	100
(*b*) *Employment* (%):							
industrial enterprises	86.86	84.81	83.47	79.63	78.15	77.99	77.03
craft enterprises	9.63	11.03	12.91	16.92	18.85	19.04	20.00
co-operatives	3.43	4.16	3.62	3.45	3.00	2.97	2.97
not classified	0.08	—	—	—	—	—	—
Total	100	100	100	100	100	100	100

Source: Compiled from *Cassa Edile* data.

These developments have had specific effects on the organization of building projects of all kinds. A general contractor, who is responsible for the whole building project, now subcontracts various phases of the building work, particularly the initial work of excavation and laying foundations, and the final finishes and installation of services. Some subcontractors are specialized building enterprises, and provide materials and equipment as well as labour. But the use of labour-only subcontracting, in all its various forms and at all stages of the building process, has become very common, and this also helps to explain the increased fragmentation of the industrial structure in the Milan district.

The spread of labour-only subcontracting since the beginning of the 1970s means that it became the usual way to organize the labour process in conditions of skilled labour shortage. No estimate exist of the actual volume of subcontracting, but employers, trade unions, and students of the sector all agree that it is important, that it has a quite clear influence on the building labour market, and that it affects the whole division of labour.[35]

Even without quantitative estimates, however, it is possible to outline some of the ways of organizing labour-only subcontracting that are in general use. It should be said, however, that practice varies from district to district with local labour market conditions.

Generally, the use of lump labour requires three agents: a main contractor, who is responsible for the whole building project; the subcontractor, who takes on part of that work; and the worker, who is hired out, on a labour-only basis, to the main contractor by the subcontractor. Lump contracts are organized in a variety of ways: (*a*) between small craft enterprises and the main contractor or subcontractor; (*b*) between gangs of self-employed workers and the main contractor or subcontractor; (*c*) between gangs of workers, formally employed by the subcontractor or by the main contractor, but who actually operate as an incentive team (i.e. fictitious hiring), and the contractor; (*d*) between a gang-leader, who takes on the contract himself and pays the other members of the gang, and the main contractor or subcontractor. In the last three cases the contract is usually negotiated informally, and illegally, between the main contractor (or the subcontractor) and the gang-leader, who agree between them a fixed fee for a set quantity of work. Payment may take the form of a lump sum handed over on completion of a specified task, or a piece-rate—for example, so much for a certain number of tiles laid. Such contracts give individual workers very high earnings,[36] but it is important to stress that these high wages depend on two basic conditions: (*a*) the pace of work is much faster than usual, and (*b*) social insurance contributions and tax payments are largely avoided. This is possible because the contract is always negotiated outside union control and, moreover, usually breaks all union agreements on hours of work, wages, and safety.

Through this system the employers are able to organize the whole labour process and control the pace of work, since the gang groups condition the pace of the entire site. As a result, gang labour gives them better control over both the timing and the total costs of production. In fact, despite the facts that (*a*) gang systems are by and large based on skilled labour, (*b*) gang workers' wages are considerably higher than the wages of other building workers, and (*c*) gang workers are supposed to be able to decide their own pace of work, all lump contract systems can be considered a special type of piece-work, or bonus system, designed to improve the organization of casual labour in the building industry in conditions of labour shortage.

Labour-only subcontracting and task work payments (the lump) are not new to the Italian building industry. Several features of the industry help to foster them. Production techniques are relatively simple and labour-intensive, and the whole building process is readily subdivided, lending itself to a high division of labour. Moreover, demand is particularly unstable, and the incentives for risk shifting are high. Labour-only subcontracting is a form of work organized to cope with variations in demand both for the product and for the various types of labour during the building cycle.

8.4.1 Subcontracting: the sources of decentralization

Subcontracting, lumping, and other 'putting-out' arrangements have a long history in the sector, with a growing trend in more recent years. It is therefore not the resort to labour-only subcontracting as such that is new, but the sheer extent of its current use. To understand this, it is necessary to explain the nature of subcontracting systems in construction, and the reasons for their recent expansion. Four different questions need to be investigated: the first is related to the structure of the industry, the second to the nature of the labour relations, the third to the conditions of labour supply, and the fourth to the role of the unions.

(i) *The structure of the industry*. The construction industry has always been characterized by a very fragmented industrial structure, with an increasing tendency towards decentralization. As Brusco (1982, pp. 171–3) has clearly pointed out, to explain decentralization it is necessary to consider the technology in use, as this constitutes the necessary condition which makes decentralization possible, that is, without having recourse to an inferior technology. In construction, the production process is the result of a series of separate stages, for which little mechanization is required. With the exception of industrialized building methods, there are no technological economies of scale for the single contractor who keeps all the stages of the production process together; therefore, the fragmentation of the productive process is possible without any reduction in productivity. Moreover, if one considers the different phases of the production process as 'complementary activities' (Richardson, 1972, pp. 889–92) with different minimum efficient scales of production, requiring different specializations and different timing, it is possible to argue that there will be some diseconomies for a single contractor to complete the whole process himself. As Richardson has explained, it is the need to coordinate closely complementary but dissimilar activities which explains the existence of a 'complex network of cooperation' between enterprises—that is, an industrial structure characterized by a high and complex division of labour between firms.

In this respect, the technological evolution in the sector[37] explains the existence of a general tendency towards increasing decentralization of the productive structure. In the old traditional building site, the bricklayer was able to work throughout the production process, on all the different tasks. And a master mason with one—or a few—building sites was able to employ him throughout the year, asking him to perform different tasks during the site life. But technological evolution has split the process into a longer series of more diversified activities, each of a temporary nature, and the tendency has been to increase the division of labour so to narrow down individual tasks—in order to increase workers' productivity. As a result, workers who specialize in doing one task quickly will only find continuous employment with those contractors who have a large number of yards. Moreover, those yards must be coordinated in the timing of their projects, so as to allow for the rotation of specialist workers between sites. In practice, this is very rarely the case: unless the enterprise has a very large number of sites, which are extremely well coordinated, the costs are simply too high. And it is this which explains the existence of a decentralized productive structure, made up of a network of small firms, each specializing in different phases of the process, and rotating between building sites.

(ii) *The labour relations.* The discussion so far has considered the industrial structure. The question that now needs to be investigated is the nature of the employment relationship (waged labour, pieceworkers, gang groups, self-employed). Given that the same technology can be used for a certain stage of the production process by contractors, subcontractors, gangs, or self-employed workers, what in any one situation makes one form of labour relations preferable to another? To understand this it is useful to refer to the debate on the rise of factory production, which has focused on the differences between the factory system and the putting-out systems. As Cohen (1981) has very clearly pointed out, the crucial change that took place in the shift from putting-out and cottage production to factory production was in the role of the capitalist. The essence of the factory system lay in the nature of the relationship between labour and capital (and not in location, machinery, size of productive units, and so on). In the putting-out system, the workers controlled the work process, while products were monitored; in the factory, the tendency was to supervise the work process as well as to monitor the product. And it is the increased output per worker brought about by the change in supervision and in the nature of supervision itself that explains the change from putting-out to factory production:

> With the introduction of factory organization, a fundamental change occured in the nature of the labour exchange. In the factory, the worker sold his/her labour power for a specific period at a given price and in return agreed to accept the authority of the factory master in matters of discipline, supervision, and organization of the work process. Not only were a whole series of costly market transactions replaced by a single, relatively simple, intentionally imprecise labour contract, but for the most part determination of speed, hours, organization, method of work all fell under the control of the factory master. To the extent that productivity gains could be achieved through a greater specialization, more rational coordination of activities, greater speed of operations, superior quality control, and so on, they could be realized most effectively in a factory type setting. (Cohen, 1981, p. 30).

The same argument can be reversed to explain the survival and the expansion of putting-out systems in construction. It is possible to argue that—given, on the one hand, the characteristics of the production process (the changing working conditions, the small size of many operations, the relatively large number of workers employed on a site), and on the other, the fact that jobs are spread over a large area—the supervision of the labour force and the securing of uniform quality and amounts of services from it are made difficult and expensive. Consequently, the contractor is often faced with the dilemma of supervising a large number of workers performing a miscellany of diversified activities, each with a short time-span. Since it would be physically impossible to control all the workers employed on a site at all times, waged labour paid on an hourly basis would be free to work hard only when the contractor or his assistants were around. However, by tying compensation directly to production—entirely, as in the case of the lump, or partially, as in the case of piece-work—the problem of supervision is largely eliminated. Piece-work, lumping, and subcontracting have therefore to be considered as a substitute for supervisors, and they tend to be used by contractors if this allows productivity gains and/or a greater control of total costs (in order to protect a contract bid), with the exception of those works and those sequences of the production process for which the quality of the workmanship is considered crucial. In such cases it might be more advantageous for the contractor to do the work directly, through the hiring of skilled and loyal workers, and possibly by tying them to the enterprise.

(iii) *The conditions of labour supply.* Nevertheless, the economic advantage to employers of using nonwaged labour cannot alone explain the variety of labour relations found in any one part of the work process. It has to be set against the availability of workers willing to be employed in the sector as nonwaged labour. For such a working arrangement implies not only greater freedom from supervision and increased earnings, but also a noticeable increase in the pace of work, hours of work, and the workload in general, and without the security provided by waged labour relations. In this context, it is useful to consider the contrast between labour market conditions in the sector, on the one hand, in the 1950s and 1960s and, on the other, in the 1970s, which had very different implications for the organization of the labour force.

In the 1950s and early 1960s, the labour market was characterized by an excess of labour supply: unskilled workers, just arrived in the northern urban areas, were willing to be employed for very little money.[38] In a situation where, historically, unions had no control at all over the labour market (see section 8.3.5), where demand for labour was high in an expanding product market, and where there was a continuous flow of unskilled immigrants with no knowledge of the market, labour-only subcontracting developed as a way of hiring workers at very low wages and for short periods of time.[39] Given the relative shortage of skilled workers, some skilled tradesmen, with wide experience of the market (the so-called *capocottimisti*), could use their priviliged position and knowledge to organize unskilled labour. The *capocottimista* knew the product market and knew how to bid, evaluating costs and time by sight. He also had a good network of contacts with his own region or village, so that he was well known among the workers. Typically, the workers gathered outside the railway station very early in the morning (for example, at Lambrate until quite recently), and waited to be hired. The gang-leader might be an employee himself, or self-employed. In the first case, he was paid to recruit the workers, organize and control their work, and pay them. As a self-employed worker, he contracted personally with the employers, agreeing the price for specific work, and then paid the other workers. In all cases, wages were arbitrarily fixed. A large mass of immigrants was passing through the district at this time. Given their lack of knowledge of the market and the need to earn money immediately, the new immigrants had to rely on this system. At the same time, developments in technology helped to reinforce this organizational trend. The introduction of reinforced concrete, and the increased division of labour it brought with it, made the use of labour-only subcontracting easier. While the features of the building cycle and the new characteristics of the site cycle called for casual and intermittent jobs, the subcontracting systems made it possible to organize this casual employment at a time when demand for labour was expanding.[40]

In the late 1960s and early 1970s, the labour market came to be characterized by a shortage of skilled labour (see Chapter 5, sections 5.2, 5.4). The inflow of immigrants into the northern areas tailed off, and the industrial structure began to fragment, making the traditional on-the-job training pattern more difficult. In such conditions, some groups of skilled workers, given their individualistic attitude and their small business mentality, found (and indeed still find) advantages in working in gangs or as self-employed, i.e. they were willing to work very hard to get high earnings. In a situation of tight markets, they could exploit the conditions to increase their earnings, and have the greater freedom of 'being their own boss'. And it is precisely the willingness of skilled workers to work on the lump which is crucial in explaining the expansion of this system of labour relations in the second period.

(iv) *Social relations*. Last, but not least, the role of the unions has to be mentioned. The contrast with what has happened in other industrial sectors in Italy is quite remarkable. As Brusco (1982) has pointed out, in general the increased union power at the place of work (and therefore the increased rigidities imposed on the use of labour), as well as the constraints imposed by legislation on dismissals, have led to a process of decentralization in those sectors where the technology is use has made it possible. In construction, however, it is not the increased power of the unions which has led to a process of fragmentation of the industrial structure. Rather, the weakness of the unions has tended to reinforce a process of fragmentation that was already taking place.

Subcontracting arrangements have spread, in the teeth of strong union opposition, because of a general lack of control by unions at the place of work. And this in turn has further reduced the power of the unions. In other words, trade union action has acted as a self-reinforcing mechanism: subcontracting arrangements have spread because of trade union weakness at the workplace, and this has made the union position, at the workplace, even weaker. Unionized workers are of course against subcontracting and lumping for political, cultural, and ideological reasons, as it breaks the class solidarity and interest, and weakens bargaining power. Therefore, they are bitter towards their fellow workers organized in gangs, and it is common for them to boycott their work, when they work side by side in the same yard, but under different employment conditions. In this context, the existence of different strategies among workers, as well as between workers and unions, has to be pointed out, as well as the situation of conflict over the issue of the control of the work process. It is in fact the 'individualistic' attitude of gang workers, which aims at direct and individual control over the work process, that makes the 'collective' control of the work process difficult. Indeed, the impact of the upheaval of the Italian labour movement in the late 1960s and early 1970s in the construction industry has been quite the opposite of that in the steel industry (see Chapter 7, section 7.4). For, except in the very large building enterprises, the power relationship within the sites has not changed appreciably. The following section will discuss in more detail why unions have not succeeded in increasing their control over the organization of the labour process.

To conclude, it is not possible to say that any one factor alone—economic, technological, or institutional—accounts for the forms of labour relations found in particular circumstances at particular points in the construction industry. Instead, as suggested in Chapter 6, there is a complex interaction between different factors at different levels. In the examples discussed here, technology can be taken as a given (where the characteristics of the technology in use make possible the fragmentation of the production process), but the actual form of labour relations will depend on a struggle between its profitability to the employer and its attractiveness to individual workers, mediated by the conditions of labour supply. In this context the unions play a 'facilitating' role, since it would seem that where unions are weak, the likelihood of workers being prepared and able to work on the lump is by definition greater. And the role of the unions is historically weak as a result of the overall economic and technological conditions prevailing in the industry.

8.4.2 Fragmentation and trade union organization

In 1970, a law on workers' rights was passed as a result of pressure from the trade union movement (see Chapter 7, note 29). This law established rules for trade union organizations at the workplace, and thereafter it became possible for the unions to organize workers directly on the building sites. Construction unions made a considerable effort to encourage and strengthen trade union organization on the building sites, in order to centralize all union activity (information, meetings, recruitment) there. Since then, the actual organization has been based on the *delegati di cantiere*, elected by workers employed on a site by the same building contractor and representing the unions at this decentralized level, and on the workers' councils, where all issues related to the site and other more general trade union problems are discussed by the workers employed there.

But, given the institutional limits set by the law to trade union organization within the sites, and the high degree of fragmentation in the sector, it has not been easy to make such a structure work, and the district union remains very important. There are several reasons for this. First, legal protection for trade union organization is limited to building sites with 15 or more employees all working for the same contractor, and thus leaves out a large number of enterprises and sites.[41] Secondly, the fragmented structure of the sector, the mobility and temporary nature of building activity, and the high labour force turnover (due to the fact that when a construction is finished the site will vanish and the workers will move elsewhere) all imply that trade union organization at the place of work is always temporary. A continuous effort is therefore needed to establish contacts with the workers and to organize them. The more workers move from job to job, from site to site, the more difficult it is to unionize them, and to obtain 'reliable' shop stewards. Site organization is therefore very casual and, on many small sites, does not exist at all. Where it does exist, it is often the result of determined militancy on the part of a few. Moreover, quite apart from the impact of the institutional limits set by law, the fragmented structure of the sector places a limit on the physical possibility of trade union officials in the district contacting and organizing workers in all enterprises, as a large number of small sites are hard to identify and almost impossible to reach. Nevertheless, in those situations where the workers' movement is strongest, the union structure at the site exerts a real influence on the labour process. In the 1970s, particularly in the large and medium-sized enterprises, the unions had major successes at the place of work, and established more regular employment contracts, better working conditions (i.e. changing rooms, canteens, showers, toilets), and improved health and safety provisions. However, these changes were confined to medium and large firms. The rules regulating workers' rights are not applicable to enterprises with less than 15 employees, and large enterprises could avoid them by fictitious division into small firms. And, in this context, the breaking up of large enterprises into small ones has been interpreted by the building unions as an attempt to evade the law, and thereby weaken the workers' organization.

8.4.3 Fragmentation and the new mobility patterns

It seems possible to argue that the substantial changes that have occurred in the building industry in the last 10 to 15 years have been brought about by the decline in numbers, and the exhaustion of the secondary labour force that previously filled male manual jobs. This big change has had a series of consequences, which have been most strongly felt where local labour markets are tight. The most remarkable among them has been the increasing number of building workers on lump wage contracts. This in turn has had a major impact on the whole nature of work on site.

First of all, where previously the unitary labour process had fostered a relatively simple, hierarchical division of labour, the introduction of lump labour organized in specialized rotating gangs has cut across all existing horizontal and vertical divisions in the labour force. Secondly, the fact that workers on the same site are employed by different enterprises, or are employed under different arrangements, affects all aspects of worker experience. In particular, it means that, on any one site, competing systems coexist in all the major areas of work organization—working conditions, the division of labour, payment system, level of earnings, and degree of unionization. Lastly, the fact that some workers are attached to the site throughout the project and others are present only for short periods means that there is no common interest in improving general working conditions.

This situation has led to further fragmentation of the labour force employed within the same production process. There are now four main groups of workers:

(1) Very skilled workers (traditional skills). They tend to be quite old, and well-integrated into the enterprise. High job stability and good earnings are found in this group.
(2) Very skilled workers (modern skills). This group is quite small and all the workers in it are young. They have a higher level of formal education than those in the first group, and some previous experience in the industrial sector (chiefly in engineering).

(3) Unskilled manual workers. This group is still quite large, and includes both young and very young workers (who are waiting for better jobs outside construction), as well as older workers who have not been able to acquire a skill and are now trapped in this segment of the labour market. Job instability and high turnover characterize this group of workers.

(4) Gang workers, who include skilled workers at their physical peak (25–35 years old) organized in small groups working on lump contracts. Their earnings can be extremely high, compared with the average earnings of the sector, but this depends on a very fast pace of work. They work in this way until they are almost exhausted, and when they start getting older they either try to find a job outside the sector or try to get themselves employed directly by a building contractor.

The actual labour market structure can be sketched as in Figure 8.6.

In order to understand the changes that have occurred in the labour market structure of the building industry, it is also necessary to analyse the increasing outflow of workers from the sector, and the ways in which recruitment to the industry has changed.

(i) *Inter-sectoral mobility*. High inter-sectoral mobility has always been a feature of the building industry. In fact, in periods of expansion, when demand for labour in construction is high, the industry depends on attracting unskilled labour from outside. This is because these workers will only stay in the sector for short periods, moving to better jobs as soon as this is possible. The high turnover recorded in construction seems to a large extent due to such mobility between the building industry and the other sectors of the economy. Indeed,

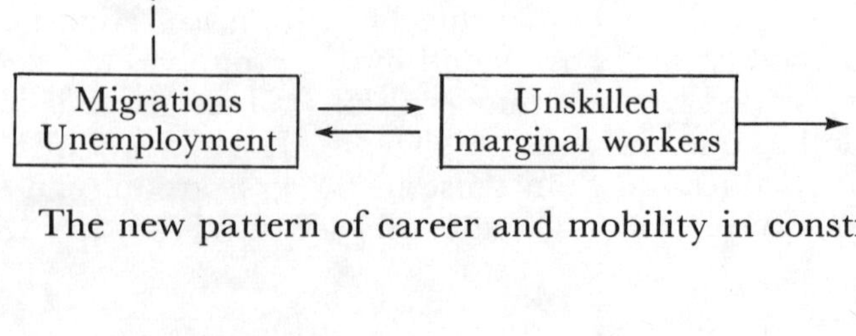

FIG. 8.6 The new pattern of career and mobility in construction

turnover tends to increase when employment is expanding, especially when this happens rapidly and in the context of large-scale migrations.

(ii) *Horizontal mobility.* For some groups of workers, and in particular market conditions, horizontal mobility can be much more important than vertical mobility, since it allows them to exploit market conditions to their own advantage. This was the case in the 1960s. Unskilled workers had little interest in training and job promotions, but set out to take advantage of the construction boom to improve their earnings by working overtime and by moving from enterprise to enterprise, from area to area, until they could earn high wages. Nowadays, skilled workers organized in gang groups show a similar mobility pattern. When skilled labour is scarce in a district, these workers take advantage of their skill to work on the lump and move around the district looking for the best paid contracts.

(iii) *Vertical Mobility.* In spite of what has just been said, a building worker can have a stable job, good working conditions, career prospects, and continuity of employment, providing he can acquire a degree of skill. The process of acquiring skill is not a straightforward one, and has changed over time. The general conditions of the market—the market structure and product demand conditions, the degree of subcontracting, technology in use, division of labour, and labour market conditions—all affect the training process, so that the process of acquiring a skill varies considerably depending on the time workers enter the sector.

It has always been a characteristic of the industry that there was no formal training procedure, and that unions played no part in the acquisition or reward of skills. Instead, this has depended chiefly on the worker's own experience, and on the current mobility pattern within the industry (see Chapter 5, section 5.4). In contrast with those industries where skill is a byproduct of long service with one employer, in the building industry, staying with a single contractor is unimportant. On the contrary, it is when a worker has acquired some skill that he is more likely to stay with one employer. Skilled workers show a lower level of mobility than unskilled, and building contractors try to strengthen their links with skilled labour, given that they are indispensable and in short supply. The most common way to attach skilled workers to the enterprise is to pay them personal bonuses, which often do not appear on the books.

8.5 Conclusions

The transformation of the Italian economy from an agricultural to an industrial economy required large population movements. The north/south dual economic development, the continuous outflow of population from the peasant areas, the process of development, and finally the large internal migrations created such a fluidity of labour supply as to permit a *continuous labour turnover* in construction. This was possible while (*a*) a surplus labour supply existed, (*b*) this consisted of cheap labour (unskilled, young, immigrants, peasants), and (*c*) unionization levels were low. The rationalization introduced into building activity in the 'second phase' made it possible to cut down employment requirements, and these reductions mainly affected unskilled labour. But changes in the demand for labour were not sufficient to meet those in the conditions of labour supply. Thus, the labour market environment for construction differed widely in the two cycles.

During the period 1951–65, the expansion in building activity gave rise to a large increase in employment in what was a typical labour-intensive sector. This increase in the building labour force was greater than that in all other sectors, in spite of the fact that the latter, too, were expanding. Throughout the whole period, construction performed a precise 'social function' with respect to the Italian labour market: it was a pool where the industrial reserve army was contained and given a first rough training, and from which it was then channelled towards the industrial sector. Starting with the end of the 1960s, the relationship between demand and supply in the building labour market was modified quite drastically. On the supply side, four changes can be seen: (*a*) the emergence of alternative jobs in the extra industrial sectors (*b*) an increase in average personal income (*c*) an increase in schooling, and its effects in terms of labour supply and job expectations, and finally (*d*) the lessening of internal migration. All these factors served to reduce labour supply for the building industry. At the same time, manpower mobility, both between sectors and between areas, largely declined.

From 1965 onwards, the level of building activity was low. The industry responded by reorganizing production, and by restructuring the labour process. Building activity was further subdivided into a connected series of specific tasks, and these were increasingly organized by subcontractors or gangs (small groups of skilled workers working as an incentive team). Direct employment by building contractors was reduced to a few skilled trades, as employment of marginal/unskilled workers was drastically cut with the slow down in building programmes and the reorganization of the building process. The demand for skilled labour, both for the traditional trades and for the new ones, increased with the restructuring of the industry. Moreover, the reorganization of all sequences of the building process through subcontracting interrupted existing forms of on-the-job training, with the result that skilled labour became even scarcer. The growing labour shortage in turn encouraged the gang system as a way of organizing and controlling labour.

Thus, cumulative changes in market, technology, skills, labour market environment, and trade union organization have interacted continuously to restructure the labour market.

Notes

1. Data on the housing census show quite clearly this shift; see Appendix E. 37.
2. See Barp *et al.*, 1975; Barp, 1976; ANCE, 1980, pp. 47–51.
3. It is possible to foresee the diffusion of industrialized methods of production only when a new expansionary cycle takes place. It is in this persepctive that the study of the impact of the new techniques on the labour process (see Brusco *et al.*, 1981) becomes extremely interesting. For a discussion of technical innovation and diffusion in the Italian construction industry, see Appendix C.
4. See Appendices E. 31, E. 32, E. 33, E. 34, E. 35, E. 36, E. 37.
5. Erection consisted in superposing bricks (or stones or other materials, according to the local building materials available) on a layer of mortar. The crucial difference between walls was related to their load-bearing capacity, and difficulties increased with the architectonic complexity of the building (vaultings, escalators, balconies, re-entering parts, and so on).
6. *Ministero di Agricoltura, Industria e Commercio, Censimento della Popolazione del Regno d'Italia al 1' febbraio 1901*, Vol. V, Table 30, pp. 124–5, Roma (1904); Procacci, 1970.
7. Rossi (1926, p. 557) in analysing the wage structure per industry and trade in the Milan district, acknowledged 11 groups of trades in the construction industry: *muratori* (bricklayers), *cementisti* (cement workers), *pittori ed imbianchini* (painters), *stuccatori di platfonds* (stucco workers), *fumisti* (stove setters), *marmisti* (marble workers), *lavoranti pavimenti in legno* (wood-floor workers), *tappezzieri in carta* (paper hangers), *imprese lavori stradali* (roadworkers), *suolini, asfaltatori* (asphalt workers).
8. Mereu (1972, p. 257) estimated that out of 12–15,000 workers employed in the Milan district, 3,500 were bricklayers, 4,000 labourers, and navvies, 4,500 boys (*garzoni*).
9. This created extremely crowded building sites with a high risk of accidents.

10. A large number of minors were employed in the sector. According to the statistics for workers on strike, for the period 1901 and 1905, between 10 to 20 per cent and up to 40 to 48 per cent of the workers recorded in construction strikes were minors (Andreasi, 1968, p. 225).
11. See *Libro Ricordo Storico*, 1906, p. 160; Procacci, 1970, p. 14; Saba, 1978, p. 29.
12. See Schiavi, 1910, p. 376; Procacci, 1970, p. 22; De Vecchi and Treu, 1979, p. 26.
13. The *Società di Mutuo Soccorso* were voluntary associations of workers, for the most part characterized by an inter-class and paternalistic nature. They were financed by the members themselves through a subsidy fund, which aimed to preserve workers' earnings in cases of involuntary interruption of employment (illness and unemployment). They developed in the years 1869–80, mainly among the skilled urban workers and craftsmen. Among their leaders were many honorary members belonging to a different social class, who contributed both financially and in terms of the public image of the association. On the experience of the *Società di Mutuo Soccorso* see Saba, 1978, pp. 7–17; Procacci, 1970; Merli, 1970; and De Vecchi and Treu, 1979, pp. 43–9.
14. Membership of FIOE was small if compared with the over half a million workers in the sector, but quite a considerable number if compared with the other major federations: 50,000 in the federation of metal workers; 41,000 in the federation of railwaymen; 18,000 in the federation of textile workers (Procacci, 1970, pp. 25–53).
15. Such piece-work was, by contrast, permitted for digging and transporting bricks (Schiavi, 1910, p. 377).
16. This worker was called *poussà*, a word that in the local dialect means 'pushing'.
17. De Vecchi and Treu, 1979, pp. 28–9; Cipollini, 1979, p. 17; Schiavi, 1910, p. 379.
18. See Cipollini, 1979, pp. 19, 24–5.
19. See Appendices E. 24, D. 25.
20. See Bianchi, 1952, p. 315; Cipollini, 1979, p. 42.
21. Paci (1963a, p. 111), in analysing the immigration of labour into the construction industry of the Milan district, concluded: 'it is our conviction that this process of training is longer and more difficult than it was in the past.'
22. The data at the national level on the structure of the labour force by classification grade give an idea of the weight of the different groups of workers. For 1951 and 1961, foremen and skilled workers accounted for 10 per cent and 13.3 per cent and unskilled workers for 65.5 per cent and 60.1 per cent, respectively for the two years. See Appendix E. 24.
23. In the construction site analysed by Pellicciari (1963, p. 46), these workers were relatively old (one aged over 60; four between 50 and 59; three between 40 and 49; and one younger than 40), all with long experience in the sector (seven had over 20 years experience, three between 10 and 19; two between five and nine); and with a long length of

service with the same building contractor (two had over 20 years of service, six between 10 and 19, and four between five and nine).

24. Overtime work was used extensively from the spring till the end of the summer, up to 12–14 and even 16 hours a day (Pellicciari, 1963, pp. 15, 19).
25. Paci (1963*a*, pp. 79–80), for this purpose, quotes from a paper prepared by a commission of the construction employers' association of the Milan district. The problem of labour shortage was set out and explained, together with the considerable mobility of workers towards other industrial sectors and abroad, and this was related to the greater continuity of employment in the other sectors. See also Pinchera and Veneziani, 1965, p. 109.
26. Paci calculated, on the basis of the census data, that employment in construction increased over the period 1951–61 by 64 per cent for the country as a whole, by 82.96 per cent for the north of Italy, by 499.82 per cent for Lombardia, by 132.25 per cent for the Milan district, and by 246.63 per cent for the city of Milan (Paci, 1963*a*, pp. 76–83 and Appendix, Table 1).
27. Of which 300,000 people moved to Turin alone, and 250,000 to Milan (Alasia and Montaldi, 1975, pp. 28–9).
28. As Paci (1963, pp. 110, 112) pointed out: 'The carpenters, the wood workers and the miners, they all are from the mountains. First, Friuli and Veneto, and then Abruzzo and Calabria. This specialization seems connected with their experience of wood-working, typical of the people from the mountains. From the plain, instead, there came the bricklayers, experts in working with stones and bricks . . . . These groups were following a geographical and professional itinerary, already experienced by other seasonal workers, that is, the oldest and most expert workers of their villages.'
29. The biographies of immigrants into the Milan district collected in 1960 by Alasia and Montaldi (1975) show very clearly and sharply the phenomena just described.
30. This highly centralized structure was the result of (*a*) the ideological basis of the Italian trade union movement, its class nature, and therefore the idea of the unions as general representatives of all workers, and (*b*) the objective circumstances in which the unions were reorganizing, that is, the lack of trade union officials with bargaining experience, and the lack of direct bargaining activity between employers and workers in the previous years, as the fascist corporative system was based on collective agreements settled centrally. In this respect, there was some continuity, as the trade unions began to renegotiate the industrial national agreements set by the fascist unions.
31. This workers' representative body was allowed only on sites with no less than 40 workers and, in any case, with very limited power.
32. In the 1950s as a result of the anti-union discriminatory practices followed by many industrial enterprises, a considerable number of trade union activists were dismissed. Some of them were then hired by the

trade union organizations as their officials. In this connection, it is interesting to notice that while I was interviewing a trade union official of FLC of Milan, Mr Trezzi, I discovered that he was one of the members of the Internal Commission at Falck sacked in 1952, in the years of heavy anti-union policies. He then started working for CGIL as a trade union official in the construction industry of the Milan district.

33. Data are not available on unionization for this period, and this is a rough estimate from trade union sources.
34. *Il Giornale dei Costruttori*, 1968; Torri, 1969.
35. Estimates are not available, but it is possible to argue that various arrangements for subcontracting are employed to organize most building activity. For example, skilled workers interviewed for the ISFOL (1977) research on training were employed as follows: 55.7 per cent in direct employment, 28.1 per cent subcontracting, and 16.2 per cent self-employed. It should be added that 63.6 per cent of the workers directly employed had previously experienced some sort of subcontracting arrangements. Finally, while 28.1 per cent of the sample (national basis) were working on a subcontracting basis, this was true of 36.6 per cent of workers in the Milan district (ISFOL, 1977, p. 56).
36. No data is available on lump payments and wages informally bargained. In an interview with some workers directly employed, but actually working on the lump (*lavoro a misura*), it turned out that their earnings tended to be twice, or even more than twice, the average regular wages (Pizzigani, 1980).
37. In particular, the early introduction of reinforced concrete, the subsequent introduction of some capital-intensive equipment in the first sequences of the process, in more recent times the increased specialization of labour and firms, and finally the tendency to rationalize production in order to have less integrated and more independent sequences of work (see Appendix C).
38. See Paci, 1963*b*; Cipollini, 1979, pp. 49–70; Picollo, 1955.
39. On the problem of labour-only subcontracting in the Milan district, see FLC Milano (1974); and the article published by ASSIMPREDIL, the Milan building employers' association, in *Il Giornale dei Costruttori*, 1968.
40. Other types of subcontracting systems were found at that time (i.e. small co-operatives, or associations of skilled workers, small craft enterprises, etc.) but the peculiarity of this period was the widespread development of labour-only subcontracting of unskilled labour.
41. Moreover, since the enterprise remains the point of reference for the law, there is no trade union organization for workers employed by different contractors on the same site, or for workers employed by the same contractor on different sites.

CHAPTER NINE

Conclusions: The Structuring of Labour Markets

The hypothesis underlying this work, as discussed in Chapter 1, is that the labour market should be analysed in terms of a segmented market, where the persistence of low pay is explained in terms of the existence of non-competing markets. It is argued that the labour market as a whole is divided into separate segments, where each segment is distinguished from the others by the fact that workers are treated differently, independently of their own characteristics. This analysis of the structuring of the labour market rejects as misleading any attempt to identify and isolate one single explanatory variable, since different factors interact.

The empirical findings on the steel and construction industries presented in this work have shown, first, how labour market structures differ (Chapters 2, 3, 4, 5), and secondly, the factors determining the structuring of labour markets (Chapters 6, 7, 8). The main conclusion, as anticipated in the discussion in Chapter 6, is that economic and technological conditions are crucial in the structuring of the labour market, but that they are not sufficient to account for existing differences, as social relations have to be taken into account. Economic factors, such as product market conditions and industrial structure, and technological factors, such as the nature of technology in use and technical change, define the *economic/technological framework* (i.e. the realm of possibilities) within which employer/worker/union interaction takes place. In other words, to understand the process of determination of the labour market structure, the analysis of *labour/management relations* has to be considered. But the actions and motivations of employers, workers, and unions are constrained by the economic and technological circumstances within which they operate; moreover, economic and technological conditions affect trade union organization, since labour is organized on the basis of the existing conditions of production. At the same time there is a *feedback effect*: the interplay between management, workers, and unions affects in turn the economic and technological conditions under which employers operate, workers are employed and trade unions organize labour, thus giving rise to a continuous and iterative process of change in labour market structures.

This concluding chapter reconsiders the question of the structuring of labour markets by referring back to the points raised by the LMS debate as presented in Chapter 1, and in the light of the empirical findings on the steel and construction industries presented in the later chapters. The aim is to develop a general framework for the analysis of labour market structures. The starting point, presented in section 9.1, is a discussion of the concept of *labour market*. The view is presented that a main problem underlying the LMS debate is the lack of an intelligible definition, so that a certain ambiguity persists in what is meant by 'labour market'. On the one hand, the LMS debate originated in a critique of the traditional concept of labour market.[1] On the other hand, its own definition of the labour market has never been made explicit. As a result, the concept of the labour market tends to be assimilated to the traditional one in terms of the functions the labour market fulfils, thus restricting the concept of the labour market. Section 9.2 proposes a more general approach to the definition of the labour market. By discussing and describing the functions the labour market fulfils, an attempt is made to single out the interrelations structuring it.

9.1 The labour market and the LMS approach

The LMS debate lacks a precise and accurate definition of 'the labour market'. Everybody talks about it, but what is really meant by it is never made explicit. The different hypotheses advanced in the literature to account for segmentation seem to assume, implicitly, a definition of the labour market that, on the one hand, points towards employment and wages as the result of two distinct processes, and, on the other hand, refers to the problem of allocation of workers as the function of the labour market. In other words, it is assumed that the labour market fulfils the same function identified by the traditional theory, with the only difference being that the processes described are not the same, given that the market is not supposed to work in a competitive way.[2]

But, I would argue, the labour market has to be interpreted and analysed within a more general framework which takes into account different levels of analysis and the interrelations between them. That is, the labour market operates in such a way as to allocate workers to jobs, but this problem of allocation cannot be isolated from the other extremes of the spectrum: on the one hand, the process of production of labour power, that is, the system of social reproduction; and, on the other hand, the process through which labour power is consumed, that is, the labour process.

When the analysis of the labour market is limited to the problem of the allocation of workers to jobs, it is not just that the analysis is partial, because restricted to one aspect of a set of complex phenomena that are interrelated, but it also loses its explanatory power. To understand fully the situation of the southern peasant, who emigrates to the north of Italy and is employed as a labourer on a temporary basis under a labour-only subcontractor in the construction industry; of his wife, who, once arrived in the north, works—intermittently—as a domestic help; of the worker in his 40s married and with children, employed in a stable and well-paid job in a steel plant; of his daughter, employed in a small factory producing for a larger enterprise; and so on, we need to understand in detail both the differences in their position in the structure of the supply of labour, thus incorporating into the analysis the social reproduction of labour, and the differences in the labour processes within which they are employed. Thus, if we define segmentation as the separation of the market into different segments within which workers are treated differently, independently of their own characteristics, then we have to explain the different structures of the labour market. Therefore, we have to look at the labour market as a complex phenomenon within which different structuring relations interact. What is needed is a comprehensive conceptual framework, capable of including different levels of analysis, from the social reproduction of labour power to the transformation of labour power, and their interrelations. It is with this intention that I turn to the discussion of the labour market in the following section.

9.2 The labour market and its functions

This section presents a discsussion of the labour market in an attempt to define the interrelations structuring it. Four different levels of analysis are singled out, each focusing on a specific function the market fulfils: (*a*) the social reproduction of the labour force, (*b*) the determination of existing and changing employment opportunities, (*c*) the allocation of workers to jobs available, and (*d*) the transformation of labour power into labour. Within this approach, the problem of the determination of rewards can be considered as incorporated into the previous levels of analysis, since it is assumed that wage rates are determined by the job, and therefore on the basis of the economic, technological, and institutional factors that define the characteristics of these jobs. In other words, my argument is that wage structures are attached to jobs and not to workers. And since these wages are paid on the basis of the jobs the workers hold, in order to explain how workers are paid it is crucial to explain *possible differences in access to jobs*. For each level of analysis a chart is provided (see Figures 9.1 to 9.5) pointing out the main factors involved and their interaction. A final summarizing chart (Figure 9.6) reassembles the different levels of analysis.

Before discussing the different functions the labour market fulfils, it is necessary to point out that in the course of this chapter a simplification has been made with respect to the possible forms of organization of social reproduction and production. More precisely, the analysis is carried out in terms of the *family* as the unit of social reproduction and the *firm* as the unit of production. However, as the work presented here has shown, these are only particular forms of organization. In fact, the construction industry provides evidence of forms of organization different from the traditional ones. On the one hand, the immigrant community constitutes the social unit for the reproduction of labour; on the other, the building site, with its interrelation of firms and gang groups working on subcontracting, constitutes the unit of production. Thus, by taking into account the family and the firm only, and limiting the discussion to two particular forms of organization, the analysis is greatly simplified. In fact, the issues involved here are very complex; the discussion presented does not pretend to be exhaustive, but to outline the main interrelations structuring the labour market, as sketched in Figures 9.1 to 9.6.

9.2.1 *The social reproduction of labour*

The debate[3] on the role and position of women within the production system has put the family at the core of the analysis. This is no longer considered as a decision-making unit based on maximizing principles,[4] but as a social institution, with attention focused on its role in the reproduction of labour power. Without entering into the debate, and therefore without considering the existing divergences, it is possible to say that there are two basic questions raised by the social reproduction analysis: first, the definition of the supply of labour in quantitative terms, given the family as a system of social reproduction, where the inputs are the wages the family gets and housework, and one of the outputs is the labour power sold in the market;[5] and, secondly, the determination of the position of the supply of labour in the labour market, given the sexual division of labour within the family and in the labour market, and their interrelations.[6] The main conclusion of this debate, with respect to the problem of the definition of the labour market, seems to be that the supply of labour, both quantitatively and qualitatively, has to be derived in social terms, 'social terms' meaning the power relationship between social classes historically determined, and therefore including the division by sex.

The starting point of this approach is social reproduction as related to production and therefore as part of the economic system. At the centre of the system of social reproduction is the family. This is the basic unit of reproduction of labour and, as such, secures for all members of the family the necessary standards of living. This concept is based on (*a*) a pull of different incomes (wages, benefits, pensions), where wages are the main source of income, and (*b*) the services provided by housework.[7] Wage bundles and housework are strictly interdependent, and so are the subjects providing them: the providers of wage bundles need housework, just as houseworkers need wages, so that it is argued that labour power is a joint product of wage goods and housework (Picchio del Mercato, 1981, p. 200). Moreover, we could say that the standards of living, as defined above, and their repartition between wages and housework, depend (*a*) with respect to wages, on the jobs, and their employment conditions—including wages—accessible to every member of the working-class population (see section 9.2.3), and (*b*) with respect to housework, on the services provided by the market, and their costs, and/or by the state. Therefore, it is suggested that who will be—or will not be—in the market is determined by (*a*) the household's standard of living, and (*b*) its distribution between waged (wage labour) and non-waged (housework) activities.

The same kind of reasoning could be repeated for immigrant labour, with the difference that in this case the process of the social reproduction of labour takes place outside the economic system that employes that labour power. As a result, the economic and social cost of reproduction of labour is not paid for by the economic system which consumes the labour power. We could say that, in the case of immigrants, it is the very low standard of living in their place of origin that induces them to emigrate, and to supply their labour power.

The state plays a fundamental role in the reproduction of labour, its action affecting standards of living, and shaping the legal structures regulating the reproduction and employment of the labour force (see Figure 9.1).[8] Benefits (supplementary incomes, pensions, social security benefits) and services (all social services, including, in a broad definition, education, health, housing, etc.) are provided by the state to integrate wages and/or housework, if either or both are not sufficient for an 'adequate' standard of living.[9] Moreover, state intervention takes place also through legal structures, in the regulation of both the system of social reproduction (i.e. family law) and the labour market system (i.e. employment legislation).[10] To conclude,

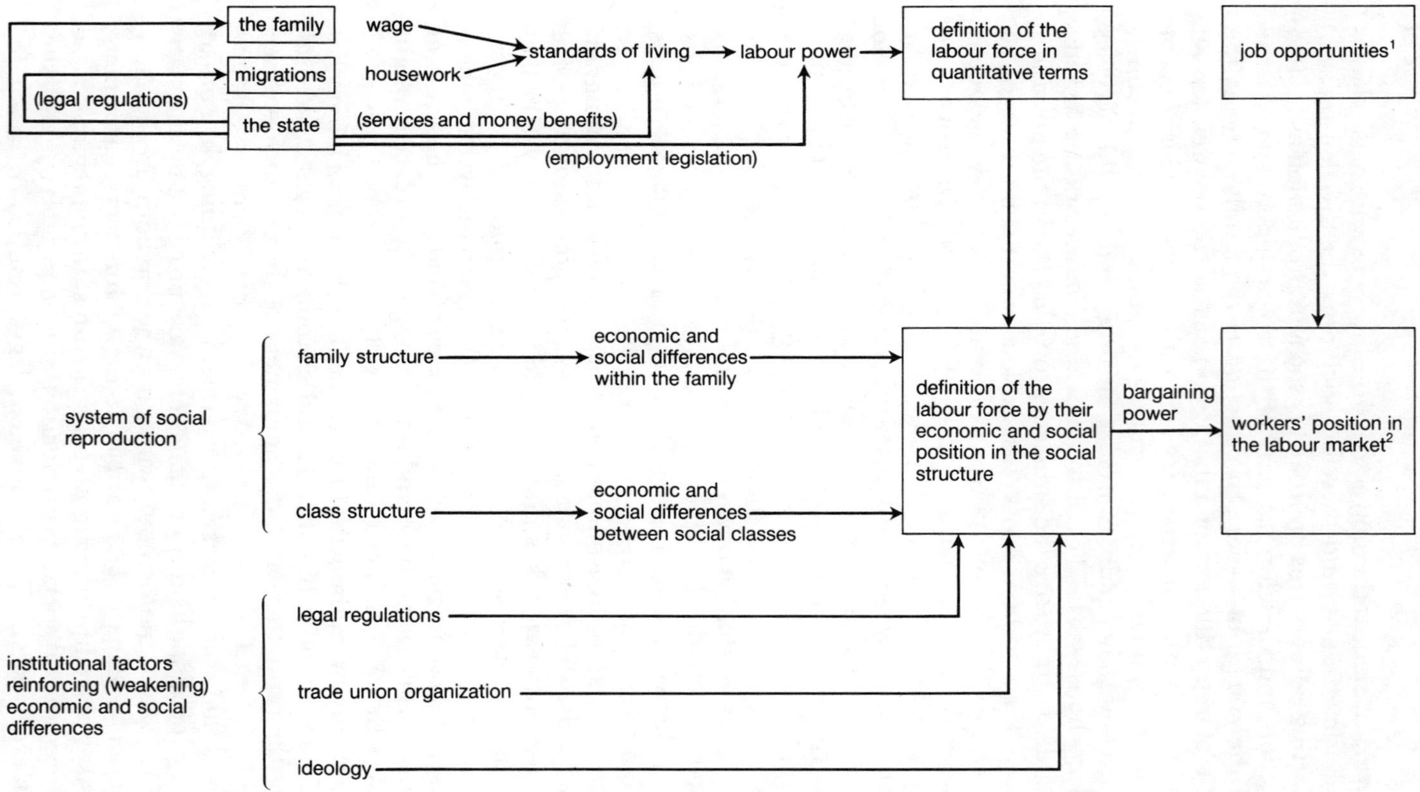

FIG. 9.1 The system of social reproduction

Notes:
1. See Figure 9.2.
2. See Figure 9.3.

the state, by affecting on the one hand the standards of living and its distribution between incomes and services, and on the other the legal structures for the regulation of both the social reproduction of labour power (the family) and its consumption (the labour market), can exert a control on the supply of labour, particularly the supply of low-paid labour.

The work done on the system of social reproduction has shown that the labour force is not homogeneous. Women, men, old people, juveniles, immigrants, and ethnic minorities differ substantially, not so much in terms of skills, education, and physical conditions, but with respect to the position they occupy in the labour market. And, it has been argued, their position in the labour market must be explained by reference to the existing *economic and social* differences in the system of social reproduction. I would argue that differences in the economic and social status of workers are a reflection of (*a*) the position workers occupy in the system of social reproduction, with respect to the existing class structure; and (*b*) the position workers occupy within the family.

The social and economic position of the worker's family, that is the *social class* to which he/she belongs, is crucial in determining the worker's access to occupations and trades. Following the classical argument of non–competing groups, differences in education, information, work connections, relations, and so on, differentiate the access to occupations and trades for each stratum of the work force. At same time, the social class, given the class culture background and ethic of work, defines what is considered as a 'socially acceptable' occupation, in terms of both working conditions and wage level.

In this respect, the case of the construction industry underlines the need to consider the changes in the system of social reproduction (i.e. the changes in the social structure) in order to explain the evolution in the labour market structure. During the 'first phase', 1949–64, large internal migrations made available in the northern urban districts a large supply of cheap unskilled labour, willing to be employed under almost any conditions. The construction industry expanded dramatically by recruiting almost exclusively among immigrants recently arrived in the north, or, in other words, amongst those in the lowest social strata and willing to accept the worst jobs. The labour market structure was hierarchical, and structured in two superposed groups: the group of stable and skilled workers; and the group of the casual and unskilled workers. The 'second phase', 1964–81, saw a change in the system of social reproduction. The slow-down of internal migrations reduced the inflow of cheap and casual labour, while the workers settled in the north were no longer willing to be employed in the construction industry. A quite different labour market structure characterizes this second phase. Groups of skilled workers, organized in gangs, supply their labour directly, bearing the risk of uncertainty and exploiting product market conditions.

Moreover, *within the family,* members differ in their economic and social position. As already said, waged labour and houseworkers depend on each other for subsistence: the wage worker exchanges wage goods for housework, and houseworkers exchange housework for wage goods. But this is not an equal relation of exchange, for the provision of wage goods is waged and that of housework is unwaged. The balance of power is not equal, since housewives have no independent wage. This difference in the economic position of the members of the family has a mirror image in their position in the social structure and consequently, given the jobs available, in the labour market.[11] This has led, historically, to men's supremacy in the labour market, on the basis of the claim of being the breadwinners.[12] And this supremacy has been reinforced through labour organizations and activities,[13] and through laws and ideologies, thus reinforcing the weaker economic status of women.[14]

In this respect, the steel industry is a clear example of this imbalance of power between male and female labour. The jobs in the sector have always been characterized as hard and tiring, but at the same time as secure, stable, well-paid, and with career prospects. The labour force employed has always been male, in its prime. The existing legislation on hiring has reinforced this policy by allowing employers to discriminate against women, at least up to 1977 (see Chapter 4, section 4.2.4.). The hiring of a few women at Breda in more recent years supports the hypothesis of an imbalance of power between male and female workers in the labour market, as their recruitment has reflected primarily the deterioration of the position of Breda in the product market, and hence in the labour market, and not a more even balance between male and female labour, in terms of job opportunities.

In a very similar way, with respect to the *social structure,* it is possible to say that trade union practices, state legislation, and ideology can be very important in weakening or strengthening the economic and social status of different social groups, since they can affect the conditions under which these groups of workers are willing to supply their labour. For example, as discussed in Chapter 8 (section 8.3.4), the legislation on residence and employment existing in the 1950s weakened the economic and social position of immigrants. On the other hand, the legislation providing for equal rights for women at work passed in 1977 has strengthened the position of women in the labour market, at least in the sense that direct discrimination against them is no longer possible.

To conclude, as a result of (*a*) differences in the system of social reproduction, in terms both of social structure and of family structure, and (*b*) social and institutional forces reinforcing existing differences, some social groups are constructed as crucially weaker sections of the labour force. Thus, the location and forms of the work of different social groups reflect, given the jobs available to them (see next section), their *social bargaining power,* that is, their willingness and ability to accept jobs at certain wages and in certain working conditions.

9.2.2 Existing and changing employment opportunities

The level of employment, following Keynes's approach, is determined by effective demand. The amount of labour that entrepreneurs decide to employ depends on aggregate demand. Various post-keynesian developments have reinforced the keynesian proposition that changes in demand normally affect the level of activity, hence employment, but not prices. These include precisely the studies on the oligopoly sector; studies on the nature of technology, characterizing prevailing technology in terms of fixed technical coefficients of production; and studies on the process of price formation, and particularly those on the pricing decisions of firms with market power. The argument relates demand for labour to the level of output that firms plan to produce, without reference to the marginal productivity theory. Since, in industrial production, full capacity is reached only in boom periods and in a limited number of sectors, an expansion of demand affects not industrial pricing, but the amount of employment.

As a first approximation, we could say that, given the state of technology, existing capital equipment, and the structure of the product market, as well as social relations, the level of employment is determined by expected aggregate demand for output (see Figure 9.2).

The structure of effective demand by sector, industry, and firm will determine the structure of employment, that is, jobs available by sector, industry, and firm. But jobs are found to differ in terms of their working conditions: skill, training involved, career prospects, stability, certainty, earnings and earnings prospects, dirtiness, fatigue and exertion, monotony, and so on. In this attempt to explain the structure of employment, and more precisely the structuring of the labour market in segments characterized by jobs governed by different rules, the LMS debate has pointed out, with different emphases in the various hypotheses advanced, three main groups of factors affecting

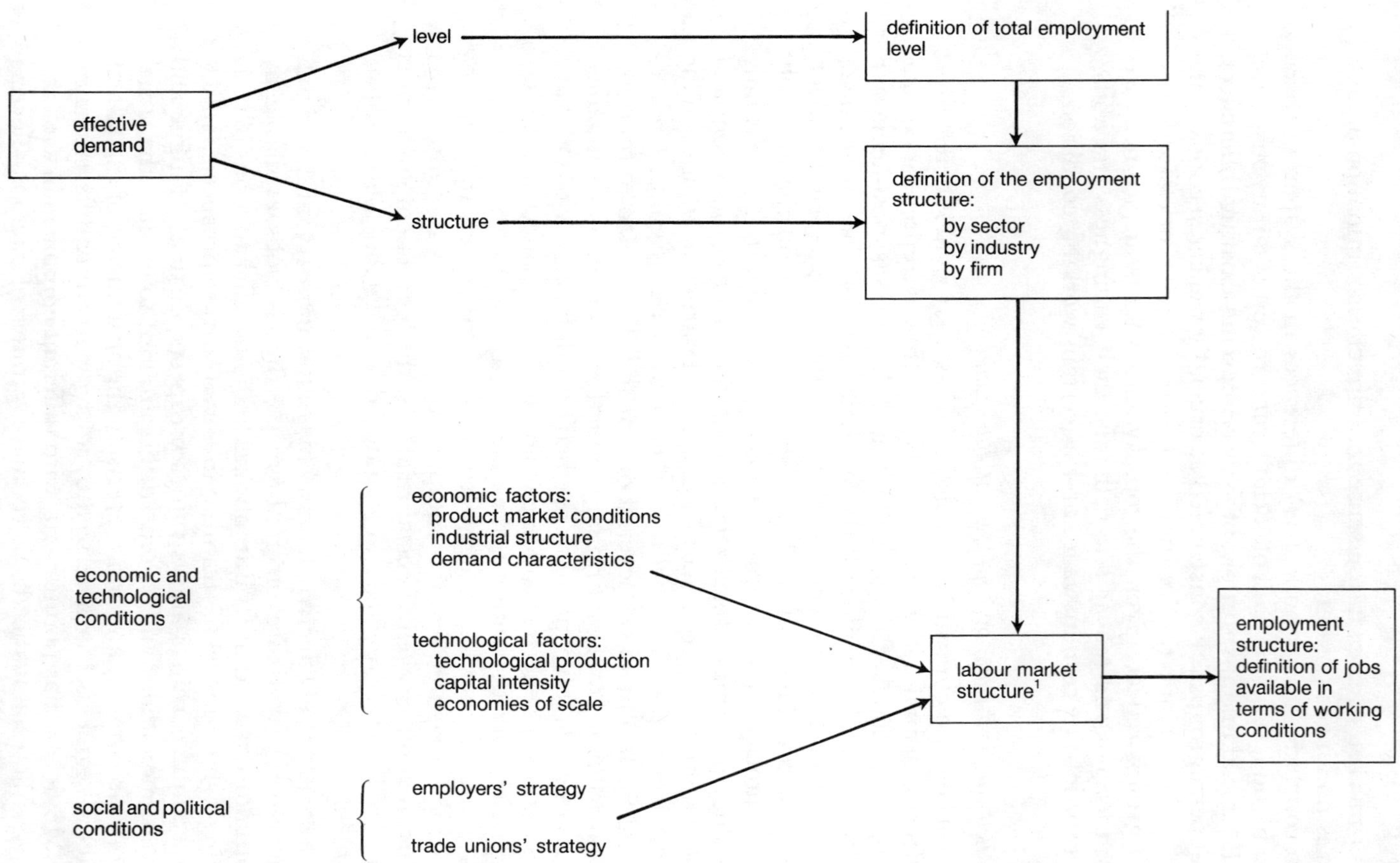

FIG. 9.2 Existing and changing employment opportunities

Note:

1. See Figure 9.4.

employment conditions: economic factors, technological factors, and institutional factors.

The institutionalists have pointed out the role of the formal and informal rules developed in the large industrial firms to substitute for the market process; the dual labour market theory has emphasized the role of technology and existing differences between sectors and firms to account for differences between internal and external markets; the radical approach has underlined the existence of class conflict, and the consequent capitalists' strategy to 'divide and rule' the working class; finally a more comprehensive approach, incorporating institutional, economic, and technological factors, takes into account the role of labour—as organized in trade unions—in the process of segmentation. The debate, as discussed in Chapter 1, has also pointed out that the identification and isolation of one single variable is misleading, since it is the interaction between different variables that has to be considered. This necessarily, brings into evidence the relation between the jobs available, in terms of their employment conditions (given aggregate demand), and the organization of the labour process, and thus the structure of the labour market. Anticipating what will be discussed next, we could argue that the nature of the product, the industrial structure, and the technology in use all affect the functioning of the labour market, by defining the framework within which employer/worker strategies interact. That is, they define the 'realm of possibilities' within which employer/worker interaction takes place, thus defining the labour market structure in terms of jobs available and their characteristics.

The structure of the labour market, defined in terms of segments with different characteristics and processes, has to be related, finally, to the cyclical fluctuations of the economic system.[15] Macroeconomic analyses of the evolution of the labour market have pointed out how a rise or a fall in aggregate demand not only affects the level of employment in different segments of the market (given the structure of product demand), but can lead to a modification in the structure of the labour market itself, i.e. the characteristics of the segment. And this, too, has to be related to the strategies adopted by employers, labour, and the state to deal with fluctuations in economic activity.

In this respect, the rapid and continuous expansion in demand for steel has led to the strengthening of internal markets, where the labour force employed is protected from cyclical fluctuations. As a result of the previous policies, even during the recent slump, steel workers have not been affected by redundancies. The case of construction is quite different. During the expansion, the sector increased the numbers of workers employed on a temporary and casual basis. Then, during the recession, these large firms changed their policy, preferring to employ a smaller labour force, and using subcontracting for the organization of the production process.

9.2.3 Workers' position in the labour market

Effective demand will determine the level and the structure of demand for labour, and therefore, given the historically determined social relations, the jobs available in the economy. In order to understand the process by which workers find employment, and thus the process by which jobs are filled, we have to analyse the interaction between the supply of labour—as defined by the system of social reproduction—and the demand for labour—as defined by the level and the structure of effective demand—at the level of the firm. Before elaborating this, a few points need to be made clear.

A discussion about the structure of employment which explains which workers are employed will also explain who are the unemployed. The questions to be answered in order to understand the concentration of unemployment in certain specific groups are: (*a*) who are these workers? (*b*) what kind of jobs do they usually fill? and (*c*) why is the level of unemployment high in these jobs? Thus, in order to understand the different position of workers with respect to the labour market (that is, employed in primary and secondary jobs, unemployed with brief spells/long spells/frequent spells, or not in the labour force) two processes need to be considered: how vacancies are filled, and how redundancies are made.

It is well-known that most jobs are found by persons who move directly from another job. This includes both the case of internal mobility (within a firm or a plant) and the case of mobility from one firm to another. In both cases, workers move when a vacancy occurs in a somewhat better job, and they can move either because they have been granted the right to move (and this is denied to other workers) or because they have acquired, previously, the necessary cognitive skills.[16] In fact, most skills (using this term in a broad sense to include ability, knowledge, and required behaviour), either specific or general, are acquired formally or informally through on-the-job training *after* a worker finds entry to a job. This is the case in both steel and construction, but with a crucial difference. In the case of the steel industry, all skills (general and specific) are learned on the job, and workers move upward along job ladders when vacancies occur. Thus, once a worker has gained access to a steel plant he can be assured of the possibility of acquiring a skill and developing his career (Chapter 4, section 4.4). In the case of the construction industry, all skills are learned on the job, with new recruits working side by side with skilled workers. But a permanent position in the sector does not ensure the possibility of training and advancement for all workers, so that it is possible to find workers with a long tenure in the sector and no skill (Chapter 5, section 5.4). This implies that workers' position in the labour market changes as a result of their past experience, since affects both their characteristics and the job opportunities open to them. At the same time, the lack of appropriate job opportunities, and particularly the lack of good jobs, affects not only workers' present income and working conditions, but also their future position in the labour market. And this explains why some workers employed in secondary jobs are trapped there,[17] as is the case for some of the southern peasants who emigrated to the north of Italy and became employed in the construction industry.

Workers have to move out of situations (local markets, industrial sectors, plants) where jobs have been destroyed by declining demand or technical change, and this results in lay-offs and discharges. There are some *sectors* which, because of the conditions of demand (mature sector, declining demand, cyclical and seasonal fluctuations) are more prone than others to employment variation. In this sense, the construction industry is quite typical. There are some *firms* that, given the sector in which they operate and their characteristics (dimension, location, integration), show a higher birth/death rate. There are also some *jobs* that, because of the trends of technical change, are more prone to be destroyed. Labour-saving techniques are increasingly applied in labour-intensive processes. Thus, the fact that some workers are more prone than others to suffer from uncertainty and discharge depends (*a*) on the demand side, on the characteristics of these sectors, firms, and jobs that make them more prone than others to be affected by employment fluctuations; and (*b*) on the supply side, on the process through which certain groups of workers are employed there, and on the process through which it is decided which workers to discharge first in these jobs. Indeed, the latter is determined, by and large, by the power relationship between employers, trade unions, and different groups of workers. Therefore, the process through which workers are allocated to jobs, as well as the process by which they are excluded and laid off, have to be analysed, as already pointed out (see above) both on the demand and supply side. Figure 9.3 gives a sketch of the factors involved, and their interaction in determining workers' position in the labour market.

I would argue on the basis of the work done on the steel and construction industries, that the position of workers in the labour market depends, on the one hand, on the *job opportunities available*

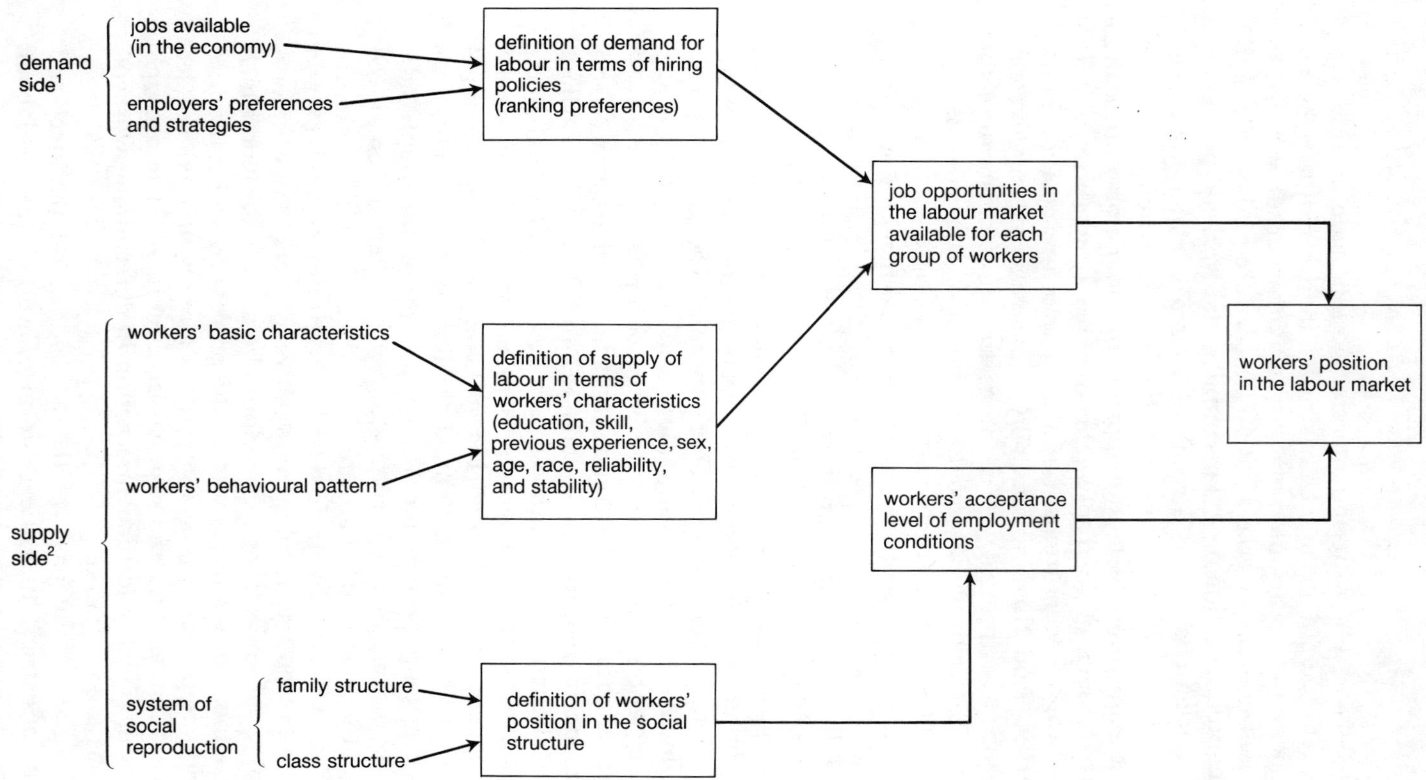

FIG. 9.3 Workers' position in the labour market (allocation of workers to jobs available)

Notes:

1. See Figure 9.2.
2. See Figure 9.1.

to them and, on the other hand, on the *worker's terms of acceptance* of the working conditions, by which I mean their social bargaining power.

Given the jobs available in the market, as determined by effective demand (as discussed in the previous section), employers will define their hiring policies for the different types of jobs. Workers' basic characteristics (such as sex, race, age, and marital status as well as skill, educational attainment, and previous training), together with workers' behavioural patterns (in terms of stability, reliability, obedience, diligence, and so on), tend to be used by employers as screening devices to define their ranking preferences for each type of job. This implies that, given the level of demand for labour (i.e. the total number of jobs available) and given employer strategy, various features of individual workers (including basic characteristics and behavioural patterns) define the employment opportunities available for each group of workers.[18] The position of workers in the social structure (i.e. economic and social status) affects their place in the labour market by defining what I would call their 'acceptance level' of working conditions in terms of earnings, earning prospects, security, stability, training, career prospects, and so on. The system of social reproduction differentiates workers by economic and social status (see section 9.2.1) (*a*) within the family, reflected in differences by sex, age, and marital status, and (*b*) between classes of families, reflected in the different status attached to different groups of workers (such as peasant/industrial workers, labourers/skilled workers, blue-collar workers/foremen/white-collar workers/professionals/managers), and also expressed in differences in work habits and work ethic. And it is precisely this differentiation that delimits the position of workers in the labour market, by defining their 'acceptance level' of employment conditions, below which they would tend to consider the employment opportunities available to them as 'socially' unacceptable. In other words, this defines their *social bargaining power*.

To conclude, the position of workers in the labour market depends on (*a*) employment opportunities available to them, given the level of aggregate demand and employers' policies, and (*b*) workers' relative position in the social structure, differentiating workers in terms of their bargaining power, i.e. acceptance level of working conditions. The main implication of this differentiation of the labour supply, which occurs at the level of definition of both job opportunities and workers' acceptance level, is that similar categories of workers are available at radically different minimum supply prices, *independent of their potential/real productivity*.

9.2.4 The transformation of labour power into labour

From what has been argued in the previous pages, it follows that, in order to understand the process of the allocation of labour—i.e. which worker gets which job—employers' policy and strategy, at the firm level, have to be discussed. And this leads to the analysis of the labour process.

The picture of the labour market given by traditional theory is very unsatisfactory, not only because it gives a picture of the workings of the labour market that is continuously contradicted by empirical evidence, but also because it leaves out what should be at the core of the analysis: that is, the organization of the labour process. The firm is perceived as a 'black box' where inputs enter and outputs exit, but the process of transforming inputs into outputs is not analysed. In my approach, it is precisely *the labour process that plays a crucial role in the process of labour market structuring*.

The process of allocation of workers to jobs, as discussed in the previous section, is the mirror image of the process of allocation of workers within the firm. This is the outcome of a longer series of interrelated processes, through which it is determined which workers to recruit, how to select and train them, and how to promote and pay them. As it has been shown in the course of this work, these questions cannot be treated separately: the problem of allocation is strictly

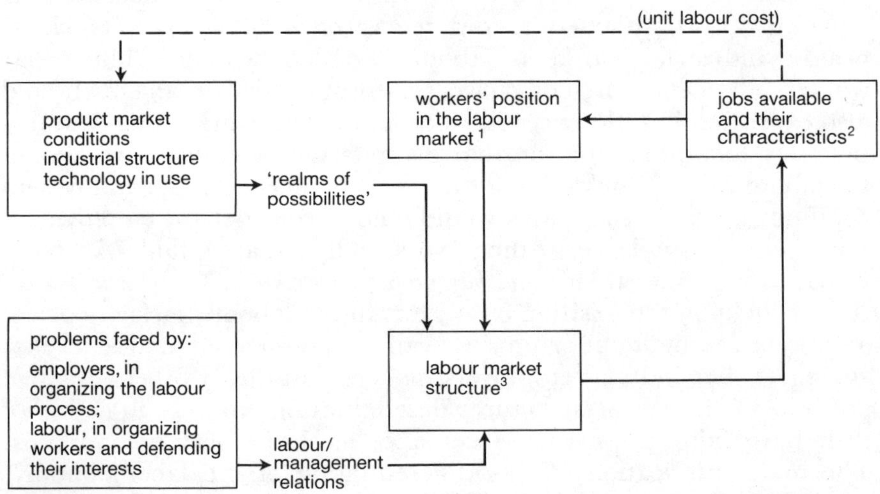

FIG. 9.4 Factors shaping the structure of the labour market

Notes:

1. See Figure 9.3.
2. See Figure 9.2.
3. See Figure 9.5.

related to the question of the organization of the labour process. The entrepreneur has to employ workers in order to organize the production process. More precisely, employers have to fill jobs with workers selling their labour power, and they have to organize the labour process in order to transform labour power into labour. Thus, the process of allocation of labour (the employment of labour power) is directly related to the organization of the labour process (the use of labour power).

This implies, on the one hand, that a change in the way the labour process is organized might cause a change in the process of allocation of workers to jobs—for example, through an adaptation in the recruitment process. This has been the case in the Italian steel industry, where the strengthening of labour organization within the steel plants imposed restriction on capital in its use of labour. Management had to modify the internal labour policy, as the previous systems of organization of the labour process were no longer suitable for pursuing the goals they were designed for. The result was a modification in the division of labour, and an adjustment in the recruitment of labour. Mature workers with little education and long industrial experience were no longer recruited, while young workers with little experience and high educational attainment were preferred (as discussed in Chapters 4 and 7).

On the other hand, a change in the process of allocation of labour inevitably changes the way the labour process is organized. For example, this can be the case where modifications in the characteristics of the supply of labour mean that some groups of workers are no longer available (in quantitative terms) or are no longer willing to play a certain role (for example, because of changes in their 'acceptance level', reflecting a process of collective consciousness and organization). This might result in a change in the way the labour process is

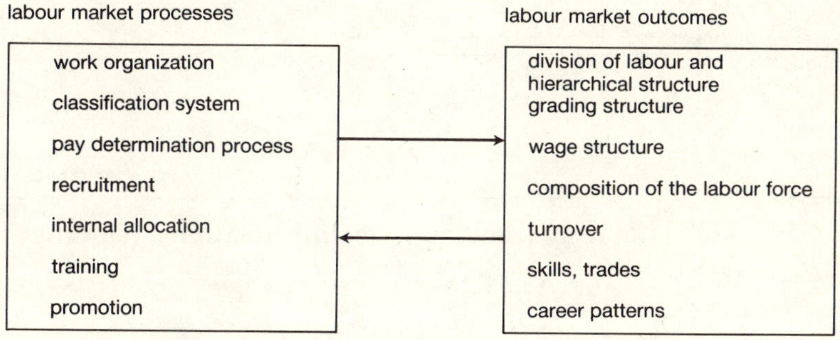

FIG. 9.5 The labour market structure

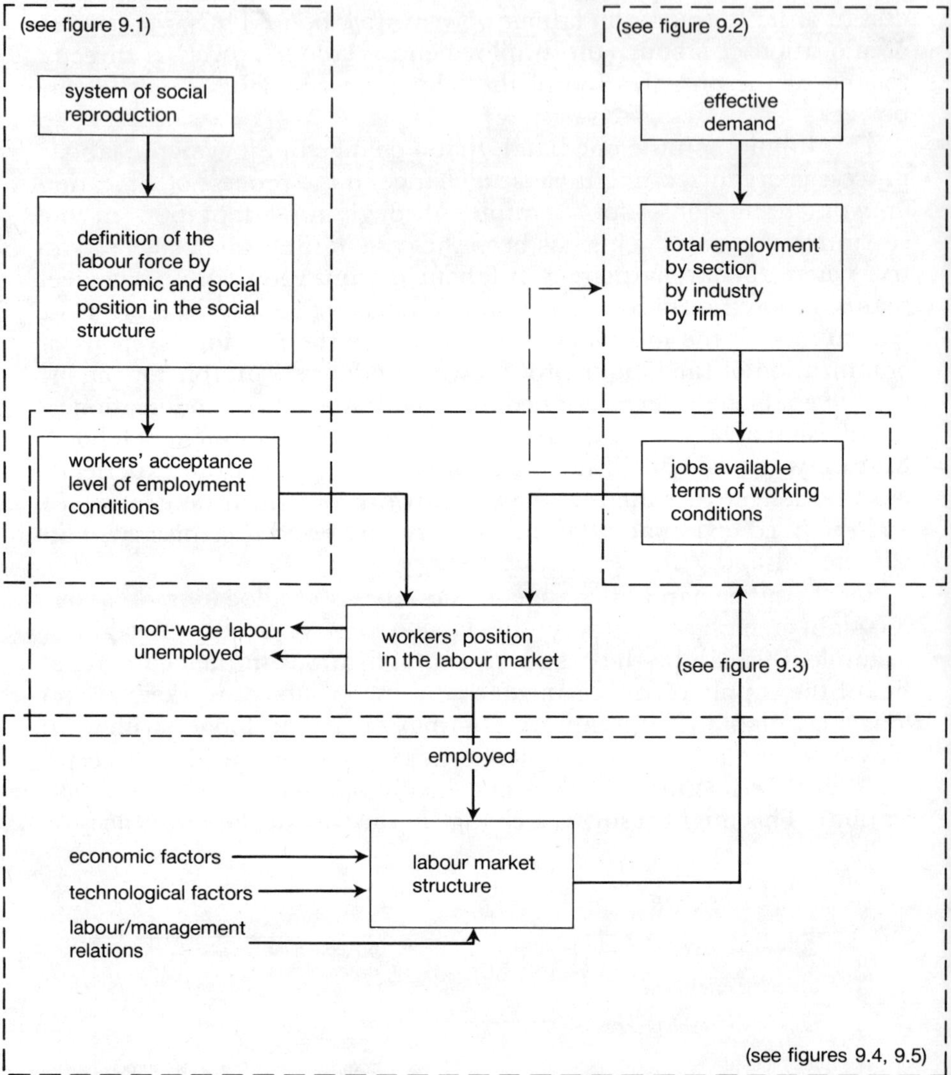

FIG. 9.6 The labour market and its interrelations (summarizing chart)

organized. The case study of the construction industry in Italy describes this. The lack of skilled workers willing to stay in the sector, in recent years, has made it difficult for employers to organize the labour process in the usual way. As a result, the labour market structure has changed from a system based on large building enterprises, organized in teams of workers distinguished by trade, to a complex system of contractors, subcontractors, and gang groups, where workers of similar characteristics, working in the same site, are employed under different conditions (as discussed in Chapter 8).

To conclude, in order to understand fully the workings of the labour market, and why certain groups of workers are employed in and confined to certain jobs, while for others the access to some jobs implies a defined career pattern, it is crucial to analyse the labour process as discussed in Chapter 6, and here represented in Figure 9.4. Within this approach, I refer to the *labour market structure* as the set of mechanisms and institutions through which the labour process is organized (see Figure 9.5). The mechanisms and institutions through which labour is hired, trained, promoted, and paid can best be analysed in terms of the interaction between processes and outcomes. This implies not only that changes in any process (work organization, classification system, payment system, recruitment, training, promotion) might produce changes in the labour market structure in terms of its outcomes (division of labour and hierarchy, grading structure, wage structure, composition of the labour force, turnover, skills and trades, career patterns), and vice versa; but also that a change in any of the processes will not only affect the interrelated outcome, but will call for adjustment in the other processes too.

But labour market structures (as defined above) do not exist in a vacuum: economic and technological factors differ between historical periods, economic systems, sectors, industries, and firms. The economic and social costs of *possible different labour market structures* are defined by the specifics of the economy, in terms of development, growth rate, and business cycle; the specifics of the industry, in terms of product market conditions, industrial structure, techniques of production, and technical innovation; the specifics of the firm, in terms of competitive position in the market structure, past history, and management tradition; and finally, the specifics of the factory, in terms of geographical location, physical dimension, past history, and methods of production. Economic and technological factors can be analysed as defining the problems faced by managers and workers, respectively, in the organization of the labour process. Thus, technological and economic factors can be analysed as *constraints*, delimiting the boundaries within which the labour process has to be organized.

Within these constraints the *balance of power* between the different actors operating within the labour process, employers and employers' association, workers and labour organization, will determine the labour market structure over time.

Notes

1. In fact, the origin of the debate on LMS can be traced back to the empirical findings of the 1950s and early 1960s, showing that employment and wages are not simultaneously determined in a market process, but are rather the result of two distinct processes. See Kerr, 1950; Reynolds, 1951; Bakke and Hauser, 1954; Taylor and Pierson, 1957; Reddaway, 1959; OECD, 1965. For a more recent discussion, within the LMS debate, see Tobin, 1972; Thurow, 1975; Kerr, 1978; Piore, 1979; Appelbaum, 1979.
2. See Burawoy (1979, pp. 95–7) as an example of an interpretation of the LMS hypothesis, in which it is suggested that the problem of allocation of workers between jobs remains the core of the analysis of the labour market. In his approach, the idea of the labour market is confined to the problem of matching jobs and workers. The allocative function is no longer fulfilled by the interrelations between demand and supply through adjustment via wages, but is still considered as the *function* of the labour market; and therefore segmentation seems to be interpreted as the result of allocative processes that are different from the traditional one.
3. This section draws mainly on the work by Picchio del Mercato (1981) and Kenrick (1981). The ideas expressed here developed in the course of joint study sessions I had with Antonella Picchio and Francesca Bettio, to whom I am grateful for the very stimulating discussions.
4. Mincer, 1962; Becker, 1965.
5. Harrison, 1974; Seccombe, 1974; Gardiner, 1975; Humphries, 1977; Himmelweit and Mohun, 1977; Barrett and McIntosh, 1980; Picchio del Mercato, 1981.
6. Milkman, 1976; Breughel, 1979; Beechey, 1977; Hartmann, 1979; Sen, 1980; Kenrick, 1981; Bettio, 1984.
7. Humphries, 1977, in Amsden 1980, pp. 142–5; Picchio del Mercato, 1981, p. 199.
8. Kenrick, 1981; Picchio del Mercato, 1981; Moore and Walker, 1983.
9. See Moore and Walker, 1983, for an analysis of the role of the state in the provision of social services, and their effect on the labour market.
10. Institutional regulations define, through legislation, numerous fields, such as the legal position of women both in the family and in the employment relationship, the school leaving age, retirement age, the legal status of different groups of workers (immigrants), hours of work legislation, wage fixing legislation, and immigration policy.
11. Picchio's argument is that men's control over the system of social reproduction where housewives have no independent wage 'provides the basis

for men's command over housework' (Picchio del Mercato, 1981, p. 201).

12. The idea that it is a male breadwinner who earns the principal wage, and who, therefore has to be protected and privileged, has always been very well-rooted. In the present period this still implies that, whenever there is the possibility of lay-offs, the first workers to be fired will be women, juveniles, and the old. See Kenrick, 1981 for a historical analysis.
13. Kenrick (1981, pp. 172–4) discusses in this context the work done by Hartmann, Rubery and Sengenberger on the question of discrimination practices by male workers against female workers in the fight for jobs.
14. A historical discussion of the way in which patriarchal control embodied in common law helped to determine the location and nature of women's labour is presented by Kenrick (1981). She concludes: 'I have referred only to three aspects of politics that have impinged on the economic position of women: family law, craft organization and national economic regulation. Together they provide clear examples of how the reproduction of structures at a national, institutional and individual level has weakened the terms under which women supply their labour. The effects of these structures are mutually reinforcing.' (p. 187.)
15. See Sengenberger, 1979, 1981; Tarling, 1981; Tarling and Garonna, 1979.
16. Reynolds (1951) recognized, a long time ago, that workers move not because of wage differentials but because of the availability of jobs. People move out of situations where jobs have been made redundant by declining demand or technical change, and move to a place where new jobs are opening up.
17. Rosenberg (1977) examined the career pattern of a sample of male workers in order to explain why some particular groups of workers are concentrated in secondary jobs throughout their lives. His main conclusion was that many people beginning in secondary jobs seemed to be confined to this type of employment throughout their working career; but it was apparent that barriers to upward mobility were not based on a lack of stable work habits (as suggested, for example, by Doeringer and Piore and the radicals): holding a secondary job strongly suggested that one would continue to do so.
18. With the difference that, while physical, educational, and skill requirements can be directly related to job characteristics, others such as sex, race, marital status and to some degree, education are used as screening devices, on the basis of which employers set their hiring standards.

APPENDIX A

Production Process and Technology in Use in the Steel Industry

Pig-iron is an alloy of iron and carbon obtained by direct reduction of the ore with the enrichment of carbon (1.7 per cent). Pig-iron is smelted in the blast-furnace, a vertical cylinder lined with protective fire-bricks.[1] The blast-furnace is continuously charged from above with a mixture of iron ore, limestone, and coke. The charge, in its slow descent, is subject to a series of chemical and physical transformations due to the blast of air blown in at the bottom, and to the consequent generation of heat. Iron separates from the earthy matter of its ore, and this combines with the limestone to form slag. Molten iron sinks to the bottom and the liquid slag floats on top of it. The whole process is continuous; at intervals, the iron and the slag are tapped out at the bottom at two different levels, and the raw materials are fed in at the top to keep the furnace full. The pig-iron is then run into special ladles for transport to the steel mills in a liquid state, where it is refined.

The refining of pig-iron into steel consists in the reduction of carbon content and the removal of impurities. During the conversion, additives and alloy elements are added in order to obtain steel of the required quality. Two phases may be distinguished in the steel-making process: oxidation and the reduction of the molten metal. Oxidation is obtained by a blast of air (Bessemer process) or of pure oxygen (LD converters, open-hearth, and electric furnaces), or by the addition of minerals (open-hearth and electric furnaces), or by the combination of different systems. During this phase, most of the elements of the charge, apart from iron, are oxidized and almost completely eliminated. Then the reduction of the metal follows: the metal bath is deoxidized, usually by the addition of ferro-manganese alloys in order to achieve the required chemical composition of the steel. As this account suggests, different steel-making processes can be used to produce steel; in Italy, open-hearth furnaces, electric furnaces, and LD converters are employed, but while the first process is now technically obsolete and in decreasing use, the other two are technically efficient and becoming more common (see Table A.1 and Figure A.1).

The *open-hearth process* (OH) was developed towards the end of last century, and was rapidly introduced in those areas lacking iron ore deposits, given the ability of the process to deal with a high proportion of scrap. With this technique, the charge can be liquid (molten pig-iron), cold (scrap), or a mixture of the two, and as a result this process can be used both in integrated steel plants and in steel mills only. Pig-iron and scrap, in varying proportions, are placed in the furnace bath, and flames from burning gas, tar, or oil

TABLE A.1
Characteristics of three different steel-making processes

	Open-hearth furnaces		Electric furnaces			Basic oxygen converters	
	I	II	I	II	III	LD	OBM
productive capacity per casting (tons)	280	65	140	56	20	300	250
% of molten pig-iron per charge	60	—	—	—	—	100	80
total time required (hrs./mins.)	7/40	6/30	2/20	2/10	2/15	0/45	0/50
steel produced per hour (tons)	37	10	58	26	9	330	275
steel produced per day (tons)	888	240	1,392	624	216	7,900	6,600

Source: Nicodemi and Zoia, 1980, pp. 150–1, 166, 192.

are directed down onto the metal from above. Oxidizing agents, such as lime, are then introduced, and these combine with the impurities and float as slag on the metal. Heat is supplied externally, and this allows the temperature of the furnace and the speed of the reaction to be carefully controlled, a feature of the process which fits it for the production of special (as well as common) steel. However, the productivity of this process is low, compared with other processes, as shown in Table A.1 (p. 277).[2] For a 250 ton furnace, eight hours are required to complete the whole process. The use of oxygen, recently introduced to speed up the refining of the bath, can reduce the time required to five to six hours. Despite this, the process is obsolete, and it has been increasingly replaced over the last 15 years by electric furnaces or basic oxygen converters (see Figure A.1).

Electric furnaces developed in areas lacking in coal but rich in hydroelectric power in the first decade of this century. With this technique the charge is cold, and melted by heating. Carbon electrodes are used to carry an electric current from a supply transformer to the steel charge in the furnace. As soon as the circuit is made, an electric arc is struck between the metal and the electrodes. This arc generates a very high temperature, which causes the steel to melt.[3] Electric furnaces have the following advantages: (*a*) a cold charge, composed entirely of scrap, can be used, (*b*) the use of electricity for heating excludes all oxidizing gases, and (*c*) the melting process can be precisely controlled. All these points make the technique particularly good for the production of alloys, special steels, and quality steel.[4] The volume of electric furnaces can vary from a few tons up to over 200 tons per casting, and the complete process is concluded in six hours or less.[5] The introduction of very powerful transformers over the last decade, to turn electric furnaces into

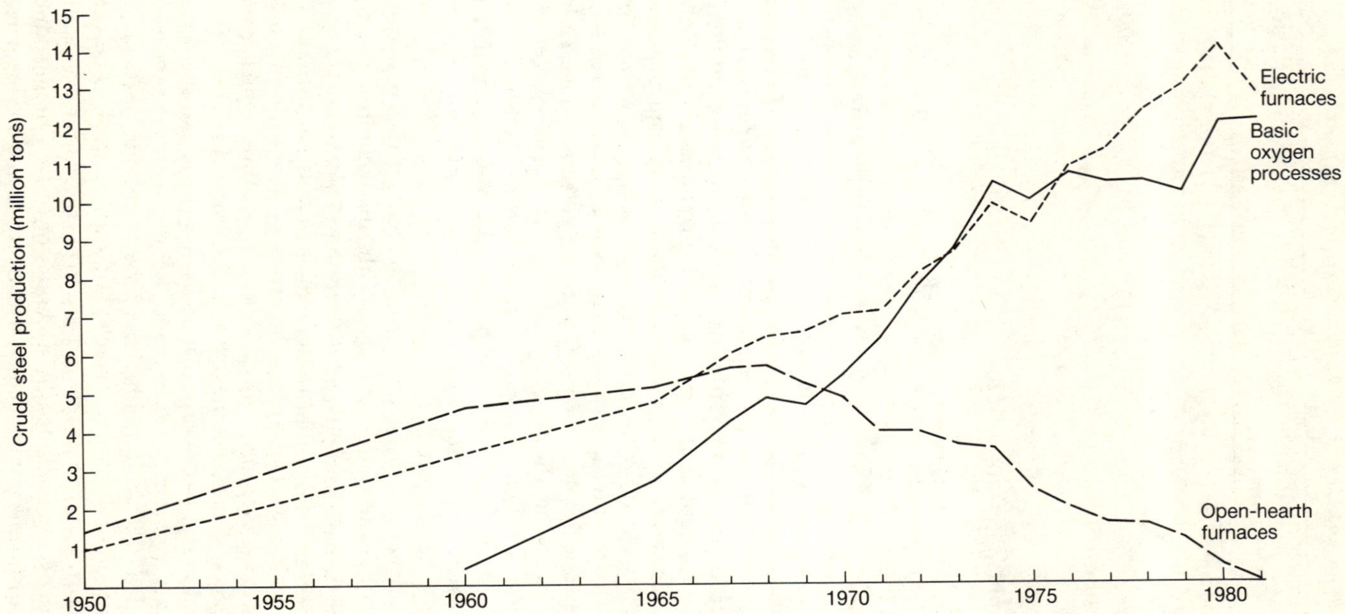

FIG. A.1 Crude steel production by process, 1950–81 (thousand tons)
Source: ASSIDER data.

UHP furnaces (ultra-high-power), has made the process even more rapid (reducing the time required to two to three hours), thus increasing its competitiveness and making it efficient for the production of common steel too.

Steel refining in basic oxygen systems (BOS), such as LD, Kaldo, Rotor and OBM converters, involves the blowing of oxygen at high velocity onto the surface of the metal. This combines with the impurities of the charge, and thc process is completed in one to two hours. This technique has the advantage of high productivity, as a result both of the large capacity of the converter (up to 300 tons per casting) and of the speed of the process (one hour). The first basic oxygen converter, the LD converter, was introduced for the first time in Austria at the end of the 1950s, as a development of the old traditional converters (Bessemer and Thomas).[6] Given its very high productivity, this process developed rapidly, but in integrated plants only, since a liquid charge (molten pig-iron) is required. The refining reaction is extremely rapid, the process being concluded in only 40–45 minutes. The large size of LD converters and the speed of the process allow the production of vey large quantities of steel, unknown in the other processes. Moreover, the versatility of this process, in the sense that different combinations of charge (characteristics of the bath) are possible, allows for differences in raw materials. A process computer, on real time, is usually installed with it to determine the weight and composition of the charge, and the oxygen necessary to produce a given quantity of steel of a certain chemical composition and temperature (given the chemical composition of the charge).

When the steel-making cycle is completed—whatever the process used—the molten metal is ready to be cast, in large ingot moulds or, increasingly, in a continuous casting machine. First the steel is tapped from the furnace, or converter, into a ladle—a very large container in steel sheet with a fire-proof lining. This is transported by means of a crane to the casting area, where the molten metal is cast, from the bottom of the ladle into the casting pits. Here, it is poured into ingot moulds and allowed to solidify. The ingot moulds are then sent to the stripping area, where the ingots are extracted from the moulds by means of a special crane (a stripper) equipped with a pair of large tongs, which grip the ingots and lift them out. The ingots are then sent to the soaking pits (heat furnaces) to be re-heated uniformly before passing to the rolling area. If the continuous casting process is used, the molten metal is tapped from the furnace and poured directly into the casting machine, from which it emerges as solid semifinished slabs, billets, or blooms. The continuous caster produces directly from the molten metal to the semifinished product, without going through the ingot stage, cooling, stripping, reheating, and rolling into a semifinished form.

The rolling and finishing processes change the shape of the ingots into semifinished slab, blooms, or billets, and then into finished products, i.e. sheets, bars, or other structures. The rolling mill consists of a feeding machine, for the transportation of the ingots, the soaking pits, where the ingots are reheated before rolling, a blooming stand (or slabbing stand)—a rolling train that transforms ingots into semifinished products (blooms or slabs)—various other rolling trains, which transform by further rolling the semifinished products into finished products of the required section, and a finishing area, for further treatment and finishing operations.

A rolling train is made up of a series of rolling stands, shafting gears, and pieces of electrical equipment. A stand is a strong metal structure ('housing') which supports the rotating rolls through which the metal is passed. The rolling process consists in the compression of the steel ingot between two rolls, rotating in opposite directions. As the ingot is fed into the stand between the cylinders, which are placed one on top of the other and rotate at a given speed, this impels the ingot to advance by attrition while it is reduced. If the rotation of the rolls is reversed, and the distance between them reduced at the same time, the ingot passes back again through the rolls, and its thickness is reduced still further. It is then cut into the required lengths and passed to other trains for further rolling. Here the rolls have the section required to obtain finished products with a certain structure.

Notes

1. The most modern blast-furnaces can have a diameter of over 10 and up to 14 metres, producing between six and eight thousand tons of pig-iron a day (Nicodemi and Zoia, 1980, pp. 8, 98).
2. The largest open-hearth available may produce up to 900 tons of steel per casting, but such furnaces usually have much smaller dimensions (about 200 tons or less). Nicodemi and Zoia, 1980, pp. 156–66.
3. The carbon electrodes are fitted in the roof, and can be raised from and lowered to the surface of the metal automatically. Specially selected scrap, the composition of which is accurately known, is loaded into the furnace; the electrodes are then lowered to the surface of the metal. The generated heat causes the charge to melt under oxidizing conditions, the slag is skimmed off, and carbon is added. The bath is then refined with a strongly reducing slag, and alloys are added.
4. The other processes (Bessemer, Thomas, open-hearth, LD) suffer from some certain limitations when special steels are produced.
5. Further refining, such as vacuum de-gassing, can be required for special steels, thus requiring more time.
6. The first industrial converters were installed at Linz and Donawitz in 1952 and 1953, and from the initials of these two towns (LD) the process takes its name. The first Bessemer converter was built by Bessemer in 1856, for the conversion and refining of molten pig-iron, therefore installed in integrated plants only. Molten pig-iron is placed in the converter, and air is blown through it from the bottom. This causes violent chemical reactions, and the impurities of the molten metal are rapidly oxidized out. The converter is then tipped to remove the slag. A very similar process, the Thomas, was introduced in 1870. This is usually used when phosphorous iron ore is employed. The decarburation of the pig-iron takes place in this process through the addition of lime. Thomas converters have never been used in Italy, since ion ore is not found there. This process is now disappearing, being progressively replaced with new coverters in which the blast of air has been replaced by pure oxygen.

APPENDIX B

The Industrial Structure of the Italian Steel Industry

The Italian steel industry consists of a public and a private sector, with marked differences in specialization.

(i) *The public sector.* In the public sector, the main holding company is IRI (Istituto per la Ricostruzione Industriale), set up in 1933, and subject to public law, through which the state intervenes in economic activity.[1] IRI controls its companies through subsidiary financial holding companies (*società finanziarie*). These financial holding companies issue equity shares, of which IRI owns a majority interest, and they in turn control the companies in their sector, sometimes owning 100 per cent of the equity capital.[2]

FINSIDER[3] is the holding company that groups together all the main enterprises in the iron and steel industry. It controls 11 operating companies, for the production of iron and steel, plus a large number of other companies (such as commercial companies, financial companies, project companies) whose activities are related to the iron and steel operating companies. FINSIDER companies account for 100 per cent of pig-iron, 54 per cent of crude steel, and 52 per cent of hot rolled products (see Table B.1).

The biggest firms in this group are Italsider, Acciaierie di Piombino, Dalmine, and Terni. *Italsider* is the major company, and was formed in 1961 by an earlier amalgamation of two other FINSIDER subsidiaries. It owns three of the four large integrated coastal plants (Cornigliano, Bagnoli, Taranto) and seven other iron and steel works, accounting for about 87 per cent of the total production of pig-iron and 43 per cent of the total production of crude steel. The *Acciaierie di Piombino* is the fourth integrated coastal plant of the FINSIDER group. *Dalmine* is a company grouping one medium-sized steelworks plant (a scrap-based mill) and six other plants for the production of tubes and pipes. It accounts for about 60 per cent of seamless tubes and 13 per cent of welded tubes produced in Italy. *Terni* is a medium-sized steel making plant (with scrap-based mills) concentrated on the production of quality steels. IRI directly controls a number of other companies of varying nature. Among these there are two medium-sized iron and steel enterprises, *Breda Siderurgica* and *Nazionale Cogne*, producing special steels. They were previously controlled by a different public law corporation (EGAM), abolished by law in 1977. A large project to rationalize the special steel enterprises has been put forward by IRI in recent years. This provides for the technical and productive restructuring of the special steel enterprises, carried out through a large merger of the main special steel companies (plus other auxiliary companies). This project involves both the two ex-EGAM enterprises, Breda and Cogne, and the *Acciaierie di Piombino*. Thus, the public

TABLE B.1
FINSIDER's main products and markets shares

	1977		1978		1980	
	tons '000	%	tons '000	%	tons '000	%
pig-iron	11,238	98.5	11,122	98.1	12,144	100
crude steel	12,928	55.4	12,956	53.4	14,267	53.8
hot rolled products	9,657	50.3	9,560	48.0	10,806	52.3
cold rolled products	2,045	51.9	1,935	49.1	2,381	56.0
welded tubes	1,246	54.9	1,135	48.6	1,164	46.1
seamless tubes	459	59.4	479	57.3	554	63.0
cold galvanized sheets	171	92.8	191	91.7	181	92.0

Source: Mediobanca (various issues).

sector (IRI's holding), grouping the four integrated coastal plants, some medium-sized steel enterprises, and quite a few small specialist enterprises, accounts for all pig-iron and over half of crude steel produced.

(ii) *The private sector*. The private sector is responsible for quite a large share of total steel production. It is distinguished by a considerable product diversification, so that each single private producer tends to concentrate on a few steel products. On the whole, private enterprises produce high-quality steels and special steels, the smaller scale of their works allowing for better control, and electric furnaces allowing for higher quality. In 1977, private enterprises supplied about 42 per cent of crude steel and 40 per cent of special steel, but their share rises to 67 per cent if we consider non-alloy steels only (see Table B.2.)

The private sector is far from uniform. There are two large holdings, Falck and Teksid, with a productive capacity of over one million tons of crude steel a year each. Heading the privately owned Falck group is AFL Falck, founded in 1908. All its steelworks are located in Lombardia, and they produce mainly plates, hot rolled strips, sections, hot rolled and cold drawn seamless tubes and pipes, wire and wire products, and second processing products. The other large privately owned company is Teksid. After a considerable amount of time engaged in the manufacturing of steel for FIAT, it has recently made a vigorous appearance on the steel market, particularly on the special steel market. These two private holdings together supply quite a significant relevant share of output of flat products (heavy plates, cold rolled plates, hot rolled strips, and wide strips). Quite a large proportion of their crude steel production consists of special steels, so that their product market share is higher for special steel product (see Table B.2). Moreover, there is a large number of medium small and small firms, most of which are single-plant firms. They produce crude steel from scrap in electric furnaces, and

TABLE B.2

Crude steel and special steel production (1977) (% distribution)

	Crude steel	Special steel: non-alloy		Special steel: alloy		Special steel: total		Ratio crude steel/ special steel
Public sector:	58.6		33.2		70.4		60.6	
(IRI's holding)								
FINSIDER:								
Italsider		4.6		49.7		37.8		
Terni	48.6	0.1	4.7	5.3	57.1	3.9	43.3	18.4
Dalmine		—		2.1		1.6		
Acc. Piombino	6.4		21.2		2.0		7.1	22.9
Ex–EGAM:								
Cogne Naz.	3.6	3.8	7.3	6.0	11.3	5.4	10.2	58.2
Breda Sid.		3.5		5.3		4.8		
Private sector:	41.4		66.8		29.6		39.4	
Falck holding:								
AFL Falck	5.0	20.9	22.3	3.8	9.0	8.3	12.5	51.6
Acc. Bolzano		1.4		5.2		4.2		
Teksid	3.4		6.4		12.8		11.1	67.9
Redaelli	0.8		9.2		2.0		3.9	97.0
Others	32.2		28.9		5.8		11.9	7.6
Total	100		100		100		100	20 .65
('000 tons)	(23,334)					(4,818)		

Source: *Ministero dell'industria*, 1979.

quite a few produce for the special steel market only (special high-quality steel and ferro alloys). Their production tends to be quite diversified, and they tend to concentrate more on certain specific products. Finally, there is a large group of single-plant enterprises producing common grades of steel, but characterized by high product specialization and standardization, concentrating on a few products, and often only one. In addition to the enterprises producing and finishing steel, there is a large group of small firms who are re-rollers, spread all over the country.

Notes

1. In Italy, state intervention in economic activities is carried out chiefly through the state shareholding system (*Partecipazioni Statali*). The fundamental feature of this system is that IRI is not a nationalized company, but a public law corporation, wholly owned by the State and therefore responsible to the government for its operations, through the Ministry of State Holdings. It has considerable legal and financial autonomy but special control procedures allow the government to ensure that its economic directives are followed. The companies that IRI controls, directly or indirectly, remain joint stock companies operating under private law. As a result, the Italian public industrial sector has the same legal structure and the same 'modus operandi' as the private sector (see Posner and Woolf, 1967).
2. IRI's holdings are quite diversified, and they can be divided into three main categories: (*a*) the industrial operating companies grouped under the six financial companies; (*b*) the banks owned by IRI, and (*c*) a number of directly controlled participations in companies of varying nature. The six financial companies, in their turn, control their companies by sector: (i) STET, the telephone holding company, controls the enterprises operating telephones within the country, (ii) FINMARE groups together IRI's shipping transport companies, (iii) FINMECCANICA groups all the main engineering firms; (iv) FINSIDER groups most the the IRI's enterprises in the iron and steel industry, (v) FINCANTIERI controls the shipbuilding sector, and (vi) SME groups together the enterprises in the food industry.
3. FINSIDER was created in 1937 to organize the IRI's holdings in the iron and steel industry, the result of a major bank salvaging operation in the early 1930s. This holding company was originally owned wholly by IRI; the IRI's share fell to 55 per cent at the end of the 1960s but has now risen once more to 92.5 per cent (1979). In addition to private shares in the financial holding company, private participation is also to be found in the individual operating companies.

APPENDIX C

Technical Innovation and Diffusion in Construction

Since the second world war there has been some technical innovation in the building industry in Italy. A mixture of traditional and industrialized techniques are now used, though traditional techniques still dominate.

Under *traditional techniques* we classify all methods of production that operate mainly through the use of the traditional craft trades (bricklayer, carpenter, steel fixer, plasterer, painter, scaffolder), employed at the yard for the manual assembly of traditional building inputs (bricks, mortar, steel, timber and concrete, plaster, tiles, paint) and the necesary preparatory work (such as timber cutting and shaping, steel bending and fixing).[1]

The introduction of small components, machinery and hand power-tools tends to result in the simplification, i.e. the *rationalization,* of the building process by the elimination of some operations and tasks, the reduction of the necessary physical strength, and the simplification of some jobs.[2] For example, as far as the erection of the superstructure is concerned, standardized timber carpentry and metal carpentry are now available: the traditional timber shutters, manually cut and assembled by the carpenters, within which concrete is allowed to solidify, can be replaced with re-usable and standardized timber or metal moulds and forms, so that the operations of preparing and dismantling the shutters become simpler and more rapid. Precast units such as precast beams, columns, and floors, can be employed, eliminating some operations and thereby accelerating construction activity. For example, when precast beams are used in floor framing, the operation of floor building is vastly speeded up. As far as the finishing stage is concerned, a large variety of prefabricated small components can be bought directly from specialist producers and then assembled, eliminating part of the finishing work (joining, woodworking, plastering, painting, etc.). For example, the large use of panels for internal partitions eliminates brickwork, cladding, and plastering. On the whole, all innovations have served to reduce labour requirements, to speed up the process, to give greater accuracy, and to improve the quality of construction, simplifying and accelerating site work. But, on the whole, they have not—where and when applied—modified or altered the basic features of the production process, in the sense that it remains labour-intensive, consisting in the manufacture through manual assembly of different materials, and the traditional trades are still employed. Data on the diffusion of rationalized systems of production are not available. The empirical findings available seem to suggest that they are employed only to a small extent by few enterprises, mainly working in the urban areas. Nevertheless, this tendency is an indication of a process of rationalization—of the substitution for building work of inputs manufactured by other industrial sectors and assembled by skilled workers employed directly by their non–building enterprises.[3]

Industrialized building methods, such as industrialized casting methods and prefabricated systems of production, have also been made available, radically affecting the organization of the production process and the trades employed.

(i) With industrialized casting methods, the construction is realized by the casting 'on site' of large vertical sections and slabs. Concrete is cast in large and complex metal coffers internally reinforced with steel, having the shape of a large flat surface ('table banches'), or of an L ('demi-tunnel'), or of an inverted U ('tunnel'). These are, basically, complex metal carpentry, that can be changed from an upright position, for the casting of concrete, to a flat position, that makes it possible—with the help of special oils—to slip off the metal coffer when the concrete has hardened. The product cycle, usually planned to be completed in a day, starts with the undoing, slipping off, and cleaning of the metal coffer, which is then lifted and moved by special cranes. A team of workers than places and fixes it, prepares and fits the electro-weld wire-nettings, and fixes the negatives for doors and windows, and pipes and other installations for water, gas, electricity, and heating. Then concrete is pumped into it; special equipment rapidly heats and dries the surfaces overnight, for the equipment to be ready to restart the product cycle the following day.[4]

(ii) The use of prefabricated large components has to be considered an industrialized method when these components are used to such an extent that site work is reduced to a minimum. The quantity of factory work on the building components is increased, site work is reduced, and the process is speeded up considerably. In such cases the whole building process changes, so that the prevailing operations are concerned more with lifting and assembling large units (reinforced concrete panels one or two storeys high), than with construction.[5]

Despite the availability of industrialized systems of production, building contractors in Italy largely adopt construction methods of the traditional type,[6] i.e. reinforced concrete structure, bricklaying for external walls and partitions, cladding of external walls by plastering, painting, decorating, and finally internal installations after the completion of the main structure. On the whole, industrialized techniques are very rarely used for housing, while they are more developed for general buildings. Innovation has been limited to the introduction of some rationalization in production (such as standardized timber shutters for carpentry) and the replacement of old with more up-to-date equipment. The little innovation that has been introduced has implied by and large the utilization of different inputs only; actual work remains largely manual, and little capitilization is still required. By contrast, considerable changes have taken place in the division of labour and the organization of the sector.[7] Industrialized techniques (particularly

TABLE C.1

New buildings by dimensions and technique of construction of the main structure (1976) (volume = cubic metres, '000)

	Up to 1,000	1,001/ 5,000	5,001/ 10,000	Over 10,001	Total building
Housing:					
1. *Dimensions*					
brick	27.73	55.18	9.39	7.70	100
reinforced concrete	2.84	19.81	25.73	51.62	100
other systems	38.12	50.12	11.66	—	100
prefabricated	9.21	28.95	9.21	52.63	100
Total	6.57	25.04	23.30	45.09	100
2. *Technique*					
brick	61.11	31.80	5.84	2.47	14.48
reinforced concrete	36.80	67.30	93.95	97.40	85.08
othe systems	1.93	0.77	0.17	—	0.33
prefabricated	0.16	0.13	0.04	0.13	0.11
Total	100	100	100	100	100
General buildings					
1. *Dimensions*					
brick	10.48	33.55	14.10	41.87	100
concrete	0.56	8.02	10.93	80.49	100
other systems	1.45	12.62	12.28	73.65	100
prefabricated	0.87	8.23	10.48	80.42	100
Total	1.07	9.37	11.07	78.49	100
2. *Technique*					
brick	43.42	15.88	5.63	2.37	4.43
concrete	41.42	68.59	79.04	82.13	80.09
other systems	5.95	5.51	4.55	3.83	4.09
prefabricated	9.21	10.02	10.78	11.67	11.39
Total	100	100	100	100	100

Source: ISTAT, *Annuario Statistico delle Attività Edilizie* (1978).

prefabricated systems) were tried in housing in the 1960s, but since then have been progressively abandoned, as too expensive for the Italian market.[8] Industrialized building methods need careful planning and the maximum of standardization. The low level of building activity recorded in the last 15 years, the instability of the building cycle, and the lack of rational and standardized technical legislation in terms of building standards[9] have made the use of prefabricated systems difficult and expensive. Data on the techiques employed for the erection of the main structure for housing and general buildings clearly shows the very restricted use of industrialized methods (see Table C.1): in housing, prefabrication is used very little (0.11 per cent), and then almost exclusively for very large buildings; reinforced concrete is the most common technique (85.08 per cent), but brickwork is still largely employed for the erection of small cottages and houses (61.11 and 31.8 per cent respectively). Prefabrication is therefore employed only for general buildings (11.39 per cent) and then only to a limited extent.

Technical innovation has also been confined to certain types of firms. Large building contractors, with the exception of contractors specializing in civil engineering, have played no role in the process of technological innovation. They largely adopt construction techniques of the traditional type, limiting innovation to the introduction of labour-saving equipment and the reorganization of the labour process through an increasing division of labour and subcontracting.[10]

The co-operatives (cooperatives of production where the partners are the workers themselves), particularly those acting in the Emilia Romagna region, are the only relevant example of technological innovation. They use industrialized techniques, mainly the coffrage tunnel system.[11] The rapid diffusion of this industrialized construction method among the cooperatives can be explained by taking into account their productive size,[12] and their technical and organizational structure. On the one hand, technical assistance is given by the ICIE (*Istituto Cooperativo Industrializzazione Edilizia*) to the cooperatives willing to use industrialized systems; on the other hand, the cooperatives are largely organized in *consorzi* (associations) which perform the important function of planning the building activity of their members at the regional level. Building projects are directly tendered through the *consorzio*, and this allows them to work for large projects on a continuous basis. These seem to be the two crucial conditions for the application of industrialized building methods. This industrialized technique (the coffrage tunnel) was also tried out by the private sector at the beginning of the 1970s, but was gradually abandoned. It is still used by some large building contractors, but in general its use has always been very limited and locally restricted.[13]

Notes

1. A large set of prefabricated standardized components have been made available by other industrialized sectors. This process has involved a large number of works and trades: brickwork (standardized bricks and blocks), shuttering (standardized timber shutters, moulds, and forms), steelworking (electro-weld wire-nettings), concrete (prestressed and prefabricated concrete components such as precast beams and columns, ramps, and balconies), woodworking (door frames, window frames, sections and ceiling joists, timber frames, standardized wooden components, and floor boarding), plumbing (introduction of mass-produced universal systems for pipework, joints, cisterns, in

plastic, nylon, or copper). Brickwork is still the main technique in repair and modernization, in the erection of non-load-bearing walls and internal partitions, and in the erection of the loadbearing structure, when small houses, individual family cottages, and similar are to be built. Reinforced concrete is more common for large buildings. This has to be considered as a traditional technique when the load-bearing structure is erected by casting concrete into timber shutters internally reinforced with steel (see below). In the finishing stage, walls are treated by plastering, painting, and so on.

2. For a discussion of the rationalization of traditional techniques in the erection of the superstructure, see Frison, 1979, pp. 27–30; for the finishing and fixing stage, see FLC Lombardia, 1981.
3. A research study of the technology for fixing and finishing in 72 construction yards in the Lombardia region reached the concluson that, despite the existence of a large variety of components, the processes remain by and large traditional. Nevertheless, the tendency is towards the hiving off some traditional activities from the building industry to other industrial sectors: the chemical industry, plastics industry, and metal industry. Typical in this respect is the example of floor covering: carpet and linoleum coverings are now installed by the employees of these specialist firms (FLC Lombardia, 1981).
4. For a discussion of the coffrage tunnel system, see Frison, 1979, pp. 31–8; Brusco and D'Alessandro, 1979, pp. 32–7; Cicconi, 1980, pp. 75–80, *II Modulo,* 1978, pp. 19–43.
5. A wide variety of prefabricated building methods can be used. Usually the main distinctions are in terms of off-site or on-site methods, heavy or light prefabrication, and open or closed systems of prefabrication.
6. It is generally agreed among the students of the sector that the Italian building industry—apart from a very small number of cases—is technologically backward, both with respect to other industrial sectors in Italy and with respect to the building industry in other industrialized countries. See Petrini, 1971; ISFOL, 1977, pp. 12–29; Roscelli, 1978, pp. 50–1; Cicconi, 1980, pp. 10–12; FILCA CISL Lombardia, 1980*b* p. 6; FLC Lombardia, 1981, p. 138. In this respect, it is important to point out that (*a*) industrialization implies not only the introduction of new techniques of production, but a different planning and organizational structure and, (*b*) there are some cases (building enterprises working in the national or international market for civil engineering, very large building contractors working mainly in public building) in which the process of industrialization is well advanced, but their experience is still very limited.
7. In fact, a process of vertical disintegration, matched by an increasing use of subcontracting and lump systems, and an increasing division of labour—technology remaining substantially the same—has been recorded as the main change occurring over the last decade.
8. In the area around Milan, where a large number of enterprises producing prefabricated building components developed in the 1960s,

only a few are still producing, and their output is almost exclusively used for industrial and commercial buildings.

9. There is no national technical regulation for building requirements but every single district has to define them, so that there are over 8,000 regulations. See Frison, 1979, p. 42; Cicconi, 1980, p. 11.
10. For a discussion of the low rate of technical innovation in the Italian construction industry see Petrini, 1971; Indovina, 1972; Barp, 1976, pp. 16–7; Crosta, 1976, pp. 65–8; Scarpini, 1981, pp.94–9.
11. On the experience of the cooperatives see *Il Modulo,* 1978; Cicconi, 1980, pp. 21–32.
12. In 1977, the average size of the cooperatives associated with ANCPL was 200 employees; and 20 cooperatives employed over 500 people (Cicconi, 1980, p. 22).
13. This was the case with the council houses built in Rome by the IACP (*Istituto Autonomo Case Popolari*) in the period 1972–6. About 50 per cent of the flats contracted (out of 75,000 rooms) were built with industrialized techniques, mostly coffrage tunnel (Brusco *et al.*, 1981, pp. 39–40).

APPENDIX D

Tables on the Steel Industry

The data which provide the empirical material for the analysis of the steel industry are included in this Appendix. The data are derived from the archives of these four enterprises: Breda Siderurgica, AFL Falck, Dalmine S.p.A., and Italsider S.p.A.

Besides data, the enterprises in question provided copies of the collective agreements which have been quoted in the text. Interviews with representatives of management provided additional information.

TABLE D.1

The four steel enterprises examined: main characteristics, 1980

	Breda Siderurgica		AFL Falck		Dalmine		Italsider	
Year of construction of the first steel works	1915		1906		1906		1897	
Ownership	state-controlled enterprise, IRI holding (ex EGAM)		private enterprise, Falck holding		state-controlled enterprise, FINSIDER, IRI holding		state-controlled enterprise, FINSIDER, IRI holding	
Output of main products (000 tons) and market shares (%), 1980:	tons	%	tons	%	tons	%	tons	%
pig-iron	—	—	—	—	—	—	10,355	85.2
crude steel	320	1.2	1,166	4.4	550	2.1	10,829	40.9
of which								
special steel	279	5.2	483	9.0	n.a.[1]	n.a.	n.a.	n.a.
seamless tubes	—	—	131	14.9	554	63.0	—	—
welded tubes	—		86	3.4	323	12.8	755	29.9
coils	—	—	—	—	—	—	6,503	94.2

Steel productive capacity/year (000 tons)	410	1,600	620	17,095
main technology in use	scrap-based steel equipped with OH and electric furnaces	scrap-based steel equipped with UHP electric furnaces, integrated with with continuous casting	scrap-based steel works equipped with UHP electric furnaces, integrated with continuous casting	integrated steelworks equipped with LD and OBM furnaces, integrated with continuous casting
Steel plants: by technology in use and total employment * integrated steelworks † scrap-based steelworks ‡ re-rollers	† Breda 3,169	† Unione 3,553 † Concordia 1,505 ‡ Vittoria 800 ‡ Porta Romana 127 † Arcore 1,688 ‡ Vobarno 1,454 Novate 190	† Dalmine 5,983 ‡ Massa 1,683 Piombino 1,016 ‡ Costa Volpino 1,671 Torre Annunziata 886 Sabbio 810	* Taranto 21,251 * Bagnoli 7,681 * Cornigliano 8,670 ‡ Novi Ligure 1,971 † Campi 2,786 Trieste 1,799 † Lovere 2,780 ‡ Marghera 1,528 ‡ S. G. Valdarno 820 Savona 1,012
Total employment:				
managers	17	81	103	439
clerical workers	563	1,650	2,572	12,037
manual workers	2,589	9,583	10,328	40,314
Total	3,169	11,314	13,003	52,790

Note: 1. n.a. = data not available

TABLE D.2

The four steel plants examined: technology in use and employment structure (1980)

(*a*) *Breda Siderurgica*:

Year of construction: 1915
Location: Sesto San Giovanni, Milano
Crude steel productive capacity: 410,000 tons/year

Total employment (31.10.79):

	No.	%
managers	17	0.53
clerical workers	452	14,18
foremen	114	3.58
manual workers	2,604	81.71
Total	3,187	100

Main works:[1]

(i) *Steel-making department:*

no. 2	Open-hearth basic furnaces with blast of oxygen	1956; (1963)	60 tons/casting; 300 tons/day; 4h 40′/casting
no. 2	three phase electric furnace with blast of oxygen	1956 (1970)	60 tons/casting; 500 tons/day; 2h 55′/casting
no. 1	degassing unit	1967; (1969)	60 tons/casting
no. 1	refining plant with argon	(1979);	60 tons/casting
no. 1	additives blasting unit	1978;	60 tons/casting

(ii) *Rolling department:*

no. 1 roughing-billet-section mill	1957; (1972)	5 stands; 400 tons/shift; 12 reheating furnaces
no. 1 section mill	1958; (1979)	4 stands; 150 tons/shift; 1 reheating furnace
no. 1 round-wire rod mill	1958; (1976)	30 stands, 320 tons/shift; 2 reheating furnaces

(iii) *Other facilities:*
furnaces for thermic treatment
drawing facilities
finishing shop

Employment structure by department:

	Managers	Clerical workers	Foremen	Manual workers	Ratio manual workers/ foremen
steel-making department	1	21	16	389	24.3
rolling department					
rolling	1	11	13	344	26.5
finishing	1	22	10	356	35.6
finishing department	—	9	13	444	34.2
maintenance	1	43	27	531	19.7
quality control service	1	59	5	102	20.4
other services					
administrative	5	139	—	45	—
technical service	2	28	—	4	—
internal transport and storage	3	70	22	246	11.2
personnel	2	50	8	143	17.9
Total	17	452	114	2,604	22.8

TABLE D.2. *(continued)*

(*b*) *AFL Falck, Concordia works:*

Year of construction: 1906
Location: Sesto San Giovanni, Milano
Crude steel productive capacity: 600,000 tons/year

Total employment (31.12.79):

	Concordia works		AFL Falck total works	
	No.	%	No.	%
managers	5	0.34	86	0.72
clerical workers	139	9.37	1,987	16.71
foremen	39	2.63		
manual workers	1,301	87.66	9,820	82.57
Total	1,484	100	11,893	100

Main works:
(i) *Steel-making department:*

no. 1	three-phase electric furnace with blast of oxygen	1964;	135 tons/casting; 900 tons/day; 3h 40′/casting
no. 1	" "	1964; (1970)	135 tons/casting; 1,100 tons/day; 3h 40′/casting

no. 1 refining plant with argon	1978;	135 tons/casting
no. 1 refining plant by emulsion	1964;	135 tons/casting
no. 1 continuous casting machine	1970;	1,000 tons/day

(ii) *Rolling department:*

no. 1 reversing heavy and medium plate mill	1955;	no. 1 stand reheating furnaces; 1,300 tons/day

(iii) *Other facilities:*
thermic treatment
dressing shop
sand-blasting shop

Employment structure by department:

	Managers	Clerical workers	Foremen	Manual workers	Ratio manual workers/ foremen
steel-making department	n.a.[2]	16	19	340	17.9
rolling department	n.a.	13	1	348	348.0
maintenance	n.a.	15	6	325	54.2
services	n.a.	95	13	288	22.1
Total	5	139	39	1,301	33.4

TABLE D.2. *(continued)*

(*c*) *Dalmine, Dalmine works:*

Year of construction: 1913
Location: Dalmine, Bergamo
Crude steel productive capacity: 600,000 tons/year

Total employment (31.1.80):

	Dalmine		Dalmine total works	
	No.	%	No.	%
managers	15	0.25	100	0.77
clerical workers	604	10.09	2,487	19.08
foremen	176	2.95		
manual workers	5,189	86.71	10,448	80.15
Total	5,984	100	13,035	100

Main works:
(i) *Steel-making department:*

no. 2 three-phase electric furnace with blast of oxygen	1947 (1979)	50 tons/casting; 280 tons/day; 4h 20′ casting
no. 2 three-phase electric furnace with blast of oxygen	1958 (1976)	50 tons/casting; 280 tons/day; 4h 20′/casting
no. 1 three-phase electric furnace with blast of oxygen (UHP)	1976	90 tons/casting; 819 tons/day; 2h 40′ casting
no. 1 vacuum arc degassing unit	1976	90 tons/hour
no. 1 continuous casting machine	1976	280 tons/day

(ii) *Seamless tube mill:*

no. 1 continuous mandrel mill		no. 9 stands; 140 tons/shift
no. 1 pilger mill		no. 2 stands; 200 tons/shift
no. 1 press piercing mill multi-stand pipe mill	1978	no. 8 stands; 535 tons/shift

(iii) *Other facilities:*

furnaces for thermic treatment
hot draw benches and finishing shops
dressing shop
pylon making shop

Employment structure by department (manual workers only):

steel-making department	
1947 and 1958 furnaces	450
1976 UHP furnaces	170
rolling department	
continuous mill	791
pilgrim mill (incl. finishing, coating)	1,179
PPM—MPP	280
maintrnance	
process department maintenance	429
central workshops	371
specialized workshops	450
other maintenance services	260
services	
quality control	387
technical and administrative services	73
internal transport and storage	330
personnel	260
Total	5,430

TABLE D.2. *(continued)*

(*d*) *Italsider, Cornigliano works:*

Year of construction: 1953
Location: Cornigliano, Genova
Crude steel productive capacity: 2,400,000 tons/year
Total employment (31.12.80):

	Cornigliano		Italsider total works	
	No.	%	No.	%
managers	41	0.46	439	0.83
clarical workers	1,858	20.76	12,037	22.80
foremen	140	1.56		
manual workers	6,910	77.22	40,314	76.37
Total	8,949	100	52,790	100

Main works:

(i) *Pig-iron department:*		
no. 1 blast furnace	1953; (1980)	diameter = 6.3m; volume = 647m^3; 1,400 tons/day
no. 1 blast furnace	1955; (1980)	diameter = 6.3m; volume = 647m^3; 1,400 tons/day
no. 1 blast furnace	1962	diameter = 8.6m; volume = 1,360m^3; 3,300 tons/day
no. 1 coke plant		30 cells; 1,1000,000 tons/year
(ii) *Steel-making department:*		
no. 2 OBM converters (with oxygen injection, working alternatively)	1980;	250 tons/casting; 6,600 tons/day; 50′ casting
no. 1 vertical continuous casting machine,	1980;	3,300 tons/day; 1,200,000 tons/year

(iii) *Rolling department:*

no. 1 slabbing mill	1953 (1959)	1 stand; 24 reheating furnaces; 2,000 tons/shift
no. 1 semi continuous mill,	1953 (1971)	7 stands; 3 reheating furnaces; 1,950 tons/shift
no. 1 cold rolling mill	1955 (1964)	5 stands; 600 tons/shift
no. 1 cold rolling mill	1980	5 stands; 500 tons/shift

(iv) *Other facilities:*

no. 2 electrolytic tinning lines
no. 2 continuous galvanizing lines

Employment structure by department:

	Managers	Clerical workers	Foremen	Manual workers	Ratio manual workers/ foremen
pig-iron department					
coke plant	n.a.	37	—	312	—
sintering	n.a.	19	—	142	—
blast-furnaces	n.a.	31	13	206	15.85
steel-making department	n.a.	56	43	446	10.37
rolling department					
blooming mill	n.a.	22	11	335	30.45
finishing mill	n.a.	28	15	351	23.40
cold rolling mill	n.a.	34	24	381	15.87
coating	n.a.	37	15	487	32.47
cylinder turning	n.a.	16	—	147	—
quality control	n.a.	120	4	65	16.25

maintenance					
process department maintenance	n.a.	170	—	1,062	—
central workshops	n.a.	104	—	680	—
specialized workshops	n.a.	92	—	437	—
automation and instrument.	n.a.	69	—	116	—
other maintenance services	n.a.	31	4	226	56.50
services					
auxiliary services	n.a.	30	4	168	42.00
technical services	n.a.	400	1	79	79.00
administrative services	n.a.	290	4	208	52.00
internal transport and storage	n.a.	144	1	724	724.00
personnel	n.a.	128	1	338	338.00
Total	41	1,858	140	6,910	49.36

Notes: 1. In the 'Main works' sections of this table, the first dates in each entry indicate the year when the capital equipment was set up. Dates in parentheses indicate the year of modernization of the capital equipment.
2. n.a. = data not available.

TABLE D.3

Newly-hired workers by age group in four steel plants

	Breda Siderurgica Breda works (1979)			AFL Falck Concordia works (1979)			Dalmine Dalmine works (1979)			Italsider Cornigliano works (1980)		
	No.	%		No.	%		No.	%		No.	%	
< 21	27	16.5		19	17.3		15	3.5		21	4.7	
21–5	76	46.3	59.7	38	34.6	51.9	247	57.9	79.3	241	54.3	77.5
26–30	22	13.4		19	17.3		91	21.4		103	23.2	
31–5	15	9.2	15.3	11	10.0	24.5	37	8.7	13.2	44	9.9	15.5
36–40	10	6.1		16	14.5		19	4.5		25	5.6	
41–5	8	4.9		3	2.7		4	0.9		5	1.1	
46–50	5	3.0	8.5	4	3.6	6.3	11	2.6	4.0	2	0.5	2.3
> 50	1	0.6		—	—		2	0.5		3	0.7	
Total	164	100		110	100		426	100		444	100	

TABLE D.4

Manual workers by age group in four steel plants

	Breda Siderurgica Breda works (Dec. 1979)		AFL Falck Concordia works (Sept. 1980)		Dalmine Dalmine works (Dec. 1979)		Italsider Cornigliano works (Dec. 1980)	
	No.	%	No.	%	No.	%	No.	%
< 21	20	0.8	35	2.7	17	0.3	29	0.4
21–5	165	6.4	240	18.6	342	6.6	558	8.1
26–30	269	10.4			743	14.3	865	12.5
31–5	376	14.5	286	22.1	735	14.2	910	13.2
36–40	394	15.2			785	15.1	915	13.2
41–5	504	19.5	459	35.6	902	17.4	1,116	16.9
46–50	496	19.2			785	15.1	1,124	16.3
51–5	268	10.3	271	21.0	608	11.7	893	12.9
56–60	94	3.6			272	5.3	449	6.5
> 60	3	0.1	—	—	—	—	—	—
Total	2,589	100	1,291	100	5,189	100	6,910	100
Average age	42		41		40		41	

TABLE D.5

Newly-hired workers by educational level[1] in four steel plants

	Breda Siderurgica Breda works (1979)	AFL Falck Concordia works (1979)		Dalmine Dalmine works (1979)		Italsider Cornigliano works (1980)	
	No.	No.	%	No.	%	No.	%
licenza scuola superiore	data not available	—	—	28	6.6	79	17.8
licenza media		85	77.3	249	58.7	218	49.1
licenza elementare		25	22.7	143	33.7	136	30.6
< 5 years of schooling		—	—	4	1.0	11	2.5
Total	164	110	100	424	100	444	100

Note:
1 . See Table D. 6, note 1.

TABLE D.6

Manual workers by educational level[1] in four steel plants

	Breda Sigerurgica Breda works (Dec. 1979)		AFL Falck Concordia works	Dalmine[2] Dalmine works (Jan. 1980)		Italsider Cornigliano works (Dec. 1980)	
	No.	%		No.	%	No.	%
university degree	—	—	data not	—	—	3	—
licenza scuola superiore	35	1.3	available	5	0.9	329	4.8
licenza media	352	13.6		145	26.6	1,548	22.4
licenza elementare	1,694	65.5		285	52.2	3,821	55.3
< 5 years of schooling	508	19.6		111	20.3	1,209	17.5
Total	2,589	100		546	100	6,910	100

Notes:

1. Five years of education are required for *licenza elementare*, a further three for *licenza media*, and a further five for *licenza scuola superiore*.

2. Figures for Dalmine are based on a sample of jobs 1 every 10, for all departments.

TABLE D.7

Manual workers by educational level[1] and by department in two steel plants (% distribution)

(*a*) *Breda Siderurgica*[2] *(December 1974)*

	Steel dept.	Rolling dept.	Finishing dept.	Maintenance	Qual. cntrl.	Trans. serv.	Other servs.	Total	(No.)
licenza media	2.6	9.6	9.0	24.9	9.4	2.1	5.0	11.3	(321)
less than *licenza media*	4.4	7.1	6.5	11.9	46.3	3.1	6.5	7.3	(209)
licenza elementare	68.4	64.4	68.3	55.9	13.4	74.1	64.0	64.4	(1,836)
< 5 years of schooling	24.6	18.9	16.2	7.3	30.9	20.7	24.5	17.0	(486)
Total	100	100	100	100	100	100	100	100	
(No.)	(386)	(646)	(675)	(506)	(149)	(290)	(200)		(2,852)

TABLE D.7. *(continued)*

(b) Dalmine, Dalmine works[3] *(January 1980)*

	Steel dept.	Rolling dept.	Maintenance	Services	Total	(No.)
lincenza scuola superiore	—	0.4	3.3	—	0.9	(5)
licenza media	16.3	22.0	40.8	29.0	26.6	(145)
licenza elementare	2.2	67.4	52.5	62.6	52.2	(285)
< 5 years of schooling	81.5	10.2	3.4	8.4	20.3	(111)
Total	100	100	100	100	100	
(No.)	(92)	(227)	(120)	(107)		(546)

Notes:
1. See Table D.6, note 1
2. Figures for Breda are compiled from Facchini and Umidi, 1980.
3. See Table D.6, note 2.

TABLE D.8

Manual workers recruited by educational[1] level, Italsider, Cornigliano works, 1974–80 (% distribution)

	1974	1975	1976	1977	1978	1979	1980
university degree	—	—	—	—	—	0.21	—
licenza scuola superiore	2.21	3.70	6.09	4.97	48.00	23.45	17.79
licenza media	18.19	28.89	35.09	42.86	36.00	49.47	49.10
licenza elementare	57.85	8.89	33.40	35.40	12.00	22.82	30.63
< 5 years of schooling	21.75	58.52	25.42	16.77	4.00	4.05	2.48
Total	100	100	100	100	100	100	100
(No.)	(1,039)	(135)	(476)	(161)	(25)	(469)	(444)

Note:
1. See Table D.6, note 1

TABLE D.9
Manual workers recruited by age group, Italsider, Cornigliano works, 1974–80 (% distribution)

	1974	1975	1976	1977	1978	1979	1980
< 21	4.04	6.66	6.51	3.11	8.00	4.90	4.73
21–5	26.76	26.67	39.29	39.13	72.00	64.18	54.28
26–30	20.60	17.04	18.49	21.12	8.00	20.04	23.20
31–5	17.42	9.63	13.03	17.39	8.00	5.54	9.91
36–40	16.27	11.85	10.50	14.29	4.00	2.35	5.63
41–5	6.35	10.37	6.09	3.72	—	2.56	1.12
46–50	4.33	5.19	3.15	1.24	—	0.43	0.45
> 50	4.23	12.59	2.94	—	—	—	0.68
Total	100	100	100	100	100	100	100
(No.)	(1,039)	(135)	(476)	(161)	(25)	(469)	(444)

TABLE D.10
Newly-hired workers by place of origin in two steel plants

(a) Breda Siderurgica (1979)

	No.	%
Milan district	28	17.07
other districts in Lombardia	22	13.42
other regions	114	69.51
Total	164	100

(b) Dalmine, Dalmine works (1979)

	No.	%
Bergamo district	393	92.25
other districts	33	7.75
Total	426	100

TABLE D.11

Manual workers by place of origin in three steel plants

(a) Breda Siderurgica[1] *(Dec. 1974)*

	No.	%
Milan district	337	11.78
other districts in Lombardia	884	30.91
other northern regions	243	8.50
central Italy	168	5.87
southern Italy	1,211	42.34
abroad	17	0.60
Total	2,860	100

(b) Dalmine, Dalmine works[2] *(Jan. 1980)*

	No.	%
Dalmine	78	14.23
Bergamo district	431	78.65
other districts	39	7.12
Total	548	100

(c) Italsider, Cornigliano works[3] *(Dec. 1976)*

	No.	%
Liguria	5,467	46.49
Piemonte	1,362	11.58
other northern regions	1,067	9.07
central Italy	833	7.08
southern Italy	2,686	22.84
abroad	346	2.94
Total	11,759	100

Notes:

1. Figures for Breda are compiled from Facchini and Umidi, 1980.
2. See Table D.6, note 2.
3. Data refer to all employees, including the labour force employed at Campi works.

TABLE D.12

Manual workers by residence in four steel plants

(*a*) *Breda Siderurgica (Jan. 1980)*

	No.	%
Sesto San Giovanni	772	27.57
Monza	121	4.62
Milano	280	10.69
Milan district	886	33.83
Bergamo district	578	22.07
other districts	32	1.22
Total	2,619	100

(*b*) *Falck Concordia, workers recruited (1979)*

	No.	%
Sesto San Giovanni	25	22.73
Milan	8	7.27
Milan district	30	27.27
Bergamo district	37	33.64
other districts	10	9.09
Total	110	100

(*c*) *Dalmine, Dalmine works*[1] *(31.1.80)*

	No.	%
Dalmine	103	18.79
Bergamo district	418	76.28
other districts	27	4.93
Total	548	100

(*d*) *Italsider, Cornigliano works (31.12.78)*

	No.	%
Genova	7,342	85.98
Genova district	897	10.51
Savona district	238	2.79
La Spezia district	2	0.02
Alessandria district	60	0.70
Total	8,538	100

Note:

1. See Table D.6, note 2.

TABLE D.13

Newly-hired workers by hiring system[1]

(*a*) *Breda Siderurgica*[2] *(1.1.80–30.6.80)*

	No.	%
direct hiring	88	38.26
numerical hiring	142	61.74
Total	230	100

(*b*) *AFL Falck, Sesto San Giovanni*[2] *works (1.1.80–30.6.80)*

	No.	%
direct hiring	145	99.32
numerical hiring	1	0.68
Total	146	100

(*c*) *Dalmine, Dalmine works (1.1.79–31.12.79)*

	No.	%
direct hiring	299	70.85
direct hiring from subcontractors	43	10.19
numerical hiring	66	15.64
compulsory hiring	14	3.32
Total	422	100

Notes:

1. 'Direct hiring' refers to the hiring of workers directly from other enterprises; 'numerical hiring' refers to the hiring of workers registered at the local labour office for manual non-skilled jobs; 'compulsory hiring' refers to mandatory hiring of handicap workers through the local labour office.
2. Figures made available from the labour office *(Ufficio di collocamento)* of Sesto San Giovanni.

TABLE D.14

Newly-hired workers by previous employment position

(*a*) *Breda Siderurgica (1974 and 1976)*

	1974		1976	
	No.	%	No.	%
work experience in:				
manufacturing	270	77.8	73	59.3
construction	72	20.7	27	22.0
agriculture	3	0.9	1	0.8
service sector	2	0.6	22	17.9
no previous experience	—	—	—	—
Total	347	100	123	100

(*b*) *AFL Falck, Concordia works (1979)*

	No.	%
work experience as:		
bricklayer	25	44.54 (bricklayer, labourer)
labourer	24	
welder	16	35.46 (welder, turner, electrician, fitter)
turner	10	
electrician	8	
fitter	5	
carpenter	4	20.00 (carpenter, others)
others	18	
no previous work experience	—	—
Total	110	100

(*c*) *Italsider, Cornigliano works (1974–80)*

	No.	%
work experience	1,986	72.25
no previous work experience,	763	27.75
of which:		
school leavers	695	25.28
vocational training	68	2.47
Total	2,749	100

TABLE D.15

Newly-hired workers by entry grade and department before (1970–6) and after (1977–9) the introduction of the new classification system, Breda Siderurgica (% distribution)

	Steel dept.	Rolling dept.	Finish. dept.	Maintenance	Quality control	Transport service	Other services	Total
(a) 1970–6:								
skilled	0.25	—	—	14.09	—	—	6.41	3.05
semi-skilled	1.51	2.89	0.31	73.64	2.78	2.03	8.97	16.32
unskilled	98.24	97.11	99.69	12.27	97.22	97.97	84.62	80.63
Total	100	100	100	100	100	100	100	100
(No.)	(397)	(622)	(326)	(440)	(72)	(295)	(78)	(2,230)
(b) 1977–9								
grade 4, 5	1.72	10.35	2.78	37.73	—	—	—	12.19
3	3.45	13.79	11.11	54.72	—	5.55	72.73	23.42
2	13.79	55.17	36.11	7.55	—	55.56	—	24.88
1	81.04	20.69	50.00	—	—	38.89	27.27	39.51
Total	100	100	100	100	—	100	100	100
(No.)	(58)	(29)	(36)	(53)	—	(18)	(11)	(205)
TOTAL LF[1] (average no.)	455	651	362	493	72	313	89	2,435

Note:
1. LF = labour force.

TABLE D.16

Manual workers by length of service and by plant

	Breda Siderurgica Breda works (Jan. 1980)		AFL Falck Concordia works (Sept. 1980)		Dalmine[1] Dalmine works (Jan. 1980)		Italsider Cornigliano works (Dec. 1980)	
	No.	%	No.	%	No.	%	No.	%
< 1 year	146	5.54	103	8.28	42	7.66	426	6.16
1–2	15	0.57			20	3.65	428	6.19
2–3	26	0.99	499	40.11			23	0.33
4–5	154	5.85			63	11.50	480	6.95
6–10	1,004	38.12			150	27.37	2,360	34.16
11–15	644	24.45	454	36.50	98	17.88	766	11.09
16–20	468	17.77					918	13.28
21–30	141	5.35	109	8.76	138	25.18	1,463	21.17
> 30	36	1.36	79	6.35	37	6.76	46	0.67
Total	2,634	100	1,244	100	548	100	6,910	100
average length of service	10.88		12.23		14.24		12.17	

Note:

1. See Table D.6, note 2.

TABLE D.17

Manual workers by length of service and by department in two steel plants

(*a*) *Dalmine, Dalmine works,*[1] *January 1980*

	Steel dept.	Rolling dept.	Maintenance	Services	Total	(No.)
< 1 year	8.60	9.65	6.67	3.74	7.66	(42)
1–3	5.38	0.88	6.67	4.67	3.65	(20)
4–5	15.05	10.09	12.50	10.28	11.50	(63)
6–10	39.79	23.68	30.83	20.56	27.37	(150)
11–20	15.05	18.86	15.83	20.56	17.88	(98)
21–30	13.98	28.51	19.17	34.58	25.18	(138)
> 30	2.15	8.33	8.33	5.61	6.76	(37)
Total	100	100	100	100	100	
(No.)	(93)	(228)	(120)	(107)		(548)
Average length of service	9.91	15.36	13.29	14.59	14.24	

(*b*) *AFL Falck, Concordia works, December 1977–December 1979*

	Steel dept.	Rolling dept.	Maintenance	Services	Total
average length of service:					
in 1977	11	15	13	15	13
in 1978	11	14	13	15	13
in 1979	11	14	13	15	13

Note:
1. See Table D.6, note 2.

TABLE D.18

Manual workers by classification grade: a comparison between large enterprises in the engineering and steel industries, 1977 (% distribution)

	Engineering industry	Steel industry				
	A sample of public enterprises (1976) (1)	Italsider Cornigliano (1977) (2)	Dalmine[1] Dalmine works (1977) (3)	Terni Terni works (1977) (4)	Breda Siderurgica Breda works (1977) (5)	AFL Falck[2] total works (1977) (6)
6	—	2.88	0.20	—	—	—
5	12.10	43.74	33.40	33.00	23.24	17.37
4	29.30	42.52	54.02	44.00	38.43	37.50
3	51.10	10.14	11.13	17.40	31.29	40.94
2	6.40	0.72	1.22	5.50	6.99	4.19
1	1.10	—	0.03	0.10	0.05	—
Total	100	100	100	100	100	100
(No.)	(58,061)	(6,916)	(5,904)	(4,327)	(2,732)	(9,941)

Notes:

1. The figures include workers employed in the head office, in Milan.
2. The figures refer to the three steel works located in Sesto San Giovanni (Unione, Concordia, and Vittoria).

Source: (1 and 4) Segatori and Torresini, 1979, pp. 71, 64–5.

TABLE D.19

Manual workers by classification grade, Breda Siderurgica, 1972–9 (% distribution)

	31.7 1972	31.12 1973	31.12 1974	31.12 1975	31.12 1976	31.12 1977	31.12 1978	31.12 1979
6	—	—	—	—	—	—	—	—
5	8.29	10.40	12.18	16.85	19.42	23.24	28.80	30.94
4	24.41	30.17	31.08	36.27	35.03	38.43	41.30	39.51
3	43.13	44.82	40.03	38.01	34.62	31.29	25.80	23.83
2	20.86	13.07	16.50	8.80	9.93	6.99	4.10	5.45
1	3.31	1.54	0.21	0.07	0.10	0.05	—	0.27
Total	100	100	100	100	100	100	100	100
(No.)	(2,847)	(2,847)	(2,915)	(2,807)	(2,880)	(2,732)	(2,585)	(2,589)
average grade	3.13	3.35	3.39	3.61	3.62	3.78	3.95	3.95

TABLE D.20

Manual workers by classification grade, Dalmine, Dalmine works, 1971–9 (% distribution)

Old classification system[3]	31.12.71 (1)	31.6.72 (2)	1.7.72 (3)	New classification system	1.7.72[1] (4)	31.12.77[2] (5)	31.12.79 (6)
				6	—	0.20	0.46
OSP	0.62	1.20	38.30	5	6.40	33.40	38.85
OS	17.18	22.80		4	32.00	54.02	46.15
OQ	28.01	32.80	60.50	3	50.00	11.13	11.74
OC1	52.56	41.50		2	9.80	1.22	2.74
OCs	0.87	1.20	1.20	1	1.80	0.03	0.06
MC	0.76	0.50					
Total	100	100	100	Total	100	100	100
(No.)	(5,770)	(n.a.)	(n.a.)		(6,208)	(5,904)	(5,189)

Notes:

1. Figures include all employees, manual workers, foremen, clerical workers.
2. Figures include Sabbio works.
3. With the old classification system (*sistema delle qualifiche*), OSP (*operai specializzati di prima*) refers to highly skilled workers; OS (*operai specializzati*) to skilled workers; OQ (*operai qualifacati*) to semiskilled workers; OC (*operai comuni*) to unskilled workers employed for simple but specific tasks, distinguished in two groups (OC1 and OC2) according to the characteristics of the tasks performed; finally MC (*manovali comuni*) to unskilled workers employed for general and unskilled tasks.

Source: For the figures in columns 1, 2, 3, and 4: *Coordinamento sindacale del gruppo Dalmine*, in Abbatecola, 1975, pp. 100–2.

TABLE D.21

Manual workers by classification grade, AFL Falck, Concordia works, 1974–80 (% distribution)

	31.12.74	31.12.75	31.12.76	31.12.77	31.12.78	31.12.79	31.12.80
5	12.3	14.15	16.50	19.50	20.60	21.22	21.70
4	29.7	33.90	35.90	36.30	38.50	39.20	39.70
3	44.9	47.70	42.30	37.60	33.80	32.59	32.20
2	12.9	4.14	5.30	6.60	7.10	6.99	6.40
1	0.2	0.11	—	—	—	—	—
Total	100	100	100	100	100	100	100
(No.)	(1,348)	(1,329)	(1,334)	(1,321)	(1,312)	(1,301)	(1,312)
average grade	3.41	3.58	3.64	3.69	3.73	3.75	3.77

TABLE D.22

Manual workers by classification grade, AFL Falck, Sesto San Giovanni, 1.6.80 (% distribution)

	Unione works	Concordia works	Vittoria works	Total[1]
5	30.35	21.23	24.89	26.83
4	41.98	39.19	53.28	42.40
3	25.53	32.65	19.54	27.37
2	2.14	6.93	2.29	3.40
1	—	—	—	—
Total	100	100	100	100
(No.)	(2,801)	(1,314)	(655)	(4,908)
average grade	4.01	3.75	4.01	3.93

Note:

1. The figures include also the labour force employed at Geva and Cerco, two small non-steel plants located in Sesto San Giovanni.

TABLE D.23

Manual workers by classification grade, Italsider, Cornigliano works, 1977–80 (% distribution)

	31.12.77	31.12.78	31.12.79	31.12.80
6	2.88	4.16	4.30	4.66
5	43.74	52.28	61.26	64.07
4	42.52	36.28	25.00	21.75
3	10.14	6.74	7.60	8.26
2	0.72	0.54	1.84	1.26
1	—	—	—	—
Total	100	100	100	100
(No.)	(6,916)	(6,690)	(6,843)	(6,910)
average grade	4.38	4.52	4.58	4.63

TABLE D.24

Manual workers by classification grade in the Italsider steel plants, 1979 (% distribution)

	1	2	3	4	5	6	Total	(No.)
Taranto	—	2.40	12.61	35.95	44.63	4.41	100	(16,430)
Cornigliano	0.01	1.83	7.60	25.00	61.26	4.30	100	(6,843)
Novi	—	4.10	14.81	41.56	38.37	1.16	100	(1,634)
Bagnoli	—	0.42	10.38	33.62	52.68	2.90	100	(5,934)
Campi	0.58	1.51	5.38	24.08	66.19	2.26	100	(2,251)
Trieste	1.39	3.69	13.00	39.85	41.59	0.48	100	(1,438)
Lovere	1.77	4.09	6.20	28.78	58.86	0.30	100	(2,370)
Marghera	0.15	4.86	8.08	37.49	47.30	2.12	100	(1,275)
S. Giovanni	1.13	10.87	16.81	25.00	43.93	2.26	100	(708)
Savona	—	2.06	7.40	21.21	68.24	1.09	100	(825)

TABLE D.25

Manual workers by classification grade and length of service, Italsider, Cornigliano works

Length of service	1	2	3	4	5	6	Total	(No.)
(a) % distribution (31.12.80):								
< 1 year	—	0.97	3.21	1.78	0.20	—	6.16	(426)
1–2	—	0.26	3.65	1.80	0.82	—	6.53	(451)
3–4	—	0.02	0.17	4.37	2.39	—	6.95	(480)
5–9	—	0.01	0.32	9.78	23.56	0.48	34.15	(2,360)
10–14	—	—	0.06	1.16	9.61	0.26	11.09	(766)
15–19	—	—	0.27	1.01	10.84	1.16	13.28	(918)
20–4	—	—	0.33	1.16	10.54	1.51	13.53	(935)
25–9	—	—	0.22	0.62	5.62	1.19	7.64	(528)
> 29	—	—	0.03	0.07	0.49	0.07	0.67	(46)
Total	—	1.26	8.26	21.75	64.07	4.66	100	
(No.)	(—)	(87)	(571)	(1,503)	(4,427)	(322)		(6,910)
(b) Average length of service by classification grade (1977–80):								
31.12.77	—	14.3	5.7	10.4	14.7	20.7	12.2	
31.12.78	—	16.8	5.8	9.2	14.6	20.5	12.3	
31.12.79	0.5	4.3	4.2	8.2	14.4	21.1	12.2	
31.12.80	—	0.8	3.6	7.7	13.9	21.1	11.9	

TABLE D.26

Manual workers by classification grade and age group, Italsider, Cornigliano works

Age	1	2	3	4	5	6	Total	(No.)
(a) % distribution (31.12.80):								
< 21	—	—	0.10	0.03	—	—	0.13	(9)
21–5	—	0.46	3.13	1.88	0.62	—	6.09	(421)
26–30	—	0.45	3.01	4.72	3.82	0.03	12.03	(831)
31–5	—	0.14	0.52	4.30	8.70	0.20	13.86	(958)
36–40	—	0.12	0.27	2.62	9.16	0.28	12.45	(860)
41–5	—	0.01	0.12	3.36	11.81	0.62	15.92	(1,100)
46–50	—	0.03	0.25	2.03	13.18	1.43	16.92	(1,169)
51–5	—	0.03	0.51	1.49	10.54	1.28	13.85	(957)
56–60	—	0.02	0.35	1.28	6.23	0.80	8.68	(600)
>60	—	—	—	0.04	0.01	0.02	0.07	(5)
Total	—	1.26	8.26	21.75	64.07	4.66	100	
(No.)	(—)	(87)	(571)	(1,503)	(4,427)	(322)		(6,910)
(b) Average age by classification (1977–80):								
31.12.77	—	43.8	35.4	38.5	43.1	47.3	40.5	
31.12.78	—	47.3	34.9	38.8	43.8	48.3	41.6	
31.12.79	23.5	30.9	31.7	37.7	43.6	48.7	41.2	
31.12.80	—	28.6	29.8	37.0	43.5	48.6	41.0	

TABLE D.27

Manual workers by classification grade and by grade of job performed, Breda Siderurgica (January 1980)

Job grades	Workers' grade													
	1	2	3	4	5	Total	%	1	2	3	4	5	Total	%
	(a) Steel department:							*(b) Rolling department:*						
1	—	—	1	5	1	7	1.9	—	3	5	3	—	11	1.6
2		13	6	3	9	31	8.3		9	15	5	2	31	4.5
3		6	47	21	3	77	20.7		1	185	105	1	292	42.3
4				101	11	112	30.1				165	54	219	31.7
5					145	145	39.0					137	137	19.9
Total	—	19	54	130	169	372		—	13	205	278	194	690	
%	—	5.1	14.5	35.0	45.4		100	—	1.9	29.7	40.3	28.1		100
	(c) Finishing department:							*(d) Maintenance services:*						
1	—	13	8	—	—	21	4.4	—	3	5	4	2	14	2.8
2		24	27	12	2	65	13.7		—	8	—	1	9	1.8
3		10	54	109	2	175	36.9			33	9	3	45	9.0
4				141	14	155	32.6				143	3	146	29.1
5					58	59	12.4					287	287	57.3
Total	—	47	90	262	76	475		—	3	46	156	296	501	
%	—	9.9	18.9	55.2	16.0		100	—	0.6	9.2	31.1	59.1		100

	(*e*) *Quality control:*							(*f*) *Transport services:*						
1	—	—	1	2	1	4	4.0	—	6	1	—	—	7	3.0
2		—	—	—	—	—	—		33	19	5	1	58	25.2
3			5	10	2	17	17.0		1	100	25	—	126	54.8
4			1	36	7	44	44.0				25	2	27	11.8
5					35	35	35.0					12	12	5.2
Total	—	—	7	48	45	100		—	40	120	55	15	230	
%	—	—	7.0	48.0	45.0		100	—	17.4	52.2	23.9	6.5		100
	(*g*) *Other services:*							(*h*) *Total:*						
1	—	36	25	12	5	78	36.3	—	61	46	26	9	142	5.5
2		5	6	4	2	17	7.9		84	81	29	17	211	8.2
3			54	40	3	97	45.1		18	478	319	14	829	32.1
4				13	—	13	6.0			1	624	91	716	27.7
5					10	10	4.7			1		684	685	26.5
Total	—	41	85	69	20	215		—	163	607	998	815	2,583	
%	—	19.1	39.5	32.1	9.3		100	—	6.3	23.5	38.6	31.6		100

TABLE D.28

Upgrading by department and by system of upgrading, Breda Siderurgica, 1973–9 (number of workers)

	Total upgrading (1973–9)						Average upgrading per year (No.)	Average upgrading per year (per 100 workers)
	Promotion		Rotation and substitution		Total			
	No.	%	No.	%	No.	%		
steel dept.	874	91.14	85	8.86	959	100	137.00	36.44
rolling dept.	843	77.13	250	22.87	1,093	100	156.14	22.47
finishing dept.	352	62.08	215	37.92	567	100	81.00	18.12
maintenance	715	99.44	4	0.56	719	100	102.71	19.53
quality control	101	82.79	21	17.21	122	100	17.43	17.26
transport serv.	206	78.03	58	21.97	264	100	37.71	16.40
other services	86	76.79	26	23.21	112	100	16.00	7.41
Total	3,177	82.82	659	17.18	3,836	100	548.00	21.15

TABLE D.29

Upgrading by grade and by system of upgrading, Breda Siderurgica, 1973–9

	1/2			2/3			3/4			4/5			Total			%		
	P	R	Tot	P	R	Tot	P	R	Tot	P	R	Tot	P	R	Tot	P	R	Tot
1973	217	—	217	223	4	227	159	—	159	50	—	50	649	4	653	99.39	0.61	100
1974	311	1	312	187	40	227	218	23	241	105	3	108	821	67	888	92.45	7.55	100
1975	32	—	32	193	26	219	210	62	272	119	16	135	554	104	658	84.19	15.81	100
1976	139	—	139	83	36	119	114	85	199	134	19	153	470	140	610	77.05	22.95	100
1977	36	—	36	92	16	108	104	111	215	100	20	120	332	147	479	69.31	30.69	100
1978	3	—	3	14	12	26	56	65	111	81	23	104	154	100	254	60.63	39.37	100
1979	40	—	40	34	10	44	37	54	91	86	32	118	197	96	293	67.24	32.76	100
Total	778	1	779	826	144	970	898	400	1,298	675	113	788	3,177	658	3,835			
%	99.9	0.1	100	85.2	14.8	100	69.2	30.8	100	85.7	14.3	100				82.8	17.2	100
%		20.31			25.29			33.85			20.55			100				

Note:
P = promotion; R = rotation.

TABLE D.30

Manual workers by classification grade, by system of acquisition of the grade and by department, Dalmine, Dalmine works[1], January 1980

	(a) No. of workers						(b) Distribution					
	Newly hired 2	As per job 3	*ad personam* 4	Rot. substit. 5	Down-graded 6	Tot.	Newly hired 2	As per job 3	*ad personam* 4	Rot. substit. 5	Down-graded 6	Tot.
Grade 6:												
steel dept.	—	—	—	—	—	—	—	—	—	—	—	—
roll dept.	—	—	—	—	—	—	—	—	—	—	—	—
mainten.	—	—	—	3	—	3	—	—	—	100	—	100
services	—	—	—	—	—	—	—	—	—	—	—	—
Total	—	—	—	3	—	3	—	—	—	100	—	100
Grade 5:												
steel dept.	—	32	8	16	2	58	—	55.2	13.8	27.6	3.4	100
roll dept.	—	45	8	13	2	68	—	66.2	11.8	19.1	2.9	100
mainten.	—	68	—	1	—	69	—	98.6	—	1.4	—	100
services	—	14	4	7	7	32	—	43.7	12.5	21.9	21.9	100
Total	—	159	20	37	11	227	—	70.0	8.8	16.3	4.9	100
Grade 4:												
steel dept.	—	19	1	4	2	26	—	73.1	3.8	15.4	7.7	100
roll. dept.	—	51	8	67	4	130	—	39.2	6.2	51.5	3.1	100
mainten.	—	28	—	3	1	32	—	87.5	—	9.4	3.1	100
services	—	28	3	19	6	56	—	50.0	5.4	33.9	10.7	100
Total	—	126	12	93	13	244	—	51.7	4.9	38.1	5.3	100

Grade 3:												
steel dept.	4	2	—	—	—	6	66.7	33.3	—	—	—	100
roll. dept.	—	20	1	2	—	23	—	87.0	4.3	8.7	—	100
mainten.	1	8	—	1	1	11	9.1	72.7	—	9.1	9.1	100
services	—	9	—	—	5	14	—	64.3	—	—	35.7	100
Total	5	39	1	3	6	54	9.3	72.2	1.9	5.5	11.1	100
Grade 2:												
steel dept.	3	—	—	—	—	3	100	—	—	—	—	100
roll. dept.	7	—	—	—	—	7	100	—	—	—	—	100
mainten.	5	—	—	—	—	5	100	—	—	—	—	100
services	1	2	2	—	—	5	20.0	40.0	40.0	—	—	100
Total	16	2	2	—	—	20	80.0	10.0	10.0	—	—	100
Total:												
steel dept.	7	53	9	20	4	93	7.5	57.0	9.7	21.5	4.3	100
roll. dept.	7	116	17	82	6	228	3.1	50.9	7.4	36.0	2.6	100
mainten.	6	104	—	8	2	120	5.0	86.7	—	6.7	1.6	100
services	1	53	9	26	18	107	1.0	49.5	8.4	24.3	16.8	100
Total	21	326	35	136	30	548	3.8	59.5	6.4	24.8	5.5	100

Notes:

1. See Table D.6, note 2.
2. Newly hired workers are given a grade lower than that of their job until they acquire some training.
3. Here the workers are given the grade that applies to the job, always through promotion.
4. These are workers who are temporarily moved to a lower grade job for personal reason (e.g. illness) but who keep their original grade.
5. Workers who are given a higher grade than that of their job after a certain number of rotations or substitutions.
6. 'Downgraded' workers have been permanently moved to a lower-grade job, as they are no longer able to perform their job; but they keep their original grade.

TABLE D.31

Annual average turnover rates by category of employment, Breda Siderurgica, 1972–9 (%)

	Entries			Departures		
	Hirings	Internal promotion from a different category	Total entries	Departure from the plant	Internal promotion to a different category	Total departures
managers	n.a	n.a.	15.54	22.30	—	22.30
clerical workers	n.a.	n.a.	8.68	n.a.	n.a.	10.23
foremen	—	7.93	7.93	n.a.	n.a.	11.46
manual workers	6.96	—	6.69	5.80	1.43	7.23
Total	n.a.	n.a.	7.08	n.a.	n.a.	7.92

TABLE D.32

Annual average turnover rates by category of employment Dalmine, Dalmine works, 1970–9 (%)

	Entries			Departures		
	Hirings	Internal promotion from a different category	Total entries	Departure from the plant	Internal promotion to a different category	Total departures
managers	3.62	8.70	12.32	7.97	—	7.97
clerical workers	6.58	2.75	9.33	8.74	0.20	8.94
foremen	0.91	8.05	8.96	8.42	4.25	12.67
manual workers	5.72	—	5.72	5.82	0.44	6.26
Total	5.66	0.56	6.22	6.22	0.54	6.76

TABLE D.33

Annual average turnover rates by category of employment, Italsider, Cornigliano works, 1976–80 (%)

	Entries				Departures			
	Hirings	Intra-company transfer	Internal promotion from a different category	Total entries	Departure from the plant	Intra-company transfer	Internal promotion to a different category	Total departures
managers	0.54	6.52	7.07	14.13	4.35	5.43	—	9.78
clerical workers	0.28	3.35	5.36	8.99	3.82	1.61	0.16	5.59
foremen	—	—	7.36	7.36	4.82	0.20	13.21	18.23
manual workers	4.57	0.14	—	4.71	3.72	0.51	1.10	5.33
Total	3.64	0.25	1.24	5.13	3.77	0.73	1.24	5.74

TABLE D.34
Annual average turnover rates, manual workers only: a comparison of steel and manufacturing (%)

	Entry rate	Departure rate
Breda Siderurgica (*1972–9*)	6.69	7.23
AFL Falck, Concordia works (*1973–9*)	6.38	6.78
Dalmine, Dalmine works (*1970–9*)	5.72	6.26
Italsider, Cornigliano works (*1976–80*)	4.71	5.33
steel industry, Italy[1] (*1978–80*)	7.78	8.35
manufacturing, Italy[1] (*1978–80*)	12.01	13.53

Note:
1. *Ministero del Lavoro* data, based on the enterprises with over 50 employees.

TABLE D.35

Internal and external turnover rates by department, manual workers only, Breda Siderurgica, 1970–9

	Entries			Departures			
	Hirings	Intra-department transfers[1]	Total entries	Departures from the plant	Promotion to other categories	Intra-department transfers[1]	Total departures
(a) Total no. of workers:							
steel	455	5	460	312	20	81	413
rolling	651	62	713	408	38	120	566
finishing	362	89	451	385	14	71	470
maintenance	493	118	611	388	41	13	442
quality control	72	47	119	103	38	83	224
transport service	313	15	328	196	25	147	368
other services	89	179	268	146	34	—	180
Total internal turnover		515				515	
Total external turnover[2]	2,435		2,435	1,938	210		2,148

(*b*) *Annual average rates per 100 workers:*							
steel	11.39	0.12	11.51	7.81	0.50	2.03	10.34
rolling	8.53	0.81	9.34	5.34	0.50	1.57	7.41
finishing	7.59	1.87	9.46	8.07	0.29	1.49	9.85
maintenance	9.81	2.35	12.16	7.72	0.81	0.26	8.79
quality control	5.14	3.35	8.49	7.35	2.71	5.92	15.98
transport service	11.88	0.57	12.45	7.44	0.91	5.58	13.93
other services	4.24	8.53	12.77	6.96	1.62	—	8.58
Total internal turnover		1.87				1.87	
Total external turnover[2]	8.84		8.84	7.04	0.75		7.79

Notes:

1. These data are calculated on the basis of differences between the yearly labour force employed by department and external turnover by department.
2. Total external turnover refers to total departures excluding intra-departmental transfers.

TABLE D.36

Annual labour turnover rates for manual workers, Breda Siderurgica, 1970–9

	No. of workers					Per cent	
	Departure from the plant	Intra-company transfer	Promotion to other categories	Total departures	Total employment	Departure rate[1]	Net departure rate[2]
1970	335	—	45	380	2,609	14.56	12.84
1971	220	—	13	233	2,709	8.60	8.12
1972	182	—	29	211	2,885	7.31	6.31
1973	221	—	5	226	2,846	7.94	7.76
1974	248	18	44	310	2,915	10.63	8.51
1975	125	1	21	147	2,807	5.24	4.45
1976	160	—	17	177	2,870	6.17	5.57
1977	170	—	10	180	2,732	6.59	6.22
1978	150	—	14	164	2,585	6.34	5.80
1979	123	—	19	142	2,589	5.48	4.75
annual average (1970–9)	193.4	1.9	21.7	216.8	2,754.7	7.87	7.02

Notes:

1. The annual average departure rate in this table(7.87%) differs from the rate calculated in Table D.35 (7.79%), as intra-company transfers have been included.
2. Excluding promotion to other categories of employment and intra-company transfers

TABLE D.37

Internal and external turnover rates by department, manual workers only, Dalmine, Dalmine works, 1970–9

	Entries			Departures			
	Hirings	Intra-department transfers[1]	Total entries	Departures from the plant[2]	Promotion to other categories[2]	Intra-department transfers[1]	Total departures
(*a*) *Total no. of workers:*							
steel	898	—	898	432		444	876
rolling	1,295	147	1,442	1,686		132	1,818
maintenance	583	187	770	694		20	714
services	452	313	765	758		51	809
Total internal turnover		647				647	
Total external turnover[3]	3,228		3,228	3,318	252		3,570

TABLE D.37. *(continued)*

(b) Annual average rates per 100 workers:							
steel	8.79	—	8.79		4.23	4.35	8.58
rolling	5.25	0.60	5.85		6.84	0.53	7.37
maintenance	5.10	1.64	6.74		6.07	0.20	6.25
services	4.30	2.97	7.27		7.21	0.48	7.69
Total internal turnover		1.14				1.14	
Total external turnover[3]	5.68		5.68	5.84	0.44		6.28

Notes:

1. See Table D.35, note 1.
2. Available data by department do not allow the distinction of departures from the plant from promotion to other categories; this distinction is available for the total labour force only.
3. See Table D.35, note 2.

TABLE D.38

Annual labour turnover rates for manual workers, Dalmine, Dalmine works, 1970–9

	No. of workers					Per cent	
	Departures from the plant	Promotion to white-collar jobs	Promotion to foremen jobs	Total departures	Total employment	Departure rate	Net departure rate[1]
1970	304	25	27	356	5,714	6.23	5.32
1971	234	3	6	243	6,029	4.03	3.88
1972	234	8	25	267	6,159	4.34	3.80
1973	240	1	19	260	6,107	4.26	3.93
1974[2]	854	1	25	880	5,861	15.01	14.57
1975	197	6	12	215	5,783	3.72	3.41
1976	270	13	15	298	5,625	5.30	4.80
1977	280	6	12	298	5,363	5.56	5.22
1978[2]	452	4	6	462	5,000	9.24	9.04
1979[2]	251	9	29	289	5,189	5.57	4.84
annual average (70–9)	331.6	7.6	17.6	356.8	5,682.9	6.28	5.83

Notes:

1. Excluding promotion to other categories of employment.

2. The high level of departures in 1974 and 1978 is the result of an administrative decision to treat as an independent unit a small plant that had previously been part of the Dalmine works; a small number of these 'administrative departures' are recorded in 1979.

TABLE D.39

Turnover rates by department, manual workers only, AFL Falck, Concordia works, 1979 (%)

	Hirings	Departures
steel	7.06	6.47
rolling	11.21	10.63
maintenance	9.23	10.77
services	5.92	8.33
Total	8.46	9.07

TABLE D.40

Annual labour turnover rates for manual workers, AFL Falck, Concordia works, 1973–9 (%)

	Entry rate	Departure rate
1973	8.13	6.37
1974	7.49	8.98
1975	2.33	3.69
1976	5.44	6.07
1977	5.75	6.75
1978	7.09	6.48
1979	8.46	9.07
annual average (1973–9)	6.38	6.78

Note:
Departures include promotions to different categories of employment.

TABLE D.41

Internal and external turnover rates by department, manual workers only, Italsider, Cornigliano works, 1976–80 (annual average rates per 100 workers)

	Empl. 1975	Empl. 1980	Δ 1975–80	Entry rates		Departure rates	
				Internal[2]	External[3]	Internal[4]	External[5]
Pig-iron dept.							
coke plant	296	312	+16	1.33	7.94	5.67	2.47
sintering	162	142	−20	5.19	5.87	9.96	3.42
blast-furnace	282	206	−76	1.40	3.20	8.29	2.29
Steel dept.	564	446	−118	0.82	2.10	5.65	2.95
Hot rolling							
blooming	315	335	+20	5.14	3.80	4.53	3.00
hot rolling	402	351	−51	5.43	5.69	9.78	3.56
Cold rolling							
cylind. turn.	120	147	+27	4.84	4.69	0.47	4.84
cold rolling	302	381	+79	7.96	7.08	9.10	2.46
finishing	417	487	+70	6.93	5.96	6.49	3.55

TABLE D.41. *(continued)*

Dept. maintenance							
pig-iron dept.	232	238	+6	1.86	5.40	3.37	3.80
steel dept.	296	279	−17	2.51	5.17	3.16	5.75
hot rolling	238	262	+24	2.65	6.09	2.97	4.13
cold rolling	217	283	+66	2.74	13.31	4.66	4.57
Quality control	183	65	−118	6.14	0.18	23.28	3.79
Central maintenance							
automation	129	116	−13	0.84	7.07	5.55	3.20
centr. maint.	672	680	+8	1.44	4.49	1.61	4.11
workshops	342	437	+95	5.76	2.29	2.48	6.81
Auxil. services							
auxil. serv.	216	168	−48	2.40	1.40	5.10	4.00
maint. AS	93	102	+9	4.42	5.06	1.31	6.86
Other services							
transport serv.	883	724	−159	0.98	5.06	4.32	2.98
maint. TS	119	124	+5	1.47	4.42	1.99	4.08
other services	627	625	−2	15.27	1.26	7.79	8.91
Total	7,107	6,910	−197	4.27	4.69	5.39	4.18

Notes:

1. Δ = absolute variation.
2. Intra-department transfers.
3. Hirings and intra-company transfers.
4. Promotion to other categories of employment and intra-department transfers.
5. Departures from the plant.

TABLE D.42

Annual labour turnover rates for manual workers, Italsider, Cornigliano works, 1975–80

	No. of workers					Per cent	
	Departure from the plant	Intra-company transfer	Promotion to other categories	Total departures	Total employment	Departure rate	Net departure rate[1]
1975	178	44	78	300	7,108	4.22	2.50
1976	373	36	92	501	7,116	7.04	5.24
1977	190	76	100	366	6,916	5.29	2.75
1978	174	18	61	253	6,690	3.78	2.60
1979	233	36	50	319	6,843	4.66	3.40
1980	315	12	78	405	6,910	5.86	4.56
Annual average (75–80)	243.8	37.0	76.5	357.3	6,930.5	5.16	3.52

Note:

1. Excluding promotion to other categories of employment and intra-company transfers.

TABLE D.43

Labour turnover by reason for departure, manual workers only, a comparison of four steel plants (% distribution)

	Breda Siderurgica (1970–9)	AFL Falck Concordia works (1979)	Dalmine Dalmine works (1979)	Italsider Cornigliano works (1975–80)
retirement	19.32	36.44	19.47	20.62
death and illness	3.91	6.78	7.63	5.27
dismissal[1]	8.70	—	4.96	1.63
resignation	58.29	40.68	54.96	40.58
intra-company transfer	—	—	—	10.35
promotion to other categories	9.78	7.63	12.98	21.41
other reasons	—	8.47	—	0.14
Total	100	100	100	100

Note:

1. Data include also 'resignation by mutal consent'. This is part of company policy in Dalmine, where management is keen to avoid direct dismissals.

TABLE D.44

Labour turnover by reason for departure and department, manual workers only, Breda Siderurgica, 1970–9

	Steel dept.	Roll. dept.	Finish. dept.	Maintenance	Quality control	Transp. serv.	Other serv.	Total
(a) Labour turnover by reason for departure (% distribution):								
retirement	14.46	20.18	14.53	22.14	12.77	13.12	42.78	19.32
death	1.81	3.81	3.26	3.50	1.42	6.34	9.44	3.91
dismissal	17.17	6.73	10.78	5.13	7.09	9.05	2.78	8.70
resignation	60.54	60.76	67.92	59.67	51.77	60.18	26.11	58.29
promotion	6.02	8.52	3.51	9.56	26.95	11.31	18.89	9.78
Total	100	100	100	100	100	100	100	100
(b) Annual average labour turnover rate (%):								
entry rate	11.39	8.53	7.59	9.81	5.14	11.88	4.24	8.84
departure rate	8.31	5.84	8.36	8.53	10.06	8.39	8.58	7.79
net depart. rate[1]	7.81	5.34	8.07	7.72	7.35	7.44	6.96	7.04

Note:

1. Excluding promotion to other categories of employment.

TABLE D.45

Labour turnover by reason for departure and department, manual workers only, Dalmine, Dalmine works, 1979

	Steel dept.	Rolling dept.	Maintenance	Services	Total
(a) Labour turnover by reason for departure (% distribution):					
retirement	15.15	22.45	6.58	34.55	19.47
death	9.09	11.23	2.63	7.27	7.63
dismissal[1]	12.12	6.12	2.63	1.82	4.96
resignation	51.52	46.94	71.05	49.09	54.96
promotion	12.12	13.26	17.11	7.27	12.98
Total	100	100	100	100	100
(b) Annual average labour turnover rates 1970–79 (%):					
entry rate	8.79	5.25	5.10	4.30	5.68
departure rate	4.23	6.84	6.08	7.21	6.23
net depart. rate[2]	n.a.	n.a.	n.a.	n.a.	5.82

Notes:

1. Including 'resignation by mutual consent' (see Table D.43, note 1).
2. Excluding promotion to other categories of employment.

TABLE D.46

Labour turnover by reason for departure and department, manual workers only, Italsider, Cornigliano works, 1976–80 (% distribution)

	Retirement	Other reasons for departure	Intra-company transfer	Promotion to other categories	Intra-department transfer	Total departures
Pig-iron dept.						
coke plant	2.46	22.95	4.92	9.02	60.65	100
sintering	4.08	21.43	—	4.08	70.41	100
blast-furnace	5.43	14.73	1.55	2.32	75.97	100
Steel dept.	2.56	20.00	3.08	5.13	69.23	100
Hot rolling						
blooming	12.20	22.76	4.88	10.57	49.59	100
hot rolling	9.69	14.73	2.33	4.26	68.99	100
Cold rolling						
cylinder turn.	35.30	55.88	—	2.94	5.88	100
cold rolling	5.46	13.66	2.19	15.30	63.39	100
finishing	9.17	21.83	4.37	3.06	61.57	100
Dept. maintenance						
pig-iron	4.70	44.71	3.53	21.18	25.88	100
steel dept.	2.42	30.65	31.45	8.06	27.42	100
hot rolling	10.99	43.86	4.39	17.68	23.08	100
cold rolling	9.01	37.84	2.70	33.33	17.12	100
Quality control	4.67	8.00	1.33	11.33	74.67	100

TABLE D.46. *(continued)*

Central maintenance						
automation	11.54	21.15	3.85	61.54	1.92	100
centr. main.	13.06	40.20	18.59	9.05	19.10	100
workshops	12.82	58.47	2.05	11.79	14.87	100
Auxil. services						
auxil. services	12.09	31.87	—	13.19	42.85	100
main. AS	8.00	56.00	20.00	4.00	12.00	100
Other services						
transp. serv.	7.66	29.93	3.28	6.94	52.19	100
maint. TS	29.03	48.39	3.22	3.23	16.13	100
other serv.	26.48	23.63	3.26	14.87	31.76	100
Total turnover	11.10	27.48	5.13	11.31	44.98	100

TABLE D.47

Total employment and labour turnover by length of service and by plant, manual workers only (%)[1]

Length of service	AFL Falck Concordia works (1979)			Dalmine[2] Dalmine works (1979)			Italsider[3] Cornigliano works (1980)		
	Employment	No. departures	Dep. rate (%)	Employment	No. departures	Dep. rate (%)	Employment	No. departures	Dep. rate (%)
< 1 year	103	14	13.59	420	9	2.14	426	45	10.56
1–5	499	33	9.42	830	8	0.96	931	16	1.72
6–10		14		1,500	27	1.80	2,360	54	2.29
11–15	454	8	4.41	980	19	1.94	766	5	0.65
16–20		12					918	31	3.38
21–5	109	2	3.67	1,380	83	6.01	935	38	4.06
26–30		2					528	31	5.87
>30	79	33	41.77	370	82	22.16	46	15	32.61
Total	1,244	118	9.48	5,480 (5,189)	228 (228)	4.16 (4.39)	6,910 (6,910)	235 (315)	3.40 (4.56)

Notes:

1. Departures from the plant, excluding intra-company transfers.
2. Data on employment by length of service are based on a sample of jobs (1 in every 10). Data in parentheses refer to total actual employment.
3. Data on departures by length of service do not include 80 workers who retired in 1980. Data in parentheses refer to total departures, including retirements.

TABLE D.48

Total employment and labour turnover by age group and by plant, manual workers only (%)

Age group	AFL Falck Concordia works (1979)			Dalmine Dalmine works (1979)			Italsider Cornigliano works (1980)		
	Employment	No. departures	Dep. rate (%)	Employment	No. departures	Dep. rate (%)	Employment	No. departures	Dep. rate (%)
>30	103	1	0.97	17	—	—	29	—	—
21–5	499	30	8.02	342	4	1.17	558	32	5.73
26–30		10		743	13	1.75	865	32	3.70
31–5	454	14	5.07	735	21	2.86	911	26	2.86
36–40		9		785	9	1.15	915	13	1.42
41–5	109	7	7.34	902	7	0.78	1,166	14	1.20
46–50		1		785	6	0.76	1,124	10	0.89
<50	79	46	58.23	880	168	19.09	1,342	188	14.01
Total	1,244	118	9.49	5,189	228	4.39	6,910	315	4.56

TABLE D.49

Number of manual workers per foreman, Italsider, Cornigliano works, 1960–80

	Foremen (1)	Manual workers (2)	(2)/(1) (3)
1960	243	5,820	23.9
1961	308	6,426	20.9
1962	356	6,612	18.6
1963	373	6,454	17.3
1964	404	6,176	15.3
1965	417	6,074	14.6
1966	407	5,962	14.6
1967	391	5,860	15.0
1968	371	5,672	15.3
1969	353	5,928	16.8
1970	353	5,948	16.8
1971	347	6,384	18.4
1972	321	6,712	20.9
1973	293	6,676	22.8
1974	281	7,262	25.8
1975	266	7,108	26.7
1976	233	7,116	30.5
1977	193	6,916	35.8
1978	188	6,690	35.6
1979	175	6,843	39.1
1980	140	6,910	49.4

TABLE D.50

Manual workers by classification grade[1] in the steel industry and manufacturing, Italy, 1963–77 (% distribution)

	1963	1965	1968	1971	1974	1977
(*a*) *Steel industry*:						
skilled	12.9	19.1	21.4	28.5	35.7	48.4
semiskilled	27.8	32.4	35.0	36.1	40.5	32.3
unskilled	39.8	33.1	31.0	26.4	19.2	15.8
labourers	4.7	3.6	3.4	1.9	3.3	2.3
apprentices	0.7	0.5	1.0	0.2	0.1	0.1
other categories	14.1	11.3	8.2	6.9	1.2	1.1
Total	100	100	100	100	100	100
(*b*) *Manufacturing*:						
skilled	17.0	17.6	18.3	20.4	24.4	29.9
semiskilled	37.9	38.1	36.2	38.2	40.1	43.0
unskilled	27.1	25.0	26.0	27.9	26.4	21.2
labourers	9.6	9.6	10.1	7.6	5.1	3.0
apprentices	6.0	3.0	6.8	3.8	2.9	2.1
other categories	2.4	6.7	2.6	2.1	1.1	0.8
Total	100	100	100	100	100	100

Note:

The data refer to firms with ten or more employees; for the general distinction between the grades, see Table D.20, notes.

Source: Ministero del Lavoro (various issues).

TABLE D.51
Gross average wages in the steel industry and manufacturing, Italy, 1955–81
(Italian lira)

	Gross average wage per hour			Gross average earnings per month		
	Steel (1)	Manuf. (2)	(1)/(2) × 100 (3)	Steel (4)	Manuf. (5)	(4)/(5) × 100 (6)
1955	336	248	135.48	n.a.	n.a.	—
1956	364	265	137.36	n.a.	n.a.	—
1957	384	275	139.64	n.a.	n.a.	—
1958	395	288	137.15	n.a.	n.a.	—
1959	411	294	139.80	n.a.	n.a.	—
1960	430	307	140.07	n.a.	n.a.	—
1961	457	328	139.33	n.a.	n.a.	—
1962	511	379	134.83	n.a.	n.a.	—
1963	586	440	133.18	n.a.	n.a.	—
1964	630	493	127.79	n.a.	n.a.	—
1965	712	527	135.10	116,951	79,746	146.65
1966	n.a.	n.a.	—	n.a.	n.a.	—
1967	784	565	138.76	130,008	89,930	146.19
1968	818	592	138.18	133,997	92,908	144.23
1969	929	653	142.27	141,025	97,999	143.90
1970	1,122	799	140.43	171,084	119,462	143.21
1971	1,285	939	136.85	184,585	135,059	136.67
1972	1,416	1,067	132.71	201,793	148,772	135.64
1973	1,778	1,313	135.41	245,526	177,201	138.56
1974	2,211	1,684	131.29	307,981	224,465	137.21
1975	2,332	1,794	130.00	366,525	274,666	133.44
1976	2,722	2,133	127.61	435,909	334,322	130.39
1977	3,295	2,673	123.27	518,954	418,300	124.06

Note:
The data refer to firms with ten or more employees.
Source: Ministero del Lavoro (various issues).

APPENDIX E

Tables on the Construction Industry

The data which provide the empirical basis of the construction industry are included in this Appendix. The data are derived from public sources, which are not available in the UK, and from private sources, primarily the records of the *Cassa Edile* of the Milan district. Interviews with representatives of the construction unions and people who work in the sector in an official or professional capacity provided additional statistical information. As most of the information on employment and industrial structure is derived from data provided by the *Cassa Edile*, a brief description of this data source is given below.

The *Cassa Edile* is a welfare organization established by collective agreement in every district. Its main function is maintaining a reserve fund, paid in by both employers and construction workers, to provide delayed wage payments in case of holiday, illness, unemployment, accidents, and so on. All firms classified as industrial (>9 employees on average over the year) have to register both themselves and their employees with the *Cassa Edile*. In the case of the craft enterprises it is at the discretion of the employees to register with the *Cassa Edile*. In 1981, for the Milan district, the unions estimated the proportion of the workforce registered as 70 per cent.[1]

Note:

1. See FILCA CISL Milano, 1982, p. 35.

TABLE E.1

Total employment in construction by statistical source, Italy, 1951, 1961, 1971 and 1981 ('000)

	1951	1961	1971	1981
population census[1]	1,472.7	2,345.6	2,063.3	n.a.
industrial census[2]	525.4	915.8	992.9	1,199.0
employment survey[3]	—	1,823.0	1,954.0	2,117.0
national accounting[4]	1,108.7	1,896.2	1,900.0	1,770.0

Source: 1. ISTAT, *Censimento generale della popolazione.*
2. ISTAT, *Censimento generale dell'industria e del commercio.*
3. ISTAT, *'Indagini sulle forze di lavoro', Annuario di statistiche del lavoro*
4. ISTAT, *'Occupazione presente', Annuario di contabilità nazionale*

TABLE E.2
Employees, self-employed, and total employment in construction, Italy 1951–81

	No. ('000)			%	
	Employees	Self-employed	Total	Employees	Self-employed
1951	994.0	115.0	1,109.0	89.63	10.37
1952	1,145.0	122.0	1,267.0	90.37	9.63
1953	1,309.0	129.0	1,438.0	91.03	8.97
1954	1,404.0	136.0	1,540.0	91.17	8.83
1955	1,474.0	142.0	1,616.0	91.21	8.79
1956	1,440.0	150.0	1,590.0	90.57	9.43
1957	1,466.0	156.0	1,622.0	90.38	9.62
1958	1,482.0	163.0	1.645.0	90.09	9.91
1959	1,499.0	169.0	1,668.0	89.87	10.13
1960	1,558.0	244.7	1,832.7	86.65	13.35
1961	1,701.3	256.1	1,957.4	86.92	13.08
1962	1,787.0	266.4	2,053.4	87.03	12.97
1963	1,852.4	276.0	2,128.4	87.03	12.97
1964	1,879.0	278.0	2,157.0	87.11	12.89
1965	1,733.6	271.2	2.004.8	86.47	13.53
1966	1,668.0	265.5	1,933.5	86.27	13.73
1967	1,700.4	263.7	1,964.1	86.57	13.43
1968	1,713.9	264.3	1,978.2	86.64	13.36
1969	1,764.6	269.5	2,034.1	86.75	13.25
1970	1,762.8	270.5	2,033.3	86.70	13.30
1971	1,657.7	242.3	1,900.0	87.25	12.75
1972	1,594.7	243.3	1,838.0	86.76	13.24
1973	1,535.6	251.4	1,787.0	85.93	14.07
1974	1,515.7	252.3	1,768.0	85.73	14.27
1975	1,493.0	256.2	1,749.2	85.35	14.65
1976	1,456.0	262.7	1,718.7	84.72	15.28
1977	1,437.2	267.7	1,704.9	84.30	15.70
1978	1,448.8	275.2	1,724.0	84.04	15.96
1979	1,440.9	279.1	1,720.0	83.77	16.23
1980	1,452.0	287.0	1,739.0	83.50	16.50
1981	1,475.0	295.0	1,770.0	82.72	17.28

Source: ISTAT, '*Occupazione presente*', *Annuario di statistiche del lavoro*, 1982.

TABLE E.3

Total employment in construction, production industries, and all industries by region, 1981

	('000)			%	
	(1) Construction	(2) Production industries	(3) All industries	(4) (1)/(2)	(5) (1)/(3)
Piemonte	131	891	1,856	14.70	7.06
Valle d'Aosta	5	16	48	31.25	10.42
Lombardia	292	1,885	3,667	15.49	7.96
Liguria	56	176	655	31.82	8.55
Total north-west	484	2,968	6,226	16.31	7.77
Trentino-Alto Adige	38	104	351	36.54	10.83
Veneto	167	736	1,700	22.69	9.82
Friuli-Ven. Giulia	48	170	462	28.23	10.39
Emilia-Romagna	148	662	1,691	22.36	8.75
Total north-east	401	1,672	4,204	23.98	9.54

TABLE E.3. *(continued)*

Toscana	114	588	1,404	19.39	8.12
Umbria	34	115	301	29.57	11.30
Marche	61	263	612	23.19	9.97
Lazio	171	397	1,695	43.07	10.09
Total centre	380	1,363	4,012	27.88	9.47
Abruzzi	58	135	435	42.96	13.33
Molise	17	28	119	60.71	14.29
Campania	184	494	1,715	37.25	10.73
Puglia	146	335	1,267	43.58	11.52
Basilicata	37	55	203	67.27	18.23
Calabria	106	149	609	71.14	17.41
Sicilia	236	392	1,475	60.21	16.00
Sardegna	69	138	487	50.00	14.17
Total south	853	1,726	6,310	49.42	13.52
Total Italy	2,117	7,729	20,751	27.39	10.20

Source: ISTAT, '*Indagini sulle forze di lavoro, media delle quattro rilevazioni*', *Annuario di statistiche del lavoro*, 1982.

TABLE E.4

Male employment in construction, production industries, and all industries by region, 1981

	('000)			%	
	(1) Construction	(2) Production industries	(3) All industries	(4) (1)/(2)	(5) (1)/(3)
Piemonte	124	649	1,208	19.11	10.26
Valle d'Aosta	4	14	31	28.57	12.90
Lombardia	274	1,340	2,398	20.45	11.43
Liguria	54	148	445	36.49	12.13
Total north-west	456	2,151	4,082	21.20	11.71
Trentino-Alto Adige	37	89	238	41.57	15.55
Veneto	160	532	1,160	30.08	13.79
Friuli-Ven. Giulia	46	133	305	34.59	15.08
Emilia Romagna	140	469	1,074	29.85	13.04
Total north-east	383	1,223	2,777	31.32	13.79

TABLE E.4. *(continued)*

Toscana	109	416	940	26.20	11.60
Umbria	33	84	206	39.29	16.02
Marche	59	177	387	33.33	15.25
Lazio	165	344	1,228	47.97	13.65
Total centre	366	1,021	2,761	35.85	13.26
Abruzzi	56	106	291	52.83	19.24
Molise	16	25	76	64.00	21.05
Campania	179	409	1,219	44.77	14.68
Puglia	143	285	894	50.18	16.00
Basilicata	36	50	135	72.00	26.67
Calabria	104	138	438	75.36	23.74
Sicilia	232	362	1,169	64.09	19.85
Sardegna	67	130	367	51.54	18.26
Total south	833	1,505	4,589	55.35	18.15
Total Italy	2,038	5,901	14,208	34.54	14.34

Source: ISTAT, '*Indagini sulle forze di lavoro, media delle quattro rilevazioni*', *Annuario di statistiche del lavoro*, 1982.

TABLE E.5
Manual employment in construction by skill in a sample of districts, Italy, 1979
(% distribution)

	Skilled	Semiskilled	Unskilled	Apprentices	Total
Valle D'Aosta:					
Aosta	15.83	38.57	45.60	n.a.	100
Piemonte:					
Allessandria	29.31	31.92	38.77	n.a.	100
Asti	17.20	32.92	49.88	n.a.	100
Torino	29.70	32.27	34.13	3.90	100
Vercelli	25.35	31.75	42.90	n.a.	100
Liguria:					
Genova	52.94	21.80	25.26	n.a.	100
Imperia	17.16	37.87	41.35	3.62	100
Lombardia:					
Bergamo	34.72	35.41	24.39	5.48	100
Brescia	28.27	34.03	29.55	8.15	100
Cremona	28.94	31.15	39.91	n.a.	100
Como	40.05	20.01	39.94	n.a.	100
Lecco	22.45	40.36	37.19	n.a.	100
Milano	50.24	19.52	29.86	0.38	100
Sondrio	9.88	54.09	30.88	5.15	100
Trentino:					
Trento	21.19	40.06	38.75	n.a.	100
Veneto:					
Padova	17.45	47.43	28.87	6.25	100
Venezia	29.15	38.82	25.34	6.69	100
Verona	25.81	42.57	27.44	4.18	100
Emilia:					
Modena	50.40	21.60	28.00	n.a.	100
Parma	37.19	22.47	40.34	n.a.	100
Piacenza	37.68	24.53	37.79	n.a.	100
Toscana:					
Arezzo	34.05	30.48	34.15	1.32	100
Massa Carrara	40.02	19.96	40.02	n.a.	100
Pistoia	49.08	18.92	32.00	n.a.	100
Prato	39.27	21.10	37.52	2.11	100
Marche:					
Ascoli Piceno	18.19	31.32	45.68	4.81	100
Pesaro	22.56	33.04	40.56	3.84	100
Lazio:					
Frosinone	12.00	41.01	46.99	n.a.	100
Roma	49.80	17.00	33.20	n.a.	100
Viterbo	34.00	20.98	45.02	n.a.	100

Abruzzi-Molise:					
L'Aquila	34.49	24.02	41.49	n.a.	100
Campobasso	24.99	39.99	35.02	n.a.	100
Campania:					
Sicilia:					
Caltanissetta	18.62	31.28	50.10	n.a.	100
Palermo	11.68	32.81	55.51	n.a.	100
Ragusa	10.97	42.35	46.68	n.a.	100
Siracusa	13.29	33.15	53.56	n.a.	100
Sardegna:					
Cagliari	17.12	27.51	55.37	n.a.	100

Source: Casse Edili, 'Inchiesta Nazionale' (mimeo).

TABLE E.6

Manual employment in construction, average age by skill in a sample of districts, Italy, 1979

	Skilled	Semiskilled	Unskilled	Apprentices	Total
Valle D'Aosta:					
Aosta	41	36	31	n.a.	35
Piemonte:					
Alessandria	44	42	39	n.a.	41
Asti	43	40	36	n.a.	39
Torino	43	39	34	n.a.	38
Vercelli	44	39	38	n.a.	40
Liguria:					
Genova	44	41	38	n.a.	42
Imperia	n.a.	n.a.	n.a.	n.a.	41
Lombardia:					
Bergamo	38	35	33	17	35
Brescia	39	37	35	17	36
Como	44	39	36	n.a.	40
Cremona	40	38	35	n.a.	38
Lecco	42	40	33	n.a.	38
Milano	n.a.	n.a.	n.a.	n.a.	38
Sondrio	41	39	35	17	37
Veneto:					
Padova	43	40	43	17	40
Venezia	43	39	40	17	40
Verona	44	42	43	n.a.	43
Emilia:					
Parma	43	43	41	n.a.	42
Piacenza	44	43	40	n.a.	42

Toscana:					
Azezzo	45	45	46	18	45
Prato	46	43	43	n.a.	43
Marche:					
Ascoli Piceno	42	39	44	19	41
Pesaro	43	41	46	n.a.	44
Lazio:					
Roma	45	43	44	n.a.	44
Abruzzi:					
L'Aquila	41	40	41	n.a.	41
Campania:					
Napoli	41	40	37	n.a.	38
Sicilia:					
Palermo	37	39	43	n.a.	41
Ragusa	44	42	40	n.a.	41
Sardegna:					
Cagliari	42	37	31	n.a.	34

Source: Casse Edili, 'Inchiesta Nazionale' (mimeo).

TABLE E.7

Total, average, and full employment[1] in the Milan district, 1969–81

	(1) 'Total' employment	(2) 'Average' employment	(3) 'Continuous' employment	(4) (1)/(3)
1969	80,441	60,852	n.a.	—
1970	80,280	61,042	42,145	1.905
1971	68,689	53,551	38,810	1.770
1972	60,708	47,678	34,771	1.746
1973	64,157	49,438	34,588	1.855
1974	69,158	51,913	38,563	1.793
1975	67,370	52,262	37,238	1.809
1976	60,161	48,314	36,113	1.666
1977	54,074	43,601	33,167	1.630
1978	50,938	41,621	31,919	1.596
1979	48,871	39,931	30,786	1.587
1980	47,850	38,942	29,682	1.612
1981	47,568	38,623	29,183	1.630

Note:

1. For the definition of (1), (2), and (3) see Chapter 5, Figure 5.1, notes.

TABLE E.8

Manual workers entitled to the premio di professionalità[1] edile, *Milan district, 1976–81*

	Workers entitled	Workers not entitled	Total	Period considered
1976	31,982	31,341	63,323	Oct. '72–Sept. '75
1977	32,501	28,205	60,706	Oct. '73–Sept. '76
1978	31,728	22,145	53,873	Oct. '74–Sept. '77
1979	30,795	20,003	50,798	Oct. '76–Sept. '78
1980	28,851	20,007	48,858	Oct. '77–Sept. '79
1981	30,668	17,122	47,790	Oct. '78–Sept. '80

Note:
1. The *premio di professionalità edile* is a bonus related to the worker's length of stay in the sector, and to the total number of hours worked (see Chapter 5, note 15); for the years 1976, 1977, and 1978, three years and a minimum of 3,000 hours of work within this period was required; for the years 1979, 1980, and 1981, two years and a minimum of 2,100 hours of work within this period was required.
Source: Compiled from *Cassa Edile* data.

TABLE E.9

New entrants into the construction industry of the Milan district by classification grade[1] *1979, 1980, and 1981*

	Employment						Entry rates[2] (%)		
	1979		1980		1981		1979	1980	1981
	No.	%	No.	%	No.	%			
skilled	2,296	30.36	2,119	26.40	2,587	27.07	8.89	8.76	10.49
semiskilled	1,410	18.64	1,446	18.02	1,747	18.28	15.42	16.47	20.20
unskilled	3,752	49.61	4,357	54.29	5,091	53.28	27.59	32.36	37.00
apprentices	91	1.21	94	1.17	98	1.03	58.33	46.08	45.16
others	4	0.05	9	0.11	31	0.33	7.14	15.00	11.35
with no grade	10	0.13	1	0.01	1	0.01	15.87	50.00	100
Total	7,563	100	8,026	100	9,555	100	15.48	16.77	20.09

Notes:

1. For the general distinction between the grades, see Table E.13, notes.
2. Entry rates are calculated on total employment, over the year.

Source: Compiled from *Cassa Edile* data.

TABLE E.10

New entrants into the construction industry of the Milan district by age group, 1979, 1980, and 1981

	Employment						Entry rates[1] (%)		
	1979		1980		1981		1979	1980	1981
	No.	%	No.	%	No.	%			
14–18	1,277	17.85	1,761	22.61	2,083	22.66	56.68	63.28	63.33
19–20	660	9.23	855	10.98	924	10.05	31.72	38.88	40.40
21–5	1,656	23.15	1,801	23.12	2,282	24.83	29.61	31.69	36.85
25–30	896	12.52	906	11.63	1,122	12.21	18.68	19.60	24.81
31–5	637	8.90	629	8.08	757	8.24	14.09	14.46	17.52
36–50	564	7.88	480	6.16	538	5.86	10.39	10.31	13.43
41–5	529	7.39	506	6.50	561	6.10	8.11	8.26	9.85
46–50	419	5.86	387	4.97	458	4.98	6.12	5.84	7.23
51–5	330	4.61	308	3.95	308	3.35	5.89	5.48	5.45
56–60	172	2.40	137	1.76	135	1.47	4.39	3.36	3.33
>60	15	0.21	19	0.24	23	0.25	2.13	2.51	3.04
Total[2]	7,155 (408)	100	7,789 (237)	100	9,191 (364)	100	15.48	16.77	20.09

Notes:

1. Entry rates are calculated on total employment recorded over the year.
2. Parentheses denote numbers for which data are not available.

Source: Compiled from *Cassa Edile* data.

TABLE E.11

New entrants into the construction industry of the Milan district by size of enterprise, 1979, 1980, and 1981

	Employment						Entry rates[1] (%)		
	1979		1980		1981		1979	1980	1981
	No.	%	No.	%	No.	%			
1–2	509	6.73	485	6.04	592	6.20	26.14	23.32	27.22
3–5	981	12.97	1,002	12.48	1,146	11.99	19.23	19.56	22.12
6–9	1,046	13.83	1,074	13.38	1,171	12.26	16.55	17.19	18.57
10–19	1,581	20.90	1,630	20.31	1,903	19.92	14.72	16.09	19.45
20–49	1,477	19.53	1,947	24.26	2,585	27.05	12.22	15.72	19.87
50–99	1,005	13.29	1,124	14.01	1,282	13.42	15.80	17.45	21.31
100–249	557	7.37	542	6.75	605	6.33	11.11	13.32	15.99
250–459	407	5.38	222	2.77	271	2.83	31.72	16.28	20.64
>500	—	—	—	—	—	—	—	—	—
Total	7,563	100	8,026	100	9,555	100	15.48	16.77	20.09

Note:

1. Entry rates are calculated on total employment recorded over the year.

Source: Compiled from *Cassa Edile* data.

TABLE E.12

New entrants into the construction industry of the Milan district by type of enterprise, 1979, 1980, and 1981

	Employment						Entry rates[1] (%)		
	1979		1980		1981		1979	1980	1981
	No.	%	No.	%	No.	%			
industrial enterprise	5,146	68.04	5,692	70.92	6,595	69.02	16.53	18.74	22.17
craft enterprise	2,233	29.52	2,110	26.29	2,701	28.27	29.74	28.45	34.96
co-operative of producers	182	2.41	224	2.79	259	2.71	15.22	19.39	22.56
no information available	2	0.03	—	—	—	—	—	—	—
Total	7,563	100	8,026	100	9,555	100	18.99	20.61	24.74

Note:

1. Entry rates are calculated on the basis of average employment per quarter, as data on total employment per type of enterprise are not available; therefore, total entry rates in this Table differ from total entry rates in the Tables E.9, E.10, and E.11.

Source: Compiled from *Cassa Edile* data.

TABLE E.13

Construction workers' previous work experience: a sample of 519 workers

	Agriculture	Manufacturing	Services	Other sectors	No work exp.	Total	(No.)
By trade (%)							
bricklayer	23.8	0.8	7.1	19.8	48.4	100	(126)
carpenter	21.3	15.7	6.7	24.7	31.5	100	(89)
tile-layer	20.5	2.3	13.6	34.1	29.5	100	(44)
labourer	27.8	—	5.6	11.1	55.6	100	(18)
cement worker	25.0	2.1	8.3	16.7	47.9	100	(48)
machine op.	6.1	34.8	25.8	13.6	19.7	100	(66)
installator	3.3	29.5	14.8	13.1	39.3	100	(61)
other trades	35.8	1.5	4.5	9.0	49.3	100	(67)
By classification grade (%)							
skilled	17.5	14.1	12.7	17.5	38.1	100	(354)
semiskilled	11.8	5.9	5.9	32.4	44.1	100	(34)
unskilled	37.5	—	5.6	11.1	45.8	100	(72)
ungraded	20.3	11.9	6.8	23.7	37.3	100	(59)
Total (%)	20.2	11.4	10.6	18.3	39.5	100	
(No.)	(105)	(59)	(55)	(95)	(205)		(519)

Note:
The classification grades used for construction workers are: *operaio specializzato* (OS), here defined as skilled; *operaio qualificato* (OQ), here defined as semiskilled; *manovale specializzato* (MS), here defined as unskilled, referring to workers employed in simple but specific tasks; *manovale comune* (MC), here defined as ungraded, referring to workers employed in general and unskilled tasks.
Source: ISFOL, 1977, Appendix, Table 6, p. 138.

TABLE E.14

Construction workers employed in the Milan district by residence, 1979, 1980, and 1981

	1979		1980		1981	
	No.	%	No.	%	No.	%
Milan district	31,062	70.94	27,590	71.56	24,809	72.02
of which:						
city			6,330	16.42	5,583	16.21
rest of district			21,260	55.14	19,226	55.81
Total other districts in Lombardia	9,545	21.79	8,469	21.97	7,540	21.89
of which:						
Bergamo	4,739	10.82	4,252	11.03	3,717	10.79
Brescia	2,631	6.01	2,293	5.95	2,102	6.10
Como	452	1.03	410	1.06	350	1.02
Varese	601	1.37	497	1.29	434	1.26
Pavia	499	1.14	455	1.18	420	1.22
Cremona	483	1.10	426	1.10	392	1.14
Sondrio	132	0.30	126	0.33	121	0.36
Mantova	8	0.02	10	0.03	—	—
Total other regions	3,183	7.27	2,496	6.47	2,097	6.09
Total	43,790	100	38,555	100	34,446	100
(residence unknown)	(5,057)		(9,295)		(13,122)	

Source: Compiled from *Cassa Edile* data.

TABLE E.15

Manual employment in the construction industry by number of weeks worked per quarter, Milan District, 1980–1 (% distribution)

	No. of weeks								Total	No. employed per quarter
	1–4	5–6	7–8	9	10	11	12	13		
4th qtr. '80	12.5	6.6	10.8	8.4	11.4	17.4	24.2	8.7	100	37,537
1st qtr. '81	16.1	7.1	11.6	8.4	10.1	14.6	23.3	8.8	100	38,151
2nd qtr. '81	13.8	5.8	8.9	6.4	8.0	10.7	23.5	22.9	100	38,377
3rd qtr. '81	16.4	10.7	18.3	18.2	20.7	9.8	3.1	2.8	100	37,235
Average	14.7	7.5	12.4	10.3	12.5	13.1	18.6	10.9	100	37,825

Source: Compiled from *Cassa Edile* data.

TABLE E.16

Manual employment by educational level: a comparison of manufacturing and construction (% distribution)

	Manufacturing industry	Construction industry		
	Population census (1971)	Population census (1971)	ISFOL–CRESME case study of a sample of skilled workers	Gadola S.p.A (1978)
	(1)	(2)	(3)	(4)
university degree	0.1	—	—	16.0 (university degree, *licenza scuola superiore* and *licenza media*)
licenza scuola superiore	1.6	0.4	1.7	
licenza media	18.9	7.4	12.9	
licenza elementare	66.9	63.1	55.9	64.0
semiliterate	11.2	23.7	27.7	20.0 (semiliterate and illiterate)
illiterate	1.3	5.4	1.8	
Total	100	100	100	100
(No.)	(4,529,892)	(1,668,838)	(519)	(197)

Note:
Five years of education are required for *licenza elementare*, a further three for *licenza media*, and a further five for *licenza scuola superiore*.

Source: (1) and (2), ISTAT, *Censimento generale popolazione*, 1971; (3), compiled from ISFOL, 1977, Appendix; (4), FLC and C.d.D. Gadola, 1980, p. 15.

TABLE E.17

Methods of training in construction: a sample of 519 workers

	On-the-job training	Formal training	Training in other sectors	Other methods	Total	(No.)
By classification grade[1] (%)						
skilled	65.25	29.38	5.08	0.29	100	(354)
semiskilled	79.41	14.71	2.94	2.94	100	(34)
unskilled	100	—	—	—	100	(72)
ungraded	81.36	11.86	5.08	1.70	100	(59)
By trade (%)						
bricklayer	96.80	1.60	—	1.60	100	(126)
carpenter	84.30	9.00	6.70	—	100	(89)
tilelayer	88.60	11.40	—	—	100	(44)
cement worker	77.10	22.90	—	—	100	(48)
machine op.	7.60	81.80	10.60	—	100	(66)
installator	36.10	50.80	13.10	—	100	(61)
Total[2]	72.83	22.35	4.24	0.58	100	
(No.)	(378)	(116)	(22)	(3)		(519)

Notes:

1. For the general distinction between the grades, see Table E.13, note.
2. Including labourers and other trades.

Source: Compiled from ISFOL, 1977, Appendix, Table 6, pp. 135–7.

TABLE E.18

Manual workers by total time spent in the construction industry and by classification grade: a comparison between two samples

(a) CRESME sample:

	Skilled	Semiskilled	Unskilled	Labourers	Total
< 1 year	1.7	6.6	6.3	13.3	4.0
1–5 years	16.2	23.7	28.4	34.1	20.6
6–10 years	22.9	23.5	16.2	20.7	21.8
> 10 years	59.2	46.2	49.1	31.9	53.6
Total	100	100	100	100	100
(No.)	(n.a.)	(n.a.)	(n.a.)	(n.a.)	(4,400)

(b) ISFOL sample:

	Skilled	Semiskilled	Unskilled	Ungraded	Total
< 1 year	1.7	2.9	9.7	—	2.7
1–3 years	9.9	20.6	19.4	6.8	11.6
4–10 years	33.1	26.5	27.8	45.8	33.3
> years	54.2	50.0	41.7	45.8	51.3
data not available	1.1	—	1.4	1.6	1.1
Total	100	100	100	100	100
(No.)	(354)	(34)	(72)	(59)	(519)

Note:
For a general distinction between grades, see Table E.13, note.
Source: (a) CRESME, in Franciosi, 1979*a*, p. 43; *(b)* compiled from ISFOL, 1977, Appendix.

TABLE E.19

Annual labour turnover rates in the Milan district, manual workers only, 1969–81 (%)

	Average labour force turnover (1)	Entry rate (2)	Exit rate (3)
1969	32.15	—	—
1970	31.52	—	—
1971	28.27	—	—
1972	27.33	—	—
1973	29.77	34.27	25.27
1974	33.22	35.84	30.60
1975	28.51	28.84	28.98
1976	24.52	20.32	28.72
1977	24.02	21.66	26.38
1978	22.39	20.03	24.75
1979	22.39	20.88	23.90
1980	22.88	21.45	24.31
1981	23.16	22.71	23.61

Source: Compiled from *Cassa Edile* data.

TABLE E.20

Manual workers by length of service and by classification grade: a sample of 4,400 workers employed by large contractors (% distribution)

	Skilled	Semiskilled	Unskilled	Labourers	Total
< 6 months	11.7	22.9	24.4	44.5	17.4
6 months–1 year	15.5	19.7	20.4	27.3	17.6
1 year–2 years	21.5	25.3	24.4	12.5	22.5
> 2 years	51.3	32.1	30.8	15.7	42.5
Total	100	100	100	100	100

Note:
For the general distinction between grades, see Table E.13, note.
Source: CRESME, in Franciosi, 1979*a*, p. 43.

TABLE E.21

Manual employment by classification grade, Milan district, 1971–81 (% distribution)

	1971[1]	1972	1973	1974	1975	1976	1977	1978	1979	1980	1981
highly skilled	—	—	—	—	—	—	—	—	—	0.05	0.27
skilled	45.69	40.89	40.17	36.81	42.95	46.56	50.24	51.30	52.52	52.90	51.59
semiskilled	19.77	20.85	20.69	20.66	19.68	19.38	19.52	19.37	18.90	18.35	18.18
unskilled	16.82	17.02	17.53	23.08	36.78	34.01	29.79	28.51	28.11	28.14	28.93
labourers	17.18	19.88	20.03	17.73	0.46	—	—	—	—	—	—
apprentices	0.54	1.04	1.27	0.97	0.03	0.03	0.38	0.54	0.31	0.43	0.46
ungraded[2]	—	0.32	0.31	0.75	0.10	0.02	0.07	0.28	0.16	0.13	0.57
Total	100	100	100	100	100	100	100	100	100	100	100
(No.)	(68,689)	(60,708)	(64,157)	(65,158)	(67,370)	(60,161)	(54,074)	(50,938)	(48,871)	(47,850)	(47,567)

Notes: For the general distinction between the grades, see Table E.13, note

1. Data for 1971 represent a sample of the total workers registered at the *Cassa Edile*, and are not therefore directly comparable with other years.

2. Includes discontinuous and site watchmen.

Source: Compiled from *Cassa Edile* data.

TABLE E.22

Manual employment by classification grade, by size of enterprise, and by type of enterprise, Milan district, 1981

	1–2	3–5	6–9	10–19	20–49	50–99	100–249	>249	Total	(No.)
(*a*) *Industrial enterprise:*										
highly skilled	0.65	0.29	0.03	0.34	0.37	0.04	0.52	—	0.28	(101)
skilled	54.33	56.40	55.41	54.66	54.73	54.78	55.91	42.92	54.42	(19,547)
semiskilled	19.70	17.75	16.22	17.12	16.98	16.24	18.19	25.08	17.35	(6,232)
unskilled	24.24	24.68	27.59	27.01	27.49	26.81	25.29	31.70	27.14	(9,749)
apprentices	0.43	0.29	0.11	0.15	0.05	0.04	—	—	0.08	(30)
discontinuous	0.65	0.59	0.64	0.72	0.38	2.11	0.09	0.30	0.73	(262)
Total	100	100	100	100	100	100	100	100	100	
(No.)	(462)	(1,718)	(3,447)	(8,032)	(12,319)	(5,365)	(3,250)	(1,328)		(35,921)
(*b*) *Craft enterprise:*										
highly skilled	—	0.12	0.11	0.25	—	—	—	—	0.11	(11)
skilled	28.92	39.79	45.63	47.42	48.37	25.62	—	—	40.77	(4,162)
semiskilled	26.05	23.88	20.28	18.06	17.80	13.22	—	—	21.85	(2,230)
unskilled	41.98	34.44	32.12	32.59	33.33	61.16	—	—	35.37	(3,610)
apprentices	2.93	1.77	1.54	1.68	0.50	—	—	—	1.79	(183)
discontinuous	0.12	—	0.32	—	—	—	—	—	0.11	(11)
Total	100	100	100	100	100	100	—	—	100	
(No.)	(1,708)	(3,451)	(2,796)	(1,611)	(399)	(242)	(—)	(—)		(10,207)

TABLE E.22. *(continued)*

(c) Cooperative of producers:										
highly skilled	—	—	—	7.35	1.38	—	0.57	—	1.18	(17)
skilled	40.00	33.33	58.73	47.79	50.87	60.34	62.71	—	57.82	(832)
semiskilled	—	22.22	20.63	16.18	13.84	13.55	9.98	—	12.85	(185)
unskilled	60.00	44.45	20.64	28.68	33.91	26.11	25.99	—	27.87	(401)
apprentices	—	—	—	—	—	—	0.75	—	0.28	(4)
discontinuous	—	—	—	—	—	—	—	—	—	(—)
Total	100	100	100	100	100	100	100	—	100	
(No.)	(5)	(9)	(63)	(136)	(289)	(406)	(531)	(—)		(1,439)

Note:
For the general distinction between the grades, see Table E.13, notes.
Source: Compiled from *Cassa Edile* data.

TABLE E.23

Manual employment by classification grade in the districts of Lombardia, 1980 (% distribution)

	Brescia	Como Lecco	Milano	Mantova[1]	Pavia	Cremona	Bergamo[2]	Sondrio	Varese
highly skilled	0.37	—	0.05	—	0.01	—	0.10	—	—
skilled	29.29	49.73	52.90	34.90	18.44	32.39	35.68	n.a.	n.a.
semiskilled	30.95	24.47	18.35	21.80	33.18	29.30	33.74	n.a.	n.a.
unskilled	28.40	25.80	28.14	38.50	46.01	38.31	23.81	n.a.	n.a.
apprentices	9.59	—	0.43	2.20	1.51	—	6.67	n.a.	n.a.
dicontinuous	1.40	—	0.13	2.60	0.85	—	—	n.a.	n.a.
Total	100	100	100	100	100	100	100	100	100

Notes:
See Table E.21, notes.
1. 3.40% of skilled workers are foremen.
2. 0.97% of skilled workers are foremen.
Source: FILCA CISL Lombardia, 1981, p. 42.

TABLE E.24

Manual workers by classification grade[1] in the construction industry,[2] Italy, 1951, 1961, and 1971 (distribution)

	1951	1961	1971
supervisors	0.3	0.7	0.9
skilled	9.7	12.6	18.5
semiskilled	24.7	26.5	31.8
unskilled	16.8	15.7	21.9
labourers	43.7	39.8	23.6
apprentices	3.9	4.3	3.0
other categories	0.9	0.4	0.3
Total	100	100	100
(No.)	(436,289)	(706,874)	(647,587)

Source: ISTAT, *Censimento generale dell'industria e del commercio*, 1951, 1961, 1971.

TABLE E.25

Manual workers by classification grade[1] in construction[2] and manufacturing industry, Italy, 1965–77 (% distribution)

	1965	1968	1971	1974	1977
(*a*) *Construction:*					
skilled	17.3	17.7	20.4	26.1	31.0
semiskilled	32.7	33.4	34.8	33.6	33.1
unskilled	12.8	12.5	15.9	21.2	29.5
labourers	34.1	32.7	26.9	17.2	4.3
apprentices	2.4	3.0	1.4	1.3	1.4
other categories	0.7	0.7	0.6	0.6	0.7
Total	100	100	100	100	100
(*b*) *Manufacturing:*					
skilled	17.6	18.3	20.4	24.4	29.9
semiskilled	38.1	36.2	38.2	40.1	43.0
unskilled	25.0	26.0	27.9	26.4	21.2
labourers	9.6	10.1	7.6	5.1	3.0
apprentices	3.0	6.8	3.8	2.9	2.1
other categories	6.7	2.6	2.1	1.1	0.8
Total	100	100	100	100	100

Notes:

1. For the general distinction between the grades see Table E.13, notes.
2. The data refer to construction only, excluding installation.

Source: Ministero del Lavoro (various issues).

TABLE E.26

Manual employment by age group, Milan district, 1971–81

	1971[1]	1972[1]	1973	1974	1975	1976	1977	1978	1979	1980	1981
(a) Employment (total registered):											
15–18	1,467	1,364	2,761	4,275	4,271	3,259	2,538	2,291	2,253	2,783	3,289
19–20	1,020	886	2,518	3,584	3,820	2,991	2,355	2,089	2,081	2,199	2,287
21–5	4,040	3,634	6,660	7,782	8,379	6,879	5,676	5,568	5,593	5,684	6,192
26–30	4,967	4,281	6,798	7,448	7,448	6,680	5,804	5,229	4,796	4,623	4,523
31–5	7,461	6,433	8,491	8,158	7,039	5,747	5,138	4,755	4,522	4,350	4,320
36–40	8,092	7,182	9,080	8,970	8,543	7,784	6,913	6,095	5,429	4,654	4,003
41–5	7,555	7,317	8,954	9,052	8,685	8,144	7,498	6,957	6,522	6,129	5,696
46–50	6,146	5,888	7,356	7,495	7,219	7,200	7,051	6,886	6,850	6,622	6,334
51–5	3,767	3,781	5,107	5,793	5,888	5,683	5,567	5,600	5,602	5,624	5,653
56–60	4,829	4.116	4,446	3,772	3,460	3,358	3,463	3,671	3,920	4,076	4,060
61–5	741	647	1,184	1,343	1,322	1,325	1,077	823	602	661	672
>65	74	64	122	148	132	149	140	134	103	96	85
Total[2]	50,159	45,593	63,477	67,820	66,206	59,199	53,220	50,098	48,273	47,501	47,114
	(143)	(234)	(678)	(1,338)	(1,164)	(962)	(857)	(840)	(598)	(349)	(456)

TABLE E.26. *(continued)*

(b) Percentage distribution:

15–18	2.92	2.99	4.35	6.30	6.45	5.51	4.77	4.57	4.67	5.86	6.98
19–20	2.03	1.94	3.97	5.28	5.77	5.05	4.42	4.17	4.31	4.63	4.85
21–5	8.05	7.97	10.49	11.47	12.66	11.62	10.66	11.11	11.59	11.97	13.14
26–30	9.90	9.39	10.71	10.98	11.25	11.28	10.91	10.44	9.93	9.73	9.60
31–5	14.87	14.11	13.38	12.03	10.63	9.71	9.65	9.49	9.37	9.16	9.17
36–40	16.14	15.75	14.30	13.23	12.90	13.15	12.99	12.16	11.25	9.80	8.50
41–5	15.06	16.05	14.11	13.35	13.12	13.76	14.09	13.89	13.51	12.90	12.09
46–50	12.25	12.92	11.59	11.06	10.90	12.16	13.25	13.75	14.19	13.94	13.44
51–5	7.52	8.29	8.04	8.54	8.89	9.60	10.46	11.18	11.60	11.84	12.00
56–60	9.63	9.03	7.00	5.56	5.23	5.67	6.51	7.33	8.12	8.58	8.62
> 60	1.63	1.56	2.06	2.20	2.20	2.49	2.29	1.91	1.46	1.59	1.61
Total	100	100	100	100	100	100	100	100	100	100	100

Notes:

1. The data refer to a sample of workers, and are not therefore directly comparable with other years.
2. Parentheses denote numbers for which data are not available.

Source: Compiled from *Cassa Edile* data.

TABLE E.27

Unemployment rates by sex and geographical area, Italy, 1977–82

	Male						Female					
	'77	'78	'79	'80	'81	'82	'77	'78	'79	'80	'81	'82
Lombardia	2.8	2.9	2.8	2.5	3.2	n.a.	7.3	7.8	8.9	8.1	9.5	n.a.
Milan district	n.a.	n.a.	n.a.	3.0	3.6	4.4	n.a.	n.a.	n.a.	9.0	9.8	11.1
north central Italy	3.7	3.8	3.7	3.5	4.0	n.a.	10.0	10.4	11.0	10.2	11.6	n.a.
south Italy and islands	6.4	6.6	7.3	7.5	8.1	n.a.	19.0	18.1	18.9	20.2	21.5	n.a.
Total	4.6	4.7	4.9	4.8	5.4	n.a.	12.5	12.6	13.3	13.1	14.4	n.a.

Note:

Figures for the Milan district are provided by *Osservatorio del Mercato del lavoro, Provincia di Milano*, and are based on unpublished ISTAT data.

Source: ISTAT, *Annuario di statistiche del lavoro*, 1982, (data from the '*Indagine sulle forze di lavoro*', annual averages).

TABLE E.28

Registered unemployment by sector and category, Milan district, December 1980

	Manual unskilled workers			Skilled and clerical workers			Total		
	Male	Female	Total	Male	Female	Total	Male	Female	Total
Total industry	6,503	6,146	12,649	4,067	2,891	6,958	10,570	9,037	19,607
of which:									
construction	636	—	636	1,051	—	1,051	1,687	—	1,687
All other sectors	1,257	2,424	3,681	1,859	1,446	3,305	3,116	3,870	6,986
Workers not attached to any sector:									
unskilled workers	6,504	13,398	19,902	—	—	—	6,504	13,398	19,902
clerical workers	—	—	—	9,178	20,888	30,066	9,178	20,888	30,066
Total	14,264	21,968	36,232	15,104	25,225	40,329	29,368	47,193	76,561

Source: Ufficio di Collocamento, Milan.

TABLE E.29

Gross average wages and earnings in construction and manufacturing, Italy, 1965–77 (Italian lira)

	Gross average wage per hour			Gross average earnings per month		
	Construction (1)	Manufacturing (2)	(1)/(2) × 100 (3)	Construction (4)	Manufacturing (5)	(4)/(5) × 100 (6)
1965	578	527	109.68	75,936	79,746	95.22
1966	n.a.	n.a.	—	n.a.	n.a.	—
1967	610	565	107.96	82,417	88,930	92.68
1968	642	592	108.44	86,975	92,908	93.61
1969	689	653	105.51	90,463	97,999	92.31
1970	816	799	102.13	108,635	119,462	90.94
1971	918	939	97.76	118,412	135,059	87.67
1972	994	1,067	93.16	125,624	148,772	84.44
1973	1,185	1,313	90.25	151,523	177,201	85.51
1974	1,474	1,684	87.53	191,840	224,465	85.47
1975	1,521	1,794	84.78	236,772	274,666	86.20
1976	1,850	2,133	86.73	290,240	334,322	86.81
1977	2,348	2,673	87.84	365,986	418,300	87.49

Note:

The data are based on enterprises with five or more employees in construction, and ten or more in manufacturing.

Source: Compiled from *Ministero del Lavoro* data.

TABLE E.30

Manual labour turnover: a comparison of the construction and manufacturing industries, 1965–81 (%)

	Construction					Manufacturing				
	Entry rates		Exit rates			Entry rates		Exit rates		
	Hirings	Total[1]	Layoffs	Voluntary quits	Total[2]	Hirings	Total[1]	Layoffs	Voluntary quits	Total[2]
1965	65.1	88.5	72.3	12.2	94.4	15.1	21.8	10.5	8.5	23.4
1966	69.3	95.0	63.5	15.1	89.8	21.8	28.2	9.1	10.8	24.3
1967	72.1	96.9	61.0	18.3	90.3	22.5	29.6	8.6	12.8	25.6
1968	71.6	95.5	53.8	24.3	89.5	24.0	30.4	8.2	15.1	28.1
1969	70.2	92.1	50.7	27.8	88.3	28.4	35.9	6.7	17.7	28.9
1970	59.0	75.3	41.9	26.5	78.5	23.2	28.8	5.7	15.4	25.6
1971	71.2	106.5	70.7	30.0	119.4	20.2	28.3	10.6	12.6	29.0
1972	66.4	93.4	57.7	27.7	97.7	20.2	28.7	9.2	11.3	26.0
1973	53.7	75.7	45.0	27.7	81.0	19.2	23.7	6.9	13.7	26.0
1974	39.1	48.2	19.8	26.6	52.2	14.3	17.7	3.5	9.8	17.1
1975	33.0	41.3	19.8	19.3	44.7	7.8	10.7	3.3	6.5	13.8
1976	31.5	40.1	18.0	20.5	44.5	11.8	15.0	2.7	8.0	14.5
1977	31.3	40.5	21.2	19.9	47.3	10.3	11.6	2.7	7.5	13.6
1978	28.3	32.2	21.8	15.7	43.5	9.0	10.5	2.4	6.0	12.5
1979	29.5	33.3	15.3	17.0	37.9	12.2	13.7	2.9	6.7	13.5
1980	29.2	33.3	14.4	19.3	39.9	10.2	11.8	3.1	7.1	14.6

Notes:

The data are based: for the period 1965–77, on enterprises with five or more employees in construction, and ten or more in manufacturing; for the period 1978–80, on enterprises with fifty or more employees in both cases.

1. Includes intra-company transfers.

2. Includes intra-company transfers, deaths, retirements, and other causes.

TABLE E.31

Number of enterprises, productive units, and employment in construction, manufacturing, and total economy 1951, 1961, and 1971

	1951			1961			1971		
	No. of ent.	No. of prod. units	Empl.	No. of ent.	No. of prod. units	Empl.	No. of ent.	No. of prod. units	Empl.
(*a*) *Italy*:									
tot. construction	34,182	45,043	525,401	53,826	70,126	915,854	131,877	160,488	992,911
of which:									
constr. only	31,063	41,516	498,897	49,069	64,188	837,100	109,417	135,241	839,781
installation	3,119	3,527	26,504	4,757	5,938	78,754	22,460	25,247	157,130
manufacturing	606,093	636,267	3,534,496	588,931	616,830	4,533,819	605,577	642,147	5,372,979
Total economy	1,504,027	1,631,467	6,781,092	1,938,724	2,079,540	9,463,457	2,236,044	2,425,204	11,077,533
(*b*) *Milan district:*									
tot. construction	2,690	4,289	84,175	4,059	6,252	119,435	7,804	11,093	125,136
of which:									
constr. only	2,122	3,606	78,093	3,304	5,163	98,015	6,066	8,917	88,316
installation	568	684	6,082	755	1,089	21,420	1,741	2,176	36,823
manufacturing	45,238	51,572	907,403	49,869	56,206	1,097,145	50,762	59,280	1,172,489
Total economy	104,412	120,695	1,265,572	138,914	155,579	1,620,905	164,666	189,222	1,810,994

Source: ISTAT, *Censimento generale dell'industria e del commercio*, 1951, 1961, 1971.

TABLE E.32

Percentage changes in number of enterprises, productive units, and employment in construction, manufacturing, and total economy, Italy, 1951–61 and 1961–71

	1951–61			1961–71		
	Ent.	Prod. units	Empl.	Ent.	Prod. units	Empl.
(*a*) *Italy*						
tot. construction	+57.5	+55.7	+74.3	+145.0	+128.9	+8.4
of which:						
constr. only	+58.0	+54.6	+67.8	+123.0	+110.7	+0.3
installation	+52.5	+68.4	+197.1	+372.1	+325.2	+94.4
manufacturing	−2.8	−3.0	+28.3	+2.8	+4.1	+18.5
Total economy	+28.9	+27.5	+39.6	+15.3	+16.6	+17.1
(*b*) *Milan district:*						
tot. construction	+50.9	+45.8	+41.9	+92.3	+77.4	+4.8
of which:						
constr. only	+55.7	+43.2	+25.5	+83.6	+72.7	+9.9
installation	+32.9	+59.2	+252.2	+130.6	+99.8	+71.9
manufacturing	+10.2	+9.0	+20.9	+1.8	+5.5	+6.9
Total economy	+33.0	+28.9	+28.1	+18.5	+21.6	+11.7

Source: See Table E.31.

TABLE E.33

Average size of enterprises and productive units in construction, manufacturing, and total economy, 1951, 1961, and 1971 (no. employed)

	1951		1961		1971	
	Ent.	Prod. units	Ent.	Prod. units	Ent.	Prod. units
(*a*) *Italy:*						
tot. construction	15.37	11.66	17.02	13.06	7.53	6.19
constr. only	16.06	12.02	17.06	13.04	7.67	6.21
installation	8.50	7.51	16.56	13.26	6.82	6.07
manufacturing	5.83	5.55	7.70	7.35	8.87	8.37
Total economy	4.51	4.16	4.88	4.55	4.95	4.35
(*b*) *Milan district:*						
tot. construction	31.29	19.63	29.42	19.10	16.03	11.28
constr. only	36.80	21.66	29.67	18.98	14.56	9.90
installation	10.71	8.89	28.37	19.67	21.15	16.92
manufacturing	20.06	17.58	22.00	19.52	23.10	19.78
Total economy	12.12	10.49	11.67	10.42	11.00	9.57

Source: See Table E.31.

TABLE E.34

Number of productive units and employment in construction by subsector, Italy, 1951, 1961, 1971, and 1981

	1951		1961		1971		1981	
	Prod. units	Employment	Prod. units	Employment	Prod. units	Employment	Prod. units	Employment
construction only:	39,821	502,905	61,663	813,406	133,527	834,591	272,590	1,044,984
of which:								
building and maint.	22,507	364,982	39,699	617,067	87,254	602,800	192,101	802,041
road works	3,069	55,729	4,181	79,407	8,613	98,974	19,112	143,529
other civil engin.	1,189	52,899	2,171	59,881	3,188	58,338		
finishing	13,056	29,295	15,612	57,062	31,794	62,261	61,377	99,414
auxiliary works					2,678	12,218		
installation	3,578	29,150	5,787	81,001	25,026	162,943	53,410	154,029
Total constr. ind.	43,399	532,055	67,450	894,407	158,553	997,574	326,000	1,199,013

Note:
1981 data are provisional.
Source: ISTAT, *Censimento generale dell'industria e del commercio*, 1951, 1961, 1971, 1981.

TABLE E.35
Average employment by productive unit in subsectors of the construction industry, Italy, 1951, 1961, 1971, and 1981

	1951	1961	1971	1981
Construction only	12.63	13.19	6.25	3.83
building and maint.	16.22	15.54	6.91	4.18
road works	18.16	18.99	11.49	7.51
other civil engin.	44.49	27.58	18.30	} 1.62
finishing	} 2.24	} 3.66	1.96	
auxiliary works			4.56	
Installations	8.15	14.00	6.51	2.88
Total constr. ind.	12.26	13.26	6.29	3.68

TABLE E.36
Productive units and total employment in construction, Italy, Lombardia and Milan district, 1981

	No. of prod. units	Total employment	Average empl. per prod. unit
(*a*) *Italy:*			
building and maint.	192,101	802,041	4.18
civil engineering	19,112	143,529	7.51
installation	53,410	154,029	2.88
finishing	61,377	99,414	1.62
Total constr. ind.	326,000	1,199,013	3.68
(*b*) *Lombardia:*			
building and maint.	34,285	135,573	3.95
civil engineering	2,396	22,970	9.59
installation	11,198	33,580	3.00
finishing	14,212	23,186	1.63
Total constr. ind.	62,091	215,309	3.47
(*c*) *Milan district:*			
building and maint.	7,793	42,000	5.39
civil engineering	874	13,255	15.17
installation	3,379	12,958	3.83
finishing	3,613	7,215	2.00
Total constr. ind.	15,659	75,428	4.82

Note:
1981 data are provisional.
Source:
ISTAT, *Censimento generale dell'industria e del commercio*, 1951, 1961, 1971, 1981.

TABLE E.37

Manual employment in construction and average size of enterprises in the districts of Lombardia, 1971–81

	1971	1975	1978	1980	1981
(a) Employment:					
Bergamo	6,350	10,698	13,413	13,649	13,071
Brescia	20,842	21,096	20,166	20,339	20,425
Como	10,391	10,772	10,499	14,933 (Como and Lecco)	14,667 (Como and Lecco)
Lecco	5,235	5,059	5,836		
Cremona	6,000	5,500	5,155	5,111	4,791
Mantova	6,450	6,236	6,122	6,213	6,032
Milano	53,551	52,262	41,621	38,942	38,623
Pavia	9,960	8,780	8,300	7,795	7,706
Sondrio	n.a.	2,647	3,069	3,267	3,412
Varese	9,290	8,204	7,389	6,599	6,506
(b) Average size of enterprises (no. of workers):					
Bergamo	19.36	19.38	18.76	17.07	16.02
Brescia	14.59	10.53	8.43	8.03	7.86
Como	17.01	14.42	10.55	10.03 (Como and Lecco)	9.84 (Como and Lecco)
Lecco	20.61	17.81	12.18		
Cremona	12.00	9.32	8.39	8.12	7.60
Mantova	n.a.	n.a.	n.a.	7.58	7.46
Milano	20.39	17.76	11.64	10.33	9.95
Pavia	10.98	10.39	9.45	8.24	8.20
Sondrio	n.a.	9.91	5.39	5.97	6.01
Varese	14.31	12.53	8.96	7.71	7.69

Source: For 1971, 1975, 1978, FILCA CISL Lombardia, 1980*a*; for 1980, FILCA CISL Lombardia, 1981; for 1981, FILCA CISL Lombardia, 1982.

TABLE E.38

Variation in stock of housing by geographical area, 1961–81

	Δ 1961–71[1]			Δ 1971–81		
	Comuni capoluogo	*Other comuni*	Total	*Comuni capoluogo*	*Other comuni*	Total
(*a*) *Number of houses:*						
north-west	336,335	768,336	1,104,671	96,729	942,427	1,039,156
north-east	236,780	371,166	607,946	172,326	680,807	853,133
centre	433,941	332,299	766,240	244,740	587,435	832,175
south	200,021	315,377	515,398	145,977	869,035	1,015,012
islands	129,314	96,735	226,049	147,949	531,321	679,270
Total	1,336,391	1,883,913	3,220,304	807,721	3,611025	4,418,746
(*b*) *Percentage distribution:*						
north-west	10.44	23.86	34.30	2.19	21.33	23.52
north-east	7.35	11.53	18.88	3.90	15.14	19.31
centre	13.48	10.32	23.80	5.54	13.29	18.83
south	6.21	9.79	16.00	3.30	19.67	22.97
islands	4.02	3.00	7.02	3.35	12.02	15.37
Total	41.50	58.50	100	18.28	81.72	100

Note:
1. Δ = absolute variation.

Source: Compiled from ISTAT, *Censimento generale della popolazione*, 1961, 1971, 1981.

TABLE E.39

Housing stock and absolute variation, Milan (Comune), 1961–81

	No. of houses	No. of rooms
1961	534,060	1,556,858
1971	643,417	1,950,937
1981	664,530	2,124,785
Δ 1961–71[1]	109,357	394,079
Δ 1971–81	21,113	173,848

Note:

1. Δ = absolute variation.

Source: Compiled from ISTAT, *Censimento generale della popolazione*, 1961, 1971, 1981.

References

1. The labour market segmentation debate

Addison W. and Siebert, S. 1979: *The Market for Labor: and Analytical Treatment* (Santa Monica, Goodyear).

Alexander, E. 1974: 'Income, experience and the structure of internal labour markets', in *Quarterly Journal of Economics,* Vol. 88, (February).

Amsden, A. H. (ed.) 1980: *The Economics of Women and Work* (Penguin).

Appelbaum, E. 1979: 'The labour market in post keynesian economics', in Piore, 1979.

Averitt, R. T. 1968: *The Dual Economy* (New York, Norton).

Bakke, E. W. and Hauser, P. M. (eds.) 1954: *Labor Mobility and Economic Opportunity* (London, MIT Press).

Barrett, M. and McIntosh, M. 1980: 'The family wage', in *Capital and Class,* No. 11, (summer).

Becker, G. 1965; 'A theory of allocation of time', in Amsden, 1980.

Beechey, V. 1977: 'Some notes on female wage labour in capitalist production', in *Capital and Class,* No. 3, (winter).

Berger, S. and Piore, M. J. 1980: *Dualism and Discontinuity in Industrial Societies* (Cambridge University Press).

Bettio, F. 1984: 'The sexual division of labour: the Italian case' (unpublished Ph.D. thesis, Cambridge).

Blau, F. D. and Jusenius, C. L. 1976: 'Economists' approaches to sex segregation in the labour market', in Blaxall and Reagan, 1976.

Blaxall, M. and Reagan, B. (eds.) 1976: *Women and the Workplace: the Implication of Occupational Segregation* (University of Chicago Press).

Bluestone, B. 1968: 'Low wage industries and the working poor', in *Poverty and Human Resources,* (March–April).

Bluestone, B. 1970; 'The tripartite economy: labor markets and the working poor' in *Poverty and Human Resources*, (July–August).

Bluestone, B. 1971: 'The characteristics of marginal industries',in D. M. Gordon (ed.), *Problems in Political Economy: an Urban Perspective* (Lexington, Mass., D. C. Heath).

Bluestone, B. and Stevenson, M. 1981: 'Industrial transformation and the evolution of dual labor markets: the case for retail trade in the US' in Wilkinson, 1981.

Bowles, S. 1971: 'Unequal education and the reproduction of the social division of labor',in *Review of Radical Political Economy* (fall–winter).

Bowles, S. and Gintis, H. 1975: 'The problem with human capital theory, a marxian critique', in *American Economic Review, Papers and Proceedings,* Vol. 65, (May).

Braverman, H. 1974: *Labor and Monopoly Capital: the Degradation of Work in the Twentieth Century* (New York, Monthly Review Press).

Breughel, I. 1979: 'Women as a reserve army of labour: a note on recent British experience', in *Feminist Review,* Vol. 3.

Bruno, S. 1979: 'The industrial reserve army, segmentation and the Italian labour market', in *Cambridge Journal of Economics,* Vol. 3, No. 2 (June).

Brusco, S. 1982: 'The emilian model: productive decentralization and social integration', in *Cambridge Journal of Economics,* Vol. 6, No. 2 (June).

Brusco, S. and Sabel, C. 1981: 'Artisan production and economic growth', in Wilkinson, 1981.

Burawoy, M. 1979: *Manufacturing Consent* (University of Chicago Press).

Cain, G. C. 1976: 'The challenge of segmented labor market theories to orthodox theory', in *Journal of Economic Literature,* Vol. 14, No. 4, (December).

Cairnes, J. E. 1874: *Some Leading Principle of Political Economy* (New York: Augustus M. Kelley).

Craig, J. C., Rubery, J., Tarling, R. and Wilkinson, F. 1979: 'Minimum wage legislation and labour market segmentation in advanced industrial countries', in 'Low Pay and Labour Market Segmentation in Advanced Industrial Countries', 1979.

Craig, J. C., Rubery, J., Tarling R. and Wilkinson, F. 1982: *Labour Market Structure, Industrial Organisation and Low Pay* (Cambridge University Press).

Del Boca, S. 1980, 'Segmentazione e mercati del lavoro dualistici', in *Rivista Internazionale di Scienze Sociali,* Anno 88, Nos. 3–4.

Doeringer, P. 1967: 'Determinants of the structure of industrial type labour markets', in *Industrial and Labor Relations Review,* Vol. 20, No. 2.

Doeringer, P. and Piore, M. J. 1971: *Internal Labor Markets and Manpower Analysis* (Lexington, Mass., D. C. Heath).

Dunlop, J. T. 1957: 'The task of contemporary wage theory', in Taylor and Pierson, 1957.

Dunlop, J. T. 1966: 'Job vacancy measures and economic analysis', in National Bureau of Economic Research, *The Measurement and Interpretation of Job Vacancies,* (New York, Columbia University Press).

Eckstein, O. and Wilson, T. A. 1962: 'Determination of money wages in American industry', in *Quarterly Journal of Economics,* Vol. 76 (August).

Edwards, R. C. 1979: *Contested Terrain* (New York, Basic Books).

Edwards, R. C. Reich, M. and Gordon, D. M. (eds.) 1975: *Labour Market Segmentation* (Lexington, Mass., D. C. Heath).

Eisenstein, Z. R. (ed.) 1979: *Capitalist Patriarchy and Socialist Feminism* (New York, Monthly Review Press).

Elbaum, B., Lazonick, W., Wilkinson, F. and Zeitlin, J. 1979: 'The labour process, market structure and marxist theory', in *Cambridge Journal of Economics,* Vol. 3, No. 3 (September).

Elbaum, B. and Wilkinson, F. 1979: 'Industrial relations and uneven development: a comparative study of the American and British steel industries', in *Cambridge Journal of Economics* Vol. 3, No. 3 (September).

Fisher, L. H. 1951: 'The harvest labor market in California', in *Quarterly Journal of Economics*, Vol. 65 (November).
Friedman, A. 1977: *Industry and Labour* (Macmillan).
Gabriel, J. and Holzapfl, F. 1981: 'Entrepreneurial strategies of adjustment and internal labour markets', in Wilkinson, 1981.
Gardiner, J. 1975: 'The role of domestic labour', in *New Left Review*, No. 89 (January–February).
Gordon, D. M. 1972: *Theories of Poverty and Underemployment* (Lexington, Mass, Lexington Books).
Gordon, D. M. 1976: 'Capitalist efficiency and socialist efficiency', in *Monthly Review*, No. 24 (July–August).
Gordon, D. M., Edwards, R. and Reich, M. 1982: *Segmented Work, Divided Workers* (Cambridge University Press).
Harrison, B. 1972: 'Education and underemployment in the urban ghetto', in *American Economic Review*, Vol. 62, (December).
Harrison, B. and Vietorisz T. 1973: 'Labor market segmentation: positive feedback and divergent development', in *American Economic Review*, Vol. 63 (May).
Harrison, J. 1974: 'The political economy of housework', in *Bulletin of the Conference of Socialist Economists*, Vol. IV, No. 1.
Hartmann, H. I. 1979: 'The unhappy marriage of marxism and feminism: towards a more progressive union', in *Capital and Class*, No. 8 (Summer).
Hicks, J. R. 1963: *The Theory of Wages*, 2nd edition (Macmillan).
Himmelweit, S. and Mohun, S. 1977: 'Domestic labour and capital', in *Cambridge Journal of Economics*, Vol. I, No. 1 (March).
Humphries, J. 1977; 'Class struggle and the persistence of the working class family', in Amsden, 1980.
Humphries, J. and Rubery, J. 1984: 'The reconstitution of the supply side of the labour market: the relative autonomy of social reproduction', in *Cambridge Journal of Economics*, Vol. 8, No. 4 (December).
Kahn, L. M. 1976: 'Internal labour markets: San Francisco shoremen', in *Industrial Relations*, Vol. 15, No. 3 (October).
Kenrick, J. 1981; 'Politics and the construction of women as second-class workers', in Wilkinson, 1981.
Kerr, C. 1950: 'Labor markets: their character and consequences', in *American Economic Review, Papers and Proceedings*, Vol. 40, No. 2 (May).
Kerr, C. 1954: 'The balkanization of labor markets', in Bakke and Hauser, 1954.
Kerr, C. 1978: 'Industrial relations research: a personal retrospective', in *Industrial Relations*, Vol. 17, No. 2 (May).
Keynes, J. M. 1936: *The General Theory of Employment, Interest and Money* (Macmillan).
Kuhn, A. and Wolpe, A. (eds.) 1978: *Feminism and Materialism* (Routledge & Kegan Paul).
Lazonich, W. 1979: 'Industrial relations and technical change: the case of the selfacting mule', in *Cambridge Journal of Economics*, Vol. 3, No. 3 (September).

Leigh, D. 1976: 'Occupational advancement in the late 1960s: an indirect test of the dual labor market hypothesis', in *Journal of Human Resources* (spring).

Leigh, D. 1978: *An Analysis of the Determinants of Occupational Upgrading* (New York, Academic Press).

Lester, R. A. 1946: 'Shortcomings of marginal analysis for wage employment problems', in *American Economic Review*, Vol. 36 (March).

Lester, R. A. 1947: 'Marginalism, minimum wages and labour markets', in *American Economic Review*, Vol. 37, No. 1 (March).

Lester, R.A. 1951–2: 'A range theory of wage differentials', in *Industrial and Labor Relations Review,* Vol. 5.

Littler, C. 1982: *The development of the labour process in capitalist societies* (Heinemann Educational).

Livernash, E.R. 1957: 'The internal wage structure', in Taylor and Pierson, 1957.

Lorenz, E. H. 1983: 'The labour process and industrial relations in the British and French shipbuilding industries, from 1880 to 1970: two patterns of development' (unpublished Ph.D. thesis, Cambridge).

Loveridge, R. and Mok, A. L. 1979: *Theories of Labour Market Segmentations: a Critique* (The Hague, Martin Nijhoff).

'Low Pay and Labour Market Segmentation in Advanced Industrial Countries' 1979: Working papers for the Cambridge conference (Department of Applied Economics, Cambridge, mimeo).

Lucas, R. E. B. 1974: 'The distribution of job characteristics', in *Review of Economics and Statistics*, Vol. 56, No. 4.

MacCormick, B. J. and Owen Smith, E. (eds.) 1968: *The Labour Market* (Penguin).

McNulty, P. J. 1980: *The Origins and Development of Labor Economics* (Cambridge, Mass., MIT Press).

Marshall, A. 1920: *Principles of Economics,* 8th edition (Macmillan).

Marx, K. 1976: *Capital,* Vol. 1 (1887 translation) (Penguin).

Milkman R. 1976: 'Women's work and the economic crisis: some lessons from the great depression', in *Review of Radical Political Economics,* Vol. 8, No. 1.

Mill, J. S. 1909: *Principles of Political Economy* (Longmans, Green and Company).

Mincer, J. 1962: 'Labor force participation of married women: a study of labor supply', in Amsden, 1980.

Mitchell, J. and Oakley A. (eds.) 1976: *The Rights and Wrongs of Women* (Penguin).

Moore, R. 1981: 'Aspects of segmentation in the UK building industry', in Wilkinson, 1981.

Moore, R. and Walker, J. 1983: 'Privatisation of local government services', in *Studies for Trade Unionists,* Vol. 9, No. 34 (June).

Myers, C. A. 1954: 'Labor mobility in two communities', in Bakke and Hauser, 1954.

Nichols, T. (ed.) 1980: *Capital and Labour: Studies in the Capitalist Labour Process* (Fontana).

Noble, D. 1977: *America by Design: Science, Technology and the Rise of Corporate Capitalism* (New York, Knopf).

OECD 1965: *Wages and Labour Mobility* (Paris, OECD).

Oi, W. 1962: 'Labor as a quasi–fixed factor', in *Journal of Political Economy*, Vol. 70, No. 6.

Oster, G. 1979: 'A factor–analytic test of the theory of the dual economy', in *Review of Economics and Statistics*, Vol. 62 (March).

Palmer, G. L. 1954: 'Interpretating patterns of labor mobility', in Bakke and Hauser 1954.

Palmer, G. L., Parnes, H. S., Wilcox, R. C. Herman, M. W. and Brainerd, C. P. 1962: *The Reluctant Job Changer* (University of Pennsylvania Press).

Parnes, H. S. 1962: 'Workers' attitudes to job changing: the effect of private pension plans', in Palmer *et al.*, 1962.

Picchio del Mercato, A. 1981: 'Social reproduction and the basic structure of the labour market', in Wilkinson, 1981.

Piore, M. J. 1970: 'Jobs and training', in R. E. Barringer and S. H. Beer (eds.), *The State and the Poor* (Cambridge, Mass., Winthrop).

Piore, M. J. 1973: 'Fragments of a sociological theory of wages' in *American Economic Review, Papers and Proceedings,* Vol. 63, No. 2 (May).

Piore, M. J. 1975a: 'Notes for a theory of labour market stratification', in Edwards *et al.*, 1975.

Piore, M. J. 1975b: 'I fondamenti tecnologici del dualismo e il mercato del lavoro', in *Mercato del lavoro, politiche sindacali e inflazione* (Milan, Vita e Pensiero).

Piore M. J. 1978: 'Unemployment and inflation: an alternative view', in Piore, 1979.

Piore, M. J. (ed.) 1979: *Inflation and Unemployment: Institutionalist and Structuralist Views* (White Plains, New York, M. E. Sharpe).

Piore, M. J. 1980: 'Dualism as a response to flux and uncertainty', in Berger and Piore, 1980

Politics and Society 1978: 'The labour process and the working class' (special double issue), Vol. 8, Nos. 3–4.

Reddaway, W. B. 1959: 'Wage flexibility and the distribution of labour', in *Lloyd's Bank Review*, Vol. 54. Reprinted in McCormick and Smith, 1968.

Reich, M., Gordon, D. M. and Edwards, R. C. 1973: 'A theory of labour market segmentation', in *American Economic Review*, Vol. 63 (May).

Reich, M. and Wilkinson, F. 1978: 'Low pay and labour market segmentation: a research prospectus', (University of Cambridge, Department of Applied Economics, Cambridge, mimeo).

Reynolds, L. G. 1951: *The Structure of Labor Markets* (New York, Harper).

Rosenberg, S. 1977: 'The marxian reserve army of labor and the dual labor market', in *Politics and Society,* Vol. 7, No. 2.

Rosenberg, S. 1980: 'Male occupational standing and the dual labour market', in *Industrial Relations*, Vol. 19 (winter).

Rosenberg, S. 1981: 'Occupational mobility and short cycles', in Wilkinson, 1981.

Ross, A. M. 1947: 'The dynamics of wage determination under collective bargaining', in *American Economic Review*, Vol. 37, No. 4 (December).

Ross, A. M. 1948: *Trade Union Wage Policy* (Berkeley, University of California Press).

Rowthorn, B. 1980: *Capitalism, Conflict and Inflation* (Lawrence and Wishart).

Rubery, J. 1978: 'Structured labour markets, worker organization and low pay', in *Cambridge Journal of Economics*, Vol. 2, No. 1 (March).

Rubery, J. and Tarling, R. 1982: 'Women in the recession', in D. Currie and M. Sawyer (eds.), *Socialist Economic Review* 1982 (London, Merlin Press).

Rubery, J. and Wilkinson, F. 1979: 'Notes on the nature of the labour process in the secondary sector', in 'Low Pay and Labour Market Segmentation in Advanced Industrial Countries', 1979.

Rubery, J. and Wilkinson, F. 1981: 'Outwork and segmented labour markets', in Wilkinson, 1981.

Ryan, P. 1981: 'Segmentation, duality and the internal labour market', in Wilkinson, 1981.

Sabel, C. 1979: 'Marginal workers in industrial societies', in Piore, 1979.

Sabel, C. 1982: *Work and Politics* (Cambridge University Press).

Seccombe, W. 1974: 'The housewife and her labour under capitalism', in *New Left Review*, No. 83 (January–February).

Sen, G. 1980: 'The sexual division of labour and the working class family: towards a conceptual synthesis of class relations and the subordination of women', in *Review of Radical Political Economics* (summer).

Sengenberger, W. 1979: 'The cyclical behaviour of segmentation', in 'Low pay and Labour Market Segmentation in Advanced Industrial Countries', 1979.

Sengenberger, W. 1981: 'Labour market segmentation and the business cycle', in Wilkinson, 1981.

Smith, A. 1976: *An Inquiry into the Nature and the Causes of the Wealth of Nations* (1776), ed. R. H. Campbell, A. S. Skinner and W. B. Todd (Clarendon Press).

Solinas, G. 1982: 'Labour market segmentation and workers' careers: the case of the Italian knitware industry', in *Cambridge Journal of Economics*, Vol. 6, No. 4 (December).

Spence, A. M. 1973: 'Job market signalling', in *Quarterly Journal of Economics*, Vol. 87 (August).

Stiglitz, J. E. 1975: 'The theory of screening, education and the distribution of income', in *American Economic Review*, Vol. 65 (June).

Stone, K. 1975: 'The origins of job structures in the steel industry', in Edwards *et al.*, 1975.

Tarling, R. 1981: 'The relationship between employment and output: where does segmentation theory lead us?', in Wilkinson, 1981.

Tarling, R. and Garonna, P. 1979: 'A model of labour adjustment process', in 'Low Pay and Labour Market Segmentation in Advanced Industrial Countries', 1979.

Taubam, P. and Wales, T. 1973: 'Higher education, mental ability and screening', in *Journal of Political Economy* (January).

Taylor, G. W. and Pierson, F. C. (eds.) 1957: *New Concepts for Wage Determination* (New York, McGraw-Hill).

Tobin, J. 1972: 'Inflation and unemployment', in *American Economic Review*, Vol. 62 (March).

Thurow, L. 1972: 'Education and economic inequality', in *The Public Interest* (summer).

Thurow, L. 1975: *Generating Inequality* (New York, Basic Books).

Watchel, H. 1970: 'The impact of labor market conditions on hard-core unemployment: a case of study of Detroit', in *Poverty and Human Resources* (July–August).

Watchel, H. and Betsey, C. 1972: 'Employment at low wages', in *Review of Economics and Statistics*, Vol. 54 (May).

Watchel, H. 1975: 'Class consciousness and stratification in the labour process', in Edwards *et al.*, 1975.

Wilkinson, F. 1977: 'Collective bargaining in the steel industry in the 1920s', in A. Briggs and J. Saville (eds.), *Essays in Labour History: 1918–1939* (Croom Helm).

Wilkinson, F. (ed.) 1981: *The Dynamics of Labour Market Segmentation* (London, Academic Press).

Wood, S. (ed.) 1982: *The Degradation of Work* (Hutchinson).

Zeitlin, J. 1979: 'Craft control and the division of labour: engineers and compositors in Britain 1890–1930', in *Cambridge Journal of Economics*, Vol. 3, No. 3 (September).

Zimbalist, A. (ed.) 1979: *Cast Studies on the Labour Process* (New York, Monthly Review Press).

2. The Steel Industry

Accornero, A. 1974: 'Le strutture di base negli anni '50', in *Quaderni di Rassegna Sindacale*, No. 49.

Abbatecola, G. 1975: 'Dalmine', in Pizzorno, 1975.

Ancona, L., Jacono, G. and Quadrio, A. 1957: 'Iron and steel workers attitudes in the face of technological change', Report on the research carried out by the Institute of Psycology of the Milan Catholic University, European Productivity Agency, project 164 (mimeo).

Assessorato al Lavoro della Regione Lombardia 1974: *Conferenza Regionale sui Movimenti Migratori*, Varese, 20–30 March (mimeo).

ASSIDER: *Sintesi dell'attività svolta dall'ASSIDER*, annual report (various issues) (Milan, ASSIDER).

ASSIDER 1977: *Steel in Italy*, 11th ISII Conference, Rome (Milan, ASSIDER).

ASSIDER 1980: *Repertorio delle industrie siderurgiche* (Milan, ASSIDER).

Beccalli Salvati, B. 1972: 'The rebirth of Italian trade unionism, 1943–54', in S. J. Woolf (ed.), *The Rebirth of Italy 1943–50*' (Longman).

Beccalli B. 1975: 'Redaelli', in Pizzorno, 1975.

Belgrano. F. 1979: 'Sviluppo dell'automazione della produzione e del processo in Italsider', in *Informatica e Documentazione*, Nos. 2–3.

Bonel, M. 1967: *L'industria siderurgica* (Milan, Etas Kompas).

Botta, L. 1981: 'Gli anni '50 a Genova', in *Classe,* Vol. 12, No. 19.

Botta, R. 1978: 'Gerarchie professionali e competizione operaia all'Ilva di Novi Ligure: per un uso delle fonti orali', in *Movimento Operaio e Socialista,* No. 4.

Broglia, B. and Galbo, E. 1961: 'Qualifiche e mansioni all'Ilva di Bagnoli', in *Economia e Sindacato* (September).

Broglia, G. 1962: 'Le paghe di classe in Italia', in F. Momigliano (ed.), *Lavoratori e sindacati di fronte alle trasformazioni del processo produttivo* (Milan, Feltrinelli).

Butera, F. 1977: 'La ricerca intervento al laminatoio della Dalmine', in *La ricerca intervento sull'organizzazione* (Rome, Cedis).

Butera, F. 1979: *Lavoro umano e prodotto tecnico* (Turin, Einaudi).

Butera, F. (ed.) 1980: 'Le ricerche per la trasformazione del lavoro industriale in Italia: 1969–1979', in *Sociologia del Lavoro,* Nos. 10–11.

Cai, F. 1976: 'L'esperienza italiana sulla job evaluation: il caso Italsider', in Cai *et al.*, 1976.

Cai, F., Giugni, G., Garavini, S., Mattiolo, G., Veneto, G., Ichino, P., Treu, T., Visentini, L. and Peira, P. 1976: *Ascesa e crisi del riformismo in fabbrica* (Bari, De Donato).

Carabelli, G. 1975: 'Falck Unione', in Pizzorno, 1975.

Carlini, F. 1981: 'Italsider. Cambia l'organizzazione del lavoro. Analisi di un accordo controverso', in *Il manifesto* (18 September).

Castronovo, V. 1978: 'L'industria siderurgica e il piano di coordinamento dell'IRI, 1936–9', in *Ricerche Storiche*.

Castronovo, V. 1980: *L'industria italiana dall'ottocento ad oggi* (Milan, Mondadori).

CCNL Industria metalmeccanica Privata 1973 (Rome, FLM)

CCNL Industria metalmeccanica a Partecipazione Statale 1973 (Rome, FLM)

Cervetto, A. 1954: 'Le lotte operaie alla Siderurgica di Savona, 1861–1913', in *Movimento operaio*, Vol. 6 (July–August).

Chiaromonte, F., Carfora, A. M., Ciccarelli, L., Fiorelli, F. and Iovenitti, S. 1982: *La contrattazione aziendale dell'organizzazione del lavoro 1976–9* (Rome, Editrice Sindacale Italiana).

Ciborra, C. and Colombo, T. 1981: *'Siderurgia', allegato alla ricerca FAST* (1981), *'Le trasformazioni occupazionali indotte dall'evoluzione della tecnologia'* (Milan, FAST, mimeo).

CISIA 1980: *'Repertorio delle industrie siderurgiche'* (Milan, CISIA).

Cockerill, A. 1974: *The Steel Industry, International Comparisons of Industrial Structure and Performance,* (Cambridge University Press, Occasional Papers, No. 42).

Colatto, A. 1978: 'Applicazione di microcalcolatori per il controllo del processo di laminazione a caldo', in *Ansaldo Rivista,* No. 4.

Coletti, S., Caruso, F., Maccaroni, M. and Ferri, P. 1977: 'Indagine sull'inserimento e sui livelli infortunistici del personale nuovo assunto in una azienda siderurgica', in *Lavoro Sicuro* Vol. IV, No. 1.

Collettivo Dalmine (ed.) 1972: 'Lo scontro di classe nel 1969, 1970 e 1971 alla Dalmine: la linea sindacale e l'azione delle avanguardie in fabbrica' (Dalmine, January, mimeo).

Collettivo Tecnici Italsider 1979: 'Il caso Italsider', in *Sapere*, No. 816.

Confalonieri, A. 1976: 'L'esperienza della Banca Commerciale Italiana', in *Banca e Industria in Italia*, Vol. III (Milan, Banca Commerciale Italiana).

Contini, G. 1980: 'Fonti orali e fonti scritte: un confronto', in *Classe*, No. 18.

Coppola, A. 1971: 'Italsider: il padrone sconfitto due volte', in *Unità Operaia*, Vol. 2 (January).

Cremonesi, C., Dondi, L., Piccaluga, D. and Mosconi Bernardini, P. 1981: *Il lavoro delle donne e la legge di parità* (Rome, Edizioni Lavoro).

Crespi, P. 1979: *Capitale operaia* (Milan, Jaca Book).

Crouch, C. and Pizzorno, A. (eds.) 1978: *The Resurgence of Class Conflicts in Western Europe since 1968*, Vol. 1 (Macmillan).

Dal Ferro all'acciaio: La Breda Siderurgica (1967) (Turin, Autori Editori Associati).

Daneo, C. 1975: *La politica economica della ricostruzione, 1945–1949* (Turin, Einaudi).

D'Andrea, R. 1976: *Scienza operaia e organizzazione del lavoro* (Padua, Marsilio Editore).

Della Rocca, G. (ed.) 1974: 'Due documenti sulla ricerca sociale in fabbrica', in *Prospettiva Sindacale*, No. 14.

Della Rocca, G. 1982: *Sindacato e organizzazione del lavoro* (Milan, Franco Angeli).

Del Lungo, S. 1976: 'Esperienze organizzative in alcune aziende metalmeccaniche a partecipazione statale', in *Quaderni di Sociologia*, Nos. 2–3.

De Rosa, L. 1978, 'La siderurgia italiana dalla Ricostruzione al V Centro Siderurgico', in *Ricerche Storiche*.

EIU 1982: *The World Steel Industry: Structure and Prospects in the 1980s*, Special Report No. 128 July (EIU).

Facchini, C. and Umidi, G. 1980: 'Inquadramento e professionalità alla Breda Siderurgica', in *Quaderni di Battaglie del Lavoro, Rivista della Camera del Lavoro di Milano*, Anno XI, No. 109 (July).

Fantinelli, G. 1978: 'Appunti su alcuni aspetti attuali della siderurgia bresciana', in *Notiziario Economico Bresciano* (Brescia, Banca San Paolo).

Fantoli, A. 1980: 'L'approccio dell'Italsider ai temi dell'organizzazione del lavoro', in *Sociologia del Lavoro*, Nos. 10–11.

Filippi, F. 1972: 'Organizzazione del lavoro e classificazione dei lavoratori in uno stabilimento siderurgico: l'Italsider', in *Formazione e Qualifica*, No. 14.

Finsider 1948: *Sistemazione della siderurgia italiana* (Rome, Atena).

Giugni, G. 1964: *L'evoluzione della contrattazione collettiva nell'industria siderurgica e mineraria* (Milan, Giuffrè).

Graziosi, A. 1979: *La ristrutturazione nelle grandi fabbriche 1973–6* (Milan, Feltrinelli).

Hertner, P. 1978: 'La Società Tubi Mannesmann a Dalmine: un esempio di investimento internazionale (1906–17)', in *Richerche Storiche*.

Ilardi, M. 1973: 'Ristrutturazione operaia e classe operaia sotto il fascismo: la società Terni, 1928–32', in *Il Movimento di Liberazione in Italia*, No. 3.

Ilva 1948: *Altiforni e acciaierie d'Italia, 1897–1947* (Bergamo, Istituto Italiano d'Arti Grafiche).

Italia, G. 1981: 'L'organizzazione ritorna nell'accordo Italsider', in *Il Manifesto* (29 July).

Leonardi, S. 1956: 'L'industria siderurgica dall'Unità alla prima guerra mondiale', in *Movimento Operaio*, Vol. 8.

Lettieri, A. 1970: 'Factory and education', in A. Gorz (ed.), 1978, *The Division of Labour* (Harvester).

Lettieri, A. 1971: 'Inquadramento unico e strategia delle qualifiche', in *Quaderni di Rassegna Sindacale*, No. 35.

Mantero, E. 1961: 'Lotta operaia nel mezzogiorno e l'esperienza dell'Ilva di Bagnoli', in *Rassegna Sindacale*, Vol. 8, No. 46 (October).

Manzini, G. 1976: *Una vita operaia* (Milan, Einaudi).

Massi, E. and Fumagalli, S. 1977: *La geografia dell'acciaio* (Milan, Giuffrè).

Mediobanca 1980: *Ricerche e studi* (Milan, Mediobanca).

Micheli, S., Mighetto, F., Montobio, P., Parodi, E. and Rovery, S. 1976: 'Esperienza di ricerca intervento sulla organizzazione del lavoro di una grande azienda', in *Quaderni di Sociologia,* Nos. 2–3.

Ministero dell'Industria, Commercio e Artigianato 1979: *Programma finalizzato: Industria Siderurgica* (Rome: Istituto Poligrafico e Zecca dello Stato).

Mondo Economico 1976: 'Rapporto mese: siderurgia', No. 41.

Mondo Economico 1978: 'Siderurgia, dentro la crisi', No. 46

Mondo Economico 1979: 'Rapporto mese: acciai speciali', No. 46

Mondo Economico 1981: 'Il crack dell'altoforno', No. 11.

Mondo Economico 1982: 'Italsider, l'acciaio è meno rosso', No. 9.

Mondo Economico 1982: 'Siderurgia: La colata diventa rosa', Nos. 13–14.

Neufeld, M. F. 1954: *Labour Unions and National Politics in Italian Industrial Plants* (New York, Cornell International Industrial and Labour Relations Reports).

Nicodemi, W. and Zoia, R. 1980: *Processi e impianti siderurgici* (Milan, Masson Italia Editori).

Parenti, G. 1958: 'Livello di meccanizzazione e modi di remunerazione' (Florence, Università degli Sudi di Firenze, Istituto di Statistica, October, mimeo).

Peira, P. 1976: 'Esperienze aziendali in tema di classificazione unica', in Cai *et al.*, 1976.

Pesce, A. 1970: 'L'autunno '70 si chiama Italsider', in *Mondo Nuovo*, 29 (November).

Pirlone, D. 1977: 'Organizzazione del lavoro: Italsider', in *Quaderni di Rassegna Sindacale*, Nos. 64–5.

Pizzorno, A. (ed.) 1975: *Lotte operaie e sindacato in Italia (1968–72)* (Bologna, Il Mulino).

Pizzorno, A., Reyneri, E., Regini, M. and Regalia, I. 1978: *Lotte operaie e sindacato: il ciclo 1968–72 in Italia* (Bologna, Il Mulino).

Posner, M. V. and Woolf, S. J. 1967: *Italian Public Enterprise* (Duckworth).

Pozzobon, M. and Mari, R. 1978: 'Le AFL Falck (1945–48) in L. Ganapini, M. Pozzobon, R. Mari *et al.*, *La ricostruzione nella grande industria* (Bari, De Donato).

Quaderni di Rassegna Sindacale 1982: 'Organizzazione del lavoro e contrattazione collettiva', Special Issue, No. 94

Regalia, I. 1978: 'Rappresentanza operaia e sindacato: il mutamento di un sistema di relazioni industriali', in Pizzorno *et al.*, 1978.

Regalia, I., Regini, M. and Reyneri, E. 1978: 'Labour conflicts and industrial relations, in Crouch and Pizzorno 1978.

Ricerche Storiche 1978: 'La siderurgia italiana dall'unità ad oggi', *Atti del Convegno di Piombino*, 30 September–2 October 1977, Special Issue, anno 8, No. 1.

Scortecci, A. 1961: 'Rapporto sul progresso tecnologico nell'industria siderurgica italiana', in *Il Progresso Tecnologica e la Società Italiana: Effetti Economici del Progresso Technologica sulla Economia Industriale Italiana, 1938–58* (Milan, Giuffrè).

Segatori, R. and Torresini, D. 1979: *La professionalità difficile* (Rome, CEDIS Editrice).

Sette, M. 1973: Intervento di M. Sette al Convegno dell'Istituto Gramsci, 'Scienza e organizzazione del lavoro', Torino, 8–10 June, in V. Foa, 1975, *Sindacati e lotte operaie 1943–73* (Turin, Loescher).

Sinigaglia, O. 1948: 'The future of the Italian iron and steel industry', in *Banca Nazionale del Lavoro Quarterly Review*.

Surrenti, G. and Treu, T. 1971: 'Esperienze in tema di inquadramento', in *Dibattito Sindacale*, Nos. 3–4.

Tarr, D. G. 1979: 'Cyclical dumping: the case of steel products', in *Journal of International Economics*, Vol. 9, No. 1.

Torneo, C, 1970; 'Basta con le paghe di classe', in *Unità Operaia*, Vol. 1, No. 1.

Treu, T. 1971: *Sindacato e Rappresentanze Aziendali* (Bologna, Il Mulino).

Uccelli, S. E. and Amatori, F. 1978: *La Fabbrica Ristrutturata* (Milan, Franco Angeli).

Vallini, E. 1957: *Operai del Nord* (Bari, Laterza).

Veneto, G. 1974: *Contrattazione e prassi nei rapporti di lavoro* (Bologna, Il Mulino).

Vento, S. 1981: 'Portuali, siderurgici, marittimi: tradizione e nuovo protagonismo', in *Classe*, Vol. 12, No. 19.

Zanetti Polzi, G., Cimelli, D. and Zeni, S. 1975: 'Un problema di relazioni industriali: lo scaglionamento delle ferie', in *Studi Organizzativi*, No. 1.

3. The Construction Industry

Alasia F. and Montaldi, D. 1975: *Milano Corea. Inchiesta sugli immigrati*, 2nd edition (Milan, Feltrinelli).

ANCE, *Relazione del Direttivo all'Assemblea delle Associazioni Aderenti* (various issues), (Rome, ANCE).

Andreasi, A. 1968: 'La federazione edilizia e il movimento sindacale italiano, 1900–15', in *Annali della Fondazione Luigi Einaudi*, Vol. 2.

Ave, G. and Prizzon, F. 1977: 'Le immobiliari in borsa', in Barp, 1979.

Barp, A. 1976: 'Il secondo ciclo edilizio', in Barp, 1979.

Barp, A. (ed.) 1979: *Il secondo ciclo edilizio*, 2nd edition (Milan, Franco Angeli).

Barp, A., Vittadini, M. R., Potenza, S. and Secchi, B. 1975: *La riqualificazione edilizia* (Milan, Giuffrè).

Bianchi, T. 1952: 'Aspetti tecnici ed economici dell'industria edile in Italia', in *Produttività,* No. 4 (April).

Bianchi, T. 1953*a*: 'Ridurre i costi per avere più case', in *Produttività,* No. 6 (June).

Bianchi, T. 1953*b*: 'La progettazione edile e la funzione del consulente', in *Produttività,* No. 10 (October).

Bianchi, T. 1957: 'Criteri americani e criteri italiani per la esecuzione dei lavori edili', in *Produttività*, No. 3 (March).

Bruni, M. 1979*a*: 'Stagionalità, capacità utilizzata e domanda di lavoro nel settore delle costruzioni', in Bruni *et al.*, 1979.

Bruni, M. 1979*b*: 'Andamento ciclico e stagionalità nel settore delle costruzioni', in Bruni and Franciosi, 1979.

Bruni, M. and Franciosi, F. B. 1979: *Il mercato del lavoro nelle construzioni* (Padua, Marsilio).

Bruni, M., Fornari, D., Franciosi, F. B. and Frey, L. 1979: 'Lavoro e costruzioni', *Quaderni di Economia del Lavoro* (Special Issue), Vol. IV, No. 7.

Brusco, S. 1982: 'The emilian model: productive decentralization and social integration, in *Cambridge Journal of Economics,* Vol. 6, No. 2 (June).

Brusco, S. and D'Alessandro, M. 1979: 'Struttura produttiva e organizzativa del lavoro nel settore edilizio', in Brusco *et al.*, 1981.

Brusco, S., D'Alessandro, M. and Zangrandi, G. (eds.) 1981: *Casa e progresso tecnico* (Bologna, Il Mulino).

Carlino, C. 1973*a*; 'Cosa sono le scuole edili?', (Part 1), *Sindacato Nuovo,* No. 6.

Carlino, C. 1973*b*: 'Cosa sono le scuole edile?', (Part 2), *Sindacato Nuovo,* No. 7.

CCNL Edili, Settore Industria 1976 (Rome, FLC).

CCNL Edili, Settore Industria 1979 (Rome, FLC).

Cicconi, I. 1978: 'I monopoli all'assalto dell'edilizia', in *Lotta Continua* (22 September).

Cicconi, I. 1980: *Il quarto ciclo edilizio* (Milan, BEMA Editrice).

Cipollini, R. 1976: 'Industrializzazione ed organizzazione del lavoro nell'edilizia residenziale', in *Economia e Lavoro,* No. 4.

Cipollini, R. 1979: *L'organizzazione del lavoro in edilizia, 1945–77* (Milan, Franco Angeli).

Cipollini, R. and Frison, G. 1978: 'Vecchie e nuove technologie e lo scontro di classe nell'organizzazione del lavoro in edilizia', in *Sindacato Nuovo*, No. 1.

Cipollini, R. and Frison, G. 1980: 'Il salario a rendimento in edilizia', in *Quaderni ISRIL*, No. 2

Cohen, J. S. 1981: 'Managers and machinery: an analysis of the rise of factory production', in *Australian Economic Papers*, Vol. 20, No. 36 (June).

CRESME 1975: 'Ricerca sulla struttura occupazionale e imprenditoriale delle costruzioni, Sezione II, Indagine Pilota presso alcune grandi aziende' (Rome, CRESME, mimeo).

CRESME, 1976: 'Indagine su alcuni problemi nel settore dell'edilizia' (Rome, CRESME, mimeo).

CRESME, 1981: 'La carenza di manodopera' (Rome, CRESME, 25 February, abstract in FILCA CISL Lombardia, 1981).

Crosta, P. 1976: 'Le iniziative di sviluppo residenziale su larga scala: condizioni ed effetti sulle attività del settore e sulle funzioni del blocco edilizio', in Barp, 1979.

De Vecchi, G. and Treu, C. 1979: *Le organizzazioni operaie edili in Lombardia, 1980–1914* (Milan, Nuove Edizioni Operaie).

Dell'Aringa, C. 1974: *La mobilità del lavoro nell'industria* (Milan, Vita e Pensiero).

Dunlop, J. T. 1958: *Industrial Relations Systems* (New York, Holt).

FILCA CISL Lombardia 1980*a*: 'Primo rapporto esplorativo sul settore edile in Lombardia. Parte prima: la geografia economica del settore edile', in *Materiali di Lavoro,* Bulletin No. 1.

FILCA CISL Lombardia 1980*b*: 'Primo rapporto esplorativo sul settore edile in Lombardia. Parte seconda: l'analisi dei cantieri', in *Materiali di Lavoro,* Bulletin No. 2.

FILCA CISL Lombardia 1981: 'Indagine sull'attività delle Casse Edili delle province lombarde nel 1980' (Milano, October, mimeo).

FILCA CISL Lombardia 1982: 'Indagine sull'attività delle Casse Edili delle province lombarde nel 1981', in *Quaderni di FILCA CISL Lombardia* (September).

FILCA CISL Milano 1982: *L'istituto contrattuale della Cassa Edile: uno strumento moderno al servizio dei lavoratori* (Milan, Cooperativa Il Guado).

FILLEA CGIL, FILCA CISL, FENEAL UIL 1970: 'Le scandalose condizioni dei lavoratori edili' (Milan, 25 September, mimeo).

FLC Lombardia 1976: 'Situazione e prospettive della formazione professionale in Lombardia' (Milan, 8 July, mimeo).

FLC Lombardia 1977: 'Documento della Segreteria sulla formazione professionale edile' (Milan, 22 February, mimeo).

FLC Lombardia (in collaboration with Facoltà di Architettura, Dipartimento di Progettazione e Produzione Edilizia, e CNR) 1981: 'Indagine sui processi produttivi nel cantiere' (Milan, mimeo).

FLC Milano 1974: 'Convegno Provinciale: Relazione di L. Filippazzi' (Milan 13 February, mimeo).

FLC Milano 1979*a*: 'Organizzazione del lavoro, professionalità e formazione professionale in edilizia: Convegno 27–28 aprile 1979' (Milan, Centro di Formazione Professionale Edile, mimeo).

FLC Milano 1979*b*: 'L'iniziativa della FLC milanese in materia di formazione professionale (Milan, 29 January, mimeo).

FLC Milano, 1981: 'Fotografia degli occupati del settore' (Milan, 6 November, mimeo).

FLC and C.D.D. Gadola 1980: 'Elementi di riflessione in materia di contrattazione dell'organizzazione del lavoro nell'esperienza di lotta alla Gadola S.p.A. di Milano' (Milan, mimeo).

Fontanari, E. 1978: 'Organizzazione del lavoro e struttura delle mansioni nel settore delle costruzioni', Indagine ECAP CGIL Veneto, in E. Fontanari *et al.*, L'industria del Veneto (Venice, Arsenale Cooperativa Editrice).

Franciosi, F. B. 1979*a*: 'Strutture produttive e lavoro nel settore delle costruzioni', in Bruni *et al.*, 1979.

Franciosi, F. B. 1979*b*: 'Settore delle costruzioni, mercato del lavoro e politica economica', in Bruni and Franciosi, 1979.

Frey, L. 1976: 'Il potenziale di lavoro in Italia', in *Documenti ISVET*, Nos. 50–2.

Frey, L. 1979: 'Occupazione e sottoccupazione nel settore delle costruzioni', in Bruni *et al.*, 1979.

Frison, G. 1979: *L'organizzazione del lavoro in edilizia* (Rome, Nuove Edizioni Operaie).

Garonna, P. 1979: 'Mobilità e mercato del lavoro', in P. Garonna *et al.*, 1979, *La politica italiana degli anni '70* (Padua, Marsilio).

Il Giornale dei Costruttori 1968: 'Inchiesta sul problema del cottimismo–subappalto di sola manodopera', No. 11 (April).

Gruttaduria, D. 1976: 'Il nuovo cottimismo è una nuova realtà', in *Sindacato Nuovo,* No. 6 (July).

Gruttaduria, D. 1980: 'Tendenze evolutive del settore delle costruzioni', *Seminario di Lavoro* (Milan, CISEM, February, mimeo).

Indovina, F. 1972: 'Progresso tecnico e mercato del lavoro', in F. Indovina (ed.), 1972, *Lo spreco edilizio* (Padua, Marsilio).

ISFOL 1977: 'Edilizia: struttura, tendenze e bisogni di formazione', in *Osservatorio sul mercato del lavoro e delle professioni,* No. 13 (January).

ISSOCO 1975: 'Il mercato del lavoro precario: struttura e dinamica' (Rome, ISSOCO).

Libro Ricordo Storico 1906: 'Società di Miglioramento e Resistenza con Cassa Mutua fra i Lavoratori Muratori, Badilanti, Manovali e Garzoni di Milano, 20 anni, di vita della Soietà, Tipografia degli operai, Milano' in De Vecchi and Treu, 1979.

Magnani, I. and Muraro, G. 1978: *Edilizia e sviluppo urbano* (Bologna, Il Mulino).

Massarella, G. 1977: 'Intensità della recente produzione edilizia, evasione e modifiche nel vecchio patrimonio abitativo', in Barp, 1979.

Mereu, M. T. 1972: 'Origini e primi sviluppi dell'organizzazione di classe dei muratori milanesi', in *Classe,* No. 5.

Merli, S. 1970: *Proletariato di fabbrica e capitalismo industriale* Florence, Italia).

Modigliani, F. and Tarantelli, E. 1979: 'Structural and transitory determinants of labour mobility. Holt's conjecture and Italian experience', in *Banca Nazionale del Lavoro, Quarterly Review*, September.

Il Modulo 1978: 'Il coffrage tunnel nell'esperienza delle cooperative edili' (Milan, Be. Ma.).

Molinari, C. and Treu, C. 1980: 'Note sul cottimo e il subappalto' (Ufficio Studi FILCA CISL Milano, March, mimeo).

Mondo Economico 1980: 'Rapporto mese: grandi lavori all'estero', No. 8.

Mondo Economico 1981: 'La bella addormentata', No. 11.

Mondo Economico 1982: 'Cemento riarmato', No. 17.

Mondo Economico 1982: 'Grandi lavori all'estero: protagonisti d'appalto', Nos. 27–8.

Paci, M. 1962: 'Aspetti della socializzazione del lavoro in edilizia;, in *Quaderni Rossi*, No. 2 (June).

Paci, M. 1963*a*: 'Immigrazione di manodopera nel settore dell'edilizia', milanese', in 'Progetto di ricerca: l'immigrazione nell'area metropolitana VII, 2' (Milan, ILSES, mimeo).

Paci, M. 1963*b*: 'La classe operaia nell'industria edilizia', in Paci, 1973.

Paci, M. 1973: *Mercato del lavoro e classi sociali in Italia* (Bologna, Il Mulino).

Pellicciari, G. 1963: 'Condizioni di vita nelle baracche dei cantieri edili: storia di un cantiere tipo', in 'Progetto di ricerca: l'immigrazione nell'area metropolitana. VII, 3' (Milan, ILSES, mimeo).

Petrini, V. 1971: 'L'industria delle costruzioni. La misurazione del divario tecnologico', in L. Frey (ed.) *La misurazione del divario tecnologico* (Milan, Franco Milan).

Pichierri, A. 1982: 'L'organizzazione del lavoro in edilizia', in *Inchiesta,* October–December.

Picollo, A. 1955: 'Cottimismo e subappalto nell'industria edile' (Relazione al Convegno Nazionale di genova, FILEA Genova, July, mimeo).

Pinchera, M. and Veneziani, G. 1965: 'La costruzione di case in Italia. Contributo all'analisi del processo produttivo e dei problemi dell'industrializzazione' (Milan, ILSES, mimeo).

Pizzigani, O. 1980: 'Un milione al mese finchè c'è la salute', in *L'Unità*, No. 6 (March).

Procacci, G. 1970: *La lotta di classe in Italia agli imizi del XX secolo* (Rome, Editori Riuniti).

Quaderni di Rassegna Sindacale 1973: 'Sindacato ed edilizia', Special Issue, No. 43.

Regione Lombardia 1978: *Atti del Convegno 'Organizzazione del lavoro, professionalità bisogni di formazione professionale nel settore edile in Lombardia',* 27–9 June (Assessorato all'Istruzione e Formazione Professionale, Documenti di Lavoro No. 10, mimeo).

Riccardi, L. 1977: 'Scuole edili: un nodo strategico per la catergoria', in *Sindacato Nuovo,* No. 8.

Richardson, G. B. 1972: 'The organization of industry', in *Economic Journal,* Vol. 82 (September).

Roscelli, R. 1978: 'Intervento al Convegno' in Regione Lombardia, 1978.

Rosa, G. 1979: *Lo stock di capitale nell'industria italiana. Nuove stime settoriali e territoriali* (Rome, Centro Studi Confindustria, SIPI).

Rossi, E. 1926: 'I salari degli operai milanesi dal 1921 al 1' semestre 1926', in *La Riforma Sociale,* Anno 33, Vol. 37.

Saba, V. 1978: *Le Esperienze Associative in Italia, 1861–1922* (Milan, Franco Angeli).

Sabbatini, S. 1972: 'Da Milano a Bari una piattaforma dettata dagli operai', in *Sindacato Nuovo,* No. 3.

Scarpini, G. 1981: 'La qualificazione tecnologica nelle fasi a valle della struttura', in Brusco *et al.*, 1981.

Schiavi, A. 1910: 'Il problema delle abitazioni e la produttività dei muratori', in *La Riforma Sociale,* Anno 18, Vol. 22.

Talamona, M. 1958: *Fluttuazioni cicliche e cicli economici* (Rome ISCO).

Torri, G. 1969: 'Illegalità dei contratti e crisi di un settore: note sulla situazione edilizia in Italia', in *Relazioni Sociali,* No. 7.

Official Publications

ISAT, *Annuario di contabilità nazionale*, Vol. 2, edizione 1980–1.

ISTAT, *Annuario di statistiche del lavoro*, Vol. 22, edizione 1981.

ISTAT, *Annuario statistico dell'attività edilizia e delle opere pubbliche,* Vol. 24, edizione 1980.

ISTAT, *Censimento generale della popolazione*, 1951, 1961, 1971, and 1981.

ISTAT, *Censimento generale dell'industria e del commercio*, 1951, 1961, 1971, and 1981.

ISTAT, 'Occupati per attività economica e regione, 1970–1980', *Collana d'Informazioni,* No. 4 (1981).

Ministero del Lavoro e della Previdenza Sociale, *Statistiche del lavoro* (various issues).

Author Index

Subject Index